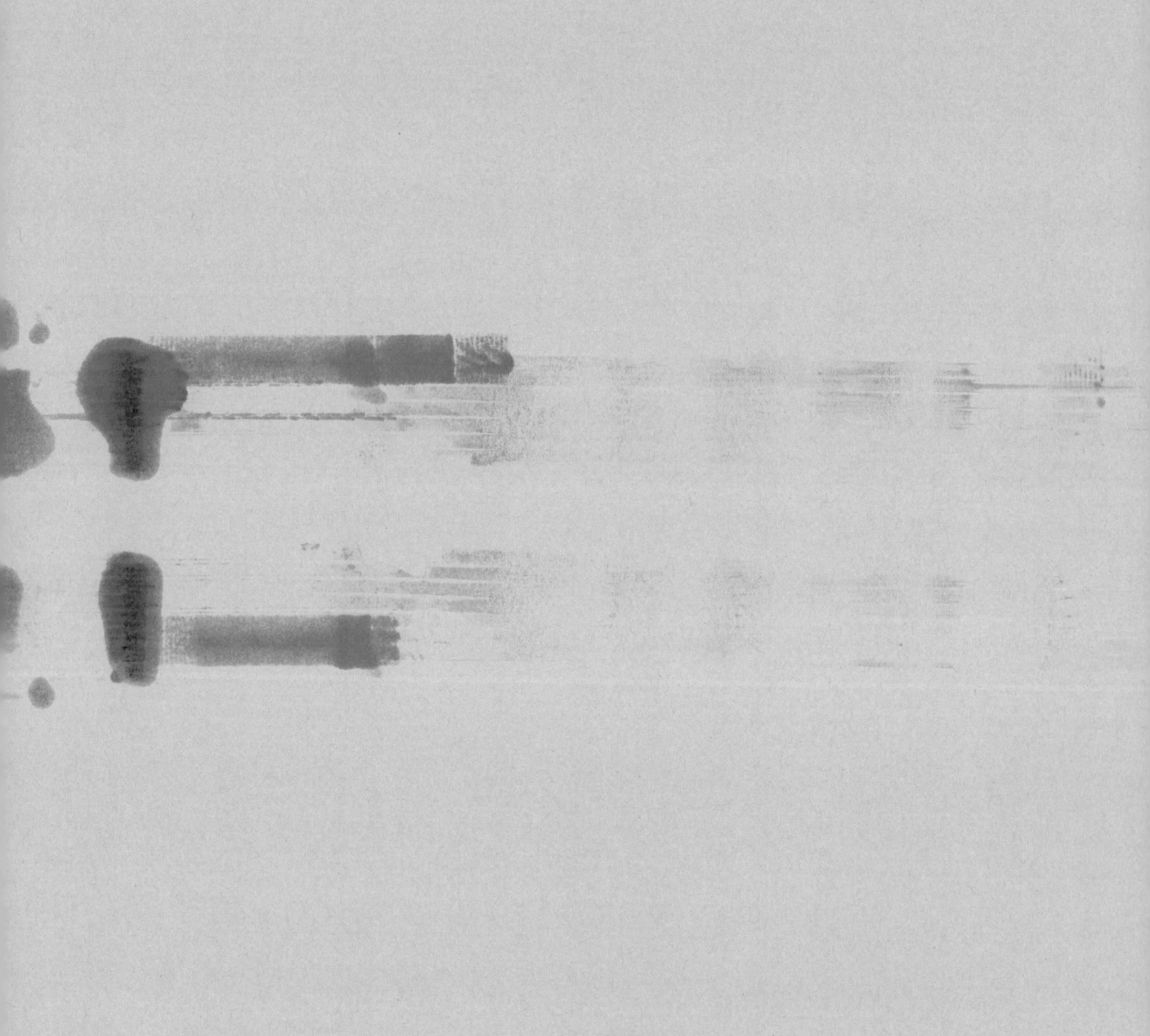

Mia's
MATH
SERIES

AP
CALCULUS AB·BC

HERMONHOUSE

Mia's AP Calculus AB & BC

발 행	2022년 01월 14일 초판 1쇄
	2024년 12월 02일 개정 2쇄

저 자	소미혜
발행인	최영민
발행처	피앤피북
주 소	경기도 파주시 신촌로 16
전 화	031-8071-0088
팩 스	031-942-8688
전자우편	hermonh@naver.com
출판등록	2015년 3월 27일
등록번호	제406-2015-31호

ⓒ 소미혜 2022, Printed in Korea.

ISBN   979-11-92520-72-8 (53410)

- 책 값은 뒤 표지에 있습니다.
- 헤르몬하우스는 피앤피북의 임프린트 출판사입니다.
- 이 책의 어느 부분도 저작권자나 발행인의 승인 없이 무단 복제하여 이용할 수 없습니다.

✤ 저자직강 인터넷 강의는 SAT, AP No.1 인터넷 강의 사이트인 마스터프랩(www.masterprep.net) 에서 보실 수 있습니다.

Why? Mia's AP calculus

'이해하기 쉬운 개념
+
다양한 example 문제
+
AP style problem'

그동안의 AP Calculus 교재에서는 볼 수 없었던 삼중 그물망구조로 AP Calculus에 필요한 모든 토픽 및 개념과 실전 능력을 한 번에 잡는다!

스스로 빈칸을 채워가며 개념을 꼼꼼히 공부할 수 있도록 설계한 교재

그저 그런 교재가 아니다! 지난 10년 간 현장에서 수많은 학생들에게 결과로 증명된 학교 GPA 및 5월 AP 시험 대비용 최적의 교재

Preface

International school의 선생님으로 일하기 시작하게 된 첫해부터 AP calculus 수업을 맡게 되었습니다. 고등학교 시절 대학수능시험을 준비하며 미적분을 가장 재미있게 공부했던 사람으로써 내가 가르치는 학생들도 개념을 알아가는 즐거움과 문제를 해결했을 때의 짜릿함을 느꼈으면 좋겠다고 생각하였습니다. 이를 위해 학생들의 입장에서 쉽고 재미있게 공부할 수 있으며 생각하는 힘을 기를 수 있는 문제들이 담긴 나만의 교재를 제작하기 시작했습니다.

교재 제작을 위해 수 많은 college board의 past paper, textbook, text prep book들의 내용들과 문제들을 연구하였습니다. 그리고 학원 및 개인지도를 통해 알게 된 국내외 많은 국제학교/외국인학교에 재학중인 학생들의 AP calculus GPA 관리를 지도하면서 각 학교 선생님들의 가르치는 방식과 내용들을 벤치마킹(Benchmarking) 하였습니다. 또한 학생들이 어려워하는 부분들을 분석하고, 학생들의 의견들을 참고하며 교재를 지속적으로 개선하며 교재수준을 향상시켰습니다. 이렇게 완성된 교재를 통해 매년 평균 80% 이상의 학생들이 5점을 맞는 성과를 얻을 수 있었습니다.

지금까지 저의 노하우를 모두 담은 강의와 교재를 더 많은 학생들과 나누고 싶어 책으로 출판하게 되었습니다.

이 책을 통해 학생들이 calculus라는 과목이 어렵지만 충분히 doable하다는 것을 깨닫고, 문제를 해결했을 때의 즐거움을 느끼며, 깊이 있는 문제들을 다루면서 사고력과 응용력이 한층 더 깊어지길 바랍니다.

마지막으로 이 책을 함께 만들기 위해 애써준 사랑하는 남편TY와 잘생긴 아들 주원이, 그 동안 함께해 준 고마운 학생들, 그리고 마스터프렙의 권주근 대표님께 감사의 마음으로 드립니다. 그리고 무엇보다도 소중한 기회를 주신 하나님께 감사와 찬양을 올려드립니다.

Mia Mihye So

Mia's AP calculus의 특징

1. 교재 내용, 문제에 대한 쉽고 명쾌한 Mia쌤의 설명, 해설강의는 유학 인터넷 강의 전문 사이트인 마스터프렙 (www.masterprep.net)에 마련되어 있습니다.

2. '이해하기 쉬운 개념 + 다양한 example 문제 + AP style Problem' 삼중 그물망구조로 개념과 실전연습을 한번에 잡아줍니다. 어려운 개념들을 쉽게 배우고 다양한 example 문제로 연습을 한 뒤, 배운 개념에 대한 AP style Problem(기출유형문제)으로 실전에 적용하는 연습까지 완벽한 개념정리를 완성시킬 수 있습니다.

3. 스스로 빈칸을 채워가며 개념을 꼼꼼하게 공부할 수 있게 설계하였습니다. 빈칸의 답은 페이지 하단에 배치하여 학생들이 필요 시 바로 참고할 수 있습니다.

4. college board에서 주최하는 AP calculus AB, BC 실전시험에 나오는 모든 토픽을 커버하였고, 실전시험에서는 출제되지 않지만 많은 학교수업에서 추가적으로 다루는 깊이 있는 내용들도 담고 *(star) 표시로 표기하였습니다. 더 깊이 calculus의 내용을 공부할 학생들은 *(star) 표기된 부분도 함께 공부할 수 있습니다.

5. 이해하기 쉽고 친근한 이미지를 활용하여 어려운 수식을 빠르게 이해할 수 있도록 작성하였습니다. 꼭 암기해야 할 개념, 공식은 shade 박스 안에 정리하였습니다.

6. 계산기 Ti 84, Ti nspire CAS (CX도 가능)를 처음 사용하는 학생들을 위한 필수 계산기 사용법을 정리하였습니다. 계산기가 필요한 실전문제들도 풀어보면서 계산기 사용법도 정복할 수 있습니다.

◆ 기호정리

* (star): AP calculus 수준 이상의 난이도 있는 문제
🖩 (calculator): calculator를 사용해야 하는 문제

$\mathbb{R}$: Real numbers $\cap$: and
$\mathbb{Z}$: Integers ∞ : infinity
$\mathbb{N}$: Natural numbers $\therefore$: Therefore
$\cup$: or $\because$: Since

저자 소개

Mia (소미혜) 선생님은 지난 14년 이상을 유학수학 현장에서 다양한 학생들과 호흡하면서 최적화된 미국 수학 및 국제학교 수학에 대한 솔루션을 제공해온 수학 전문가이다.

압구정 미국수학 전문강사라는 타이틀은 위의 노력들을 통해서 자연스럽게 얻게 된 선생님의 별칭이다.

미국에서 인증된 수학전문강사(Texas 8-12 미국수학교사자격증 content exam + PPR exam 통과)로 관련된 전문자격증을 소지하고 있으며, 특히, 해외 엄마들 사이에 입소문 난 실력파 강사이다.

AP calculus AB BC, AP Statistics, SAT 1 2 math, IB Math 등에서 14년 +의 경력을 가지고 있다. 또한 한국 수능수학 강의 경력도 4년 이상을 가지고 있어서 한국 수학과 미국/국제 학교 수학에 대해서 모두 정통한 수학 전문가이다.

- 8-12 Texas Mathematics Teacher Certificate (content exam + PPR exam 통과)
- College Board certification for AP Calculus AB, BC
- 미국텍사스고등학교, 국내국제고등학교 수학교사 경력 6년
- 용인외대부고, 경기외고, KIS, 제주KIS, SIS, 청라달튼, 브랭섬홀, 일본, 싱가포르, 베트남 국제학교 등의 학생들의 온라인/오프라인 개인지도
- (현)마스터프렙 수학대표강사, Miamath 수학대표강사
- (전) IBAdvance IB, sat 수학대표강사
- (전) 해커스유학 미국수학강사
- (전) PSU Edu AP, SAT 수학강사
- 수능수학 강의 경력 4년

※ 저 서 ※

Miamath 시리즈 : AP Calculus AB BC, AP Precalculus, Precalculus, Algebra2 (헤르몬하우스)

Contents

Formulas from Precalculus 12

Part 1. Differentiation (For both AB and BC)

1. Limit 16
2. Continuity and Discontinuity 46
3. Differentiation 54
4. Technique of Differentiation 70
5. Differentiability and Tangent line 95
   Free Response Questions (from ch1~5) 108
6. Extrema and First Derivative 110
7. Concavity and Second Derivative 123
8. Motions and Derivatives 144
9. Optimization and Related Rates 154
10. Applications of Differentiation 168
    Free Response Questions (from ch6~10) 184

Part 2. Integration (For both AB and BC)

11. Antiderivatives 190
12. Definite Integral 217
13. Fundamental Theorem of Calculus 238
14. Approximating Area 256
15. Area and Volume 270
16. More Applications and Motion 294
17. Differential Equation 306
    Free Response Questions (from ch11~17) 322

Part 3. Calculus for BC (For BC only)

18. Euler Method, Logistic Curve (for BC) 328
19. Integration for BC (for BC) 340
20. Infinite Series (for BC) 363
21. Power Series (for BC) 397
22. Taylor Series (for BC) 404
23. Parametric Equation (for BC) 431
24. Polar Equation (for BC) 451
    Free Response Questions (from ch18~24) 474

Calculator Skills 478
MCQ Mock Test for AB 502
MCQ Mock Test for BC 533

Answers 565

학생들의 후기

Mia 쌤을 만나기 전에는 학교 수업 외에 수학을 제대로 배워본 적이 없어서 대학 입시를 준비할 때 자신감도 많이 낮았고 걱정이 많았어요. 제가 고등학교를 나온 뉴질랜드와 대학 입시를 준비한 전형의 수학 진도가 거의 겹치지 않아서 처음 배우는 내용이 대부분이었는데 단기간 동안 좋은 결실을 맺을 수 있었던 건 쌤의 수업과 교재가 저 같은 초보자도 이해할 수 있도록 쉽게 설명되어 있어서였던 것 같아요. 깔끔하게 정리된 개념부터 깊이 생각해야 하는 난이도 있는 문제들까지… 도움 됐던 부분들이 너무 많아서 나열하기 힘드네요! 대학에 온 지금까지 calculus를 요하는 수업이 종종 있는데 Mia 쌤이랑 수업할 때 썼던 노트를 아직도 꺼내어 공부하고 있답니다~:)

Lee Seohyun_ NUS (National University of Singapore) Business Administration

Mia쌤의 수업과 교재는 어려운 개념 내용들도 이해하기 쉽고 깔끔하게 정리되어 있어서 여러 번 복습해가며 공부하기 좋았습니다. 기초를 다지는 기본 문제부터 실전 AP 시험 문제와 비슷한 난이도의 문제까지 골고루 제 실력에 맞게 풀 수 있어서 너무 도움되었습니다. Calculus 특성상 내용이 정말 많은데 중요한 부분들을 한번 더 강조해주셔서 효율적으로 공부할 수 있었습니다.

Jiwon Choi _University of Rhode Island PharmD

실전 AP문제 토픽별로 개념부터 응용문제까지 한번에 이해하면서 풀 수 있게 유도해줘요. 스스로 효율적으로 풀 수 있는 과정을 도출할 수 있게 단계별로 나눠 차근차근 이해시켜주고 실전에 필요한 노하우도 단원별로 한눈에 보이게 정리되어 있어요. 단원에 대해 미리 개념이 잘 안 잡혀있어도 필요한 개념들은 그때그때 remind 해주고 자연스럽게 새로운 미적분 개념까지 이해할 수 있게 자세히 설명되어 있어요. 처음부터 끝까지 수업만 잘 들어도 5점 보장해요!

Daniel Kim_University of the Pacific 3+3 Accelerated Dental Program
(Accepted school Carnegie Mellon, Case Western 4+3 dental, UCLA, UC BERKELEY, USC + others)

Mia 선생님께서 제 AP calculus BC 공부를 도와주실 때 가장 먼저 기본 개념을 충분히 다진 후 다양한 연습문제를 제공해 주셔서 배운 것들을 제 것으로 만드는 것에 많은 도움을 주셨습니다. 많은 과외와 학원을 다녔지만 실전 문제와 가장 가까운 문제들을 제공해 주셔서 시험 준비에 가장 효과적으로 많은 도움을 받아 단기간에 5점을 맞을 수 있었습니다.

Suzy Moon_ UCLA Biochemistry

쌤의 깔끔한 노트 정리, 따라가기 쉬운 설명, 그리고 어려운 문제도 쉽게 접근하여 빠르게 풀 수 있는 방법들... 다 너무 감사했어요. 쌤 덕분에 AP calculus 준비도 잘 되었고 결과도 잘 나와서 저는 너무 만족하고 좋았던 수업들이었어요~

Angela Hwang_ King's College London BSc Business Management

Mia's AP calculus textbook accentuates every important aspect of calculus while ensuring a holistic understanding of the subject. My learning was furthered refined through countless amounts of relevant practice questions that are bound to come up in the exam. I strongly recommend this book for every student who is preparing for the AP Calculus exam!

Jinhyung Kim_ University of Edinburgh LLB Law

Formulas from Precalculus

Mia's AP Calculus

1. Definition of Absolute Value

※ Absolute Value

$$|x| = \begin{cases} \boxed{①} & , x \geq 0 \\ \boxed{②} & , x < 0 \end{cases} = \sqrt{x^2}$$

"flip back to positive"

2. Properties of Logarithm

※ Properties of Log

$\log_b 1 = 0$

$\log_b b = 1$

$\log_b b^x = x$ ex) $\log 10^x =$ ③ _____ , $\ln e^4 =$ ④ _____

$b^{\log_b x} = x$ ex) $10^{\log y} =$ ⑤ _____ , $e^{\ln 5} =$ ⑥ _____

$\log_b xy = \log_b x + \log_b y$ ex) $\log 2 + \log 5 =$ ⑦ _____

$\log_b \dfrac{x}{y} = \log_b x - \log_b y$ ex) $\log 20 - \log 5 =$ ⑧ _____

$\log_b x^n = n \log_b x$ ex) $10^{2\log x} =$ ⑨ _____

$\log_b x = \dfrac{\log_c x}{\log_c b}$ Change of Base

Blank : ① x   ② -x   ③ x   ④ 4   ⑤ y   ⑥ 5   ⑦ log10 = 1   ⑧ log4   ⑨ $10^{\log x^2} = x^2$

3. Basic Trigonometry

※ Radian vs Degree

Degrees	0°	30°	45°	60°	90°	180°	270°	360°
Radians	0	$\frac{\pi}{6}$	$\frac{\pi}{4}$	$\frac{\pi}{3}$	$\frac{\pi}{2}$	π	$\frac{3\pi}{2}$	2π

※ Trigonometric ratios

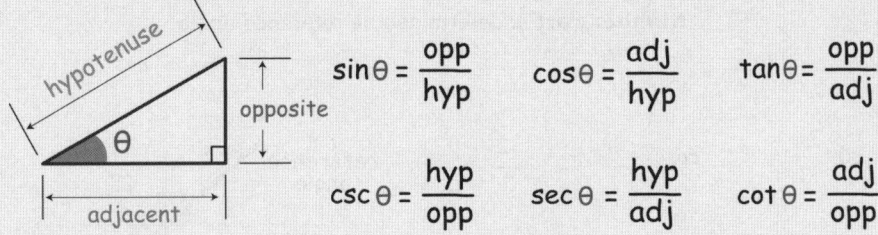

$$\sin\theta = \frac{opp}{hyp} \quad \cos\theta = \frac{adj}{hyp} \quad \tan\theta = \frac{opp}{adj}$$

$$\csc\theta = \frac{hyp}{opp} \quad \sec\theta = \frac{hyp}{adj} \quad \cot\theta = \frac{adj}{opp}$$

※ Special Values of Trigonometry Function

	0° 0	30° π/6	45° π/4	60° π/3	90° π/2
sin	0	$\frac{\sqrt{1}}{2}$	$\frac{\sqrt{2}}{2}$	$\frac{\sqrt{3}}{2}$	1
cos	1	$\frac{\sqrt{3}}{2}$	$\frac{\sqrt{2}}{2}$	$\frac{\sqrt{1}}{2}$	0
tan	0	$\frac{1}{\sqrt{3}}$	1	$\sqrt{3}$	und

※ Trig ratios

ASTC   Reference angle / triangle

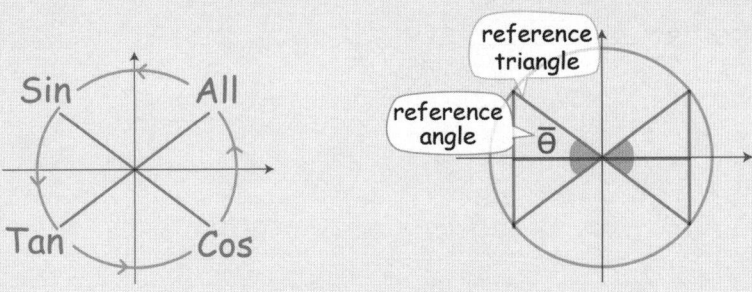

※ Evaluating Trig ratios

$$\sin\theta = (+ \text{ or } -)\ \sin\bar{\theta}$$

- sign: by ASTC
- number: by reference angle / triangle

Sign part is determined by ASTC.
Number part is determined by reference angle.

ex) $\cos\dfrac{2\pi}{3}$ = ① ____ cos ____ ② = ③ ____

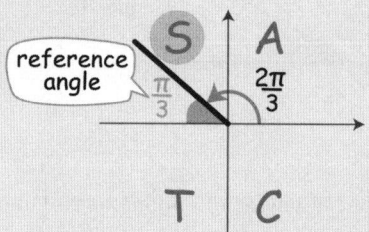

ex) Find x for $\cos x = -\dfrac{1}{2}$ for $0 \le x \le 2\pi$.

Cosine is negative in ④ ____, ____ quadrant.

The reference angle is ⑤ _____.

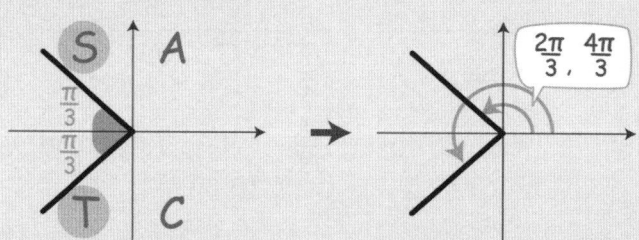

Therefore x = ⑥ _____.

Blank : ① − (negative) ② $\dfrac{\pi}{3}$ ③ $-\dfrac{1}{2}$ ④ II and III ⑤ $\dfrac{\pi}{3}$ ⑥ $\dfrac{2\pi}{3}, \dfrac{4\pi}{3}$

4. Trigonometric Identities

※ Quotient Identities

$$\tan\theta = \frac{\sin\theta}{\cos\theta} \qquad \cot\theta = \frac{\cos\theta}{\sin\theta}$$

※ Pythagorean Identities

$$\sin^2\theta + \cos^2\theta = 1$$
$$1 + \tan^2\theta = \sec^2\theta$$
$$1 + \cot^2\theta = \csc^2\theta$$

※ Odd-Even Identities

$$\sin(-\theta) = -\sin\theta \qquad \csc(-\theta) = -\csc\theta$$
$$\cos(-\theta) = \cos\theta \qquad \sec(-\theta) = \sec\theta$$
$$\tan(-\theta) = -\tan\theta \qquad \cot(-\theta) = -\cot\theta$$

※ Double Angle Formulas

$$\sin(2\theta) = 2\sin\theta\cos\theta$$
$$\cos(2\theta) = \cos^2\theta - \sin^2\theta$$
$$= 1 - 2\sin^2\theta$$
$$= 2\cos^2\theta - 1$$

※ Graph of $y = \tan^{-1} x = \arctan x$

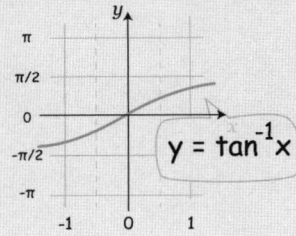

Part 1

Differentiation

Chapter 1~10
(For both AB and BC)

Mia's AP Calculus

1. Limit

1. Limit

    ① What is the value of y when $x=2$?

    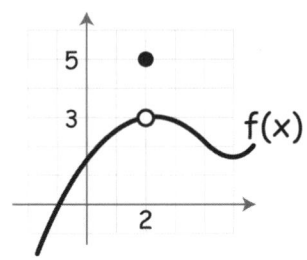

    ② What is the value of y when x **approaches to 2**?

    ① : When x = 2, the y value is 5. We can write this with function notation; f(2) = 5.

    ② : When x approaches to 2, the y value will be about 3. (y approaches to 3)

    We can write this using 'limit' notation: $\lim\limits_{x \to 2} f(x) = 3$

    ※ Notation of a Limit

    $$\lim_{x \to 2} f(x) = 3$$

    when x approaches to 2

    f(x) approaches to 3

    When you see "limit", think "approaching"

2. One-sided Limit

When x approaches to 2, we can approach in two different directions; from the negative (-) direction (from the left), and from the positive (+) direction (from the right).

$\lim\limits_{x \to 2^-} f(x) = \boxed{①}$

from (-) direction

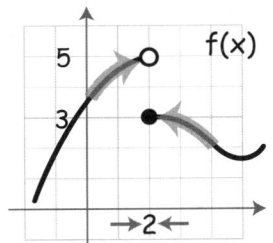

$\lim\limits_{x \to 2^+} f(x) = \boxed{②}$

from (+) direction

When x approaches to 2 from the **negative direction**, f approaches 5.
= the **left-hand limit**(-) is 5

When x approaches to 2 from the **positive direction**, f approaches 3.
= the **right-hand limit**(+) is 3

Then

$\lim\limits_{x \to 2} f(x)$ _____ ③

When you have $\lim\limits_{x \to 2} f(x)$ (with no direction sign) then you should check *both directions*. If the left-hand limit and the right-hand limit are different, then we can say the limit 'Does not exist.' So it will be $\lim\limits_{x \to 2} f(x) = DNE$.

※ Existence of a Limit

If *f* is a function and *c* and *L* are real numbers,

then $\lim\limits_{x \to c} f(x) = L$ if and only if both the left- and right- limits are equal to *L*.

$\lim\limits_{x \to c^+} f(x) = \lim\limits_{x \to c^-} f(x) = \lim\limits_{x \to c} f(x)$

from (+)   from (-)   from both

The limit ④ _____.

Blank : ① 5   ② 3   ③ Does not exist (DNE)   ④ Exists

EXAMPLE 1. Evaluate the function. And find the one-sided limit, two sided limit at each point if they exist.

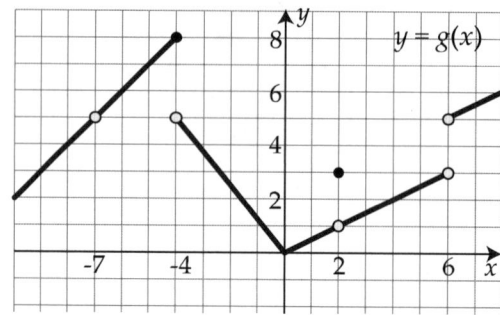

① i) $g(2)$

　ii) $\lim\limits_{x \to 2^+} g(x)$

　iii) $\lim\limits_{x \to 2^-} g(x)$

　iv) $\lim\limits_{x \to 2} g(x)$

② i) $g(-4)$

　ii) $\lim\limits_{x \to -4^+} g(x)$

　iii) $\lim\limits_{x \to -4^-} g(x)$

　iv) $\lim\limits_{x \to -4} g(x)$

③ i) $g(6)$

　ii) $\lim\limits_{x \to 6^+} g(x)$

　iii) $\lim\limits_{x \to 6^-} g(x)$

　iv) $\lim\limits_{x \to 6} g(x)$

④ i) $g(-7)$

　ii) $\lim\limits_{x \to -7^+} g(x)$

　iii) $\lim\limits_{x \to -7^-} g(x)$

　iv) $\lim\limits_{x \to -7} g(x)$

※ **Limit with infinity**

$x \to \infty$ 　　means x becomes a large positive number
(On the graph, x goes to the right endlessly...)

$x \to -\infty$ 　　means x becomes a large negative number
(On the graph, x goes to the left endlessly...)

$$\lim_{x \to -\infty} f(x) = \boxed{①}$$

As x gets larger in (−) direction

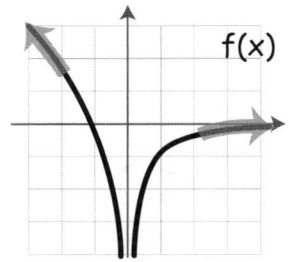

$$\lim_{x \to \infty} f(x) = \boxed{②}$$

As x gets larger in (+) direction

EXAMPLE 2. Find the limit.

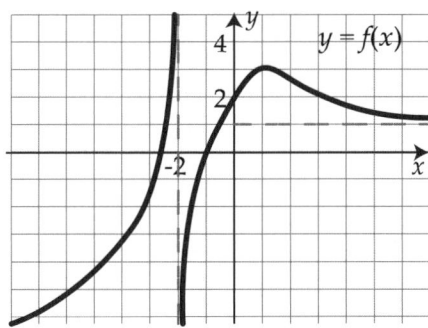

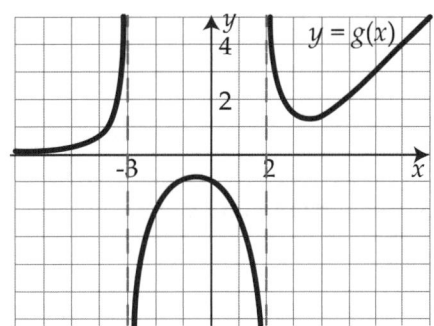

① $\lim\limits_{x \to \infty} f(x)$

② $\lim\limits_{x \to \infty} g(x)$

③ $\lim\limits_{x \to -\infty} f(x)$

④ $\lim\limits_{x \to -\infty} g(x)$

⑤ $\lim\limits_{x \to -2^+} f(x)$

⑥ $\lim\limits_{x \to -3^+} g(x)$

⑦ $\lim\limits_{x \to -2^-} f(x)$

⑧ $\lim\limits_{x \to -3^-} g(x)$

⑨ $\lim\limits_{x \to 2^+} g(x)$

⑩ $\lim\limits_{x \to 2^-} g(x)$

Blank : ① ∞ ② 0

EXAMPLE 3. Find the limit.

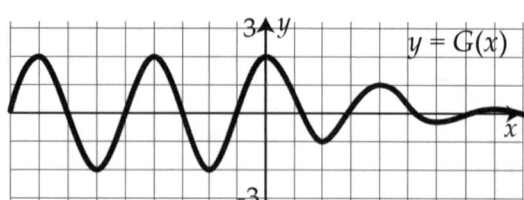

① $\lim\limits_{x \to -\infty} G(x)$

② $\lim\limits_{x \to \infty} G(x)$

③ $\lim\limits_{x \to 0} G(x)$

3. Evaluating Limits

① Direct substitution (Just put the values in)

If f is continuous at $x = c$, and c, a are any real number, then

$$\lim_{x \to c} f(x) = f(c) \qquad \lim_{x \to c} a = a$$

② Cancelation

When you do the substitution and get $\dfrac{0}{0}$, you can factor out the numerator (or denominator) and cross out.

$$\lim_{x \to 1} \frac{x^2 - 1}{x - 1} = \lim_{x \to 1} \frac{\boxed{①}}{(x-1)} = \lim_{x \to 1}(x+1) = 2$$

③ Rationalization (use conjugate)

$$\lim_{x \to 4} \frac{2 - \sqrt{x}}{4 - x} = \lim_{x \to 4} \frac{(2 - \sqrt{x})\;\boxed{②}}{(4-x)\;\boxed{③}} = \lim_{x \to 4} \frac{4 - x}{(4-x)(2+\sqrt{x})} = \lim_{x \to 4} \frac{1}{(2+\sqrt{x})} = \frac{1}{4}$$

Blank : ① (x+1)(x-1) ② 2+√x ③ 2+√x

EXAMPLE 4. Evaluate.

> Always try substitution 1ˢᵗ!

① $\lim_{x \to 2} \left(4x^2 + 3\right)$

② $\lim_{x \to 3} \dfrac{\sqrt{x+1}}{x-4}$

③ $\lim_{x \to \frac{\pi}{3}} \sin\left(\dfrac{x}{2}\right)$

④ $\lim_{t \to 2} \dfrac{t^2 - 3t + 2}{t^2 - 4}$

⑤ $\lim_{x \to 0} \dfrac{(2+x)^3 - 8}{x}$

1. Limit   21

⑥ $\lim\limits_{x \to 0} \dfrac{\sqrt{x+3} - \sqrt{3}}{x}$

⑦ $\lim\limits_{x \to 9} \dfrac{3 - \sqrt{x}}{x - 9}$

AP Style Problem

1. The graph of a function f is shown. Which of the following statements about f is true?

   A) $\lim\limits_{x \to a} f(x)$ does not exists.

   B) $\lim\limits_{x \to b} f(x) = 2$

   C) $\lim\limits_{x \to a} f(x) = 2$

   D) $\lim\limits_{x \to a} f(x) = \lim\limits_{x \to b} f(x)$

   E) $\lim\limits_{x \to b} f(x) = 1$

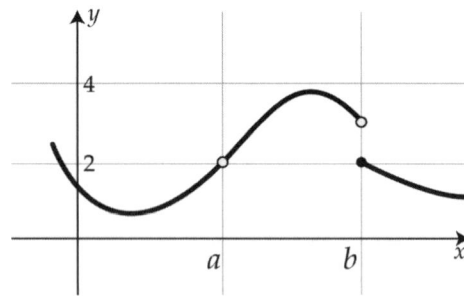

2. For what value(s) of a is it true that $\lim_{x \to a} f(x)$ exists and $f(a)$ exist, but $\lim_{x \to a} f(x) \neq f(a)$

   A) -1 only
   B) 1 only
   C) 2 only
   D) -1 or 1
   E) 1, -1, or 2

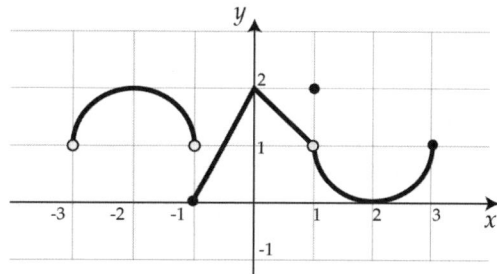

3. $\lim_{x \to a} f(x)$ does not exist for $a =$

   A) -1 only
   B) 1 only
   C) 2 only
   D) -1 or 1
   E) 1, -1, or 2

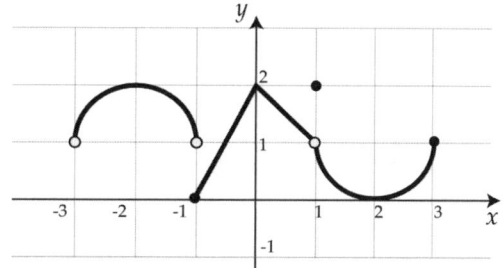

4. If $a \neq 0$, then $\lim_{x \to a} \dfrac{x^4 - a^4}{x^2 - a^2}$ is

   A) $6a^2$
   B) a^2
   C) 0
   D) $2a^2$
   E) Not exist.

1. Limit   23

5. For what value of k does $\lim\limits_{x \to 3} \dfrac{x^2 - x + k}{x - 3}$ exist?

   A) -12
   B) 7
   C) 6
   D) -6
   E) No such value exists.

4. Properties of Limits

Let b, c: real number, n: positive number, and

$$\lim_{x \to c} f(x) = L \qquad \lim_{x \to c} g(x) = K$$

then

$$\lim_{x \to c} [b f(x)] = bL$$

$$\lim_{x \to c} [f(x) + g(x)] = L + K$$

$$\lim_{x \to c} [f(x) g(x)] = LK$$

$$\lim_{x \to c} \left[\dfrac{f(x)}{g(x)}\right] = \dfrac{L}{K}, \; K \neq 0$$

$$\lim_{x \to c} [f(x)]^n = L^n$$

EXAMPLE 5. Assume that $\lim_{x \to 4} f(x) = 7$ and $\lim_{x \to 4} g(x) = -3$. Find

① $\lim_{x \to 4} (g(x) + 3f(x) + 1)$

② $\lim_{x \to 4} xf(x)$

③ $\lim_{x \to 4} \dfrac{g(x)}{f(x) - 1}$

④ $\lim_{x \to 4} \sqrt{x^2 f(x)}$

⑤ $\lim_{x \to 4} e^{f(x)}$

AP Style Problem

1. The selected values for the function $g(x)$ is given as shown.

x	2.8	2.9	2.999	3	3.001	3.1	3.2
$g(x)$	4.2	4.01	4.001	1	3.999	3.9	3.8

If $g(x)$ is not continuous at $x = 3$, what is $\lim_{x \to 3} e^{\sqrt{g(x)}} =$

A) $2e$

B) e

C) e^2

D) 4

E) 1

2. The graph of f(x) is given.

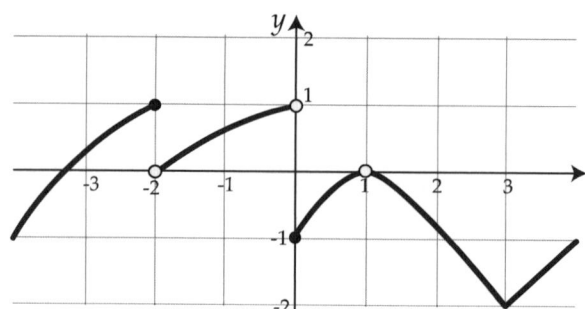

1) $\lim_{x \to 1} f(f(x)) =$

A) -1   B) 1   C) 2   D) 3

2) $\lim_{x \to 3} f(f(x)) =$

A) -2   B) 0   C) 1   D) 3

5. One sided Limits and Vertical Asymptotes

EXAMPLE 6. Find the limit.

① $f(x) = \begin{cases} 3-x, & x \leq 2 \\ \dfrac{x}{2}+1, & x > 2 \end{cases}$

a) $f(2)$

b) $\lim\limits_{x \to 2} f(x)$

c) $\lim\limits_{x \to 2^+} f(x)$

d) $\lim\limits_{x \to 2^-} f(x)$

② $f(x) = \begin{cases} \dfrac{x-1}{x^2-1}, & x \neq 1 \\ 4, & x = 1 \end{cases}$

a) $f(1)$

b) $\lim\limits_{x \to 1} f(x)$

c) $\lim\limits_{x \to 1^+} f(x)$

d) $\lim\limits_{x \to 1^-} f(x)$

③ $\lim\limits_{x \to 0^+} \dfrac{|x|}{x}$ ④ $\lim\limits_{x \to 0^-} \dfrac{|x|}{x}$

⑤ $\lim\limits_{x \to 4^+} \dfrac{x^2 - 16}{|x - 4|}$ ⑥ $\lim\limits_{x \to 4^-} \dfrac{x^2 - 16}{|x - 4|}$

※ Definition of 'Vertical' Asymptote :

To find the vertical asymptote; find where the function is undefined.

If we have a vertical asymptote at $x = a$;

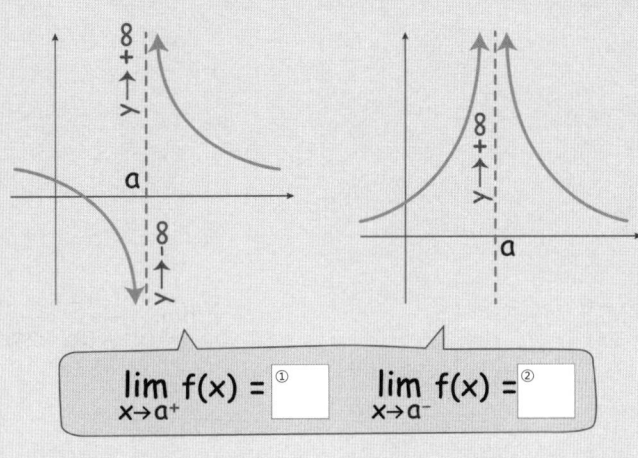

$$\lim_{x \to a^+} f(x) = \boxed{①} \qquad \lim_{x \to a^-} f(x) = \boxed{②}$$

EXAMPLE 7. Find the limit.

If you have $\dfrac{number}{0}$, use test number to decide ∞ or -∞.

$\lim\limits_{x \to 1^+} \dfrac{1}{x-1} = (-\infty \ vs \ \infty)$ ③ $\lim\limits_{x \to 1^-} \dfrac{1}{x-1} = (-\infty \ vs \ \infty)$ ④

---

① $\lim\limits_{x \to 2^+} \dfrac{1}{x-2}$ ② $\lim\limits_{x \to 2^-} \dfrac{1}{x-2}$

Blank : ① ∞ or -∞   ② ∞ or -∞   ③ ∞ (If we plug in 1.1, it is positive)   ④ -∞ (If we plug in 0.9, it is negative)

③ $\lim\limits_{x \to 3^+} \dfrac{-2}{(x-3)^3}$

④ $\lim\limits_{x \to 3^-} \dfrac{-2}{(x-3)^3}$

⑤ $\lim\limits_{x \to 1^+} \dfrac{x^2 - 5x + 6}{x - 1}$

⑥ $\lim\limits_{x \to 4} \dfrac{x - 5}{(x^2 - 10x + 24)^2}$

⑦ $\lim\limits_{\theta \to 0^+} \csc \theta$

⑧ $\lim\limits_{\theta \to 0^-} \csc \theta$

AP Style Problem

1. If $f(x) = \begin{cases} \ln x, & 0 < x \leq 2 \\ x^2 \ln 2, & 2 < x \end{cases}$, then $\lim_{x \to 2} f(x)$ is

   A) ln 8

   B) nonexistent

   C) ln 2

   D) ln 16

   E) 4

2. If $f(x) = \begin{cases} \dfrac{x^2 - x}{|x|}, & x \neq 0 \\ 0, & x = 0 \end{cases}$, then $\lim_{x \to 0} f(x)$ is

   A) 1

   B) nonexistent

   C) -1

   D) 0

   E) 2

3. A function $f(x)$ has a vertical asymptote at $x = 5$. $f(x)$ is increasing for all $x \neq 5$. Which statement is true?

   I. $\lim_{x \to 5} f(x) = +\infty$

   II. $\lim_{x \to 5^+} f(x) = +\infty$

   III. $\lim_{x \to 5^-} f(x) = +\infty$

   A) I and II only

   B) II only

   C) III only

   D) I only

   E) I and III only

6. Finding Limit when x goes to ∞

EXAMPLE 8. Find the limit.

① $\lim_{x \to \infty} \dfrac{1}{x}$

② $\lim_{x \to \infty} \dfrac{1}{x^2}$

③ $\lim_{x \to -\infty} \dfrac{1}{x}$

④ $\lim_{x \to -\infty} \dfrac{1}{x^2}$

> Try to divide the top and bottom
> by highest power of x in the denominator.

⑤ $\lim_{x \to \infty} \dfrac{x-2}{2x^2 - 4x + 3}$

⑥ $\lim_{x \to \infty} \dfrac{3x^2 - 2x + 1}{x^2 + 2}$

⑦ $\lim_{x \to \infty} \dfrac{-4x^4 + 2x^3 + 8}{x + 3}$

⑧ $\lim_{x \to \infty} \dfrac{\sqrt{4x^2 + 1}}{-x + 1}$

※ Limits at infinity

$$\lim_{x \to \infty} \dfrac{1}{x^n} = 0 \qquad \lim_{x \to -\infty} \dfrac{1}{x^n} = 0$$

7. Limit at infinity and Horizontal Asymptotes

※ Rank of the growth rate.

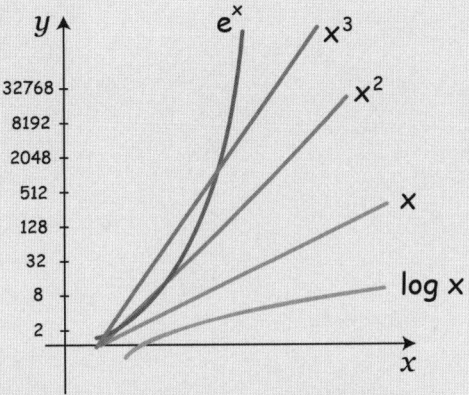

We can rank the growth rate of functions when $x \to \infty$.

$$\ln x < x^2 < x^4 < e^x < 3^x < x! < x^x$$

let $f(x)$ and $g(x)$ be positive for large x.

① If $f(x)$ grows faster than $g(x)$ as $x \to \infty$,

$$\lim_{x \to \infty} \frac{f(x)}{g(x)} = \boxed{①}$$

$$\lim_{x \to \infty} \frac{g(x)}{f(x)} = \boxed{②}$$

② If $f(x)$ and $g(x)$ grow at the same rate as $x \to \infty$,

$$\lim_{x \to \infty} \frac{f(x)}{g(x)} = L \text{ (ratio of leading coefficient)}$$

Blank : ① ∞ ② 0

EXAMPLE 9. Find the limit.

① $\lim\limits_{x \to \infty} -3x^3 + 5x^2 + 100$

② $\lim\limits_{x \to \infty} -5x^3 + 5x^4$

③ $\lim\limits_{x \to \infty} \dfrac{x-2}{2x^2 - 4x + 3}$

④ $\lim\limits_{x \to \infty} \dfrac{3x^5 - x^3 + 10}{2 + 5x^5}$

⑤ $\lim\limits_{x \to \infty} \dfrac{3x^2}{x^{1/2} + 2}$

⑥ $\lim_{x\to\infty}\sqrt{\dfrac{3x^2}{x^{1/2}+2}}$

⑦ $\lim_{x\to\infty}\dfrac{\sqrt{4x^2+1}}{1+x}$

⑧ $\lim_{x\to-\infty}\dfrac{x^2-x+100}{2x^2-2}$

⑨ $\lim_{x\to\infty}\dfrac{e^x}{x^3}+2$

⑩ $\lim\limits_{x\to\infty} -\dfrac{\ln x}{x^3} - 4$

⑪ $\lim\limits_{x\to\infty} \dfrac{2e^x}{1+3e^x}$

⑫ $\lim\limits_{x\to\infty} \dfrac{2^x}{1+3^x}$

⑬ $\lim\limits_{x\to\infty} \sqrt{x+1} - \sqrt{x}$

※ Definition of 'Horizontal' Asymptote :

If we have a horizontal asymptote at $y = b$;

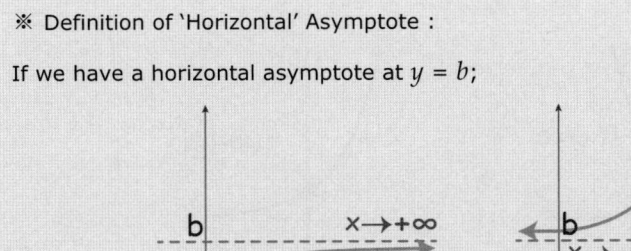

$$\lim_{x \to \infty} f(x) = b \qquad \lim_{x \to -\infty} f(x) = ①$$

To find the horizontal asymptote; find $\lim\limits_{x \to \infty}$ and $\lim\limits_{x \to -\infty}$

EXAMPLE 10. Find the horizontal asymptote of $y = \dfrac{-3x}{\sqrt{x^2+3}}$.

Blank : ① b

8. Exponential function and Limits

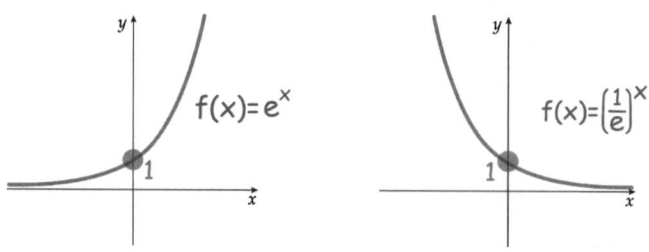

$$\lim_{x\to\infty} e^x = \boxed{①} \qquad \lim_{x\to\infty} e^{-x} = \boxed{②}$$

EXAMPLE 11. Find the limit.

① $\lim_{x\to\infty} e^x + 2$

② $\lim_{x\to\infty} e^{-x} + 5$

③ $\lim_{x\to-\infty} -2e^x - 6$

④ $\lim_{x\to\infty} -2e^{\frac{1}{x}} - 6$

⑤ $\lim_{x\to-\infty} \dfrac{3+2^x}{1+3^x}$

Blank : ① ∞   ② 0

AP Style Problem

1. In order for the line $y = t$ to be a horizontal asymptote of $G(x)$, which of the following must be true?

    A) $\lim\limits_{x \to t^-} G(x) = \infty$

    B) $\lim\limits_{x \to \infty} G(x) = \infty$

    C) $\lim\limits_{x \to -\infty} G(x) = t$

    D) $\lim\limits_{x \to t^+} G(x) = \infty$

    E) $\lim\limits_{x \to -\infty} G(x) = \infty$

2. What is(are) the horizontal asymptote of $y = \dfrac{e^x + 3}{e^x - 1}$?

    A) $y = 1$

    B) $y = 1, y = 3$

    C) $y = 1, y = -3$

    D) $y = 0, y = 1$

    E) none

9. Special Trig limits

$$\lim_{x \to 0} \frac{\sin x}{x} = \boxed{①}$$
$$\lim_{x \to 0} \frac{1 - \cos x}{x} = 0$$

$$\lim_{x \to \infty} \frac{\sin x}{x} = 0$$
$$\lim_{x \to \infty} \frac{1 - \cos x}{x} = 0$$

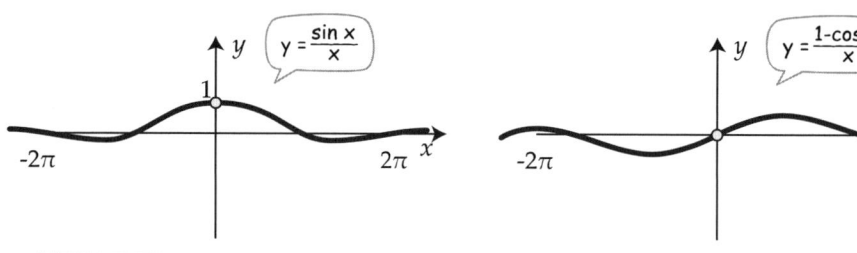

EXAMPLE 12. Find the limit.

① $\lim_{x \to 0} \dfrac{2 \sin x}{3x}$

② $\lim_{x \to 0} \dfrac{\tan x}{x}$

③ $\lim_{x \to 0} \dfrac{\sin 3x}{2x}$

Blank : ① 1

④ $\lim\limits_{x \to 0} \dfrac{\sin 4x}{\sin 8x}$

⑤ $\lim\limits_{x \to 0} \dfrac{\sin 2x}{\tan 6x}$

⑥ $\lim\limits_{x \to \infty} \dfrac{2x + \sin x}{x}$

⑦ $\lim\limits_{x \to \frac{\pi}{2}} \dfrac{1 - \sin x}{\cos x}$

⑧ $\lim\limits_{x\to 0}\dfrac{1-\cos 2x}{x^2}$

⑨ $\lim\limits_{x\to\infty}\arctan x$

10. Squeeze theorem

If $g(x) \leq f(x) \leq h(x)$
and $\lim_{x \to c} h(x) = L$, $\lim_{x \to c} g(x) = L$
then $\lim_{x \to c} f(x) = L$

EXAMPLE 13. Show that $\lim_{x \to \infty} \dfrac{\sin x}{x} = 0$ using squeeze theorem.

11. * Formal Definition of Limit

☺ Reminder

|x - a|<b means: Numbers within ①____ units of ②____

|x - a|<b (if b is a small number) means:
 Numbers really close to ③____

Assume f is defined in a neighborhood of c and let c and L be real numbers. The function f has limit L as x approaches c if, given any positive number ε(epsilon), there is a positive number δ(delta) such that for all x,

$$0 < |x - c| < \delta \quad \text{then} \quad |f(x) - L| < \varepsilon$$

If I have a number really close to c — *then f(x) has a number really close to L*

We write

$$\lim_{x \to c} f(x) = L$$

then f(x) has a number really close to L / *If I have a number really close to c*

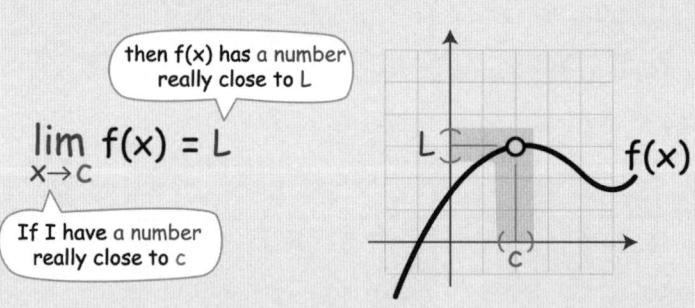

Blank : ① b   ② a   ③ a

* All in One about Evaluating Limits

Evaluate $\lim_{x \to c} f(x)$. c could be numbers, ∞ or -∞.

If we plug in c and get;	answer is / solving method	example
$\dfrac{\text{number}}{\text{number}}$	number	$\lim_{x \to 1} \dfrac{x^2+1}{x} = \dfrac{2}{1} = 2$
$\dfrac{0}{\text{number}}$	0	$\lim_{x \to 1} \dfrac{x^2-1}{x} = \dfrac{0}{1} = 0$
$\dfrac{0}{0}$	factor and reduce / use conjugate	$\lim_{x \to 1} \dfrac{x^2-1}{x-1} = \lim_{x \to 1}(x+1) = 2$
$\dfrac{\text{number}}{0}$	either ∞ or -∞	$\lim_{x \to 1^-} \dfrac{x^2}{x-1} = -\infty$
$\dfrac{\text{number}}{\infty}$	0	$\lim_{x \to \infty} \dfrac{5}{x-1} = 0$
∞ + ∞	∞	$\lim_{x \to \infty} \sqrt{x}+\sqrt{x-1} = \infty$
∞ - ∞	use conjugate	$\lim_{x \to \infty} \sqrt{x}-\sqrt{x-1} = \lim_{x \to \infty} \dfrac{1}{\sqrt{x}+\sqrt{x-1}} = 0$
∞ × ∞	∞	$\lim_{x \to \infty} \sqrt{x} \cdot \sqrt{x-1} = \infty$
$\dfrac{\infty}{\infty}$	compare the growth rate	$\lim_{x \to \infty} \dfrac{x^3+5x}{x^5-x} = 0$
e^{∞}	∞	$\lim_{x \to \infty} e^{x^2+1} = \infty$
$e^{-\infty}$	0	$\lim_{x \to \infty} e^{-x} + 3 = 0 + 3 = 3$
arctan ∞	$\dfrac{\pi}{2}$	$\lim_{x \to \infty} \arctan x = \dfrac{\pi}{2}$

Mia's AP Calculus

2. Continuity and Discontinuity

1. Continuity

Discontinuity: a graph which is not continuous

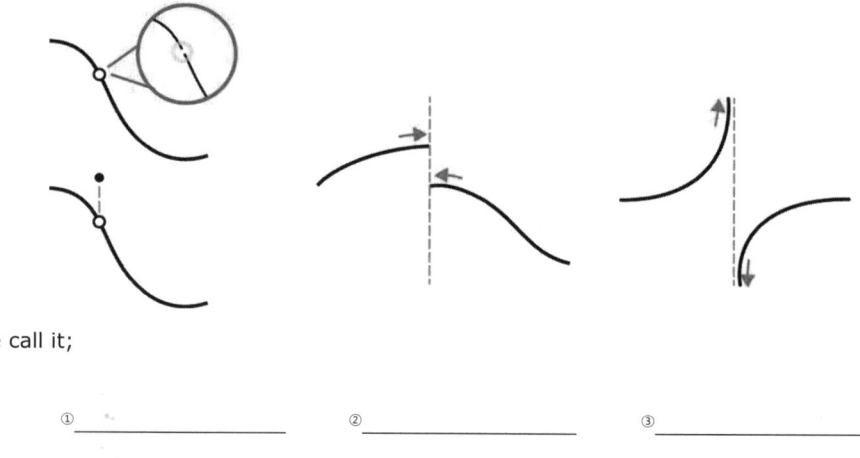

we call it;

① _____ ② _____ ③ _____
  discontinuity   discontinuity   discontinuity

Discontinuity and limit:
f is discontinuous at c. Describe each using function or limit notation.

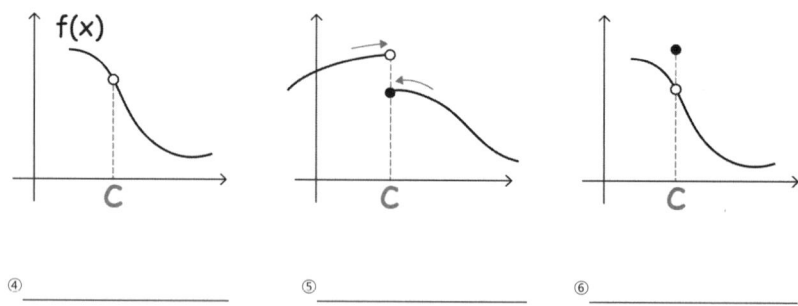

④ _____   ⑤ _____   ⑥ _____

If we think this in opposite way, then we will have a 'definition of continuity of f at c'.

Blank : ① removable ② jump ③ infinite ④ $f(c) =$ und ⑤ $\lim_{x \to c} f(x) = $ DNE ⑥ $\lim_{x \to c} f(x) \neq f(c)$

46 Mia's AP calculus AB BC

※ Definition of Continuity

The function is **continuous** at C, if

1. $f(c)$ is defined.
2. $\lim_{x \to c} f(x)$ exists.
3. $\lim_{x \to c} f(x) = f(c)$

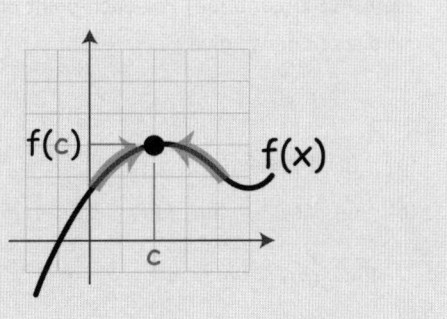

EXAMPLE 1. Find all values $x = a$ where the function is discontinuous in [-3, 3]. Name its discontinuity.

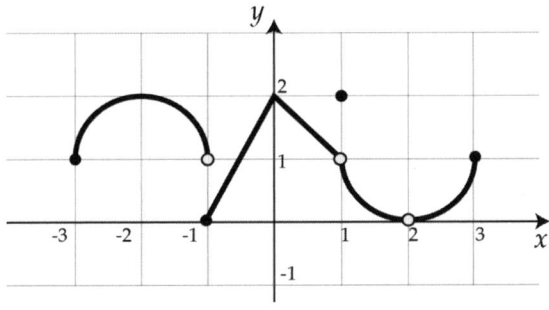

EXAMPLE 2. (*continue*) For each point of discontinuity, give ;

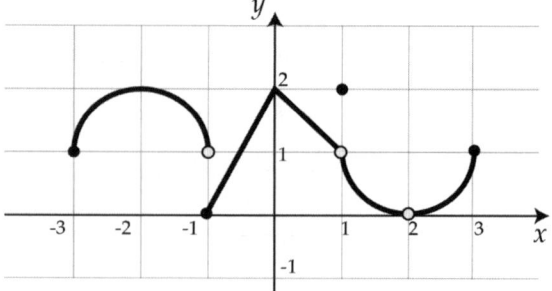

(a) $f(a)$ if it exists,

(b) $\lim_{x \to a^-} f(x)$, $\lim_{x \to a^+} f(x)$

$\lim_{x \to a} f(x)$,

(c) $\lim_{x \to a} f(x) = f(a)$, and

(d) identify which conditions for continuity are NOT met.

EXAMPLE 3. (*continue*) What value should be assigned to f(2) and to make the extended function continuous at x = 2?

EXAMPLE 4. State whether the function is continuous at the indicated point. If it is not continuous, identify which conditions for continuity are NOT met.

① $f(x) = \begin{cases} 3-x, & x < 2 \\ \dfrac{x}{2}+1, & x > 2 \end{cases}$

State whether f(x) is continuous at the point x = 2.

② $f(x) = \begin{cases} 3-x, & x \leq 2 \\ x/2, & x > 2 \end{cases}$

State whether f(x) is continuous at the point x = 2.

③ $f(x) = \begin{cases} \dfrac{x^2-x}{x-1}, & x \neq 1 \\ 1, & x = 1 \end{cases}$

State whether f(x) is continuous at the point x = 1.

④ $f(x) = \begin{cases} \dfrac{x^3-1}{x^2+2x-3}, & x \neq 1 \\ 2, & x = 1 \end{cases}$

State whether f(x) is continuous at the point x = 1.

EXAMPLE 5. Find a value for a or b so that the function is continuous.

① $f(x) = \begin{cases} x^2 - 1, & x < 3 \\ 2ax, & x \geq 3 \end{cases}$

② $f(x) = \begin{cases} \dfrac{5\sin x}{x}, & x < 0 \\ a - 3x, & x \geq 0 \end{cases}$

③ $f(x) = \begin{cases} 3, & x \leq -1 \\ ax + b, & -1 < x < 3 \\ -5, & x \geq 3 \end{cases}$

AP Style Problem

1. The function $G(x) = \begin{cases} x+3 &, x > 2 \\ 4 &, x = 2 \\ 3x-1 &, x < 2 \end{cases}$ is not continuous at $x = 2$ because

   A) $\lim\limits_{x \to 2} G(x)$ does not exist

   B) $\lim\limits_{x \to 2} G(x) \neq G(2)$

   C) $G(2) \neq 4$

   D) $G(2)$ is not defined

   E) All of the above

2. If $f(x) = \begin{cases} \dfrac{\sqrt{2x+3} - \sqrt{x+4}}{x-1} &, x \neq 1 \\ k &, x = 1 \end{cases}$, and if f is continuous at $x = 1$, then $k = ?$

   A) $\dfrac{\sqrt{5}}{2}$

   B) $\dfrac{\sqrt{5}}{10}$

   C) 1

   D) $\dfrac{\sqrt{10}}{10}$

   E) 0

3. Suppose $\lim_{x \to 2^+} g(x) = 1$, $\lim_{x \to 2^-} g(x) = 1$, and $g(2)$ is not defined. Which of the following statements is(are) true?

I. $\lim_{x \to 2} g(x) = 1$

II. g is discontinuous at $x = 2$ but continuous everywhere at $x \neq 2$

III. g has a removable discontinuity at $x = 2$.

A) I and II only
B) II only
C) III only
D) I only
E) I and III only

Mia's AP Calculus

3. Differentiation

☺ reminder
Slope shows the ①_____ of a line.

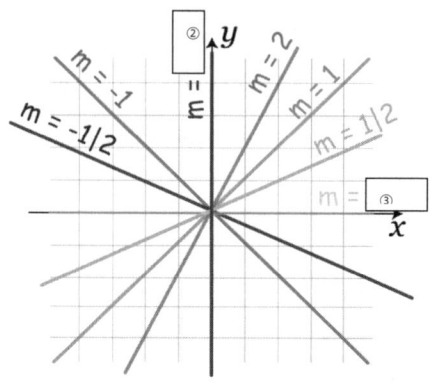

$$\text{slope}(m) = \frac{\text{rise}}{\text{run}} = \frac{\Delta y}{\Delta x} = \frac{y_2 - y_1}{x_2 - x_1}$$

1. Average rate of change

The **slope of the** ④_____ **line**

(The line that crosses ⑤_____ points on a curve)

is ;

We call it the '⑦_____ rate of change'.

※ **Average Rate of Change**

The **slope of the secant line**
that goes through two points **a** and **b**
= Average rate of change =

$$\frac{f(b) - f(a)}{b - a}$$

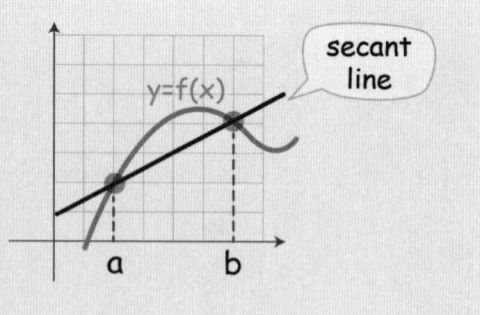

Blank : ① steepness ② undefined slope ③ 0 ④ secant ⑤ two ⑥ $\frac{f(b) - f(a)}{b - a}$ ⑦ Average

EXAMPLE 1. Find the average rate of change over the given interval.

① $f(x) = x^2 + 3x$, [2, 6]

② $f(x) = \dfrac{3}{x}$, [1, 7]

2. Instantaneous rate of change

When we have a curve...

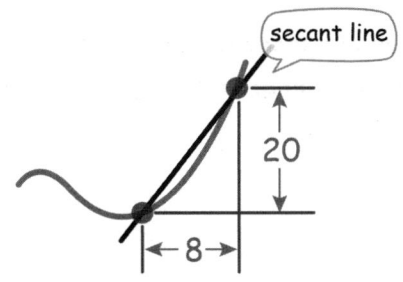

We can find an **average slope**
between two points.

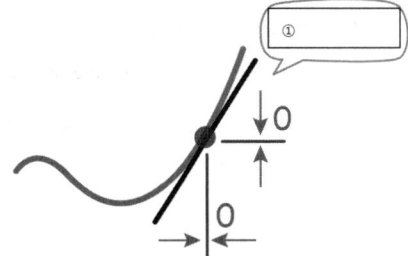

How do we find the **slope**
at one point?

Blank : ① tangent

Let's find the slope of a tangent line (The line that crosses ①_____ point on a curve) at point **x**. Assign an arbitrary point **h bigger than x**.

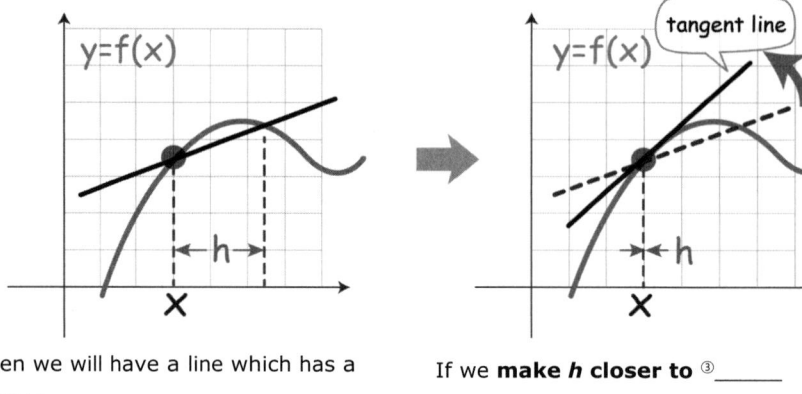

Then we will have a line which has a slope ;

②

If we **make h closer to** ③_____ then **line will become a** ④_____ line which has a slope;

⑤

We use a special notation for the **slope of a tangent line** at point **x** as ⑥_____ and call that **Instantaneous Rate of change** or ⑦_____ **of** *f* (which is 'slope function').

Blank : ① one ② $\frac{f(x+h)-f(x)}{(x+h)-x}$ ③ 0 ④ tangent ⑤ $\lim_{h\to 0} \frac{f(x+h)-f(x)}{(x+h)-x}$ ⑥ f'(x) ⑦ Derivative

※ Instantaneous Rate of change (=Derivative)

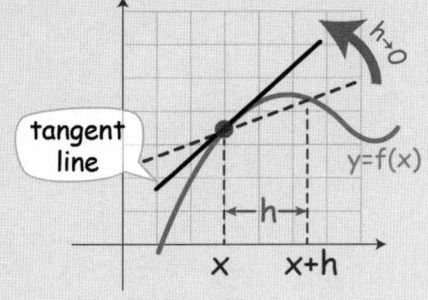

Derivative of f
$$f'(x) = \lim_{h \to 0} \frac{f(x+h)-f(x)}{h}$$

☺ **words**

You do ①_____ ...

to get a ②_____!

to find the ③_____ of change!

to find the ④_____ of the tangent line!

Notation of Derivatives

$$f'(x) \quad y' \quad \frac{d}{dx}f(x) \quad \frac{d}{dx}y \quad \frac{dy}{dx} \quad D_x[y]$$

Derivative of f(x)

dx, dy means infinitely small change of x and y

Blank : ① differentiation ② derivative ③ rate ④ slope

EXAMPLE 2. Find the indicated derivative. (by the limit process)

① $f'(x)$ if $f(x) = x^2 + 2x$

② $\dfrac{dy}{dx}$ if $y = \sqrt{x}$

③ $\dfrac{ds}{dt}$ if $s = \dfrac{t}{2t+1}$

3. Alternative Form of Derivative

When we want to the slope of the tangent line at point a, then we find $f'(a)$.

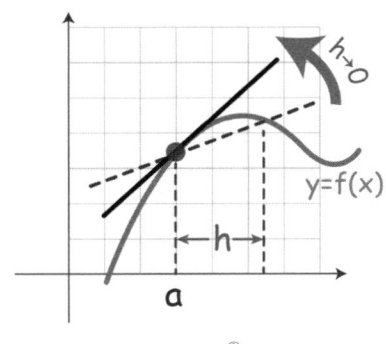

with difference ①_____

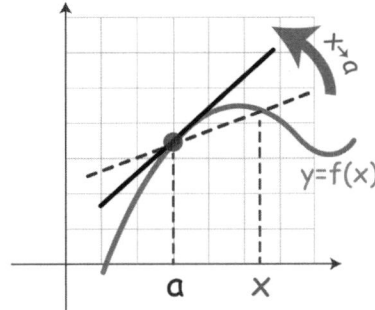

with another point ②_____

$$f'(a) = \lim_{h \to 0} \frac{\boxed{\text{③}}}{h} = \boxed{\text{④}}$$

---

slope at x=a

$$f'(a) = \lim_{h \to 0} \frac{f(a+h)-f(a)}{h} = \lim_{x \to a} \frac{f(x)-f(a)}{x-a}$$

: 'First principle of derivative'   : 'Alternative Form of Derivative'

Blank : ① h   ② x   ③ $f(a+h) - f(a)$ ④ $\lim_{x \to a} \frac{f(x)-f(a)}{x-a}$

EXAMPLE 3. Find the slope of the tangent line at x = a using
  i) the first principle of the derivative, and
  ii) the alternative form of derivative at indicated point.

① $f(x) = \sqrt{x}$, $a = 5$

② $f(x) = x^2 + 3$, $a = 2$

4. Basic Rules of Differentiation

Basic Rules of Derivatives

f(x)	f'(x)
$(x^n)'$	nx^{n-1}
$(cx)'$	c
$(c)'$	0

$(cf(x))'$	$cf'(x)$
$(f(x) \pm g(x))'$	$f'(x) \pm g'(x)$
$(\sin x)'$	$\cos x$
$(\cos x)'$	$-\sin x$
$(\tan x)'$	$\sec^2 x$
$(\sec x)'$	$\tan x \sec x$
$(\cot x)'$	$-\csc^2 x$
$(\csc x)'$	$-\cot x \csc x$
$(\arcsin x)'$	$\dfrac{1}{\sqrt{1-x^2}}$
$(\arccos x)'$	$-\dfrac{1}{\sqrt{1-x^2}}$
$(\arctan x)'$	$\dfrac{1}{1+x^2}$
$(e^x)'$	e^x
$(\ln x)'$	$1/x$
$(a^x)'$	$a^x \ln a$
$(\log_a x)'$	$\dfrac{1}{x \ln a}$

EXAMPLE 4. Find the derivative.

① $y = 7$

② $y = x^2 + \pi$

③ $y = 4x^2 + 2x + 1$

④ $y = \dfrac{1}{2}x^2 - \dfrac{x}{3} + 2$

⑤ $y = t^3 - 2t^2 + 4t + 3$

⑥ $y = x^e - ex + 8$

⑦ $y = \dfrac{1}{x} + \dfrac{1}{x^2}$

⑧ $y = \dfrac{2}{x^3} - \dfrac{1}{3x}$

⑨ $y = \sqrt{a} + \dfrac{1}{\sqrt{a}}$ ⑩ $y = 2\sqrt[3]{x^4} + \dfrac{2}{5\sqrt{x}}$

⑪ $y = \left(x + \dfrac{1}{x}\right)^2$ ⑫ $y = (2x+1)(x-1)$

⑬ $y = 4\sin x$ ⑭ $y = \pi \cos x$

⑮ $y = \dfrac{\sin x}{\cos x}$

⑯ $y = 5 + \cot x$

⑰ $y = \sec x + \csc x$

⑱ $y = -\dfrac{1}{\sin x}$

⑲ $y = x^e + e^x$

⑳ $y = \dfrac{e^x}{5}$

㉑ $y = \ln x + 1$

㉒ $y = \dfrac{2\ln x}{3}$

㉓ $y = 2^x + e^x + x^2$

㉔ $y = \log_2 x$

(use log property)

㉕ $y = \ln x^4$

(use log property)

㉖ $y = e^{x-2}$

5. Recognizing a given limit as a derivative

EXAMPLE 5. Find the limit.

$$f'(a) = \lim_{h \to 0} \frac{f(a+h)-f(a)}{h}$$

Try to find a and $f(x)$ from $f(a+h)$

① $\lim\limits_{h \to 0} \dfrac{(2+h)^4 - 2^4}{h}$

② $\lim\limits_{h \to 0} \dfrac{\sqrt{9+h} - 3}{h}$

③ $\lim\limits_{h \to 0} \dfrac{1}{h}\left(\dfrac{1}{2+h} - \dfrac{1}{2}\right)$

④ $\lim\limits_{h \to 0} \dfrac{e^h - 1}{h}$

⑤ $\lim\limits_{x \to 0} \dfrac{\sin x}{x}$

⑥ $\lim\limits_{x \to 1} \dfrac{x^5 - 1}{x - 1}$

AP Style Problem

1. If g is a function such that $\lim_{x \to 3} \dfrac{g(x)-g(3)}{x-3} = 0$, which of the following must be true?

   A) g is not defined at $x = 3$.

   B) The slope of the tangent line of g at $x = 3$ is 0.

   C) $g(3) = 0$

   D) The limit of $g(x)$ as x approaches 3 does not exist.

   E) g is continuous at $x = 0$.

2. If f is differentiable function, then $f'(a)$ is given by which of the following?

   I. $\lim_{h \to 0} \dfrac{f(a+h)-f(a)}{h}$

   II. $\lim_{x \to a} \dfrac{f(x+h)-f(x)}{h}$

   III. $\lim_{x \to a} \dfrac{f(x)-f(a)}{x-a}$

   IV. $\lim_{x \to a} \dfrac{f(a)-f(x)}{a-x}$

3. Differentiation

3. $\lim_{h \to 0} \dfrac{e^{e+h} - e^e}{h}$ is

A) $f'(e)$ where $f(x) = e^x$

B) $f'(0)$ where $f(x) = e^x$

C) $f'(x)$ where $f(x) = e^x$

D) $f'(x)$ where $f(x) = e^{x+h}$

E) $f'(e)$ where $f(x) = e^{x+h}$

4. Solve the problem.

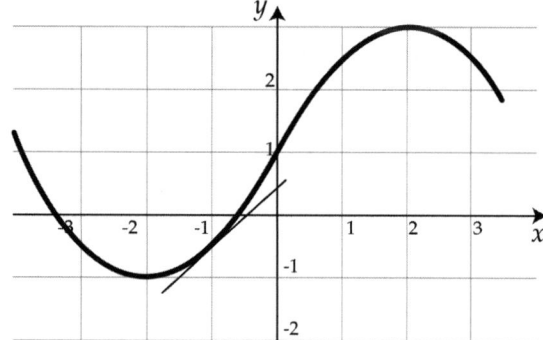

1) $f'(-1)$ is approximately

A) 0   B) 1   C) 2   D) -1   E) -2

2) $\dfrac{f(2) - f(-2)}{4}$ is approximately

A) 0   B) 1   C) 2   D) -1   E) -2

3) The rate of change is the most when x is approximately

A) 0 B) 1 C) 2 D) -1 E) -2

4) Which of the statements is(are) true?

I. $f'(-2) < \dfrac{f(1)-f(0)}{1-0}$

II. $f'(1) < \lim\limits_{h \to 0} \dfrac{f(3+h)-f(3)}{h}$

III. $f'(-1) < f(2)$

5. A differentiable function f has the values shown. Estimate $f'(0.2)$

x	0	0.4	0.8	1.2
$f(x)$	4	12	16	17

A) 0 B) 10 C) 20 D) 40 E) 80

6. For values of h very close to 0, which of the following functions best approximates $f(x) = \dfrac{\sec(x+h) - \sec x}{h}$?

A) $\tan^2 x$

B) $\sin x$

C) $\cos x$

D) $\tan x \sec x$

E) $\sec^2 x$

4. Technique of Differentiation

Mia's AP Calculus

1. Chain Rule

※ Chain rule

When we have a composite function $y = f(g(x))$, we can differentiate using **chain rule** which is

$$\frac{d}{dx} f(g(x)) = \underbrace{f'(g(x))}_{\text{out'}} \cdot \underbrace{g'(x)}_{\text{in'}}$$

$f(x)$	$f'(x)$
$(f(g(h(x))))'$ Chain rule	$f'(g(h(x))) \cdot g'(h(x)) \cdot h'(x)$
$((g(x))^n)'$	①
$(\sin g(x))'$	②
$(\sec g(x))'$	③
$(e^{g(x)})'$	④
$(\ln g(x))'$	⑤

Blank : ① $n[g(x)]^{n-1} g'(x)$ ② $\cos[g(x)] \cdot g'(x)$ ③ $\tan[g(x)] \sec[g(x)] \cdot g'(x)$ ④ $e^{g(x)} \cdot g'(x)$ ⑤ $\frac{1}{g(x)} \cdot g'(x)$

EXAMPLE 1. Find the derivative using chain rule.

① $y = 2(-x+1)^3$

② $y = \sqrt{2x-1}$

③ $y = \dfrac{1}{3x^2+1}$

④ $y = \dfrac{5}{\sqrt{(1-x^2)^3}}$

⑤ $y = \sin 2x$

⑥ $y = 2\cos 3x$

⑦ $y = \sin x^2$

⑧ $y = \sin^2 x$

⑨ $y = \sec(\tan x)$

⑩ $y = \tan(2x^2 + 1)$

⑪ $y = \csc^2 x$

⑫ $y = e^{2x/3}$

⑬ $y = \dfrac{1}{e^{-x+1}}$

⑭ $y = \dfrac{2}{e^{\sin x + 1}}$

⑮ $y = \ln\left(\dfrac{x}{3}\right)$

⑯ $y = 3\ln(2x^2)$

⑰ $y = \ln x^2 + \ln^2 x$

⑱ $y = \sqrt{\ln x} + \ln\sqrt{x}$

⑲ $y = 3^{\cos x}$

☺ Tip: Memorize!

$$\left[\sqrt{x}\right]' = \frac{1}{2\sqrt{x}} \qquad \left[\sqrt{\bigcirc}\right]' = \frac{1}{2\sqrt{\bigcirc}} \cdot \bigcirc' \text{ (using chain rule)}$$

$$\left[\frac{1}{x}\right]' = -\frac{1}{x^2} \qquad \left[\frac{1}{\bigcirc}\right]' = -\frac{1}{\bigcirc^2} \cdot \bigcirc' \text{ (using chain rule)}$$

EXAMPLE 2. Find the derivative using chain rule more than once.

① $y = \cos^3 2x$

② $f(x) = \sec^2 x^3$

③ $y = e^{\sin x^3}$

④ $y = e^{\sin^3 x}$

⑤ $y = (1+\sin^2 3x)^4$

⑥ $y = \sqrt{\sin(e^{2x})}$

2. Product Rule and Quotient Rule

※ Product rule and Quotient Rule

$f(x)$	$f'(x)$
$(f(x)g(x))'$	$f'(x)g(x) + f(x)g'(x)$
$\left(\dfrac{f(x)}{g(x)}\right)'$	$\dfrac{f'(x)g(x) - f(x)g'(x)}{g^2(x)}$

EXAMPLE 3. Find dy/dx.

① $y = (x^2 + 1)(2x+3)^2$

② $s(t) = (t^2 + 1)(1-t)^2$

③ $y = e^{2x} \sin x$

④ $f(x) = e^{-x}(\sin x + \cos x)$

⑤ $y = x \ln x$

⑥ $y = \dfrac{x^2 - 1}{x^2 + 1}$

⑦ $y = \dfrac{\sin x}{x^2}$

⑧ $y = \dfrac{\ln x}{x}$

⑨ $f(x) = \left(\dfrac{x-2}{2x+1}\right)^3$

⑩ $y = \dfrac{x}{\sqrt{x^3+2}}$

EXAMPLE 4. Find the slope of the graph of $f(x) = \ln^2(3x^2 + 1)$ at the point where $x = 1$.

EXAMPLE 5. Find x for which the function $f(x) = \ln\left(\dfrac{2}{x^2 - 12}\right)$ has a slope of 2.

EXAMPLE 6. Given $h(x) = \sin x + \cos x$, $0 \le x \le 2\pi$, find the values of x for which h has a horizontal tangent line.

EXAMPLE 7. Given that $f(x) = \dfrac{x^2 - 1}{x^2 + 2}$, find $f''(x)$ in the form $\dfrac{a - bx^2}{(x^2 + 2)^3}$.

EXAMPLE 8. Find the derivative of $\ln \dfrac{(x^3-1)^4 \sqrt{3x-1}}{x^2+4}$ using the properties of log.

3. Implicit Differentiation

When a function is not written in the form y = f(x), implicit differentiation is used. Differentiate each term separately, using the chain rule on all terms involving y:

$$\frac{d}{dx} f(y) = \boxed{①} f(y) \cdot \boxed{②}$$

※ **Implicit Differentiation**

① Take $\frac{d}{dx}$ of both sides of the equation

② Remember to multiply by $\frac{dy}{dx}$ each time you differentiate a **y** term.

③ Solve for $\frac{dy}{dx}$.

EXAMPLE 9. Find dy/dx.

① $x^2 + y^2 = 4$

② $x^3 - xy + 2y^2 = 1$

Blank : ① $\frac{d}{dy}$ ② $\frac{dy}{dx}$

③ $x^2y - xy^2 = 4$

④ $x - y = \cot y$

⑤ $\tan(x+y) = y$

⑥ $x^2 = \dfrac{x-y}{y}$

EXAMPLE 10. Find the slope of the curve $y^2 + \sin(xy) + x^3 = 4$ at the point $(0, 2)$.

EXAMPLE 11. Find the slope of $6x^2 + 3xy + 2y^2 + 17y - 6 = 0$ at the point at the point $(-1, 0)$.

EXAMPLE 12. Find the slope of the normal (perpendicular to tangent) to $y^2 + 3xy - 10x^2 = 0$ where $x = 1$, $y > 0$.

EXAMPLE 13. Find the coordinates of all the points on the curve
$x^2 + y^2 - 3y = 10$.

(a) where the curve has horizontal tangent.

(b) where the curve has vertical tangent.

4. Differentiation of Inverse Trigonometry

※ Differentiation of Inverse Trigonometry

f(x)	f'(x)
(arcsin g(x))'	①
(arccos g(x))'	②
(arctan g(x))'	③

proof☺ y = arcsin x . Find y'.

1. Write definition of inverse function.

2. Sketch a triangle.

3. Differentiate with respect to x.

4. Use triangle to substitute trig expression.

Blank : ① $\dfrac{1}{\sqrt{1-g^2(x)}} \cdot g'(x)$ ② $-\dfrac{1}{\sqrt{1-g^2(x)}} \cdot g'(x)$ ③ $\dfrac{1}{1+g^2(x)} \cdot g'(x)$

EXAMPLE 14. Find the derivative.

① $y = \arctan x$

② $y = \arctan \dfrac{x}{2}$

③ $y = \arcsin x + \sqrt{1-x^2}$

④ $y = 4x^3 \sin^{-1} x$

⑤ $y = (\tan^{-1} 3x)^2$

⑥ $y = \arcsin x + \arccos x$

EXAMPLE 15. Find the derivative.

① $6f(x) - g(x)$

② $f^2(x)$

③ $f(f(x))$

④ $g(f(x^2))$

⑤ $\dfrac{f(x^3)}{g(x)+1}$

⑥ $f(x+g(x))$

⑦ $f(x)g(x^2)$

⑧ $f(x)g^2(x)$

5. Second and Higher Order Derivatives

Higher order Derivatives

$y'' = \boxed{①}$ $y''' = \dfrac{d^3}{dx^3}$ $y^{(n)} = \dfrac{d^n}{dx^n}$ nth Derivative

Blank : ① $\dfrac{d^2}{dx^2}$

EXAMPLE 16. For the function $y = x^3 - 3x^2 - 9x + 3$, find $\dfrac{d^3y}{dx^3}$ and $\dfrac{d^4y}{dx^4}$.

EXAMPLE 17. True or False?

① If f(x) is an nth-degree polynomial, then $f^{(n+1)}(x) = 0$.

② If $y = (x+1)(x+2)(x+3)(x+4)$, then $\dfrac{d^4y}{dx^4} = 0$

EXAMPLE 18. Find d^2y/dx^2.

① $xy - x + y = 2$

② $2y^2 - x^2 = 6$

EXAMPLE 19. Let $y = \sin nx$, what is $y^{(99)}$.

AP Style Problem

1. Solve the problem using the table.

x	f	f'	g	g'
0	2	2	2	-3
1	3	2	3	-2
2	1	3	1	0
3	6	4	0	-1

1) If $A(x) = f(g(x^2))$, then $A'(1) =$

A) -16   B) -8   C) 0   D) 8   E) 16

2) If $C(x) = \dfrac{f(x^2)}{g(x)}$, then $C'(0) =$

A) -2   B) -1.5   C) 0.5   D) 1.5   E) 5

3) If $D(x) = \sqrt{f(x)}$, then $D'(2) =$

A) -1.5   B) -0.5   C) 0   D) 0.5   E) 1.5

2. If $f'(x) = x^2 - 4$ and $g(x) = f(x^2 - 4)$, what is $g'(2) = ?$

A) -16

B) 16

C) 0

D) -4

E) 4

3. The tangent to the curve $y^2 - xy + 4 = 0$ is vertical when

A) $x = \pm 2$

B) $x = \pm 4$

C) $x = 0$

D) $x = \pm \sqrt{2}$

E) none of these

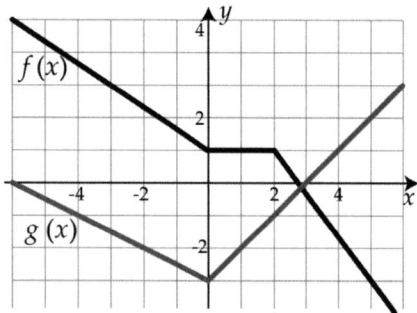

4. Graph of $f(x)$ and $g(x)$ are shown. If $h(x) = f(g(x))$, then $h'(2)$ is

A) 2/3

B) 1/2

C) 0

D) -1/2

E) -2/3

5. If f, g, and h are nonzero differentiable functions, then the derivative of $\frac{fg}{h}$ is

A) $\dfrac{f'gh + fg'h + fgh'}{h^2}$

B) $\dfrac{f'gh + fg'h - fgh'}{h^2}$

C) $\dfrac{f'gh - fg'h - fgh'}{h^2}$

D) $\dfrac{f'g'h - fgh'}{h^2}$

E) $\dfrac{f'g + fg'}{h'}$

6. If $x > 0$, and suppose $\dfrac{d}{dx} f(x) = g(x)$ and $\dfrac{d}{dx} g(x) = f(\sqrt{x})$, then $\dfrac{d^2}{dx^2} f(x^4) =$

A) $g(x^4)$

B) $f(4x^3)$

C) $4x^3 g(x^4)$

D) $4x^3 g(x^2)$

E) $16x^6 f(x^2) + 12x^2 g(x^4)$

7. All the functions below have the property of $f(x) = f^{(4)}(x)$ EXCEPT

A) $f(x) = \sin x$

B) $f(x) = \cos x$

C) $f(x) = 2e^x$

D) $f(x) = e^{2x}$

E) $f(x) = e^{-x}$

8. $\dfrac{d^n}{dx^n} x^n$ is

   A) x^n

   B) nx^{n-1}

   C) $n!x$

   D) $n!$

   E) n^n

9. If $y = \sin x$, $x = \pi$, and $dx = 2$, what does dy equal?

   A) -2   B) -1   C) 0   D) 1   E) 2

Mia's AP Calculus

5. Differentiability and Tangent line

1. Tangent line and Normal Line

Reminder☺ What do we need to find the equation of the line?

① _____ ② _____

※ Tangent Line and Normal Line

Equation of the tangent line:

$y - y_1 = \boxed{③}(x - x_1)$

Equation of the normal line:

$y - y_1 = \boxed{④}(x - x_1)$

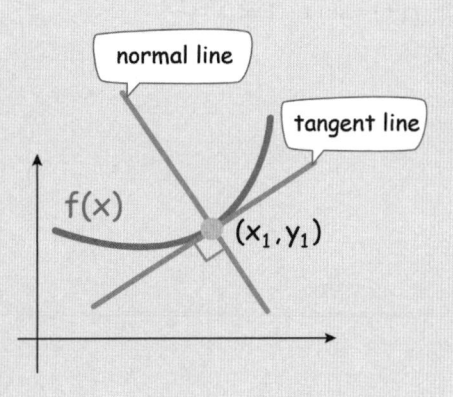

EXAMPLE 1. Find an equation of the tangent line and the normal line to the graph

① $f(x) = x + \dfrac{2}{x}$ at (2, 3).

Blank : ① point ② slope ③ $f'(x_1)$ ④ $-\dfrac{1}{f'(x_1)}$

② $f(x) = 2\ln x$ at $x = e$.

③ $f(x) = \sin x - 1$ at $x = \dfrac{\pi}{2}$

EXAMPLE 2. Find the equation of tangent to $x^2 + xy = 4$ at $x = 1$.

AP Style Problem

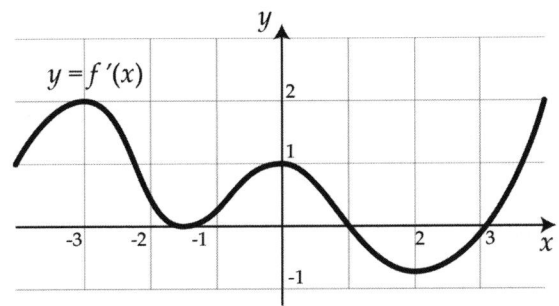

1. The graph of the derivative of f is shown above. The point (0, 2) is on the graph of $f(x)$. An equation of the line tangent to the graph of f at (0, 2) is

    A) $y = x + 2$

    B) $y = x - 2$

    C) $y = 1$

    D) $y = 2x + 1$

    E) $y = 2x - 1$

2. The line $y = x + k$ is tangent to the curve $y = \ln x$ when k is equal

    A) -1

    B) e

    C) 1

    D) 0

    E) 2

3. At what point on the graph of $y = \sqrt{(2x+3)^3}$ is the normal line parallel to the line $x + 6y + 3 = 0$?

   A) (0.5, 4)

   B) (0.5, 8)

   C) (6.5, 4)

   D) (6.5, 8)

   E) none of the above

4. The equation of the tangent line at $x = 5$ of $f(x)$ is $y = -x + 2$. Which of the following must be true?

   I. $f'(5) = -1$

   II. $f(5) = -3$

   III. $f(0) = 2$

   A) I only
   B) I, II
   C) I, III
   D) I, II, and III
   E) None of these

2. Derivatives of Inverse Function

We know that $f(f^{-1}(x)) = x$

take a derivative of both sides, then ① _____

Solve for $(f^{-1})'$: ② _____

※ Derivative of Inverse Function

$$(f^{-1})'(a) = \frac{1}{f'(f^{-1}(a))}$$

The slope of the tangent line of $f(x)$ at $(1,4)$ is 2. Then what is $\left(f^{-1}\right)'(4)$?

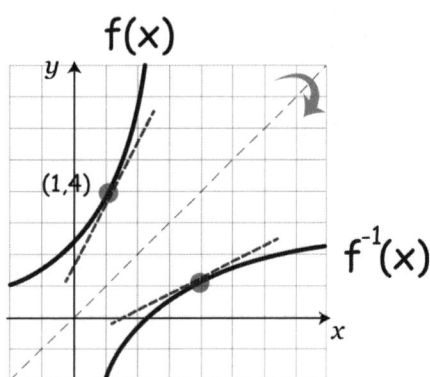

EXAMPLE 3. If $f(x) = x^2 + 4$ (for $x \geq 0$), what is the value of $(f^{-1})'(x)$ at $x = 29$?

Blank : ① $f'(f^{-1}(x)) \cdot (f^{-1}(x))' = 1$ ② $(f^{-1}(x))' = \dfrac{1}{f'(f^{-1}(x))}$

EXAMPLE 4. If $f(x) = \ln x$ and $g(x)$ is the inverse function of f, what is the value of $g'(x)$ at $x = 2$?

AP Style Problem

1. If $f(x) = x^3 - 2x^2 + 5x + 4$ and $g(x) = f^{-1}(x)$, then $g'(4) =$

   A) 1/2
   B) 1/5
   C) 2
   D) 5
   E) 4

x	f	f'
1	2	3
2	7	4

2. Using the table above, find $(f^{-1})'(2) = ?$

   A) 1/2
   B) 1/4
   C) 1/3
   D) 1
   E) 4

x	f	f'
2	3	2
3	4	4
4	5	6

3. What is the equation of the line tangent to $g(x) = f^{-1}(x)$ at $x = 3$?

A) $y - 4 = \dfrac{1}{4}(x - 3)$

B) $y - 4 = \dfrac{1}{2}(x - 3)$

C) $y - 2 = \dfrac{1}{2}(x - 3)$

D) $y - 2 = \dfrac{1}{4}(x - 3)$

E) $y - 2 = \dfrac{1}{6}(x - 4)$

3. Differentiability

※ A Function is **not differentiable** at x = a when the graph has a
1) discontinuity (removable, jump, vertical asymptote)
2) corner or cusp (sharp edges)
3) vertical tangent
4) derivative is undefined

at x = a.

※ Differentiability implies Continuity (true or false?)

If f is **discontinuous** at $x = c$, then f is **not differentiable** at $x = c$. ①_____

If f is **differentiable** at $x = c$, then f is **continuous** at $x = c$. ②_____

If f is **continuous** at $x = c$, then f is **differentiable** at $x = c$. ③_____

counterexamples:

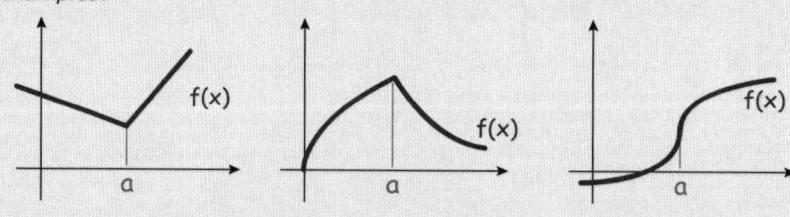

Blank : ① True ② True ③ False

EXAMPLE 5. At which point from a to h does the function appear to be

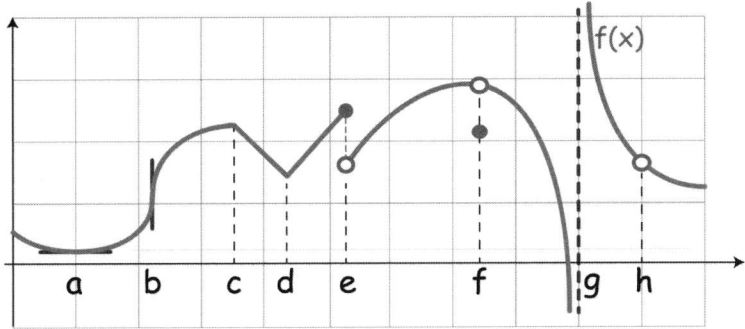

(a) limit does not exist?

(b) discontinuous?

(c) not differentiable?

(d) continuous but not differentiable?

(e) neither continuous nor differentiable?

EXAMPLE 6. Determine continuity and differentiability of the given functions at x = 0.

① $f(x) = \begin{cases} x & , x \leq 0 \\ x^2 & , x > 0 \end{cases}$

② $f(x) = \begin{cases} x^2 + 2 & , x \leq 0 \\ x^2 - 1 & , x > 0 \end{cases}$

③ $f(x) = x|x|$

④ $f(x) = x^2 - 3|x| + 2$

⑤ $f(x) = \sqrt[3]{x^2}$

⑥ $f(x) = \sqrt[3]{x^4}$

AP Style Problem

1. The graph of the function f shown in the figure has a vertical tangent at the point (-1, 1) and horizontal tangents at the points (0, 0) and (-2, 2). In $-4 \le x \le 3$, $f'(x)$ does not exist for $x =$

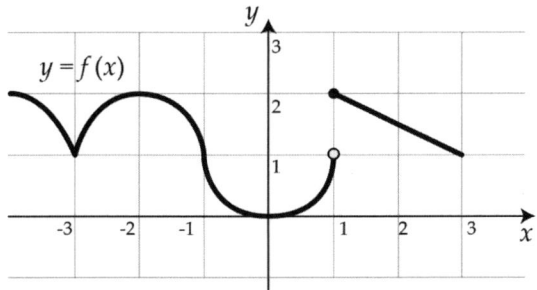

A) -3
B) -3, 1
C) -3, -1
D) -3, -1, 1
E) -3, -2, -1, 0, 1

2. If $f(x) = \begin{cases} \dfrac{2x^2-2}{x-1}, & x \neq 1 \\ 2, & x = 1 \end{cases}$, which of these statements are true?

   I. $\lim_{x \to 1} f(x)$ exists.

   II. f is continuous at $x = 1$.

   III. f is differentiable at $x = 1$.

   A) I only
   B) II only
   C) III only
   D) I and II only
   E) I and III only

3. Which of the following functions shows that the statement "If a function is continuous at $x = 0$, then it is differentiable at $x = 0$" is false?

   A) $f(x) = x^{-\frac{5}{3}}$

   B) $f(x) = x^{-\frac{1}{3}}$

   C) $f(x) = x^5$

   D) $f(x) = x^{\frac{1}{3}}$

   E) $f(x) = x^{\frac{5}{3}}$

4. Let f be a function such that $\lim\limits_{h\to 0}\dfrac{f(3+h)-f(3)}{h}=5$. Which of the following could be false?

A) f is continuous at $x = 3$

B) f is differentiable at $x = 3$

C) $\lim\limits_{x\to 3} f(x)$ exists.

D) The derivative of f is continuous at $x = 3$.

E) $\lim\limits_{x\to 3} f(x) = f(3)$

5. The graph of f' is shown here. Which of the following statements is(are) true of f ?

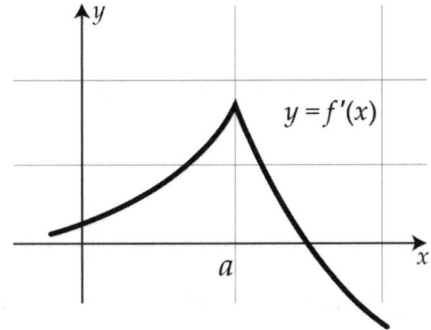

I. f is continuous at $x = a$

II. f is differentiable at $x = a$

III. f has a maximum value at $x = a$

A) I and II only

B) II only

C) III only

D) I only

E) I and III only

Mia's AP Calculus

Free Response Questions (from ch1~5)

(: Do not use calculator,   : Use calculator)

1. Limit and Continuity with graph

The graph of the function f and g are shown.

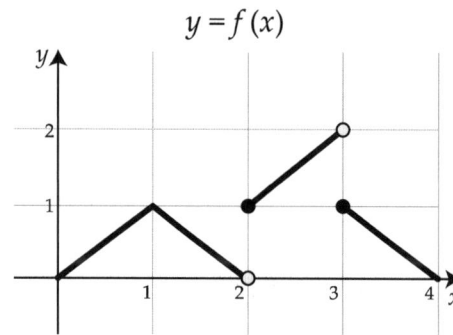

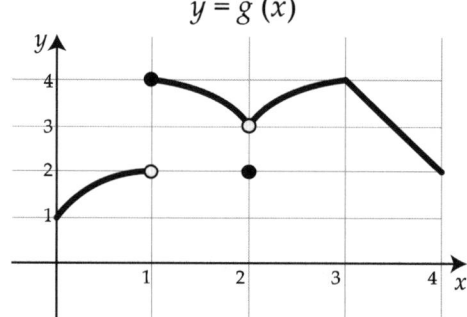

(a) Find $\lim_{x \to 1} g(f(x))$ or explain why the limit does not exist.

(b) Let $h(x) = f(x+2)g(x)$. Is $h(x)$ continuous at $x = 1$? Justify your answer.

(c) Find the $\lim_{h \to 0^+} \dfrac{f(1+h) - f(1)}{h}$ and $\lim_{h \to 0^-} \dfrac{f(1+h) - f(1)}{h}$. Use the value to explain why f is not differentiable at $x = 1$.

2. Derivatives with table

x	1	2	4	6
$g(x)$	4	1	-4	-3
$g'(x)$	1	-2	0	3

The table gives the selected values of a differentiable function g and its derivative g'. Let f be the function defined by $f(x) = x^2 e^{g(x)}$.

(a) Find $f'(2)$. Show the work that leads to your answer.

(b) Let $P(x) = \dfrac{f(x)}{g(x^2)}$. Find $P'(2)$. Show the work that leads to your answer.

(c) Let $Q(x) = f\left(\sqrt{g(x)}\right)$. Find $Q'(1)$. Show the work that leads to your answer.

(d) Let $g^{-1}(x)$ the inverse function of $g(x)$. Find the equation of the tangent line of $g^{-1}(x)$ at $x = 4$.

(e) Find the slope of the tangent line of $y^2 + 2 = g(xy + x)$ at the point $(1, 0)$.

Mia's AP Calculus

6. Extrema and First Derivative

1. Increasing and Decreasing

※ Increasing and Decreasing

graph of $f(x)$	increasing		decreasing
$f'(x)$	$f'(x) > 0$	$f'(x) = 0$	$f'(x) < 0$

Increasing: ①_____   Decreasing: ②_____

ex) Volume is increasing

③ _____

Area is decreasing

④ _____

Slope is increasing

⑤ _____

Rate is decreasing

⑥ _____

Blank : ① '>0 ② '<0 ③ V ' > 0 ④ A'>0 ⑤ f''>0 ⑥ f''<0

2. Critical Points

Find the relative (local) maxima or minima
and absolute maxima or minima of f(x), if any.

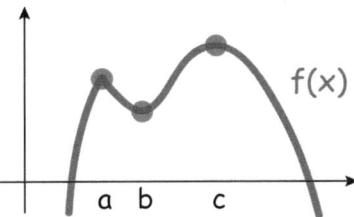

①

In a smoothly changing function, a low point (a local minimum) or high point (a local maximum) occurs

    ① where the graph of the function has ② _____

                                       (=where the slope is ③ _____.)

    ② or *sometimes*, where the slope is ④ _____.

               And we call these spots ⑤ _____.

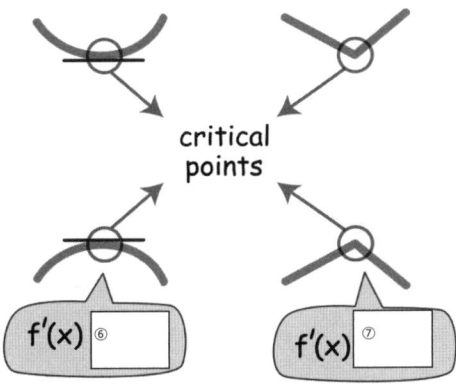

※ Critical Point

                  When f(x) is *continuous* at c

        Critical point c is where $f'(c) = 0$ or und.

                It could be a local max, min, or neither.

Blank : ① relative max : f(a), f(c)   relative min : f(b) absolute max : f(c) no absolute min
② horizontal tangent   ③ 0   ④ undefined   ⑤ critical points   ⑥ = 0   ⑦ = und

EXAMPLE 1. Find the number of critical points of the function on the graph.

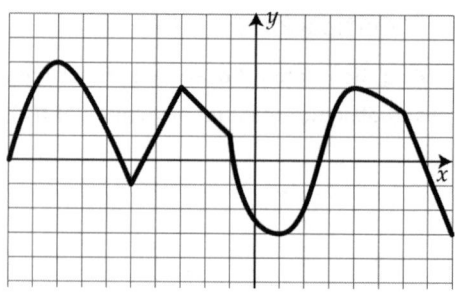

EXAMPLE 2. Determine all x values of critical point for the function.

① $y = x^3 - 3x^2 + 20$

② $y = \dfrac{x^2}{x^2 - 2}$

③ $y = (x-3)^{2/3} + 5$

3. First Derivative Test_ Finding Relative Extrema

Now it is time to find out if a critical point is a **local maximum** or a **local minimum**.

※ First Derivative Test

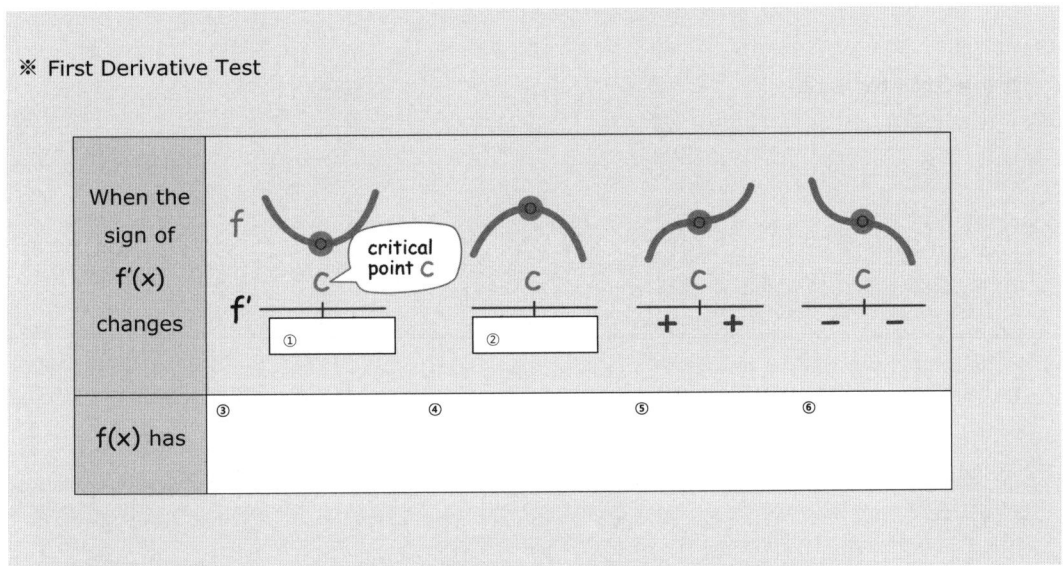

EXAMPLE 3. Find the critical numbers of (if any). Find the open intervals on which the function is increasing or decreasing and find all relative extrema.

> ※ Finding Relative Extreme Values
> ① Find the **critical points** (f' = 0 or und) and build up the intervals
> ② pick a **test points** from each intervals
> ③ and determine if it is **increasing**(f' > 0) or **decreasing**(f' < 0) on that interval by using test points.
> ④ Determine if the critical point is a **maximum** or a **minimum**

Blank : ① − +   ② + −   ③ minimum   ④ maximum   ⑤ neither   ⑥ neither

① $y = 2x^3 - 9x^2 + 12x + 5$

② $y = 3x^4 + 8x^3 + 12.$

③ $y = xe^{-x}$

④ $y = \dfrac{x-3}{x^2-5}$

⑤ $y = \dfrac{x}{2} + \cos x, \quad [0, 2\pi]$

⑥ $y = (x-1)x^{2/3}$

AP Style Problem

1. How many critical points does the function $f(x)=(x+1)^4(x-2)^5$ have?

    A) one
    B) two
    C) three
    D) four
    E) five

2. What are all values of x for which the function f defined by $f(x)=(x^2-3)e^{-x}$ is decreasing?

    A) $x < -1$ and $x > 3$

    B) $-1 < x < 3$

    C) $-3 < x < 1$

    D) There are no such values of x

    E) All values of x

3. The total number of local maximum points of the function whose derivative, for all x, is given by $f'(x)=x^3(x-2)^2(x+4)^4$ is

A) 0
B) 1
C) 2
D) 3
E) 6

4. For what value of k will $y=x+k\sqrt{x}$ have a relative minimum at $x=4$?

A) 2
B) 4
C) -2
D) -4
E) none of these

4. First Derivative Test_ Finding Absolute Extrema

Find the Absolute extreme values of the function on the interval [a, b].

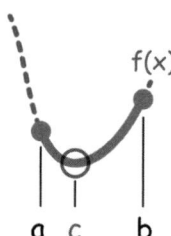

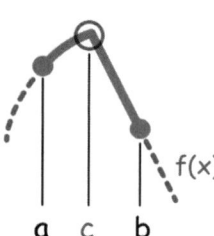

※ Finding Absolute Extreme Values (When given an ①_____)

① Find the critical numbers of *f* in [a, b]
② **Evaluate *f*** at each critical number and at each endpoints
③ The least one will be the ②_____,

and the greatest will be the ③_____.

EXAMPLE 4. Find the absolute extreme values of the function on the interval.

① $f(x) = -x^2 + 2x - 12, \ 0 \le x \le 3$

② $f(x) = e^x - x, \ -3 \le x \le 2$

Blank : ① interval [a, b] ② Absolute minimum ③ Absolute maximum

AP Style Problem

1. The maximum value of $f(x) = x^3 - 3x^2 + 12$ on the interval [-2, 1] is
   A) -9
   B) -8
   C) 0
   D) 9
   E) 12

5. Graphing f'(x)

EXAMPLE 5. The graph of f is given. Sketch the graph of $f'(x)$.

①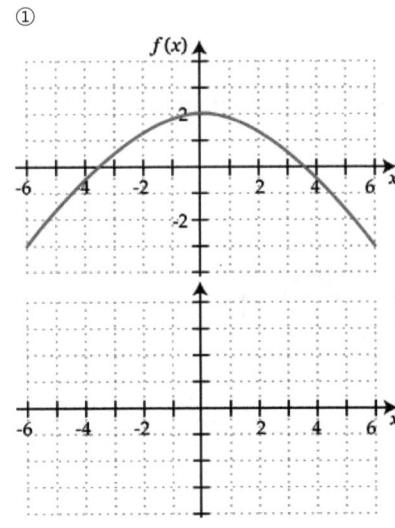

②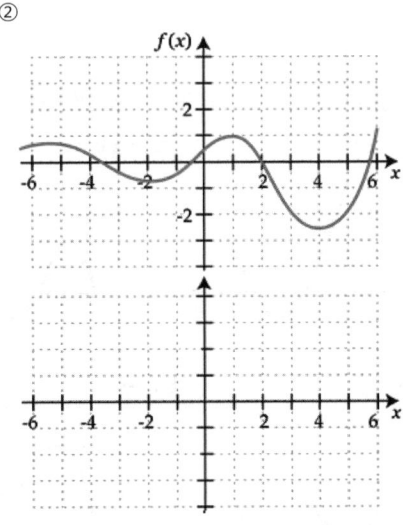

③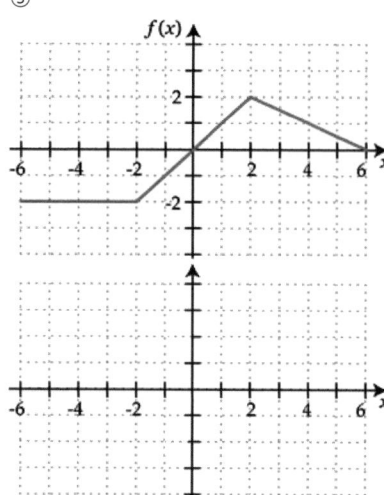

④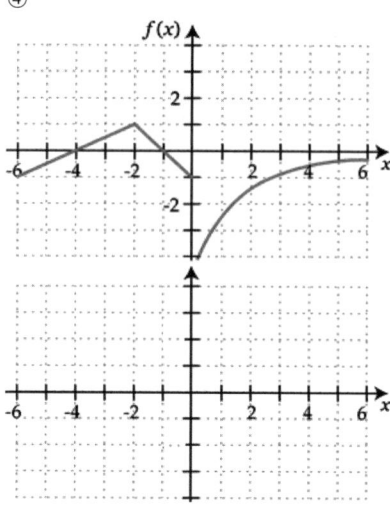

AP Style Problem

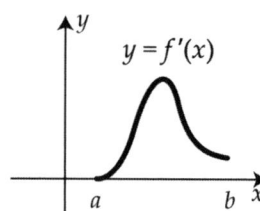

1. The graph of $y = f'(x)$ is shown. Which of the following could be the graph of $y = f''(x)$?

A) 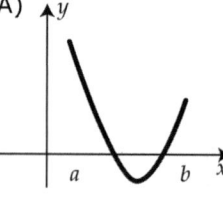   B) 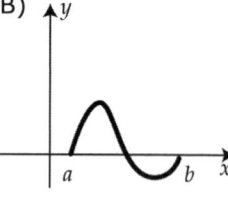   C)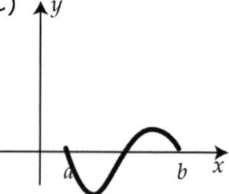

D) 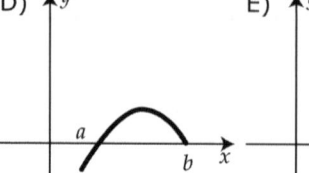   E)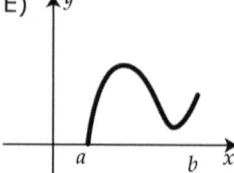

6. Interpreting Derivatives

For $Q(t)$, where Q is given as kg, t is given as hours;

Interpret $Q'(5) = 10$. ⇒ 'Q is ①_____ at the rate of 10 ②_____ at $t = 5$ ③____.'

Interpret $Q'(2) = -5$. ⇒ 'Q is ④_____ at the rate of 5 kg per hour at $t = 2$ hour.'

Unit of any derivative function is **output unit per input unit.**

EXAMPLE 6. Solve the following.

① The height of the rocket is modeled by $D(t)$ where D is in km, t is in minutes. Interpret $D'(2) = 30$.

② The time it takes for a chemical reaction can be modeled by $T(a)$, wehre T is the time in minutes, a is the catalyst used measured in milliliters. Interpret $T'(20) = 2.2$.

③ The rate at which the temperature is changing is modeled by $T(h)$, where T is measured in Fahrenheit per hour and h is in hours. Interpret $T'(5) = -10$.

Blank : ① increasing   ② kg per hour   ③ hour   ④ decreasing

EXAMPLE 7. The rate of consumption of milk in the US is given by $M(t) = 100e^{0.2t}$, where M is measured in millions of gallons per year and t is measured in years from 2000. Find $M'(10)$. Using appropriate units, interpret the meaning of it.

EXAMPLE 8. The rate of decay of radioactive substance is a differentiable function $R(t)$ where R is in grams per minutes and t is in minutes. The table shows the selected values of $R(t)$.

t (minutes)	0	4	6	8
$R(t)$ (grams per minutes)	310	240	180	155

Approximate $R'(5)$. Using appropriate units, interpret the meaning of it.

Mia's AP Calculus

7. Concavity and Second Derivative

1. Concavity

Concave up: ①_____

Concave down: ②_____

When the function **concaves upward**, the slope continually ③(decreases/increases).

When the function **concaves downward**, the slope continually ④(decreases/increases).

※ Concavity

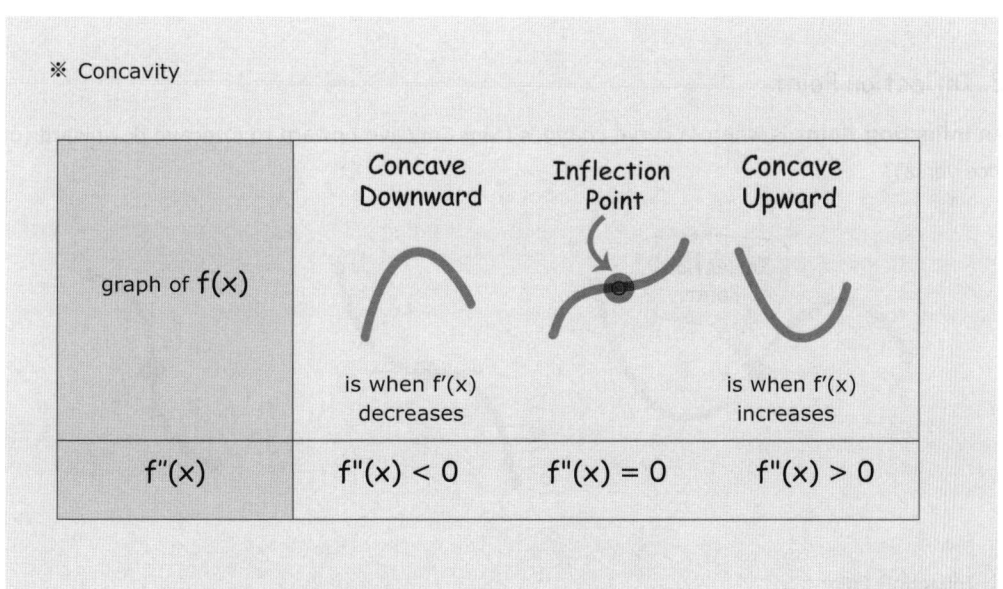

graph of $f(x)$	Concave Downward	Inflection Point	Concave Upward
	is when $f'(x)$ decreases		is when $f'(x)$ increases
$f''(x)$	$f''(x) < 0$	$f''(x) = 0$	$f''(x) > 0$

Blank : ① shape of ∪ ② shape of ∩ ③ increasing ④ decreasing

EXAMPLE 1. Fill in the sign.

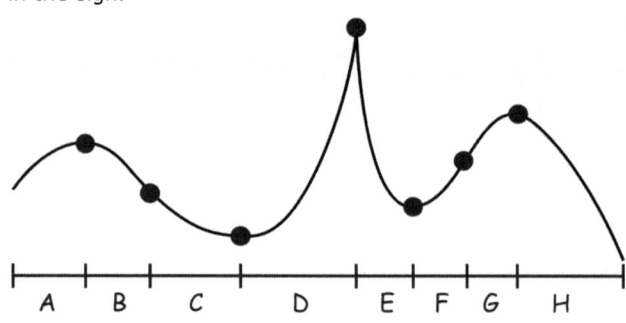

intervals	A	B	C	D	E	F	G	H
$f'(x)$								
$f''(x)$								

2. Inflection Point

An **inflection Point** is where a curve *changes* from Concave upward to Concave downward (or vice versa).

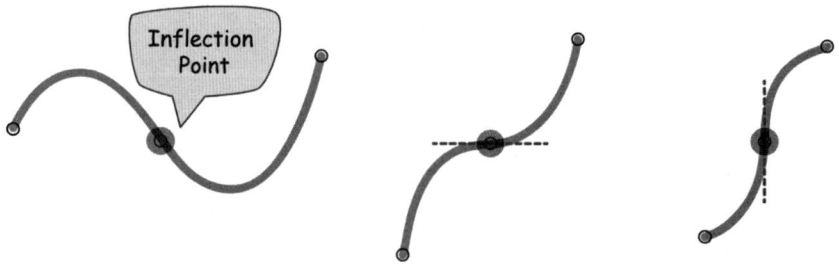

※ Inflection Point

When f(x) is continuous at c

inflection point c is where $f''(c) = 0$ or **und,**

and **the sign f'' changes**. (where concavity changes!)

EXAMPLE 2. Find the points of inflection and discuss the concavity of the graph of the function.

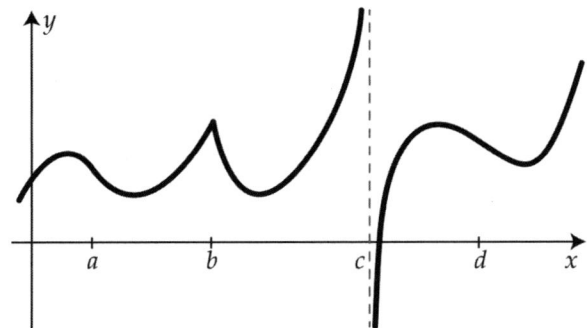

EXAMPLE 3. Find the points of inflection and discuss the concavity of the graph of the function.

※ Finding Concavity
① Find the **points where** f″ = 0 or und and build up the intervals
② pick a **test points** from each intervals
③ and determine if it is **concaving up**(f″ > 0) or **concaving down**(f″ < 0) on that interval by using test points.
④ Determine whether the point(s) is an **inflection point** or not.

① $y = x^3 - 6x^2 + 5x + 2$

② $y = x^4 - 4x^3 + 6x^2 + 7$

③ $y = (x+3)^{1/3}$

④ $y = (x+3)^{2/3}$

⑤ $y = \dfrac{\ln x}{x^2}$

EXAMPLE 4. The graph of $y = 4x^3 - ax^2 + b$ has a point of inflection at $(-1, 4)$. Find the values of a and b.

3. Basics of Curve Sketching

※ Curve Sketching

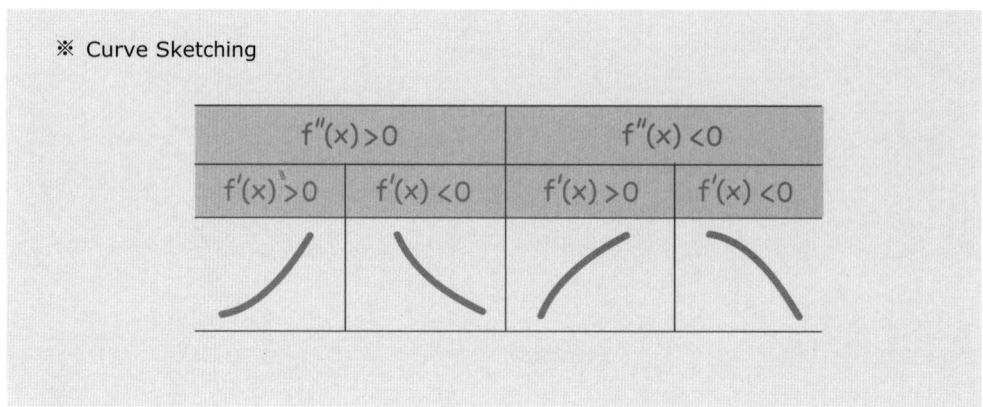

EXAMPLE 5. Let f be a continuous function on [0, 5] whose first and second derivatives have the following signs and values.

	$0 \leq x < 1$	$x = 1$	$1 < x < 3$	$x = 3$	$3 < x \leq 5$
$f'(x)$	positive	positive	positive	0	negative
$f''(x)$	positive	0	negative	negative	negative

(a) What are the x-coordinates of the relative extrema of f in the interval (0, 5)?

(b) What are the x-coordinates of the points of inflection of f in the interval (0, 5)?

(c) Sketch a possible graph of f which satisfies all the given properties.

EXAMPLE 6. Let f be a continuous function on $[0, 3]$ that has the following signs and values as in the table below.

	$0 \leq x < 1$	$x = 1$	$1 < x < 2$	$x = 2$	$2 < x \leq 3$
$f'(x)$	positive	0	negative	Not exist	negative
$f''(x)$	negative	-1	negative	Not exist	negative

(a) What are the x-coordinates of the relative extrema of f in the interval $(0, 3)$?

(b) What are the x-coordinates of the points of inflection of f in the interval $(0, 3)$?

(c) Sketch a possible graph of f which satisfies all the given properties and $f(0) = 1$.

AP Style Problem

1. For which curve shown below are both f' and f'' positive?

A) 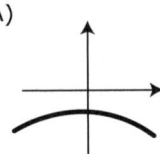 B) 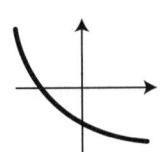 C)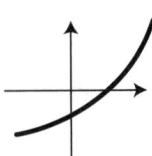

D) 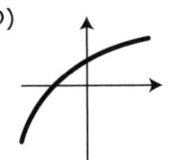 E)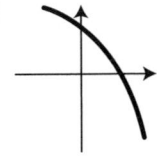

2. A function f is differentiable and f' is negative and increasing on the interval [0, 4]. Which table could be the points of f?

A)
x	0	1	2	3	4
y	0	2	4	6	8

B)
x	0	1	2	3	4
y	0	8	14	18	20

C)
x	0	1	2	3	4
y	0	2	5	9	14

D)
x	0	1	2	3	4
y	20	18	14	8	0

E)
x	0	1	2	3	4
y	14	9	5	2	0

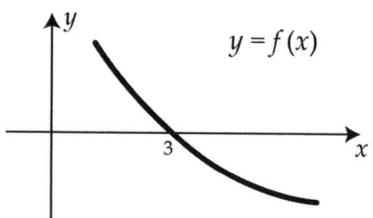

3. The graph of a twice differentiable function f is shown in the figure above. Which of the following is true?

A) $f(3) < f'(3) < f''(3)$

B) $f(3) < f''(3) < f'(3)$

C) $f'(3) < f(3) < f''(3)$

D) $f''(3) < f(3) < f'(3)$

E) $f''(3) < f'(3) < f(3)$

4. If $f''(x) = x(x+1)^2(x-2)^3$, then the graph of f has inflection points when $x =$

   A) -1 only
   B) -1, 0, and 2 only
   C) 0 and 2 only
   D) -1 and 2 only
   E) -1 and 0 only

5. If $y = x^{2/3} + 1$, which of the following is true?

   I. $f''(x)$ is negative for all x except 0.

   II. f is increasing for all x except 0.

   III. $f'(x)$ exists for all x.

   A) I and II only
   B) II only
   C) III only
   D) I only
   E) I and III only

6. Let $H(x) = f(g(x))$. Graph of f is decreasing and concave downward for all x. If g concave up at $x = a$, then which describes the graph of $H(x)$ at $x = a$?

   A) Concave downward
   B) Concave upward
   C) linear
   D) point of inflection
   E) quadratic

4. Interpreting Graph of f'

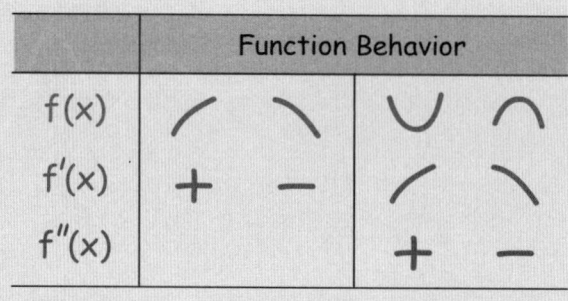

Find max and min of f.
Find inflection point of f.

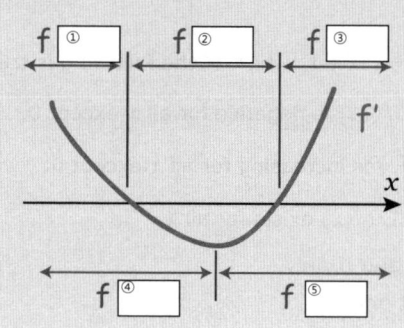

EXAMPLE 7. The graph shows $y = f'(x)$. On the graph:

(a) Mark points corresponding to a local maximum of $f(x)$ with an A. Justify.

(b) Mark points corresponding to a local minimum of $f(x)$ with a B. Justify.

(c) Mark points corresponding to a point of inflection of $f(x)$ with a C. Justify.

(d) Mark points corresponding to a zero of $f''(x)$ with a D.

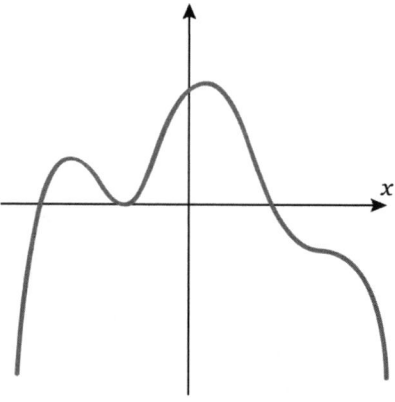

Blank : ① ↗ ② ↘ ③ ↗ ④ ∩ ⑤ ∪

EXAMPLE 8. The graph shows $y = f'(x)$. On the graph:

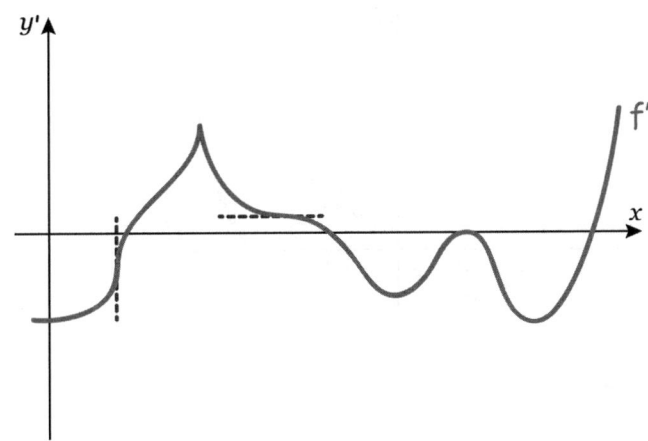

(a) Mark points corresponding to a local maximum of $f(x)$ with an A. Justify.

(b) Mark points corresponding to a local minimum of $f(x)$ with a B. Justify.

(c) Mark points corresponding to a point of inflection of $f(x)$ with a C. Justify.

(d) Mark points corresponding to a zero of $f''(x)$ with a D.

EXAMPLE 9. The graph below is the graph of the derivative of a function f in $[-3, 3]$.

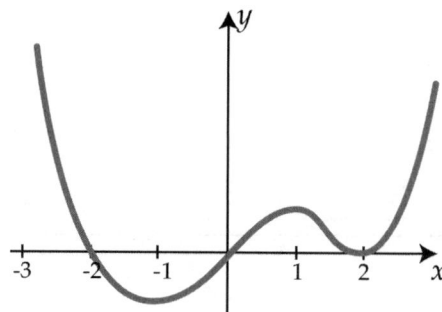

(a) Find where f is increasing. Justify.

(b) Find x where local maxima and local minima of f occur. Justify.

(c) Find where f concave up. Justify.

(d) Find inflection point of f. Justify.

EXAMPLE 10. The graph below is the graph of the derivative of a function f. f is a continuous function.

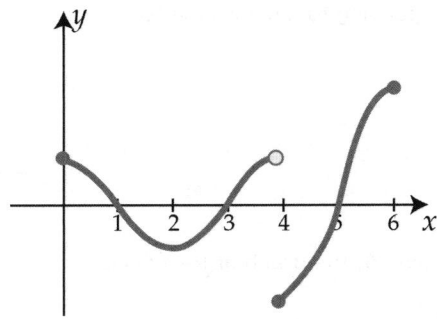

(a) Find where f is increasing. Justify.

(b) Find x where local maxima and local minima of f occur.

(c) Find where f concave up. Justify.

(d) Find inflection point of f. Justify.

EXAMPLE 11. *The graph shows $f''(x)$.

(a) Find the point(s) corresponding to a point of inflection of $f(x)$.

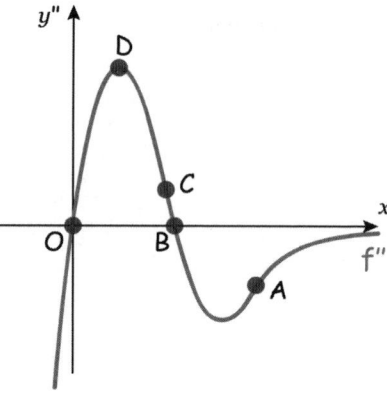

(b) State whether at the point A, the graph of $y = f(x)$ is concave up or concave down.

(c) Is $f'(x)$ increasing or decreasing at the point C?

EXAMPLE 12. The graph of $f'(x)$ is given. Sketch the graph of f.

①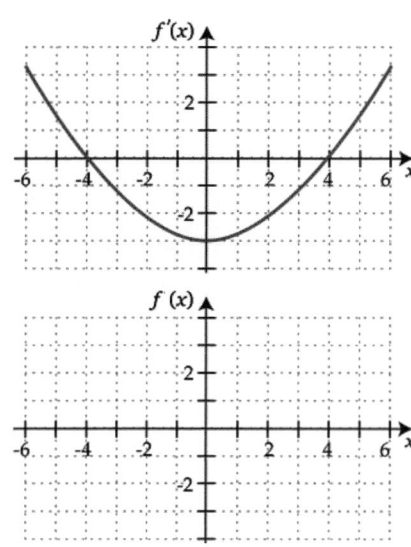

②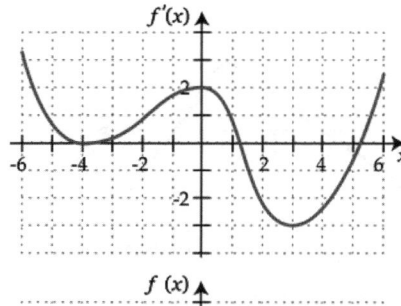

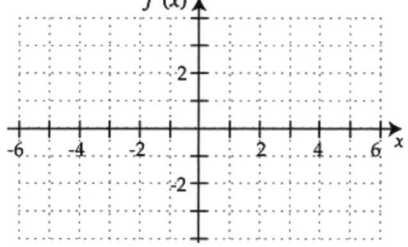

③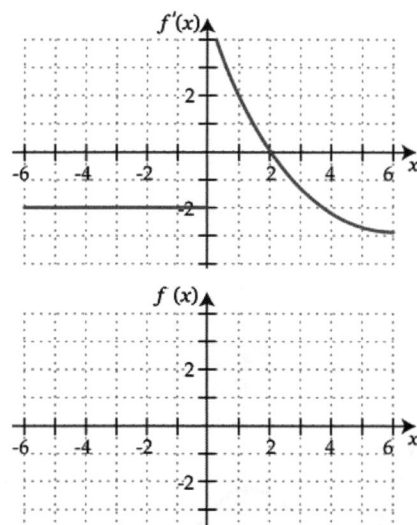

7. Concavity and Second Derivative

AP Style Problem

1. Use the graph of f'.

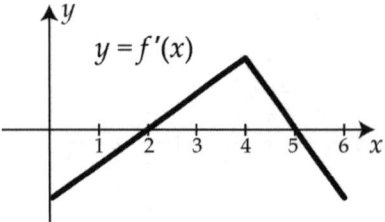

1) From the graph it follows that

   A) f has a local maximum at $x = 4$.

   B) f is constant for $0 < x < 4$

   C) f is discontinuous at $x = 4$

   D) f is decreasing for $4 < x < 6$

   E) $f(3) < f(4)$

2) Find the interval where $f(x)$ concaves downward.

   A) None
   B) (0, 2)
   C) (2, 5)
   D) (0, 4)
   E) (4, 6)

2. The graph of the derivative of f is shown above. How many points of inflection does the graph of f have in the interval $[-4,4]$?

   A) two
   B) three
   C) four
   D) five
   E) six

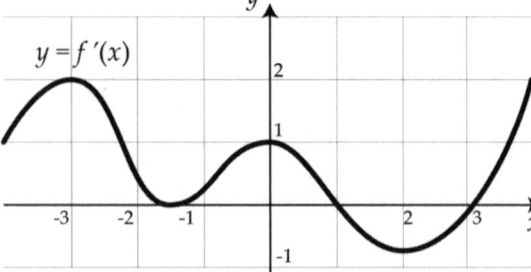

138 Mia's AP calculus AB BC

3. Graph of f' is shown. Which could be a graph of f?

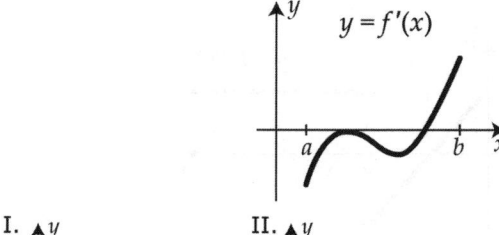

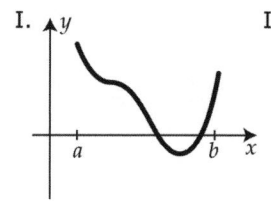 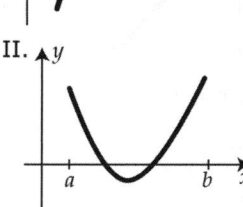 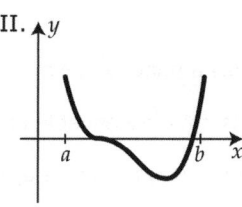

A) I only B) II only
C) III only D) I and II only
E) I and III only

4. Graph of f' is shown. Which could be a graph of f?

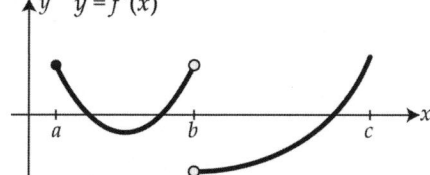

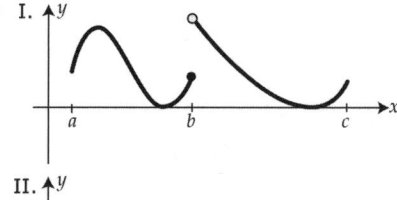

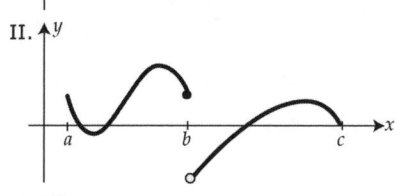

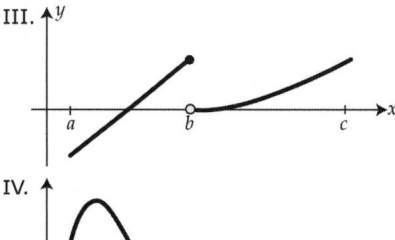

5. A continuous function f has the derivative shown. Which of the following statements is (are) true?

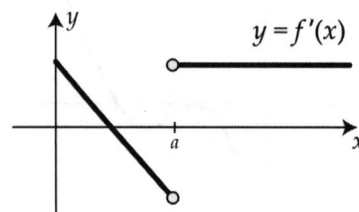

I. f has a relative minimum at $x = a$.

II. f is not differentiable at $x = a$.

III. f is always concave upward

A) I and II only
B) II only
C) III only
D) I only
E) I and III only

5. *Curve Sketching

EXAMPLE 13. Graph $f(x) = 3x^{2/3} - 2x$ on its domain.

Domain:

Asymptotes:

intercepts:

Critical points and max, min:

Inflection points and concavity:

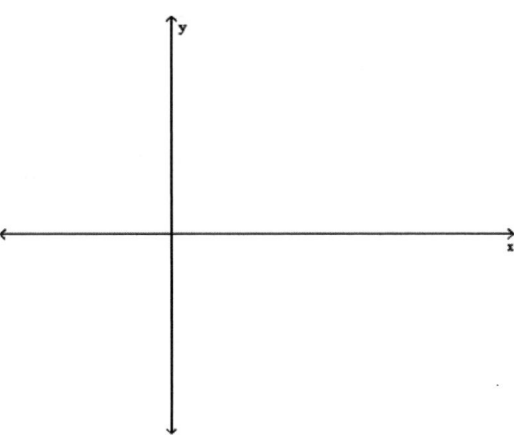

EXAMPLE 14. Graph $f(x) = e^{-x^2}$ on its domain.

Domain:

Asymptotes:

intercepts:

Critical points and max, min:

Inflection points and concavity:

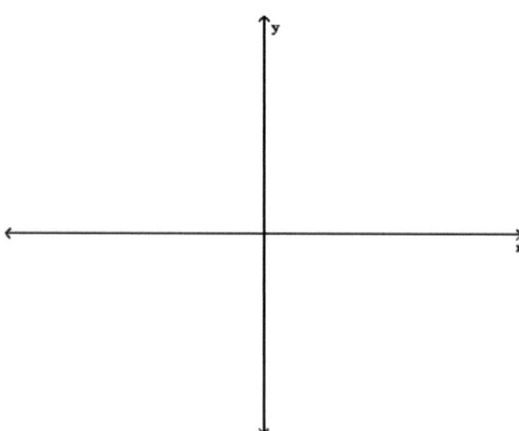

EXAMPLE 15. Graph $f(x) = \dfrac{\ln x}{x}$ on its domain.

Domain:

Asymptotes:

intercepts:

Critical points and max, min:

Inflection points and concavity:

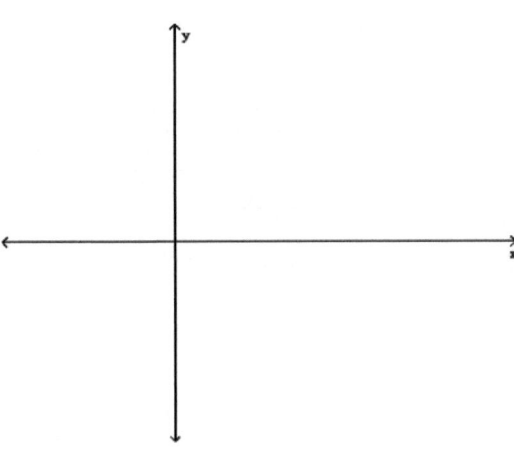

Mia's AP Calculus

8. Motions and Derivatives

1. Average Velocity

    ☺ Vocabulary
    * **Position** (①_____ of the object)
      VS **Displacement** (② _____ of _____)
      VS **Total distance** (total amount the object has traveled)

    * **Average velocity** (velocity measured over a certain time interval)
      VS **Instantaneous Velocity** (velocity at a specific moment)

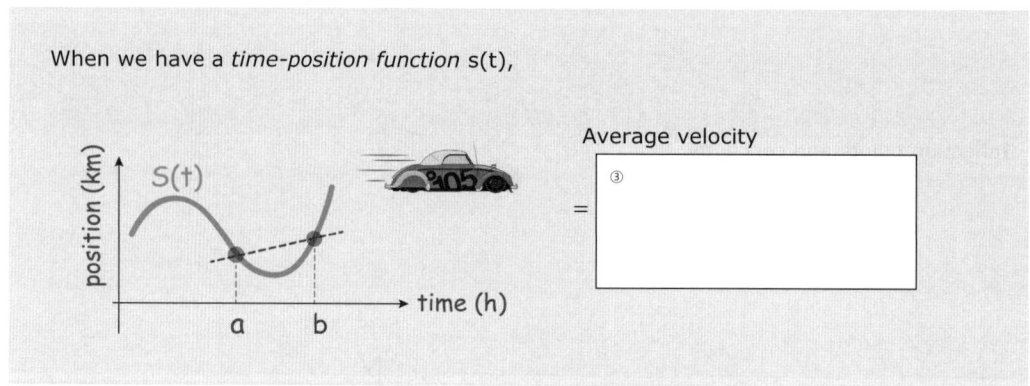

When we have a *time-position function* s(t),

Average velocity = ③

EXAMPLE 1. The coordinate s represents a moving body's position for various values of t.

t (sec)	0	0.5	1.0	1.5	2.0	2.5	3.0	3.5
s(feet)	12.5	26	36.5	44	48.5	50	48.5	44

(a) What is the body's displacement during the first 2 seconds?

Blank : ① location ② change of position ③ $\dfrac{s(b) - s(a)}{b - a}$

(b) What is the average rate of change of the moving body during the first 3 seconds?

2. Motions and Derivatives

When we have a *time-position* function $s(t)$,

$$\text{Instantaneous velocity} = \text{①}\underline{\qquad\qquad\qquad}$$

※ Motion and Derivatives

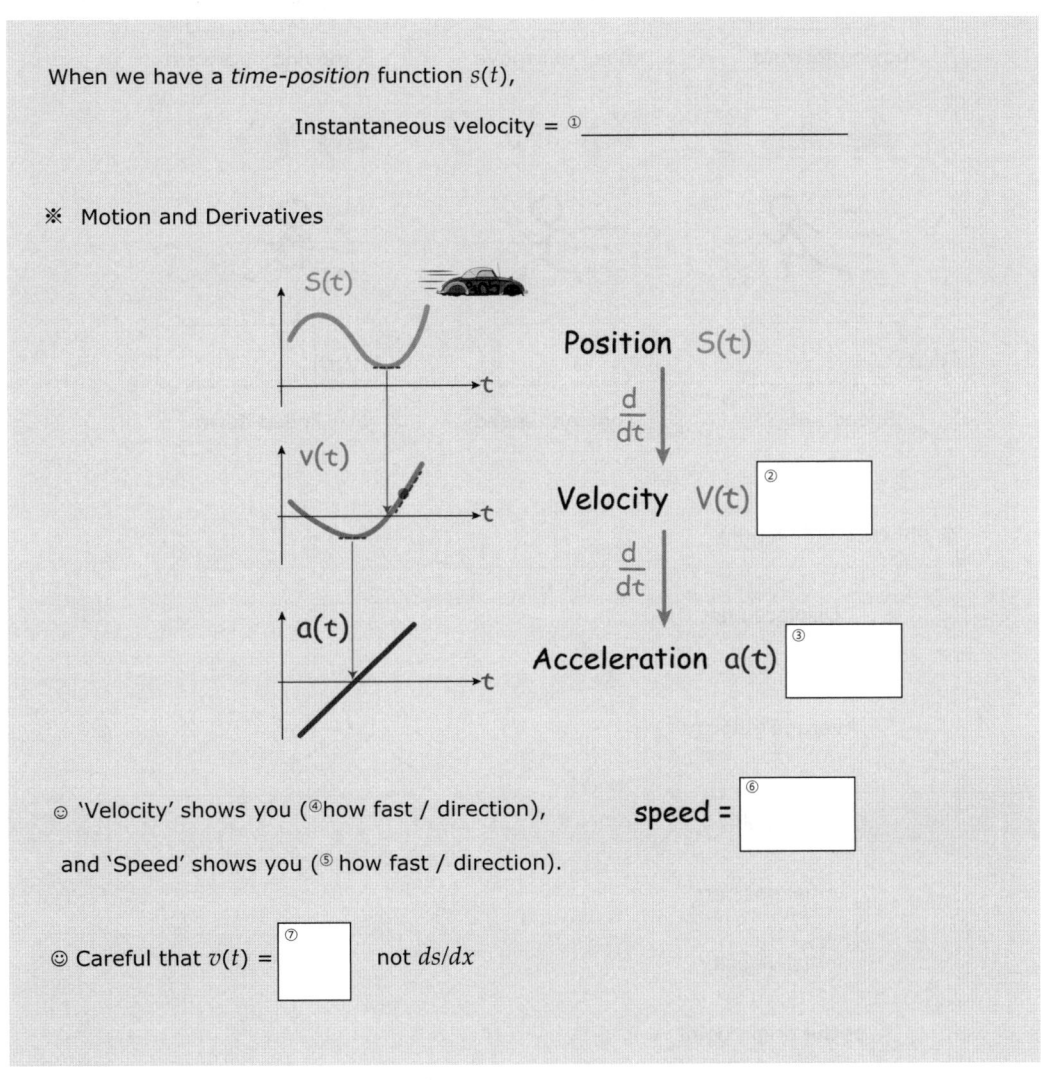

☺ 'Velocity' shows you (④how fast / direction), and 'Speed' shows you (⑤ how fast / direction).

speed = ⑥ ☐

☺ Careful that $v(t)$ = ⑦ ☐ not ds/dx

Blank : ① s'(t) ② = s'(t) ③ = v'(t) 0 ④ how fast, direction ⑤ only how fast ⑥ |v| ⑦ $\frac{ds}{dt}$

※ Movements

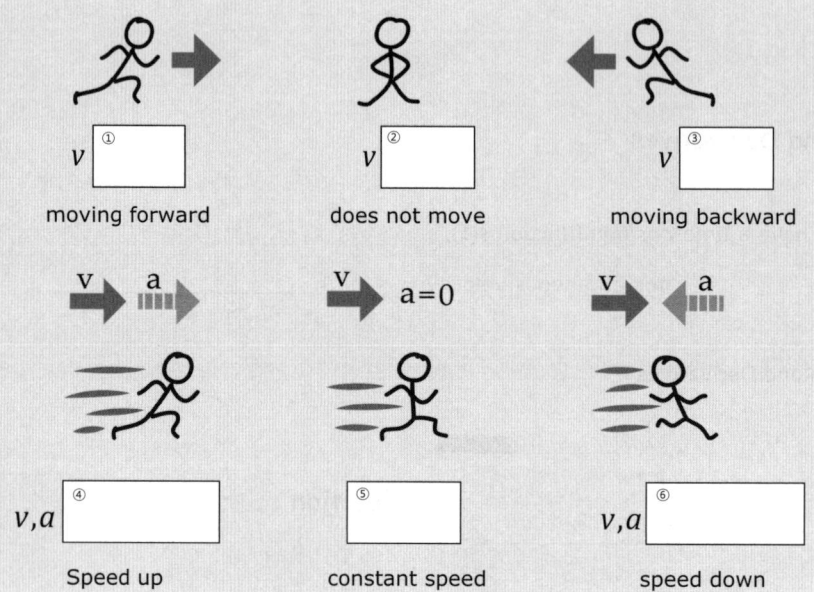

Displacement	
Average Velocity	
initial	
initial position	
initial velocity	
at the origin point	
is stationary	

※ Phrases and Motions

is at rest, is standing still	
changes direction, reverse	
reaches its maximum/minimum height	
moving forward	
moving backward	
velocity is increasing	
velocity is decreasing	
Speed up, Speed increasing	
Slow down, Speed decreasing	
constant speed	

Blank : ① > 0 ② = 0 ③ < 0 ④ has same sign ⑤ a = 0 ⑥ has different sign

※ Table Answers are in the answer section

EXAMPLE 2. Below is the graph of a particle's velocity as it moves along the horizontal line $y = 4$. The particle starts at $x(0) = 4$ at time $t = 0$.

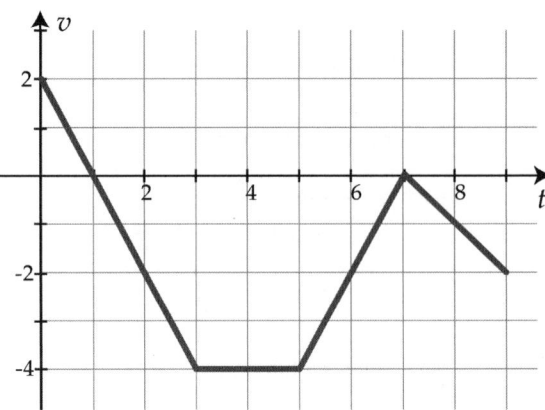

① When is the particle moving forward? backward?

② Graph the particle's speed.

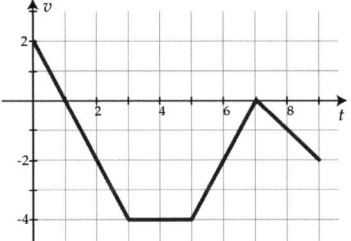

③ At what time t is the speed greatest?

④ When does the particle reverse direction?

⑤ When is the particle's velocity increasing? Decreasing?

⑥ Is the particle speeding up, slowing down, or doing neither at time $t = 6$?

EXAMPLE 3. Below is the graph of a particle's position as it moves along the horizontal line $y=5$.

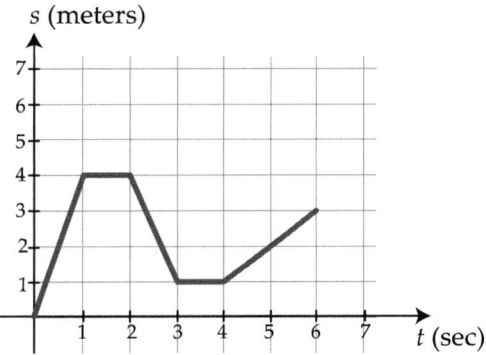

① When is the particle moving forward?

backward?

standing still?

② What is the particle's displacement when $4 \leq t \leq 6$?

③ What is the average velocity during when $4 \leq t \leq 6$?

④ What is the body's velocity when $t = 5$ sec?

EXAMPLE 4. A hiker has a position s km, at a time t hours, modeled by $s = t^3 - 4t^2 - 3t - 2$.

① Find the velocity function. And find the initial velocity.

② Find all values of t at which the hiker changes direction.

③ When is the hiker's velocity increasing?

④ When is the hiker's speed increasing?

EXAMPLE 5. A particle moves along the x-axis so that its position function at time t is given by $s(t) = -t - e^{1-t}$.

① Find the velocity function.

② Find the acceleration function.

③ Is the speed of the particle increasing at time $t = 4$?

④ Find all values of t at which the particle changes direction.

⑤ Find the displacement traveled by the particle over the time interval $0 \leq t \leq 4$.

⑥ Find the total distance traveled by the particle over the time interval $0 \leq t \leq 4$.

AP Style Problem

1. The graph shows the velocity of a particle during 8 second interval.

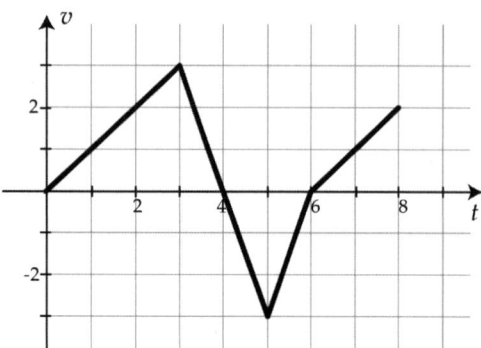

1) When does the particle reverse direction?

   A) at $t = 4, 6$ B) at $t = 4$

   C) at $t = 5, 6$ D) at $t = 6$

2) When is the particle moving forward?
   A) (0, 3) U (5, 8)
   B) (0, 4) U (6, 8)
   C) (3, 4) U (5, 6)
   D) (2, 5)

3) When is the particle's speed decreasing?
   A) (0, 3) U (5, 8)
   B) (0, 4) U (6, 8)
   C) (3, 4) U (5, 6)
   D) (2, 5)

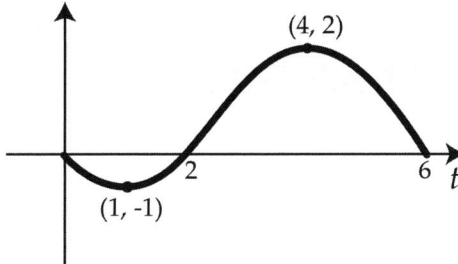

2. The particle moves along the y axis. The graph of the particle's position $y(t)$ at time t is shown. The graph has a horizontal tangent at (1, -1) and (4, 2). For what values of t is the velocity of the particle increasing?

   A) (0, 2)   B) (2, 6)
   C) (1, 4)   D) (4, 6)

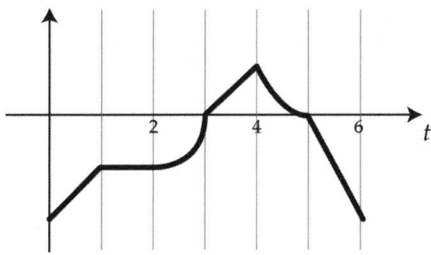

3. The graph of the particle's position $x(t)$ at time t is shown above for $0 \leq t \leq 6$. For what values of t is the speed of the particle increasing?

   A) $0 < t < 1$ B) $0 < t < 4$
   C) $2 < t < 3$ D) $3 < t < 5$

4. The particle's position is $s(t) = -3 + 6t^2 - 2t^3$. What is the open interval on which the particle speeds up?

   A) (0, 12)
   B) (1, 2)
   C) (0, 2)
   D) (2, ∞)

8. Motions and Derivatives

9. Optimization and Related Rates

Mia's AP Calculus

1. Optimization

Maximum and Minimum of f occurs at the ①_____ **of f.**

If the problem is about **MAX/MIN of f**?
First, find the function f.
Second, find the critical point C by setting ②_____.

Third, if you need to verify whether it is max or min, use ;
method 1) First derivative test : seeing slope changes

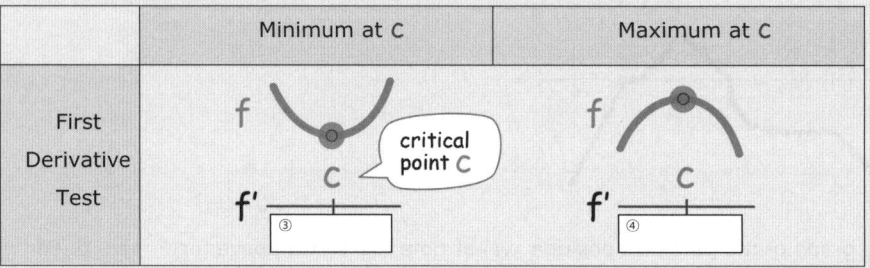

method 2) Second derivative test : using concavity

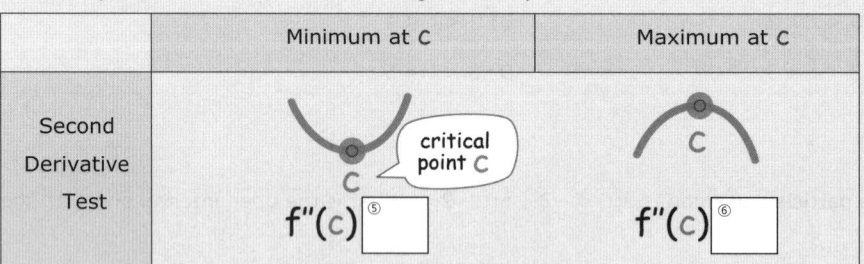

Careful what you have to answer. Is it x? or is it y(=max/min value)?
Don't forget to determine the **feasible domain**!

Blank : ① critical point   ② $f'=0$ ③ (-) to (+)   ④ (+) to (-)   ⑤ > 0 ⑥ < 0

EXAMPLE 1. Find the x value of the critical points. And use the second derivative test to determine whether it is local maximum or minimum for the function.

① $f(x) = x^3 - 6x^2 + 4$

② $f(x) = 4x^2 - \dfrac{4}{x}$

③ $y = \sqrt{x^2 + 1}$

AP Style Problem - 1 A farmer wants to fence off a rectangular pasture against his barn. The pasture must be 1000 square feet in order to provide enough grass to his livestock. What should the dimensions of the pasture be in order to use the least amount of fencing?

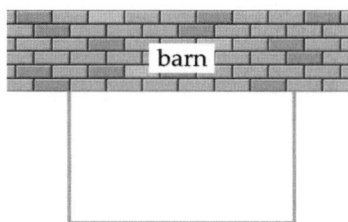

AP Style Problem - 2 A window is constructed by adjoining a semicircle and a rectangle. If the total perimeter is 12 feet, what is the radius of the semicircle that will maximize the area of the window? Show the reason why it maximizes the area.

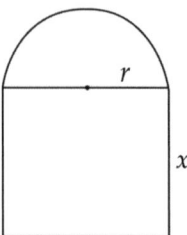

AP Style Problem - 3 A right circular cylinder can is to be designed to hold 27 cubic inches of water. If a minimum amount of material is to be used to construct the can, what must be the radius, in inches, of the can? Justify your answer.

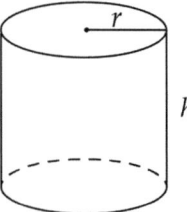

AP Style Problem - 4 A rectangle is inscribed inside the region bounded by the curve $y = 3 - x^2$ and the x axis as shown below. What is the largest area the rectangle can have, and what are its dimensions?

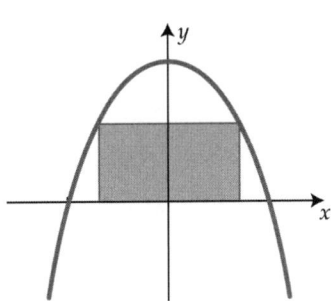

AP Style Problem - 5 A rectangle is to be drawn from the origin so that the opposite vertex is on the curve $y = 8xe^{-x}$. Find the largest possible area of the rectangle.

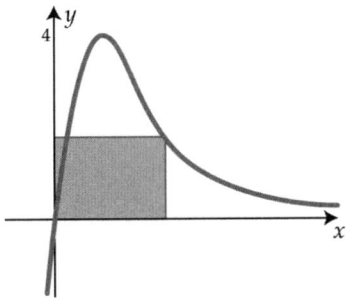

AP Style Problem - 6 What is the area of the largest rectangle that can be inscribed in the ellipse $x^2 + 4y^2 = 4$?

AP Style Problem - 7 How close does the curve $y = \sqrt{x}$ come to the point (3/2, 0)?

[Hint: If you minimize the square of the distance, you can avoid square roots.]

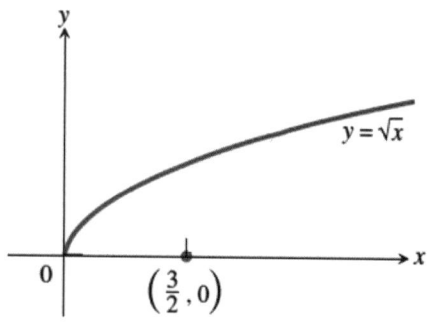

AP Style Problem - 8 A man is in a boat 3 miles from the nearest point on the coast and that point is 5 miles away from a resting place on the coast. He plans to row the boat straight to a certain point on the coast and then walk along the coast to reach the resting place. If he can row at 2 miles per hour and walk at 4 miles per hour, toward what point on the coast should he row in order to reach his resting place in the shortest amount of time?

AP Style Problem - 9 The trough in the figure is going to be made by the dimension as shown below. Only the angle θ can be varied. What is the angle θ that will maximize the trough's volume?

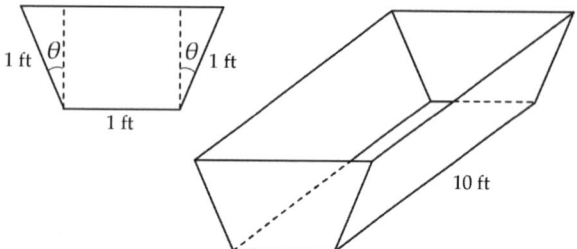

2. Related Rates

Rates is about change of a variables with respect to ①_____.

☺ words

radius is increasing at 2cm/min ②_____

diameter is decreasing at 2cm/min ③_____

water is draining at 3 cubic ft per min ④_____

Mia is walking to the right at the rate of 2m/min ⑤_____

What is the rate of change of the area? ⑥_____

How fast is the volume changing? ⑦_____

※ **Related rates** problem will always tell you about the rate at which *one quantity is changing*.
The question will then be

> how fast...
> how quickly...   *does another quantity change* as a result?
> at what rate...

※ STEPS:
① Sketch the given situation.
② Write an equation that relates the two or three quantities.
③ $\dfrac{d}{dt}$ and use **implicit** differentiation.

$\dfrac{d}{dx}x^2 =$ ⑧ ☐ $\dfrac{d}{dx}y^2 =$ ⑨ ☐ $\dfrac{d}{dt}x^2 =$ ⑩ ☐ $\dfrac{d}{dt}r^2 =$ ⑪ ☐

④ Substitute all known variables and rates and solve.

Blank : ① time ② $\dfrac{dr}{dt}=2$ ③ $\dfrac{dD}{dt}=-2$ ④ $\dfrac{dV}{dt}=-3$ ⑤ $\dfrac{dx}{dt}=2$ ⑥ $\dfrac{dA}{dt}=?$ ⑦ $\dfrac{dV}{dt}=?$ ⑧ $2x$ ⑨ $2y\dfrac{dy}{dx}$ ⑩ $2x\dfrac{dx}{dt}$ ⑪ $2r\dfrac{dr}{dt}$

EXAMPLE 2. If $x^2 + y^2 = 25$ and $\dfrac{dx}{dt} = 8$, what is the value of $\dfrac{dy}{dt}$ when $x = 3$ and $y = 4$?

AP Style Problem - 10 A circular disc is heated so that its radius increases at a rate of 2 cm/s. When the disc is 10 cm in radius, find
(a) the rate of change of the disk's circumference.

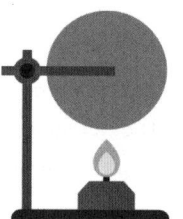

(b) the rate of change of the disk's area.

AP Style Problem - 11 Sally is making a large spherical snowball. If the volume is increasing at 10 m³/min when the radius is 5m, find the rate the radius is increasing.

AP Style Problem - 12 Sand is being poured onto a conical pile where the radius of the cone is always twice the height. If sand is being added at a rate of 50 m³/sec, how fast is the height of the pile increasing when the radius of the sand is 10m?

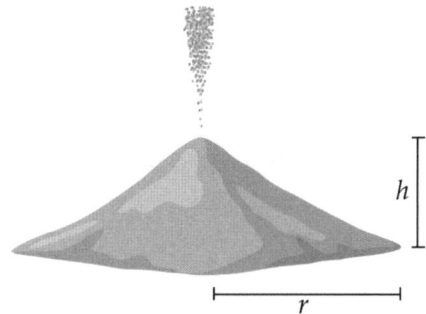

AP Style Problem - 13 A ladder 20 feet long is leaning against the wall of a house (see figure). The base of the ladder is pulled away from the wall at a rate of 2 feet per second.

(a) How fast is the top of the ladder moving down the wall when its base is 12 feet from the wall?

(b) Consider the triangle formed by the side of the house, the ladder, and the ground. Find the rate at which the area of the triangle is changing when the base of the ladder is 12 feet from the wall.

(c) Find the rate at which the angle between the ladder and the ground is changing when the base of the ladder is 12 feet from the wall.

AP Style Problem - 14 Water drains from a conical tank at the rate of 5 ft³/min. The conical tank has radius of 4 ft and height of 10 ft.

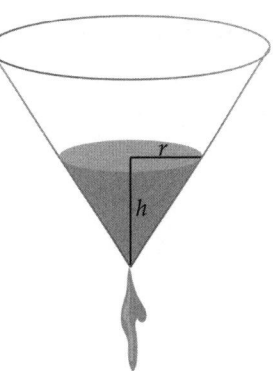

(a) What is the relation between the variables h and r?

(b) How fast is the water level dropping when $h = 5$ ft?

(c) At what rate is the exposed surface area of the water changing when $h = 5$ ft?

9. Optimization and Related Rates

AP Style Problem - 15 A space shuttle is rising vertically at a rate of 2 miles per second. A man who is 5 miles from the launch point is observing the space shuttle. If θ is the angle of elevation, find the rate of change in the angle of elevation at 5 seconds after launch.

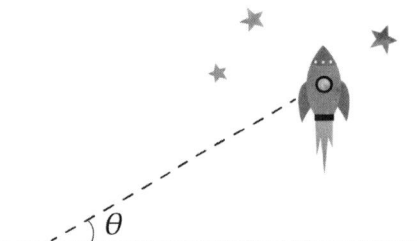

AP Style Problem - 16 The radius and height of a right circular cylinder are found at a certain instant to be 10cm and 20cm respectively. If the radius of the cylinder is increasing at the rate of 2cm/sec, what change in height will keep the volume constant?

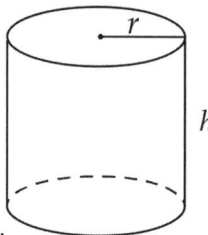

AP Style Problem - 17 When $x = 4$, the rate at which $\sqrt{x}$ is increasing is k times the rate at which x is increasing. What is the value of k?

Mia's AP Calculus

10. Applications of Differentiation

1. Intermediate-Value Theorem

※ Intermediate Value Theorem

If f is ① _____ in $[a,b]$,

and k is a number between $f(a)$ and $f(b)$,

then there is at least one number c such that

$f(c) = \boxed{\text{②}}$ in $[a, b]$.

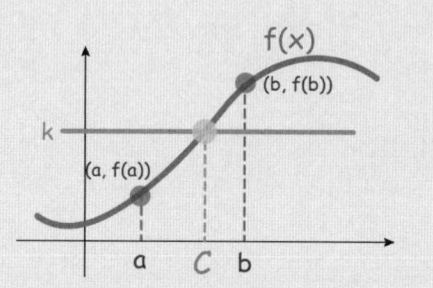

EXAMPLE 1. Show that $f(x) = x^{13} + 5x - 3$ has a zero in the interval $[0,1]$.

EXAMPLE 2. Show that $h(x) = -2e^{-x/2} \cos 2x$ has a value x that satisfy $h(x) = 0$ in the interval $\left[0, \dfrac{\pi}{2}\right]$.

Blank : ① continuous ② k

EXAMPLE 3. Show that $f(x)=4x^3-3x+1$ has a value x that satisfy $f(x)=2$ in the interval $[0,2]$.

2. Mean Value Theorem

※ Mean Value Theorem

If f is ①_____ in $[a, b]$

and f is ②_____ in (a, b),

then there is at least one number c such that

$f'(c) = \boxed{\text{③}}$ in (a, b).

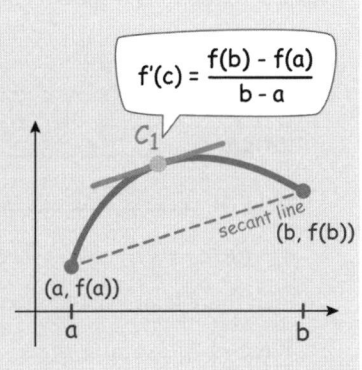

EXAMPLE 4. Find the number of c in the open interval (a, b) satisfying the Mean Value Theorem.

① 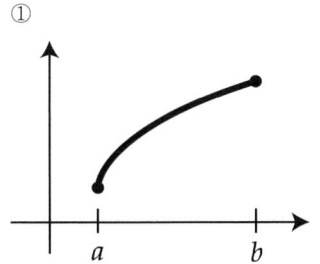   ② 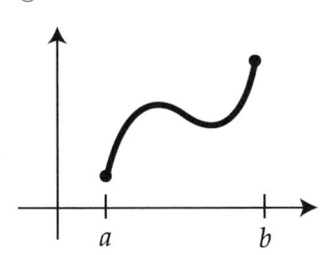   ③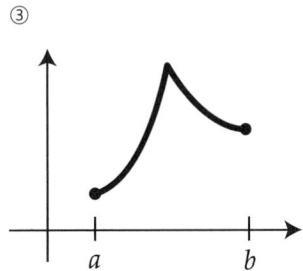

Blank : ① continuous ② differentiable ③ $\frac{f(b)-f(a)}{b-a}$

EXAMPLE 5. Given $f(x) = \ln x$ on the interval [1, 3], find all values of c in the open interval (1, 3) satisfying the Mean Value Theorem.

3. Rolle's Theorem

Rolle's Theorem is a special case of the mean value theorem.

※ **Rolle's Theorem**

If f is ①_____ in [a, b]

and f is ②_____ in (a, b),

and $f(a)$ ___ $f(b)$,

then there is at least one number c such that

$f'(c) = $ ③ ☐ in (a, b).

EXAMPLE 6. Find the value of c on the given interval that satisfies the Roll's theorem.

① $f(x) = (x^2 - 2x)e^x$ on the interval $[0, 2]$

Blank : ① continuous ② differentiable ③ 0

② $f(x) = \dfrac{x^2 - 1}{x}$ on the interval $[-1, 1]$

③ $f(x) = 3 - |x - 3|$ on the interval $[0, 6]$

EXAMPLE 7. The table below shows selected values of a differentiable function f. For $[0, 10]$,

x	0	1	3	4	6	7	9	10
$f(x)$	-2	1	7	3	-1	-2	0.5	1

① what is the fewest possible number of zeros?

② what is the fewest possible number of x where $f(x) = 2$?

10. Applications of Differentiation

③ Show that there exists at least one number c, 0 ≤ x ≤ 10, such that $f(c) = 0$

☺ Answer:
f is _____ .

_____

According to _____, there must be at least one number c such that _____ in _____.

④ Show that there exists at least one number c, 0 < x < 10, such that $f'(c) = 0.3$.

☺ Answer:
f is _____ and _____ .

_____

According to _____, there must be at least one number c such that _____ in _____.

⑤ Show that there exists at least one number c, 1 < x < 10, such that $f'(c) = 0$.

☺ Answer:
f is _____ and _____ .

_____

According to _____, there must be at least one number c such that _____ in _____.

AP Style Problem

1. The table below shows some points on a function f that is both continuous and differentiable on the closed interval [0, 20]. Which of the following must be true?

x	0	5	10	15	20
$f(x)$	10	22	40	22	10

A) $f(x)$ is increasing in $0<x<5$

B) $f'(5) > 0$

C) f has at least one zero in the interval [0, 20]

D) The maximum value of f on the interval [0, 20] is 40.

E) For some value of x on the interval (0, 20), $f'(x) = 0$

2. Let f be a function that is differentiable on the open interval [1, 9]. If $f(1) = -3$, $f(4) = 3$, and $f(9) = -3$, which of the following must be true?

    I. f has at least two values of x such that $f(x) = 0$.

    II. The graph of f has at least one horizontal tangent.

    III. For some c, $f(c) = 2$ in the interval [4, 9].

A) I and II only

B) II only

C) III only

D) I only

E) I, II, and III

3. The function $f(x) = x^{3/5}$ does not satisfy the condition of the Mean Value Theorem because

   A) $f(x)$ is not continuous at $x = 0$

   B) $f(0)$ is undefined

   C) $f'(0)$ does not exist

   D) $f'(x)$ is not defined for $x > 0$

   E) none of these

4. Let f' be a differentiable function, and the values of f' at selected values of x is given in the table below. Which of the following must be true for $0 \leq x \leq 10$?

x	0	2	3	5	10
$f'(x)$	-10	-3	2	4	10

   I. f' is increasing in $0 \leq x \leq 10$

   II. There exists c, for $0 \leq c \leq 10$, such that $f'(c) = 0$.

   III. There exists c, for $0 \leq c \leq 10$, such that $f(c) = 0$.

   IV. There exists c, for $0 < c < 10$, such that $f''(c) = 2$.

   A) II only

   B) III only

   C) I and II only

   D) II and IV only

   E) I, II, and IV

4. L'Hopital's Rule

L'hopital's Rule is a handy tool for doing limit problems.

※ L'Hopital's Rule

$$\lim_{x \to c} \frac{f(x)}{g(x)} = \lim_{x \to c} \frac{f'(x)}{g'(x)}$$

differentiate

L'Hopital's rule applies only when to quotients whose limits are indeterminate forms such as $\frac{0}{0}, \frac{\infty}{\infty}, \ldots$.

EXAMPLE 8. Find the limit. (Use L'Hopital's Rule)

① $\lim\limits_{x \to 3} \dfrac{x^2 - 9}{x - 3}$

② $\lim\limits_{x \to 0} \dfrac{\sin x}{x}$

③ $\lim\limits_{x \to 0} \dfrac{e^x - 1 + x}{\tan x}$

④ $\lim\limits_{x \to 0} \dfrac{e^{2x} - 2x - 1}{x^2}$

⑤ $\lim\limits_{x \to 0} \dfrac{\sin 2x}{\tan 3x}$

⑥ $\lim\limits_{x \to 0} \dfrac{\cos x - \sec x}{x^2}$

⑦ $\lim\limits_{x \to \infty} \dfrac{\ln x}{x}$

⑧ $\lim\limits_{x \to \infty} e^{-x} \sqrt{x}$

⑨ $\lim_{x\to\infty}\left(x\sin\dfrac{1}{x}\right)$

AP Style Problem

1. $\lim_{x\to\infty}\dfrac{\ln(e^x+x^e)}{x}=$

   A) 0
   B) 1
   C) 2
   D) e
   E) ∞

2. Let $a>0$, $b>0$. $\lim_{x\to\infty}\dfrac{\ln(ax^2+2)}{\ln(bx^3+2)}=$

   A) 0
   B) 2/3
   C) 2a/3b
   D) Not exist

5. Linearization

We know what $\sqrt{4}$ is. We want to know $\sqrt{4.01}$.

Let $f(x) =$ ①_____.

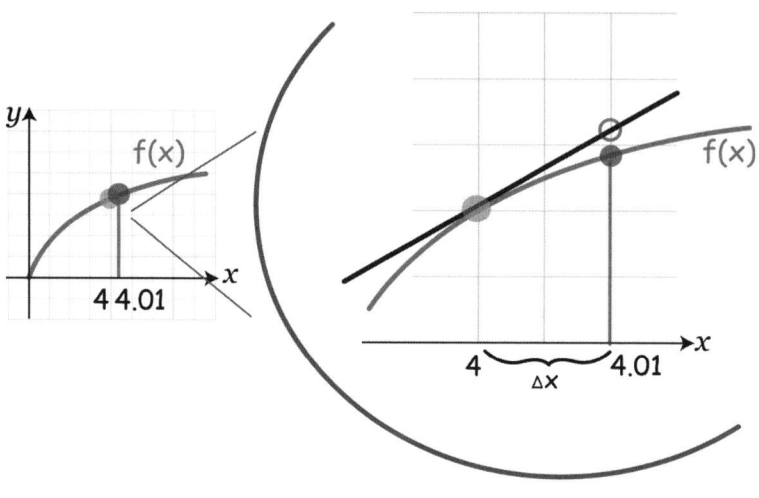

The equation of tangent line of f at $x = 4$ is ②_____

Plug in 4.01 to that tangent line.

Then we can say, $\sqrt{4.01} \approx$ ③_____

※ **Linear Approximation**

The ④ _____ of a function can be used to determine approximate values of the function. The tangent line is called the **linearization** of f at a.

Linearization

$$L(x) = f(a) + f'(a)(x - a)$$

Blank : ① $\sqrt{x}$ ② $y - 2 = 0.25(x - 4)$ ③ $2 + 0.25(4.01 - 4) = 2.0025$ ④ tangent line

EXAMPLE 9. Find the linear approximation of $f(x) = 1 + \sin x$ at x = 0.1 using the equation of the tangent line at x=0.

EXAMPLE 10. Estimate $\ln(1.02)$ using a linear approximation.

EXAMPLE 11. Estimate the $\arctan(0.9)$ using a linear approximation.

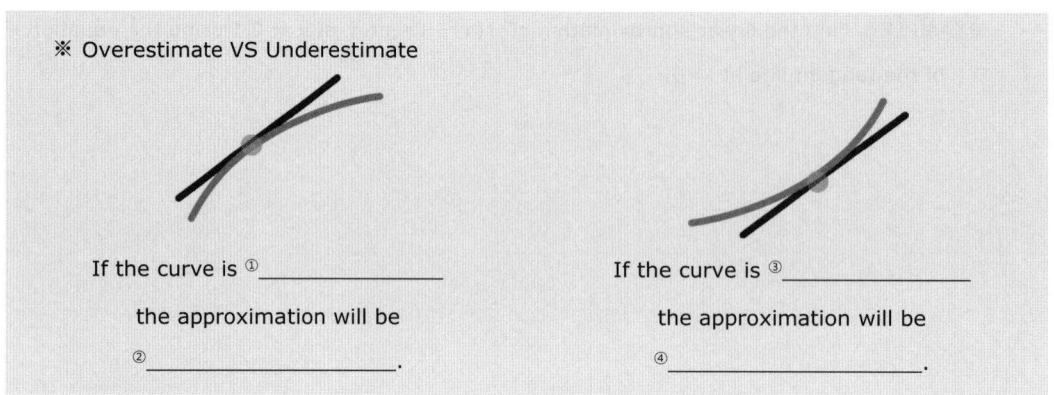

※ Overestimate VS Underestimate

If the curve is ①_____ the approximation will be ②_____.

If the curve is ③_____ the approximation will be ④_____.

EXAMPLE 12. Estimate $(4.2)^3$ using a linear approximation. Is the approximation overestimate or underestimate?

EXAMPLE 13. Use differentials to approximate $\sqrt{9.2}$. Is the approximation overestimate or underestimate?

Blank : ① concave down ② overestimated ③ concave up ④ underestimated

AP Style Problem

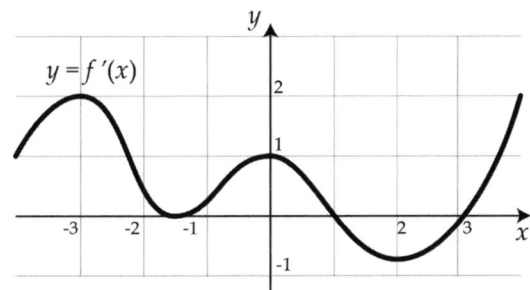

1. The graph of f' is shown above. If we know that $f(0) = 10$, then the linearization for $f(x)$ near $x = 0$ is

   A) $x + 1$

   B) $x - 1$

   C) $x + 10$

   D) $x - 10$

   E) 1

2. Let f be a differentiable function such that $g(2) = 3$ and $g'(2) = 6$. If the tangent line to the graph of g at $x = 2$ is used to find an approximation to a zero of g, that approximation is

   A) 0

   B) 0.5

   C) 1.5

   D) 7.5

   E) 9

3. Approximately how much less than 3 is $\sqrt[3]{28}$?

   A) 1
   B) 3
   C) $\dfrac{1}{3}$
   D) $\dfrac{1}{27}$
   E) $\dfrac{1}{9}$

4. If the radius of a circle increases from 5 to 5.2, what is the change in area using a linear approximation?

   A) π
   B) 2π
   C) 0.2
   D) 0.1

5. Let $f(x)$ be twice-differentiable function and $f''(x) > 0$ for all x. The graph of $y = T(x)$ is the line tangent to the graph of f at $x = 4$. Which of the following is true?

   A) $T(4.2) = f(4.2)$
   B) $T(4.2) < f(4.2)$
   C) $T(4.2) > f(4.2)$
   D) none of these

6. Suppose you have a function $f(x)$ and all you know is that $f(3) = 37$ and the graph of its derivative f' is shown.

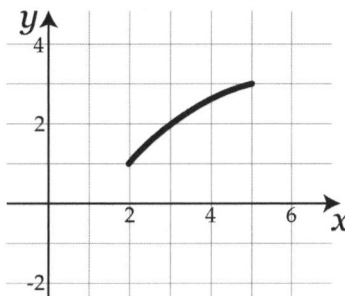

Use linear approximation to estimate $f(3.1)$. Is the approximation overestimate or underestimate?

A) 36.8, underestimate

B) 37.2, underestimate

C) 37.1, underestimate

D) 37.2, overestimate

E) 36.8, overestimate

Mia's AP Calculus

Free Response Questions (from ch6~10)

(: Do not use calculator,   : Use calculator)

1. Application of Derivative with Graph

The graph of the function f is shown in the interval $0 \leq x \leq 7$. Let $f(x) = g'(x)$.

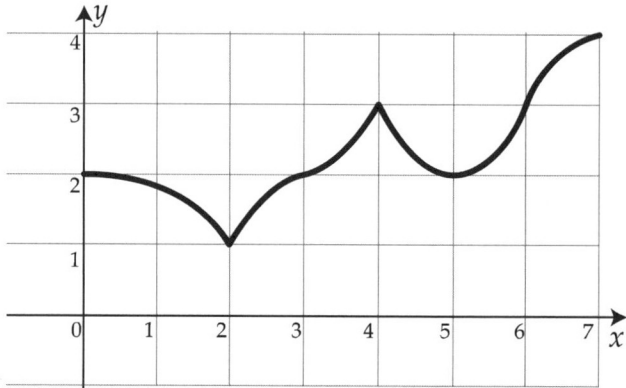

(a) Find the x value(s) of the inflection point of $f(x)$.

(b) Find the x value(s) of the inflection point of $g(x)$.

(c) Find the interval where $g(x)$ is increasing.

(d) Find the interval where $g(x)$ is concave down.

(e) Find the x value(s) of the maximum of $g(x)$ in the interval $0 \leq x \leq 7$.

2. Application of Derivative with Table

☺ Tip:

Find when Q is increasing	
Interpret $Q'(a) = +10$	
Interpret $Q'(a) = -10$	
Find when rate of Q is increasing	
Interpret $Q''(a) = +10$	

☺ Proof using theorems; When table of f is given,

Is there c in $a \leq x \leq b$ such that $f(c) = \#$?	
Is there c in $a \leq x \leq b$ such that $f'(c) = \#$?	

Blank : ※ Blank will be explained in Mia's AP calculus video from www.masterprep.net.

t	0	3	5	9	12
G(t)	5	2	1	-1	-3

The rate at which the height of the water is rising in the can is given by $G(t)$, where $G(t)$ is measured in millimeters per day and t is measured in days for $0 \le t \le 12$. $G(t)$ is differentiable function and decreasing in the interval $0 \le t \le 12$.

(a) Estimate $G'(2)$. Interpret the meaning using appropriate unit.

(b) Is there a time where the rate at which the height of the water is 0.5 millimeters per day in the interval $5 \le t \le 9$.

(c) Is there a time where $G(t)$ is decreasing at the rate of 0.5 millimeters per day per day in the interval $5 \le t \le 9$?

(d) Let the height of the water in the can as $h(t)$, which becomes $h'(t) = G(t)$. When $t = 3$, the height of the water is 6 millimeter in the can. Using the line tangent at $t = 3$, estimate the height of the water at $t = 4$.

3. Application of Derivative with Function

The amount of hay in the bin is given by $h(t)$ where h is in pounds and t is the number of hour since noon. The derivative of $h(t)$ is given by $h'(t) = \sin(t^2 - t)$, $0 \le t \le 3$.

(a) Find $h'(2)$. Interpret the meaning using appropriate unit.

(b) Find $h''(2)$. Interpret the meaning using appropriate unit.

(c) Find the t value(s) of the maximum amount of hay in the bin.

(d) Find where the amount of hay in the bin is increasing at decreasing rate.

Part 2
Integration

Chapter 11~17
(For both AB and BC)

Mia's AP Calculus

11. Antiderivatives

1. Integration

Integration is the reverse of differentiation.

We use a stylish symbol "$\int$".

ex) $\int 3x^2 \, dx$

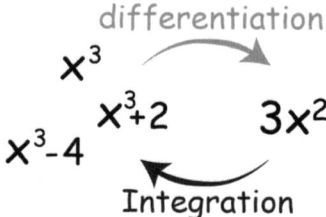

Why +c?

It is because of *all the functions* whose derivative is $3x^2$.

We can write

$$\underbrace{\int}_{\text{integral}} 3x^2 \underbrace{dx}_{\text{wrt x}} = \overbrace{x^3}^{\text{Antiderivative}} + C$$

※ Integration

When $F'(x) = f(x)$, then

$$\int f(x) \, dx = \overbrace{F(x)}^{\text{Antiderivative}} + C$$

※ Basic Rule of Integration rules

	Antiderivative F(x)
$\int x^n \, dx$	$\dfrac{x^{n+1}}{n+1}$
$\int c \, dx$	cx
$\int cx^n \, dx$	$c\dfrac{x^{n+1}}{n+1}$
$\int cf(x) \, dx$	$c \int f(x) \, dx$
$\int f(x) \pm g(x) \, dx$	$\int f(x) \, dx \pm \int g(x) \, dx$
$\int \dfrac{1}{x} \, dx$	$\ln |x|$
$\int e^x \, dx$	e^x
$\int \sin x \, dx$	$-\cos x$
$\int \cos x \, dx$	$\sin x$
$\int \tan x \sec x \, dx$	$\sec x$
$\int \sec^2 x \, dx$	$\tan x$
$\int \cot x \csc x \, dx$	$-\csc x$
$\int \csc^2 x \, dx$	$-\cot x$

EXAMPLE 1. Evaluate the integral.

① $\int x^3 \, dx$

② $\int 7 - x - 3x^2 \, dx$

③ $\int (13 - 6x^2 + x^5) \, dx$

④ $\int x^5 + \dfrac{1}{x^2} \, dx$

⑤ $\int \dfrac{3}{x^2} + \dfrac{4}{x^3} \, dx$

⑥ $\int \sqrt{x} + \sqrt[3]{x} + \sqrt[3]{x^2} \, dx$

⑦ $\int x\sqrt{x} + \dfrac{1}{2\sqrt{x}} \, dx$

⑧ $\int \left(\dfrac{x+6}{\sqrt{x}}\right) dx$

⑨ $\int \left(\dfrac{x^2+2x-3}{x^4}\right) dx$

EXAMPLE 2. Find the integral.

① $\int \dfrac{7}{x} dx$

② $\int x - 3 + \dfrac{1}{5x} - \dfrac{2}{x^2} \, dx$

③ $\int \dfrac{e^x}{3} dx$

④ $\int 3e^x + x^e \, dx$

EXAMPLE 3. Find the integral.

① $\int \sin x + \cos x \, dx$

② $\int 2\cot x \csc x \, dx$

③ $\int \sec^2 x + 1 \, dx$

④ $\int \tan^2 x + 1 \, dx$

⑤ $\int \dfrac{\sin x}{1-\sin^2 x} \, dx$

⑥ $\int \dfrac{2}{1-\cos^2 x} \, dx$

2. Reverse of Chain rule

※ Reverse of Chain rule

Since $[F(ax+b)]' = f(ax+b) \cdot a$,

$$\int f(ax+b)\, dx = \frac{1}{a} F(ax+b) + C$$

where F is the antiderivative of f.

	Antiderivative F(x)
$\int (ax+b)^n \, dx$	①
$\int \sin(ax+b)\, dx$	②
$\int \cos(ax+b)\, dx$	③
$\int \dfrac{1}{ax+b}\, dx$	④
$\int e^{(ax+b)}\, dx$	⑤

EXAMPLE 4. Find the integral

① $\int (2x-3)^2 dx$

Blank : ① $\dfrac{1}{a}\dfrac{(ax+b)^{n+1}}{(n+1)}$ ② $-\dfrac{1}{a}\cos(ax+b)$ ③ $\dfrac{1}{a}\sin(ax+b)$ ④ $\dfrac{1}{a}\ln|ax+b|$ ⑤ $\dfrac{1}{a}e^{ax+b}$

② $\int 3(x-5)^3 dx$

③ $\int 3\sqrt{1-2y}\ dy$

④ $\int \dfrac{4}{(2x+1)^3}\ dx$

⑤ $\int \sin 2x\ dx$

⑥ $\int \sec^2\left(\dfrac{x}{\pi}-2\right)dx$

⑦ $\int 2\cot\left(\dfrac{x}{2}\right)\csc\left(\dfrac{x}{2}\right)dx$

⑧ $\int \dfrac{1}{x+2}dx$

⑨ $\int \dfrac{1}{2-3x}dx$

⑩ $\int e^{-x}dx$

⑪ $\int e^{3x/2}dx$

⑫ $\int \dfrac{1}{e^{5x+4}}dx$

3. Integration by Substitution

"Integration by Substitution" (also called "**u-substitution**") is a method to find an integral, but only when it can be set up in a special way.

① Make a substitution **u = g(x)** .

$$\int f(g(x))\,g'(x)\,dx = \int f(\boxed{①})\,g'(x)\,dx$$

② Differentiate **u** wrt ②_____. Move dx to other side.

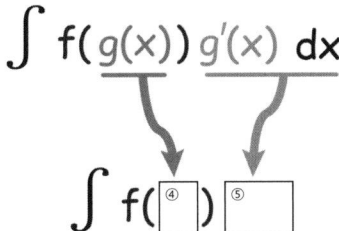

$$u = g(x)$$
$$\boxed{③} = g'(x)$$
$$du = g'(x)\,dx$$

③ Rewrite the integral in terms of u and integrate ∫f(u) du

$$\int f(\underline{g(x)})\,\underline{g'(x)\,dx}$$

$$\int f(\boxed{④})\,\boxed{⑤}$$

④ And finish up by re-inserting g(x) where u is.

Blank : ① u ② x ③ $\dfrac{du}{dx}$ ④ u ⑤ du

※ Integration by Substitution

$$\int f(g(x)) g'(x) \, dx$$

$$\int f(u) \, du$$

$u = g(x)$
$\dfrac{du}{dx} = g'(x)$
$du = g'(x) \, dx$

EXAMPLE 5. Evaluate the integral.

① $\displaystyle\int \dfrac{2x}{x^2 + 2} \, dx$

② $\displaystyle\int \dfrac{x}{x^2 + 4} \, dx$

③ $\displaystyle\int 6x(x^2 - 1)^3 \, dx$

④ $\displaystyle\int \dfrac{t}{\sqrt{t^2 + 1}} \, dt$

⑤ $\int x^2 \sqrt{(x^3-2)^3} \, dx$

⑥ $\int xe^{-x^2} \, dx$

⑦ $\int \cos^2 2x \sin 2x \, dx$

⑧ $\int \dfrac{\cos x}{\sin^2 x} \, dx$

⑨ $\int \sqrt{\cot t} \, \csc^2 t \, dt$

⑩ $\int \tan^3 y \sec^2 y \, dy$

⑪ $\int \dfrac{e^{\sqrt{x}}}{\sqrt{x}} \, dx$

⑫ $\int \left(1 + \dfrac{1}{x}\right) \dfrac{1}{x^2} \, dx$

⑬ $\int \dfrac{1}{x \ln x} \, dx$

EXAMPLE 6. *Use substitution $u = \cos\theta$ to evaluate $\int \cos\theta \sin\theta \sqrt{\cos^2\theta + 1}\, d\theta$.

EXAMPLE 7. * Use substitution to evaluate $\int \dfrac{\cos x (\ln(\sin x))^2}{\sin x}\, dx$.

EXAMPLE 8. Evaluate the integral.

> u-sub + Change x in terms of u!

① $\int x\sqrt{x+1}\, dx$

② $\int \dfrac{x^2}{(x-1)^2} dx$

③ *$\int \dfrac{1}{1+\sqrt{x}} dx$

4. Integration using Trig Identities

☺ Reminder : Trig identities

$\sin^2 x + \cos^2 x = $ ①

$1 + $ ② $= \sec^2 x$

$1 + \cot^2 x = $ ③

$\sin 2x = $ ④

$\cos 2x = $ ⑤

$= $ ⑥

$= $ ⑦

※ Integration using of trigonometric identities

When integrating $\sin^2 x$ and $\cos^2 x$, use trig identity;

	Antiderivative F(x)
$\int \sin^2 x \, dx$	$\frac{1}{2} \int 1 - \cos 2x \, dx$
$\int \cos^2 x \, dx$	$\frac{1}{2} \int 1 + \cos 2x \, dx$

EXAMPLE 9. Solve.

① $\int \sin x \, dx$

② $\int \sin^2 x \, dx$

Blank : ① 1 ② $\tan^2 x$ ③ $\csc^2 x$ ④ $2 \sin x \cos x$ ⑤ $\cos^2 x - \sin^2 x$ ⑥ $2\cos^2 x - 1$ ⑦ $1 - 2\sin^2 x$

③ * $\int \sin^3 x \, dx$

④ $\int \cos^2 x \, dx$

EXAMPLE 10. Solve.

① $\int \tan x \, dx$

② $\int \tan^2 x \, dx$

③ * $\int \tan^3 x \, dx$

④ $\int \cot x \, dx$

⑤ * $\int \sec x \, dx$

⑥ * $\int \csc x \, dx$

5. Integration using Inverse trigonometric functions

※ Integration rules

	Antiderivative F(x)
$\int \dfrac{1}{\sqrt{1-x^2}}\,dx$	①
$\int \dfrac{1}{1+x^2}\,dx$	②
$\int \dfrac{1}{\sqrt{1-(ax+b)^2}}\,dx$	$\dfrac{1}{a}\arcsin(ax+b)$
$\int \dfrac{1}{1+(ax+b)^2}\,dx$	$\dfrac{1}{a}\arctan(ax+b)$

EXAMPLE 11. Solve.

① $\int \dfrac{1}{\sqrt{1-4x^2}}\,dx$

② $\int \dfrac{1}{1+4x^2}\,dx$

Blank : ① arcsin x ② arctan x

③ $\int \dfrac{1}{\sqrt{1-x^2}} dx$

④ $\int \dfrac{x}{\sqrt{1-x^2}} dx$

※ Integration rules

		Antiderivative F(x)
$\int$	$\dfrac{1}{\sqrt{c^2-x^2}}\ dx$	$\arcsin\left(\dfrac{x}{c}\right)$
$\int$	$\dfrac{1}{c^2+x^2}\ dx$	$\dfrac{1}{c}\arctan\left(\dfrac{x}{c}\right)$

⑤ $\int \dfrac{1}{\sqrt{4-x^2}} dx$

⑥ $\int \dfrac{1}{16+x^2} dx$

☺ integrating Inverse trig

$$\int \frac{1}{\sqrt{c^2-(ax+b)^2}}\, dx \qquad \int \frac{1}{c^2+(ax+b)^2}\, dx$$

$$= \frac{1}{a}\sin^{-1}\left(\frac{ax+b}{c}\right) \qquad = \frac{1}{c}\cdot\frac{1}{a}\tan^{-1}\left(\frac{ax+b}{c}\right)$$

(flip)

⑦ $\int \dfrac{1}{4+9x^2}\, dx$

⑧ $\int \dfrac{1}{\sqrt{9-(2x-1)^2}}\, dx$

⑨ $\int \dfrac{1}{x^2 - 2x + 2} dx$

⑩ $\int \dfrac{1}{x^2 - 4x + 8} dx$

⑪ *$\int \dfrac{e^{2x}}{4 + e^{4x}} dx$

⑫ * $\displaystyle\int \frac{dx}{x(9+4\ln^2 x)}$

6. *Other strategies for integrating Quotients

Sometimes splitting the numerator helps.

EXAMPLE 12. Solve.

① $\displaystyle\int \frac{x+1}{\sqrt{1-x^2}}\,dx$

② $\int \dfrac{x+1}{x^2+1}\,dx$

③ $\int \dfrac{2x}{x^2+4x+5}\,dx$

④ $\int \dfrac{x+5}{x^2+6x+13}\,dx$

7. Finding +C

We've learned that when we are finding antiderivatives we use +C to show that we include *all* the possible antiderivatives.

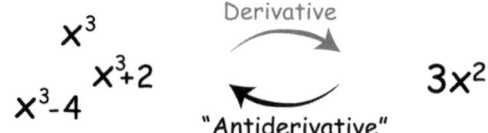

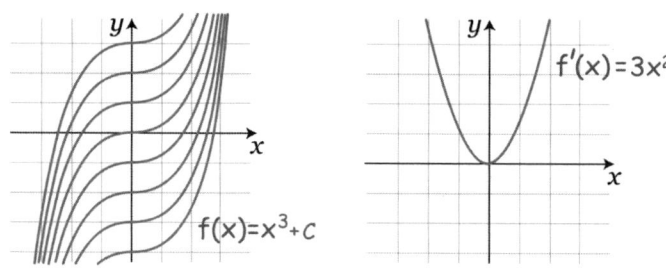

To identify a **particular** antiderivative of f we must have a **single value** which is called an initial condition.

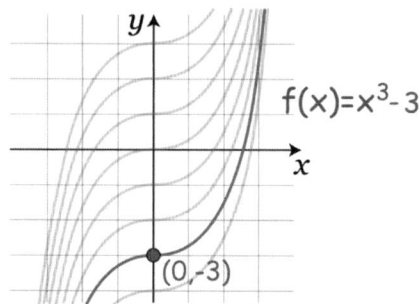

EXAMPLE 13. Find y using the given condition.

① $\dfrac{dy}{dx} = \dfrac{1}{x^2} + x, \quad y(-1) = 0$

② $\dfrac{dy}{dx} = 3x^{-2/3}, \quad y(-1) = 5$

③ $\dfrac{dy}{d\theta} = -\pi \sin \pi\theta, \quad y(0) = 0$

④ $\dfrac{d^2y}{dx^2} = 0, \quad y'(0) = 2, \quad y(0) = 4$

AP Style Problem

1. If the second derivative of f is given by $f''(x) = 3x - \sin x$, which of the following could be $f(x)$?

   A) $\dfrac{x^3}{2} + \sin x + x + 1$

   B) $\dfrac{x^3}{2} - \sin x + x + 1$

   C) $\dfrac{x^3}{2} + \cos x + x + 1$

   D) $\dfrac{3x^2}{2} + \cos x + 1$

2. Which of the following are antiderivative of $f(x) = 2\sin x \cos x$?

   I. $F(x) = \sin^2 x$

   II. $F(x) = \cos^2 x$

   III. $F(x) = -\dfrac{\cos 2x}{2}$

   A) I only
   B) I, II
   C) I, III
   D) I, II, and III
   E) None of these

Mia's AP Calculus

12. Definite Integral

1. Definite Integral

A **Definite Integral** has start and end values
: in other words there is an **interval** (from ①____ to ②____).

$$\int_a^b f(x)\, dx$$

※ Definite Integral (Second Fundamental Theorem of Calculus)
If F(x) is the antiderivative for a continuous function f(x), then

$$\int_a^b f(x)\, dx = \left[F(x)\right]_a^b = F(b) - F(a)$$

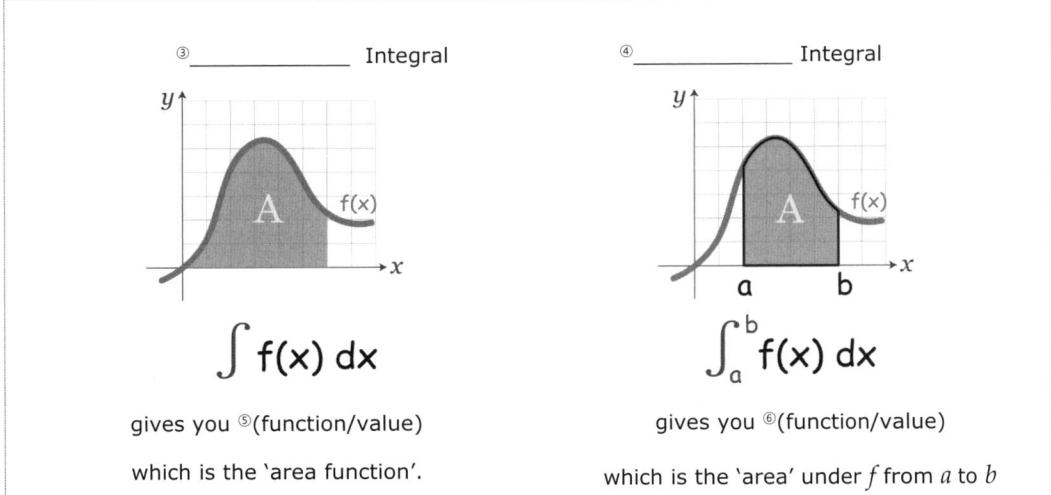

③ _____ Integral

$$\int f(x)\, dx$$

gives you ⑤(function/value)
which is the 'area function'.

④ _____ Integral

$$\int_a^b f(x)\, dx$$

gives you ⑥(function/value)
which is the 'area' under f from a to b

Blank : ① a ② b ③ Indefinite ④ Definite ⑤ function ⑥ value

EXAMPLE 1. Evaluate the integral.

① $\int_1^4 4+3x^2 \, dx$

② $\int_2^4 \dfrac{t^2 + \sqrt{t}}{t} \, dt$

③ $\int_0^4 \dfrac{4}{3x+1} \, dx$

④ $\int_0^{\pi/3} \sin(3x) \, dx$

⑤ $\int_{-\pi/4}^{\pi/4} \left(2 + 2\tan^2\theta\right) d\theta$

⑥ $\int_{0}^{\pi/2} \sin^2 \dfrac{1}{2}x \, dx$

2. Definite Integration by Substitution

※ Definite Integration by Substitution

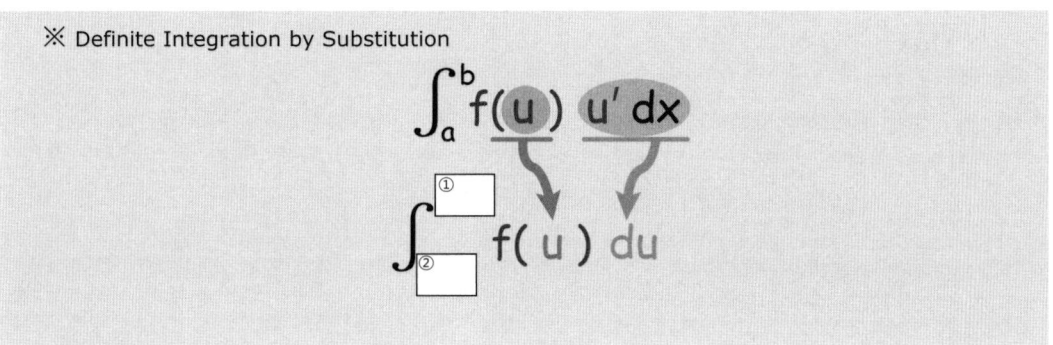

EXAMPLE 2. Evaluate the integral.

① $\int_{2}^{4} \dfrac{1}{x+4} \, dx$

Blank : ① u(b) ② u(a)

② $\int_0^2 x\sqrt{x^2+1}\ dx$

③ $\int_1^e \dfrac{(1+\ln x)^2}{x}\ dx$

④ $\int_e^{e^2} \dfrac{1}{x\ln x}\ dx$

⑤ $\int_1^2 (2x+1)e^{x^2+x-2}\ dx$

3. Properties of Definite Integral

※ Properties of Definite Integral

Reversing the interval gives the negative of the original.

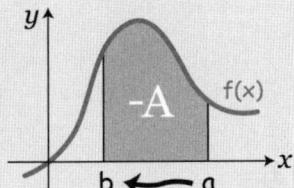

$$\int_b^a f(x)\,dx = \boxed{①} \int_a^b f(x)\,dx$$

When the interval **starts and ends at the same place**, the result is ② _____

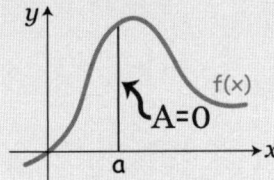

$$\int_a^a f(x)\,dx = \boxed{③}$$

You can also **add** two adjacent intervals together.

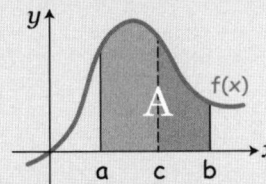

$$\int_a^b f(x)\,dx = \int_a^c f(x)\,dx + \int_c^b f(x)\,dx$$

Blank : ① -(negative)   ② 0   ③ 0

EXAMPLE 3. Given $\int_0^3 f(x)dx = 5$ and $\int_3^7 f(x)dx = 7$, evaluate

① $\int_0^7 f(x)\,dx =$

② $\int_3^0 f(x)\,dx =$

③ $\int_7^0 f(x)\,dx =$

④ $\int_3^3 f(x)\,dx =$

⑤ $\int_0^3 -f(x)\,dx =$

⑥ $\int_0^7 3f(x)\,dx =$

⑦ $\int_0^7 (f(x)+3)\,dx =$

4. Area vs Net Area

What if the graph f lies under the x axis?

※ When f(x) < 0 in [a, b], then

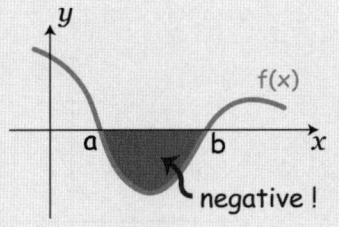

$\int_a^b f(x)\,dx$ ① _____

The integral adds the area above the axis but subtracts the area below, for a "net area":

$\int_a^b f(x)\,dx =$ (Area above x axis) − (Area below x axis)

※ Net Area VS Area

Net Area from a to d = ② _____

③ (Cal / Noncal)

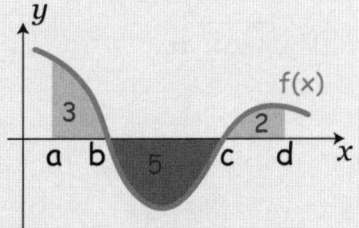

Area from a to d = ④ _____

⑤ (Cal)

⑥ (Noncal)

Blank : ① < 0 ② 3-5+2 = 0 ③ $\int_a^b f(x)\,dx$ ④ 3+5+2 = 10 ⑤ $\int_a^b |f(x)|\,dx$ ⑥ $\int_a^b f(x)\,dx - \int_b^c f(x)\,dx + \int_c^d f(x)\,dx$

12. Definite Integral

EXAMPLE 4. Graph the integrand and use areas to evaluate the integral.

① $\int_0^3 4\,dx$

② $\int_{-2}^4 \dfrac{x}{2}\,dx$

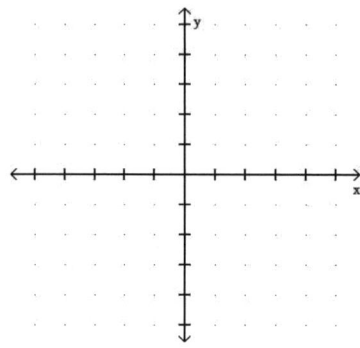
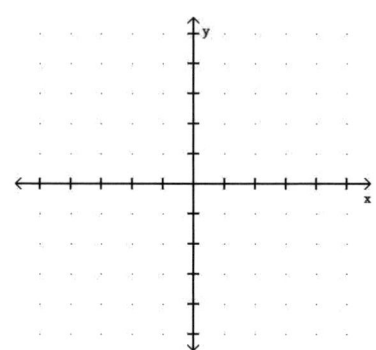

③ $\int_{-2}^2 \sqrt{4-x^2}\,dx$

④ $\int_{-1}^3 |x-1|\,dx$

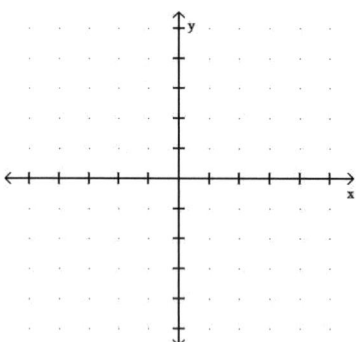
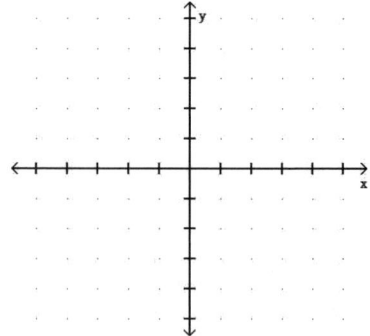

EXAMPLE 5. The graph of f is shown. Evaluate each integral.

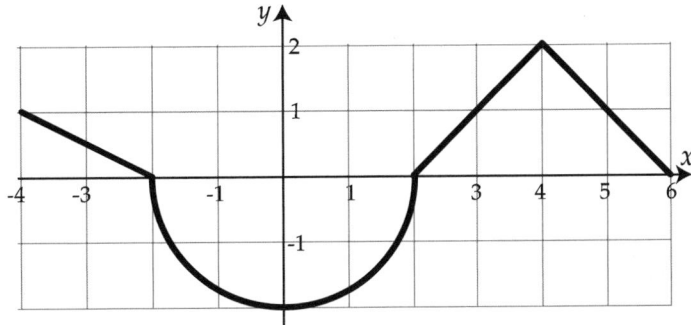

① $\int_0^2 f(x)\,dx$

② $\int_{-2}^6 f(x)\,dx$

③ $\int_6^{-4} f(x)\,dx$

④ $\int_{-4}^6 |f(x)|\,dx$

⑤ $\int_{-4}^6 (f(x)+2)\,dx$

⑥ $\int_6^0 (-2f(x)+1)\,dx$

EXAMPLE 6. Write, but do not evaluate, an integral expression that gives the area of the following shaded regions.

① $y = 2x+1$

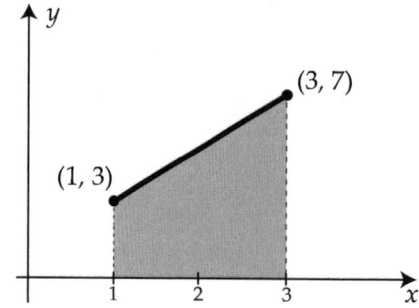

② $y = 1 - \sin\left(x - \dfrac{\pi}{2}\right)$

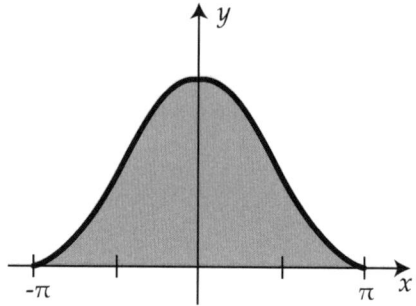

③ $y = 4 - x^2$

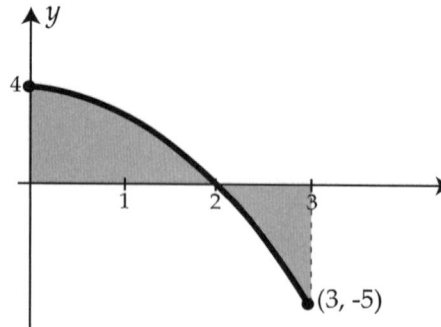

④ $y = x^2 - 4x + 3$

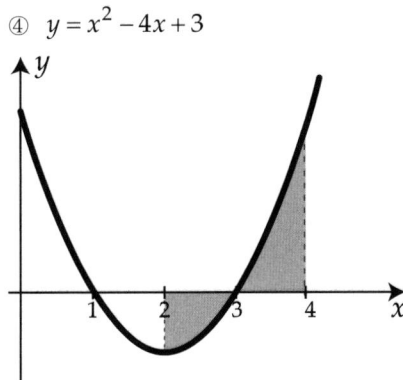

5. Integration of Odd and Even functions

※Properties of Even and Odd function

When f is even:

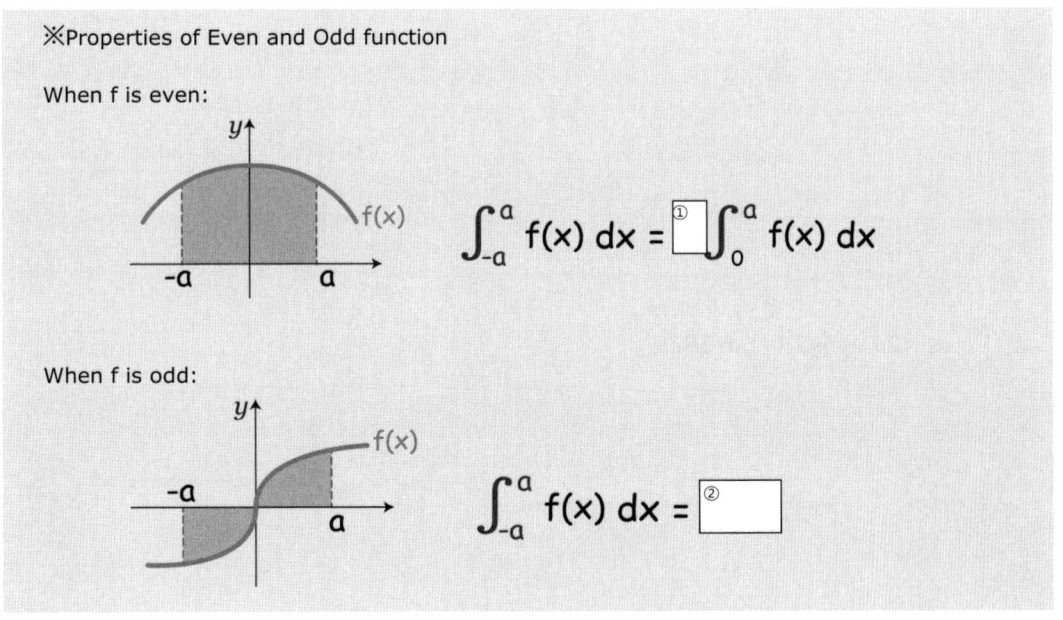

$$\int_{-a}^{a} f(x)\, dx = \boxed{①} \int_{0}^{a} f(x)\, dx$$

When f is odd:

$$\int_{-a}^{a} f(x)\, dx = \boxed{②}$$

Blank : ① 2   ② 0

EXAMPLE 7. Evaluate the integral.

① $\int_{-1}^{1} (x^3 - x) \, dx$

② $\int_{-2}^{2} (x^2 + 4) \, dx$

③ $\int_{-1}^{1} (x^5 - 4x^4 + 5x^3 - x + 1) \, dx$

④ $\int_{-\pi/4}^{\pi/4} \sin 2\theta + \cos 2\theta + \tan 2\theta \, d\theta$

AP Style Problem

1. If $\int_0^5 f(x)\,dx = 2$ and $\int_0^5 g(x)\,dx = -2$, which of the following is NOT true?

   A) $\int_5^0 f(x)\,dx = -2$

   B) $\int_0^5 f(x)g(x)\,dx = -4$

   C) $\int_0^5 f(x) - 2g(x)\,dx = 6$

   D) $\int_0^5 f(x) + 1\,dx = 7$

2. $\int_0^5 f(x+1)\,dx =$

   A) $\int_0^5 f(x)\,dx$

   B) $\int_1^6 f(x)\,dx$

   C) $\int_5^0 f(x+1)\,dx$

   D) $\int_{-1}^4 f(x)\,dx$

   E) $\int_0^6 f(x)\,dx$

3. The function f is continuous and $\int_1^{11} f(x)\,dx = 16$. What is the value of $\int_0^5 f(2x+1)\,dx$?

   A) 16
   B) 8
   C) 32
   D) 33
   E) 16.5

4. $\int_0^4 |x-2|\, dx =$

   A) -4
   B) -2
   C) 0
   D) 2
   E) 4

5. $\int_0^4 2-|x|\, dx =$

   A) -4
   B) -2
   C) 0
   D) 2
   E) 4

6. If $f(x) = \begin{cases} x+1 & ,x \geq 0 \\ x^2 - 4x - 2 & ,x < 0 \end{cases}$, then $\int_{-1}^2 f(x)\, dx =$

   A) $\dfrac{1}{3}$
   B) $\dfrac{13}{3}$
   C) $\dfrac{11}{3}$
   D) 3
   E) $\dfrac{1}{6}$

7. If $f(x) = \dfrac{|x|}{x}$, then $\int_{-2}^{2} f(x)dx =$

A) -4
B) -2
C) 0
D) 2
E) 4

8. $\int_{0}^{3} \sqrt{9-x^2}\, dx$ gives the area of

A) a circle of radius 9
B) a circle of radius 3
C) semicircle of radius 3
D) a quadrant of a circle of radius 3
E) a quadrant of a circle of radius 9

9. Let f be a function $f(-x) = f(x)$ for all x. If $\int_{0}^{2} f(x)dx = 4$, then $\int_{-2}^{2} f(x) + 2\, dx =$

A) 4
B) 8
C) 10
D) 12
E) 16

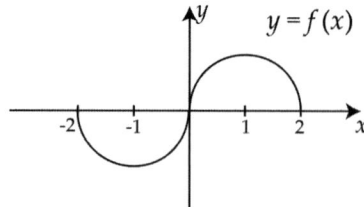

10. The graph of function f consists of two semicircles. Which of the following is (are) equivalent to $\int_0^2 f(x)dx$?

   I. $\int_0^{-2} f(x)dx$

   II. $\dfrac{1}{2}\int_{-2}^{2} |f(x)|dx$

   III. $\int_{-2}^{0} |f(x)|dx$

A) I only
B) II only
C) II and III only
D) I and II only
E) I, II, and III

6. Integrating derivatives

The Antiderivative of the $f'(x)$ is the ① _____ .

$$\int_a^b f'(x)\, dx = \boxed{②}$$

$$f(b) = \boxed{③}$$

Blank : ① f(x) ② f(b) − f(a) ③ $f(a) + \int_a^b f'(x)\,dx$

EXAMPLE 8. Graph of $f'(x)$ is given. If $f(0) = 4$ find the following.

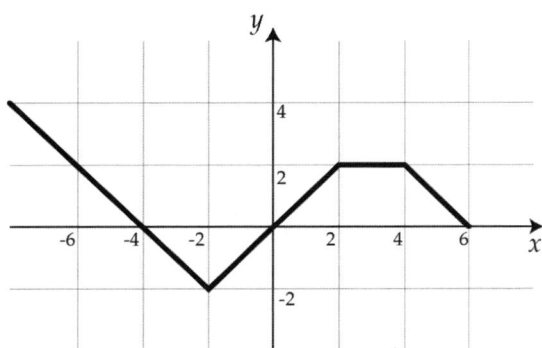

① $f(4)$

② $f(6)$

③ $f(-4)$

④ $f(-6)$

⑤ $f'(4)$

⑥ $f''(-4)$

⑦ Where f is decreasing

⑧ Where f concave up

EXAMPLE 9. The table below shows some values of two functions, f and g, and of their derivatives f and g .

x	1	2	3	4
$f(x)$	5	4	-1	3
$g(x)$	1	-2	2	-5
$f'(x)$	5	6	0	7
$g'(x)$	-6	-4	-3	4

Calculate the following.

① $\dfrac{d}{dx} f(g(x^3))$, when $x = 1$

② $\displaystyle\int_1^3 f'(x)\, dx$

③ $\displaystyle\int_1^4 g''(x)\, dx$

④ $\displaystyle\int_1^3 \left(g'(x)+6\right) dx$

⑤ $\displaystyle\int_1^2 x f'(x^2)\, dx$

AP Style Problem

1. The graph of f' is shown below. If $f(0) = 2$, then $f(4) =$

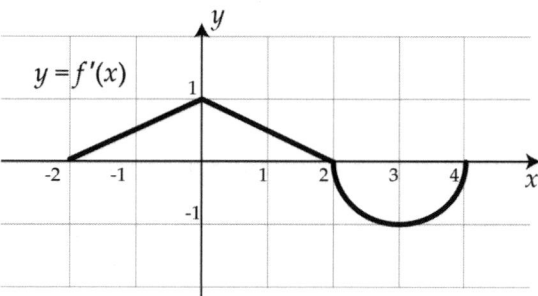

A) $3 - \dfrac{\pi}{2}$

B) $3 + \dfrac{\pi}{2}$

C) $4 - \dfrac{\pi}{2}$

D) $3 - \dfrac{\pi}{4}$

E) $4 + \dfrac{\pi}{4}$

x	1	2	4	6
$f(x)$	10	12	15	18
$f'(x)$	2	-1	-3	2

2. The table shows some values of continuous function f and its derivative. Evaluate $\int_1^4 f'(x)\,dx$.

A) -5
B) -3
C) 0
D) 3
E) 5

x	1	2	4	6
$f(x)$	10	12	15	18
$f'(x)$	2	-1	-3	2

3. The table shows some values of continuous function f and its derivative. Evaluate

$$\int_{1}^{4} \frac{f''(\sqrt{x})}{\sqrt{x}}\,dx$$

A) -10
B) -6
C) -3
D) 3
E) 5

4. The graph above shows the derivative of function f in [0, 3]. What is the value of x at which the absolute maximum of f occurs?

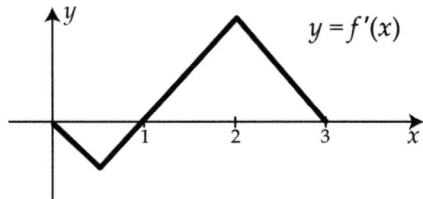

A) 0
B) 1
C) 1.5
D) 2
E) 3

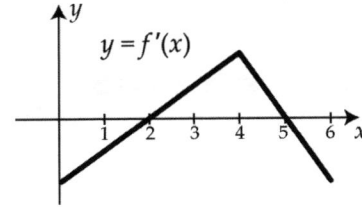

5. The graph of f' is shown. If $f(0) = 1$, which of the following must be true?

   I. $f(2) < f(0)$

   II. $f(2) > f(5)$

   III. $f(0) < f(5)$

A) I only
B) II only
C) II and III only
D) I and III only
E) I, II, and III

13. Fundamental Theorem of Calculus

1. Area Function

EXAMPLE 1. The graph of $f(t)$ is given in Figure. If $F(x) = \int_0^x f(t)\,dt$, fill in the values for $F(x)$ in the table:

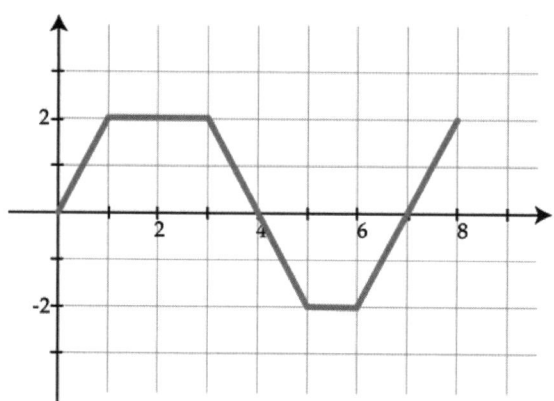

(a) Fill in.

x	0	1	3	4	5	7	8
$F(x)$							

(b) Where does $F(x)$ have its relative maximum in the interval $0 < x < 8$?

(c) Where does $F(x)$ have its relative minimum in the interval $0 < x < 8$?

※ Area Function

Area function $A(x)$ gives the net area of the region bounded by the graph of f and the t-axis on the interval $[a, x]$.

Area function
$$A(x) = \int_a^x f(t)\, dt$$

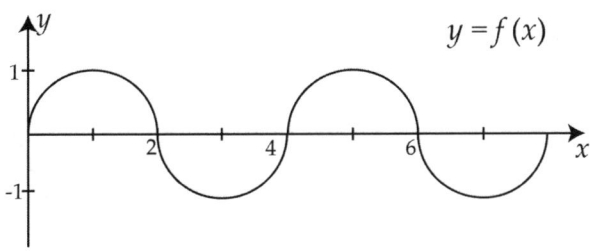

EXAMPLE 2. Consider the function f shown, its area function is $A(x) = \int_0^x f(t)\, dt$, for $0 \le x \le 8$.

Assume that the graph consists of four semicircles with same radius. Based on the graph of f, do the following.

(a) Find the zeros of A on $[0, 8]$.

(b) Find the points in the interval $0 < x < 8$ at which A has local maxima or local minima.

(c) Sketch a graph of A for $0 \le x \le 8$.

13. Fundamental Theorem of Calculus

(d) If $B(x) = \int_4^x f(t)dt$ then find x where $B = 0$.

AP Style Problem

1. The graph of function f is shown. If $g(x) = \int_{-3}^{x} f(t)\,dt$, which of the following values is greatest?

A) $g(-3)$ B) $g(-2)$ C) $g(0)$

D) $g(1)$ E) $g(2)$

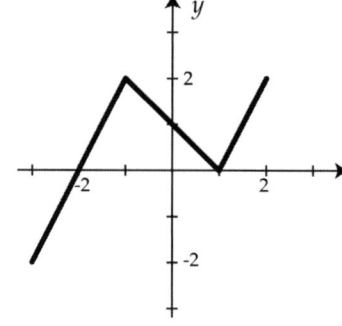

2. The graph of function f is shown. If $h(x) = \int_0^x f(t)\,dt$, where is $h(x)$ positive?

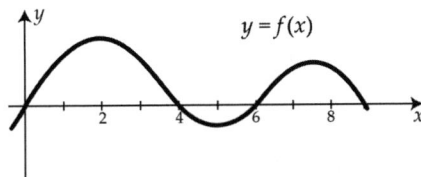

A) $0 < x < 4$

B) $6 < x \leq 9$

C) $0 < x < 4$ or $6 < x \leq 9$

D) $0 < x \leq 9$

E) none

3. For all values of x, $f(x)$ is continuous, positive and increasing. Let g be the function $g(x) = \int_1^x f(t)\,dt$. Which of the following could be a table for g?

A)

x	0	1	2
$g(x)$	-2	0	4

B)

x	0	1	2
$g(x)$	-4	0	2

C)

x	0	1	2
$g(x)$	2	0	-4

D)

x	0	1	2
$g(x)$	4	2	0

E)

x	0	1	2
$g(x)$	2	0	4

2. First Fundamental Theorem of Calculus

※ First Fundamental Theorem of Calculus

$$\frac{d}{dx}\int_a^x f(t)\,dt = f(x)$$

inverse

$$\frac{d}{dx}\int_a^{g(x)} f(t)\,dt = f(g(x))\cdot g'(x)$$

inverse

☺ Proof

Since $\int_a^x f(t)\,dt = \left[F(t)\right]_a^x =$ ①

then $\dfrac{d}{dx}\left[F(x) - F(a)\right] = \dfrac{d}{dx}F(x) - \dfrac{d}{dx}F(a) =$ ②

☺ Proof

Since $\int_a^{g(x)} f(t)\,dt = \left[F(t)\right]_a^{g(x)} =$ ③

then $\dfrac{d}{dx}\left[F(g(x)) - F(a)\right] = \dfrac{d}{dx}F(g(x)) - \dfrac{d}{dx}F(a) =$ ④

Blank : ① F(x) − F(a)   ② f(x)   ③ F(g(x)) − F(a)   ④ f(g(x)) g'(x)

EXAMPLE 3. Use the first fundamental theorem of calculus to evaluate.

① $\dfrac{d}{dx}\displaystyle\int_0^x \sqrt{2t-1}\, dt$

② $\dfrac{d}{dx}\displaystyle\int_{-5}^x \dfrac{dt}{5t+6}$

③ $\dfrac{d}{dx}\displaystyle\int_x^{\pi/2} \cos t\, dt$

④ $\dfrac{d}{dz}\displaystyle\int_{\pi/4}^z \sec^2 x\, dx$

⑤ $\dfrac{d}{dx}\displaystyle\int_0^{x^2} \sin^2 t\, dt$

⑥ $\dfrac{d}{dx}\displaystyle\int_0^{\sin x} \sqrt{t}\, dt$

⑦ $\dfrac{d}{dx}\displaystyle\int_0^{\cos^2 2x} \sqrt{t}\, dt$

⑧ $\dfrac{d}{dx}\displaystyle\int_{\ln x}^1 e^t\, dt$

⑨ * $\lim\limits_{h\to 0}\dfrac{1}{h}\displaystyle\int_{c}^{c+h} f(x)\,dx$

EXAMPLE 4. Let f be the function graphed below and let $g(x)=\displaystyle\int_{2}^{x} f(t)\,dt$.

Evaluate each of the following.

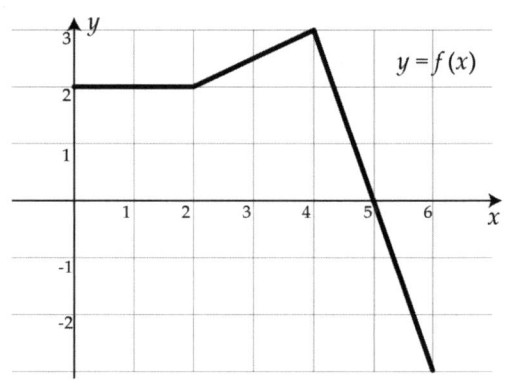

① $g(4)$ ② $g(6)$

③ $g(0)$ ④ $g(2)$

⑤ $g'(4)$ ⑥ $g'(5)$

⑦ $g''(4)$

⑧ $g''(5)$

⑨ Where is g increasing? Justify.

⑩ Where is g concave down? Justify.

⑪ Where is the inflection point of g? Justify.

⑫ Write the equation of the tangent line to g at x = 4.

⑬ What is the maximum of g on [0, 6]?

EXAMPLE 5. Let f be the function graphed below and let $g(x) = \displaystyle\int_1^x f(t)\, dt$.

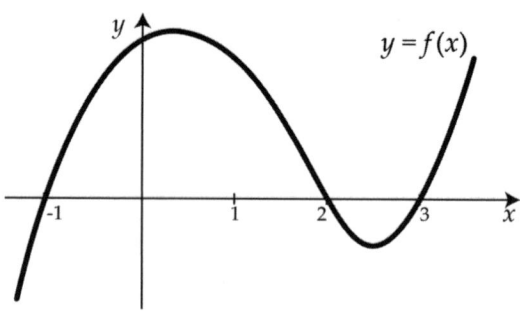

Determine the sign (whether it is positive/ negative / zero).

① $g(1)$ ② $g(2)$

③ $g(3)$ ④ $g(-1)$

⑤ $g'(1)$ ⑥ $g'(2)$

⑦ $g''(1)$ ⑧ $g''(3)$

AP Style Problem

1. If the function is given by $f(x) = \int_{2}^{x^2} (\sqrt{t}+1)\, dt$, then $f'(2) =$

   A) $\sqrt{2}+1$
   B) $\sqrt{2}+4$
   C) 3
   D) 12
   E) 24

2. If $y = \int_{-1}^{x} \sqrt{t^2+1}\, dt$, then $\dfrac{d^2y}{dx^2} =$

   A) $\sqrt{x^2+1}$
   B) $\dfrac{x}{\sqrt{x^2+1}}$
   C) $\dfrac{x}{2\sqrt{x^2+1}}$
   D) $\dfrac{x\sqrt{x^2+1}}{2}$
   E) $\dfrac{1}{2x\sqrt{x^2+1}}$

3. Let $f(x) = \int_{2}^{x} \cos 2t\, dt$ for $0 \le x \le \pi$. On which interval is f increasing?

   A) $0 < x < \pi$
   B) $\dfrac{\pi}{2} < x < \pi$
   C) $\dfrac{\pi}{4} < x < \dfrac{3\pi}{4}$
   D) $0 < x < \dfrac{\pi}{4}$ or $\dfrac{3\pi}{4} < x < \pi$
   E) $0 < x < \dfrac{\pi}{2}$

4. Let $\int_0^x g(t)\, dt = x\cos \pi x$. Then $g(0) =$

A) $-\pi$

B) -1

C) 0

D) 1

E) π

5. The graph of the differentiable function f is shown above. Let g be the function defined by $g(x) = \int_0^x f(t)\, dt$. Which of the following correctly orders $g(1)$, $g'(1)$, and $g''(1)$?

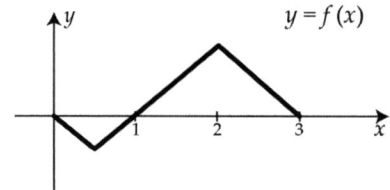

A) $g(1) < g'(1) < g''(1)$

B) $g'(1) < g(1) < g''(1)$

C) $g'(1) < g''(1) < g(1)$

D) $g(1) < g''(1) < g'(1)$

E) $g''(1) < g(1) < g'(1)$

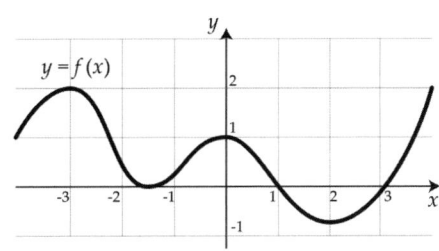

6. The graph of the function f shown above has horizontal tangents at $x = -3, -1.5, 0, 2$ in $[-4, 4]$. Let $g(x) = \int_0^x f(t)\, dt$. How many inflection points does g have in $[-4, 4]$?

A) 0
B) 1
C) 3
D) 4
E) 5

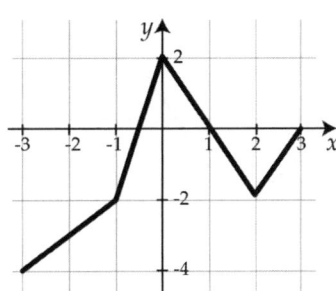

7. The graph of the function f is shown. Let h be the function defined by $h(x) = \int_0^x f(t)\, dt$. At what value of x does h has its absolute minimum in $[-3,3]$?

A) -3
B) 0
C) 1
D) 2
E) 3

13. Fundamental Theorem of Calculus

8. Let $g(x) = \int_0^x (1+e^{t^2}) \, dt$. Which of the following statements is (are) true?

   I. $g(2) < g(5)$

   II. $g(2) = g(-2)$

   III. g has no infection points.

   A) I only
   B) II only
   C) II and III only
   D) I and II only
   E) I, II, and III

9. The graph of function f is shown. If $h(x) = \int_0^x f(t) \, dt$, where is $h(x)$ positive?

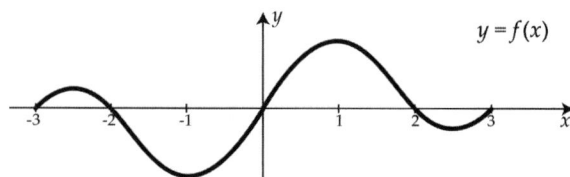

   A) $0 < x \leq 2$

   B) $-2 \leq x \leq 2$

   C) $-3 \leq x \leq -2$ or $0 < x \leq 2$

   D) $-3 \leq x < 0$ or $0 < x \leq 3$

   E) none

10. The graph of function f is shown. If $h(x) = \int_0^x f(t)\,dt$, where is $h(x)$ increasing?

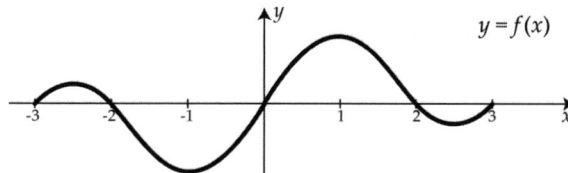

A) $0 < x \leq 2$

B) $-2 \leq x \leq 2$

C) $-3 < x < -2$ or $0 < x < 2$

D) $-3 \leq x < 0$ or $0 < x \leq 3$

E) none

3. MVT of Integration and Average Value

The **Mean Value Theorem** for definite integrals just says that $\int_a^b f(x)\,dx$ always has a ①_____ with the same area and width!

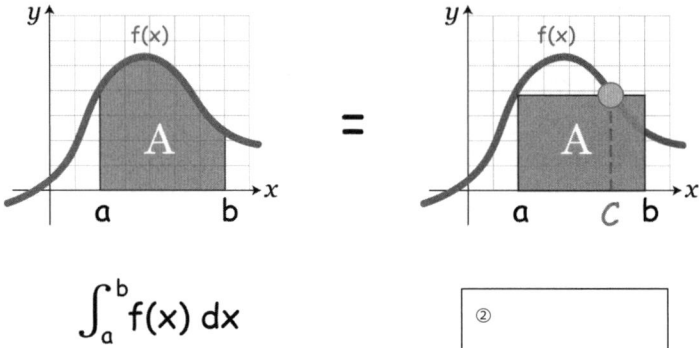

$$\int_a^b f(x)\,dx \qquad\qquad ②\boxed{}$$

※ Mean Value Theorem for integral

If f is **continuous** on the interval [a,b],

then at some point C in (a,b) such that :

$$\int_a^b f(x)\,dx = f(c)(b-a)$$

The height of the rectangle (where the top of the rectangle and f(x) intersects) is ③_____ , and we call it ④_____ value of f'.

Blank : ① rectangle ② f(c)(b − a) ③ f(c) ④ Average

※ Average Value

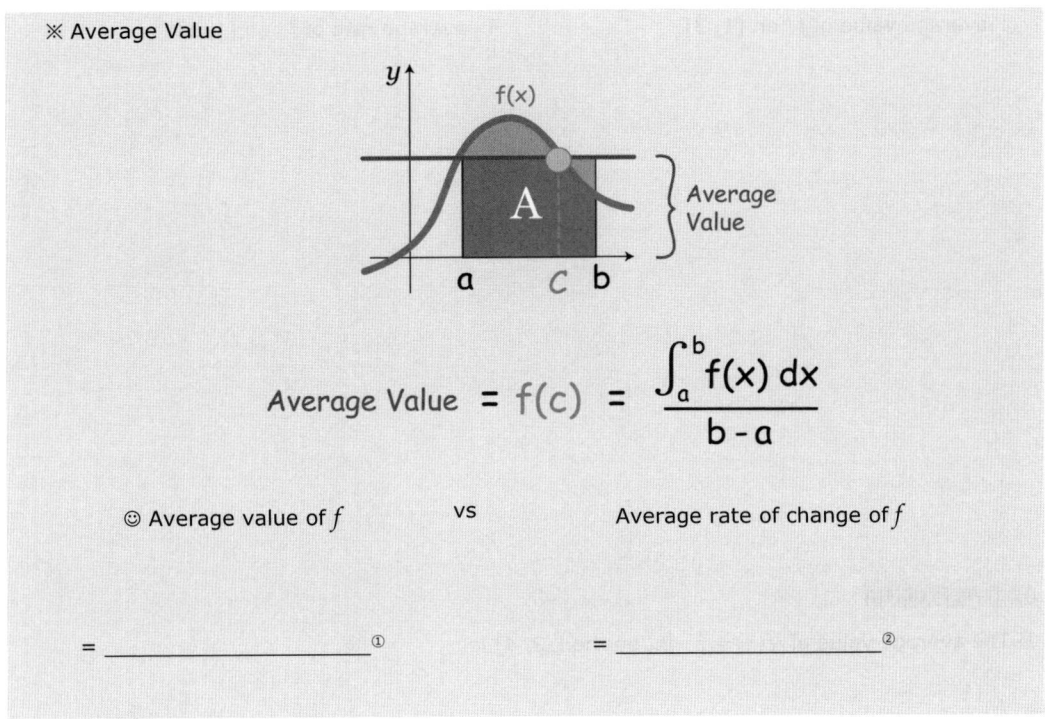

$$\text{Average Value} = f(c) = \frac{\int_a^b f(x)\,dx}{b-a}$$

☺ Average value of f vs Average rate of change of f

= _____ ①   = _____ ②

EXAMPLE 6. Let $f(x) = x^2 - 2x$.

① average value of f on [1, 3]

② average rate of f on [1, 3]

Blank : ① $\dfrac{\int_a^b f(x)\,dx}{b-a}$ ② $\dfrac{f(b)-f(a)}{b-a}$

③ average value of f' on [1, 3]   ④ average rate of f' on [1, 3]

AP Style Problem

1. The average value of $f(x) = 2 - |x|$ on the [-2, 4] is

    A) $\dfrac{1}{3}$

    B) $\dfrac{2}{3}$

    C) 1

    D) 2

    E) 4

2. The temperature t hours after 9 AM is approximated by the function $T(t) = 1 - \cos t$, where T is in degrees Fahrenheit. Find the average temperature during the time period 9 AM to 9 PM.

    A) $12 - \sin 12$

    B) $1 - \dfrac{\sin 12}{12}$

    C) $12 - \cos 12$

    D) $1 - \dfrac{\cos 12}{12}$

3. The number of bacteria in a container increases at the rate of $R(t)$ bacteria per hour. Which of the following expressions gives the average rate of the number of bacteria in the container during the first 10 hours?

A) $R(10)$

B) $\dfrac{1}{10}\displaystyle\int_0^{10} R(t)\,dt$

C) $\displaystyle\int_0^{10} R(t)\,dt$

D) $\dfrac{R(10)-R(0)}{10}$

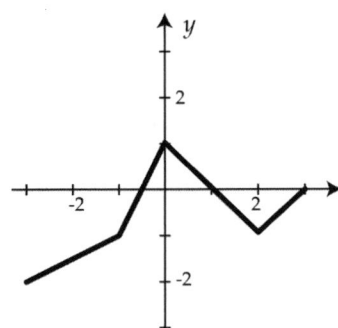

4. The graph of function f is shown. Which of the following has the greatest value?

A) Average value of f over [-3,3]

B) Average rate of change of f over [-3,3]

C) $\displaystyle\int_{-3}^{3} f(x)\,dx$

D) $f'(-0.5)$

E) $f(2)$

Mia's AP Calculus

14. Approximating Area

1. Estimating Area Using Rectangles

We have learned that **integral** was all about '①_____,' under the curve.

$$\int_a^b f(x)\, dx$$

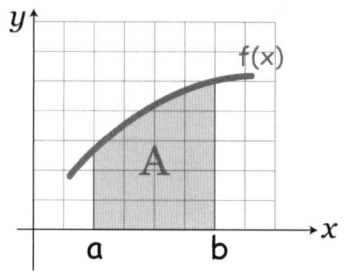

$\int$ came from the idea of **adding up many slices**.

Now we need to talk a little bit about *estimating* the area under a curve.

Let's estimate the area under the curve $f(x) = -x^2 + 5$ from $x = 0$ to $x = 2$ with 4 slices of:

1) Right-Endpoint Rectangles

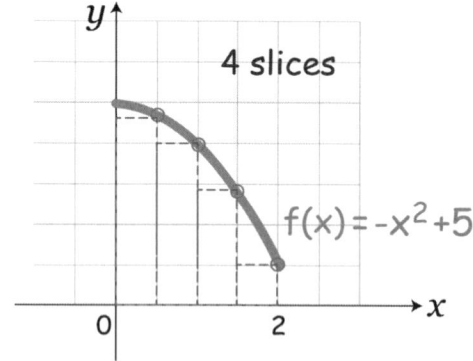

4 slices

$f(x) = -x^2 + 5$

width : all $\Delta x =$ _____ ②

③ height :

④ Area =

Blank : ① Net area   ② 0.5   ③ f(0.5), f(1), f(1.5), f(2)   ④ 0.5 [f(0.5) + f(1) + f(1.5) + f(2)]

2) Left-Endpoint Rectangles

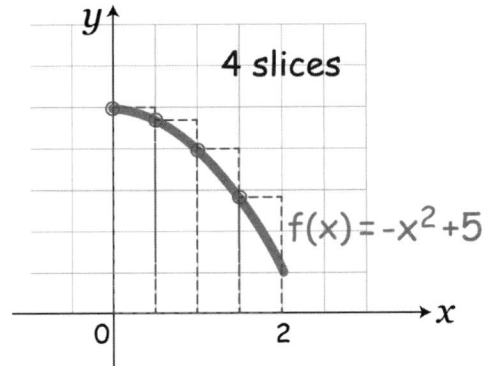

4 slices

$f(x) = -x^2 + 5$

width : all $\Delta x = $ _____ ①

② height :

③ Area =

3) Midpoint Rectangles

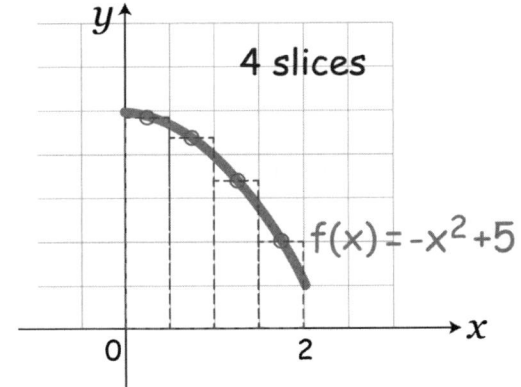

4 slices

$f(x) = -x^2 + 5$

width : all $\Delta x = $ _____ ④

⑤ height :

⑥ Area =

Blank : ① 0.5   ② f(0), f(0.5), f(1), f(1.5)   ③ 0.5 [f(0) + f(0.5) + f(1) + f(1.5)]

④ 0.5   ⑤ $f\left(\frac{1}{4}\right), f\left(\frac{3}{4}\right), f\left(\frac{5}{4}\right), f\left(\frac{7}{4}\right)$ ⑥ $0.5\left[f\left(\frac{1}{4}\right) + f\left(\frac{3}{4}\right) + f\left(\frac{5}{4}\right) + f\left(\frac{7}{4}\right)\right]$

4) Trapezoids

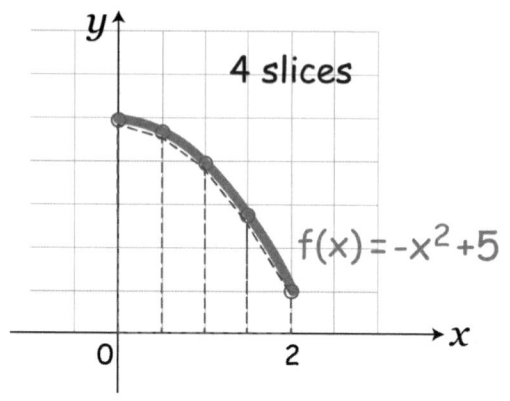

Area of the
① 1st trap:

② 2nd trap:

③ 3rd trap:

④ 4th trap:

⑤ Area =

※ Approximation Formulas

If the interval [a, b] is sliced into n subintervals, then the width will be

$$\Delta x = ⑥ \underline{\qquad}$$

The sum of the areas will be

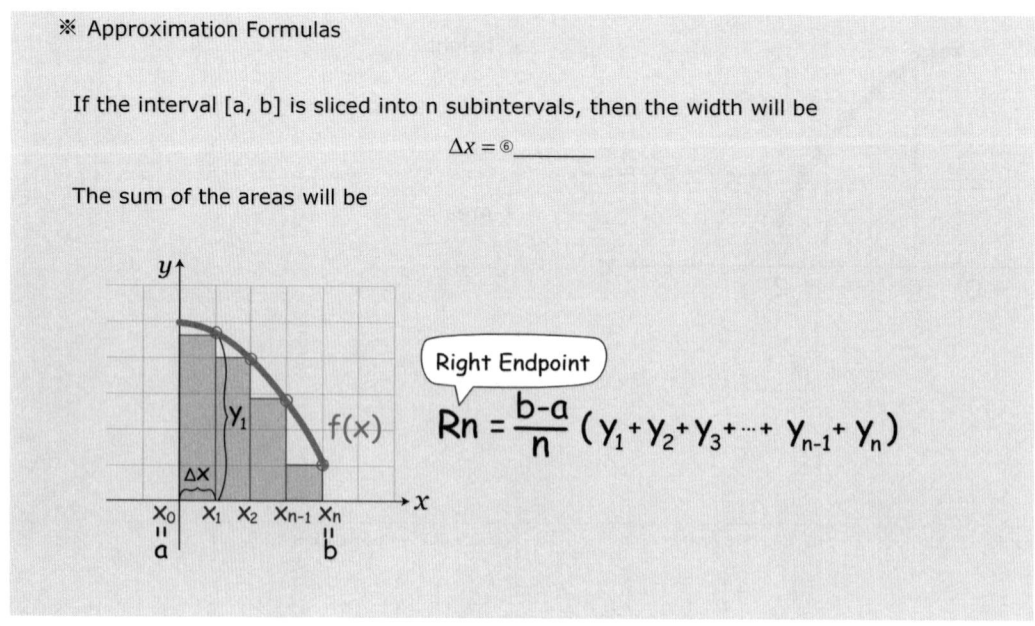

Right Endpoint

$$R_n = \frac{b-a}{n}(Y_1 + Y_2 + Y_3 + \cdots + Y_{n-1} + Y_n)$$

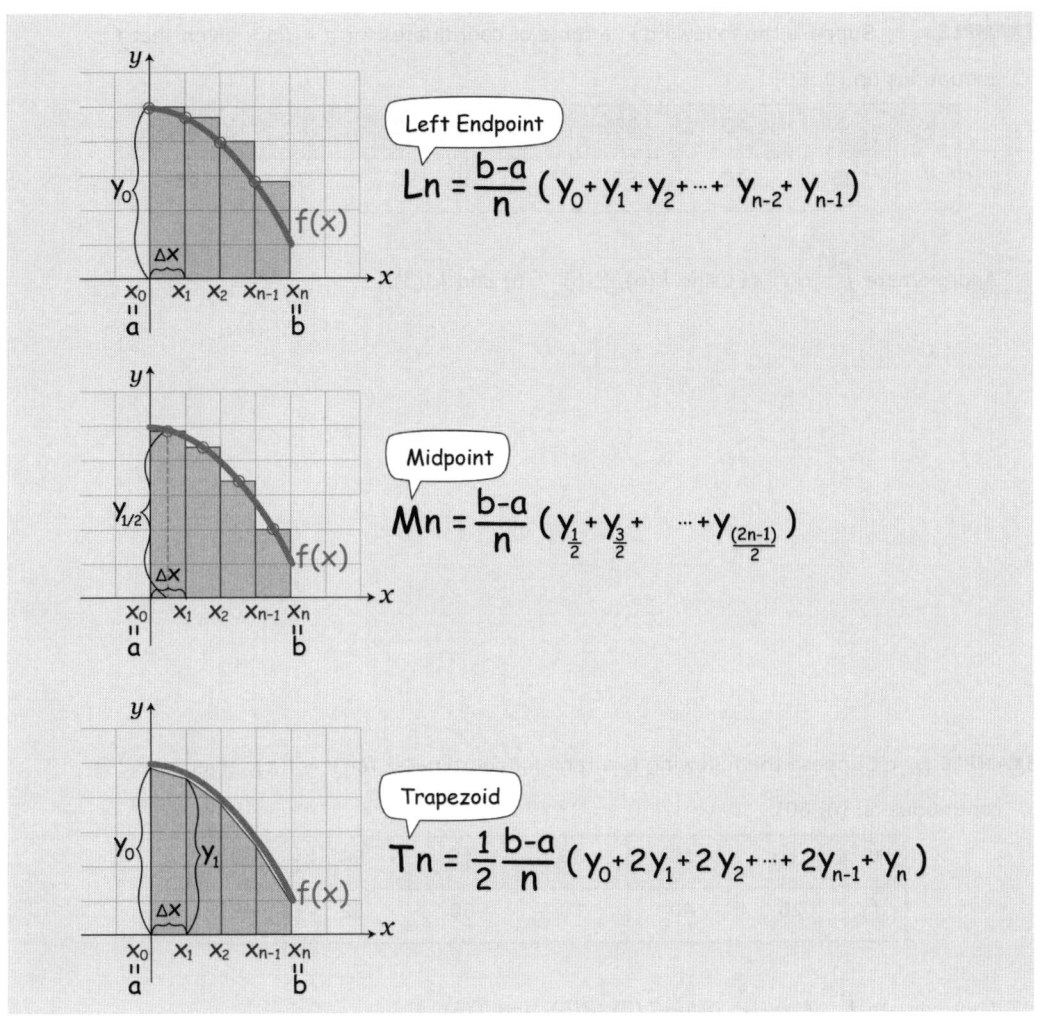

Blank : ① 0.5(0.5) [f(0) + f(0.5)]   ② 0.5(0.5) [f(0.5) + f(1)]   ③ 0.5(0.5) [f(1) + f(1.5)]   ④ 0.5(0.5) [f(1.5) + f(2)]

⑤ 0.5(0.5) [f(0) + 2f(0.5) + 2f(1) + 2f(1.5) + f(2)]   ⑥ $\dfrac{b-a}{n}$

EXAMPLE 1. Suppose the following is a table of coordinates for $y = f(x)$, given that f is continuous on [0, 60].

x	0	10	20	30	40	50	60
f	25	40	55	10	50	32	45

Approximate $\int_0^{60} f(x)\, dx$ using $L(6)$, $R(6)$, $T(6)$ and $M(3)$.

EXAMPLE 2. Suppose the following is a table of coordinates for $y = f(x)$, given that f is continuous on [0, 60].

x	0	10	30	45	50	60
f	26	40	10	60	32	45

Approximate $\int_0^{60} f(x)\, dx$, using $L(5)$, $R(5)$, and $T(5)$.

EXAMPLE 3. Find the approximation of the area of the region between the graph of $f(x)=\sqrt{x}$ and the x-axis between $x = 0$ and $x = 10$ using 5 rectangles of Right endpoint rectangle/ Left endpoint rectangle / Trapezoid.

EXAMPLE 4. Write an inequality including $L(n)$, $R(n)$, $T(n)$, and $\int_a^b f(x)dx$ for the graph of f shown in figure.

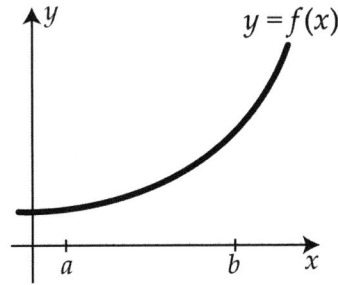

EXAMPLE 5. Write an inequality including $L(n)$, $R(n)$, $T(n)$, and $\int_a^b f(x)dx$ for the graph of f shown in figure.

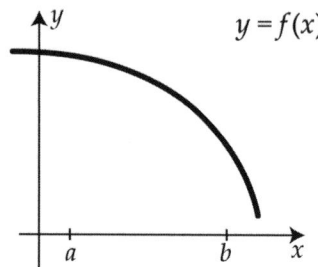

AP Style Problem

1. A continuous function f takes on the values shown in the table below. Estimate $\int_0^{10} f(x)\,dx$ using a left rectangular approximation with four subintervals.

x	0	2	5	7	10
$f(x)$	8	10	12	16	10

A) 114
B) 118
C) 110
D) 109

2. The graph of a continuous function f passes through the points (2, 1), (4, 3), (7, 5), and (8, 5).

Estimate $\int_2^8 f(x)\, dx$ using a trapezoid approximation.

   A) 8
   B) 10
   C) 21
   D) 42

3. A continuous function f takes on the values shown in the table below. Using trapezoid, we can estimate the average value of f over [0, 16] as

x	0	4	8	12	16
$f(x)$	4	6	5	9	4

   A) 6
   B) 19/4
   C) 96
   D) 16

4. The definite integral $\int_1^4 x^2\, dx$ is approximate by a left Riemann sum L, a right Riemann sum R, and a trapezoidal sum T, each with three subintervals of equal width. Which of the following is true?

   A) $L < T < \int_1^4 x^2\, dx < R$

   B) $L < \int_1^4 x^2\, dx < T < R$

   C) $R < \int_1^4 x^2\, dx < T < L$

   D) $R < T < \int_1^4 x^2\, dx < L$

2. Riemann Sums

So far we estimated the area under the curve. It was just an approximation. Now let's find out the **exact area**!

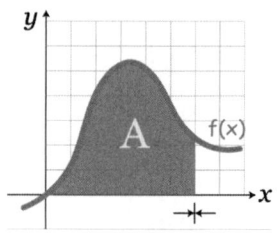

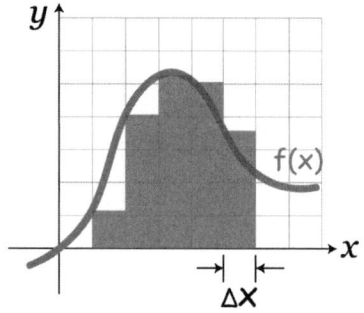

We could break the area into **slices with width Δx** like this.
(but this won't be very accurate)

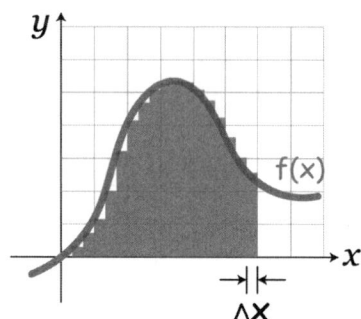

We can **make Δx a lot smaller** and **add up many small slices.**
(it's getting better)

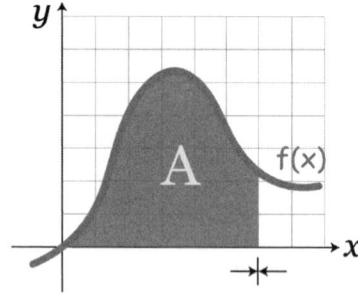

And as the **slice width Δx** approaches 0 and **add up infinite number of small slices**, it approaches the **true area**.

Let's write it mathematically!

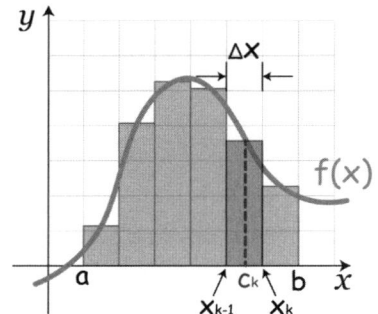

Cutting up the bound [a, b] into **n slices**, the **width of each piece** is ①_____.

If I take **one arbitrary point** (C_k) between X_k and X_{k-1} in the *kth slice*, the height of the slice will be ②_____.

So the **area of the slice** will be ③_____.

And when I **add up all the n slices**, I have ④_____.

And when I **add up infinite number of small slices** the answer approaches the **true area**.

⑤_____.

We can connect this idea with the Definite integral. (We will change c_k to x)

※ Definite Integral and Riemann Sum

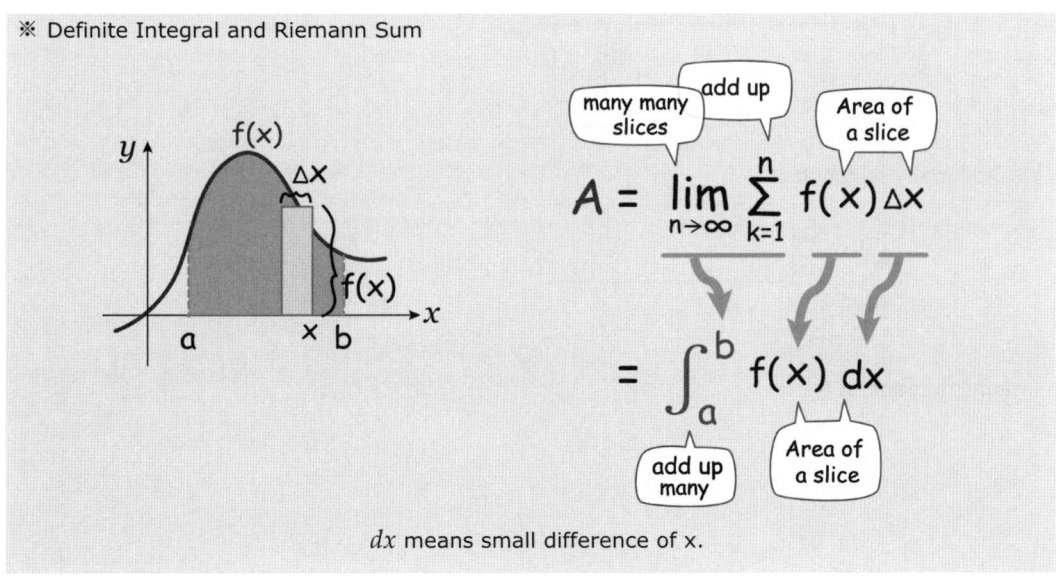

dx means small difference of x.

Blank : ① Δx ② $f(c_k)$ ③ $f(c_k)\Delta x$ ④ $\sum_{k=1}^{n} f(c_k)\Delta x$ ⑤ $\lim_{n\to\infty} \sum_{k=1}^{n} f(c_k)\Delta x$

☺ Remind

Write $\dfrac{2\sqrt{1}}{1^3}+\dfrac{2\sqrt{2}}{2^3}+\dfrac{2\sqrt{3}}{3^3}+\dfrac{2\sqrt{4}}{4^3}$ in sigma notation:

EXAMPLE 6. Find the area under the curve $f(x)$ on the interval $[1,4]$ using the limit process.
(n slices, using right-end rectangle)

① Find the width of a rectangle. $\quad \Delta x = \dfrac{\square - \square}{n} = \dfrac{\square}{n}$

② So we can make slices in the interval;

$\left[1, 1+\dfrac{\square}{n}\right], \quad \left[1+\dfrac{\square}{n}, 1+\dfrac{\square}{n}\right], \quad \left[1+\dfrac{\square}{n}, 1+\dfrac{\square}{n}\right], \ldots$

③ Using **Right** Rectangle;

Area = height · width

= $\boxed{} \cdot \boxed{}$

④ Add many rectangles!

= $\displaystyle\lim_{n\to\infty} \sum_{k=1}^{n} \boxed{} \cdot \boxed{}$

In integral notation, it is ;

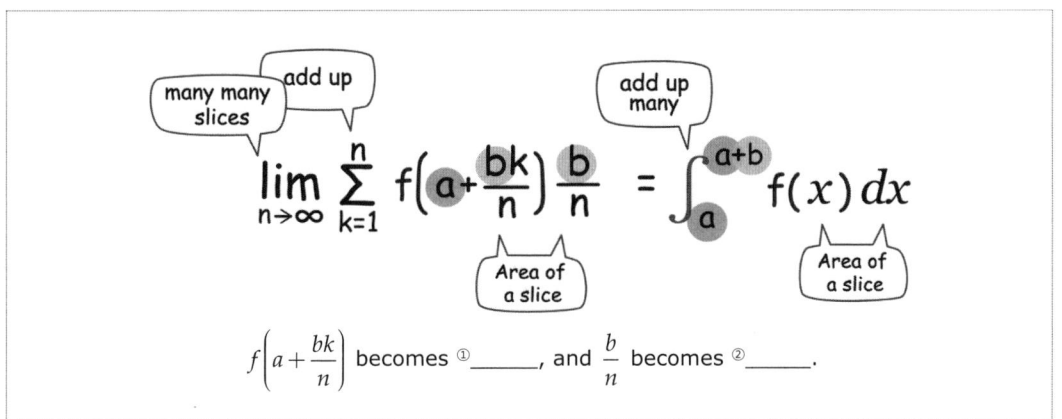

$f\left(a+\dfrac{bk}{n}\right)$ becomes ①_____, and $\dfrac{b}{n}$ becomes ②_____.

EXAMPLE 7. Express the following Riemann sums as definite integrals.

① $\displaystyle\lim_{n\to\infty}\sum_{k=1}^{n}\left(1+\dfrac{3k}{n}\right)^2\cdot\dfrac{3}{n}$

② $\displaystyle\lim_{n\to\infty}\sum_{k=1}^{n}\left(\dfrac{2k}{n}\right)^3\cdot\dfrac{2}{n}$

③ $\displaystyle\lim_{n\to\infty}\sum_{k=1}^{n}\left(1+\dfrac{3k}{n}\right)^2\cdot\dfrac{1}{3n}$

Blank : ① f(x)   ② dx

④ $\lim\limits_{n\to\infty} \dfrac{1^2+2^2+3^2+\ldots+n^2}{n^3}$

⑤ $\lim\limits_{n\to\infty} \left(\dfrac{\sqrt{1}+\sqrt{2}+\sqrt{3}+\ldots+\sqrt{n}}{\sqrt{n^3}} \right)$

⑥ $\lim\limits_{n\to\infty} \dfrac{1}{n}\left\{ \dfrac{1}{1+\dfrac{1}{n}} + \dfrac{1}{1+\dfrac{2}{n}} + \ldots + \dfrac{1}{1+\dfrac{n}{n}} \right\}$

AP Style Problem

1. Find the value of $\lim_{n\to\infty} \sum_{k=1}^{n} \left(1+\dfrac{2k}{n}\right)^2 \cdot \dfrac{3}{n}$ using a definite integral.

    A) 13
    B) 26/3
    C) 13/3
    D) 26

2. $\lim_{n\to\infty} \dfrac{1}{n}\left\{ \left(1+\dfrac{1}{n}\right)^2 + \left(1+\dfrac{2}{n}\right)^2 + \ldots + \left(1+\dfrac{n}{n}\right)^2 \right\}$ is equivalent to

    A) $\int_0^2 x^2 dx$
    B) $\int_0^1 (x+1)^2 dx$
    C) $\int_0^1 x^2 dx$
    D) $\int_0^2 (x+1)^2 dx$

Mia's AP Calculus

15. Area and Volume

1. Area Between Curves

The **definite integral** comes from the idea : ①_____ up the ② _____ of the rectangles (infinite number of)!

$$A = \lim_{n \to \infty} \sum_{k=1}^{n} f(x) \Delta x$$

$$= \int_{a}^{b} f(x)\, dx$$

add up / the area of the rectangles

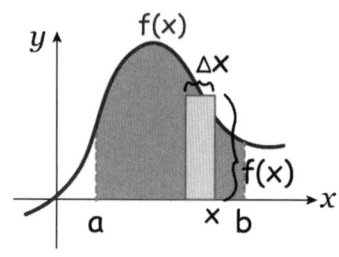

This time let's find the area of the region bounded above and below by $y = f(x)$ and $y = g(x)$, and on the left and right by $x = a$ and $x = b$.

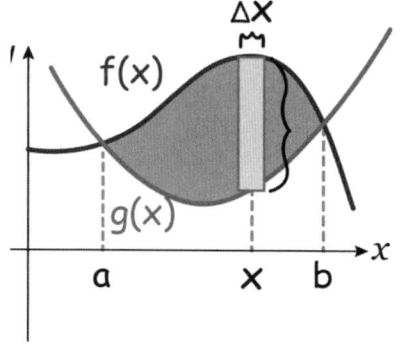

Each **rectangle** has

a height of ③_____

and a width of ④_____ (=dx)

So the area of each rectangle will be:

⑤_____

All we need is to **add up** all these **area of the rectangle** from a to b!

$$A = \boxed{\text{⑥}}$$

add up / the area of the rectangles

Blank : ① adding ② area ③ f(x) − g(x) ④ △x ⑤ [f(x) − g(x)] dx ⑥ $\int_{a}^{b} [\, f(x) - g(x)\,]\, dx$

270 Mia's AP calculus AB BC

※ Area Between Two Curves

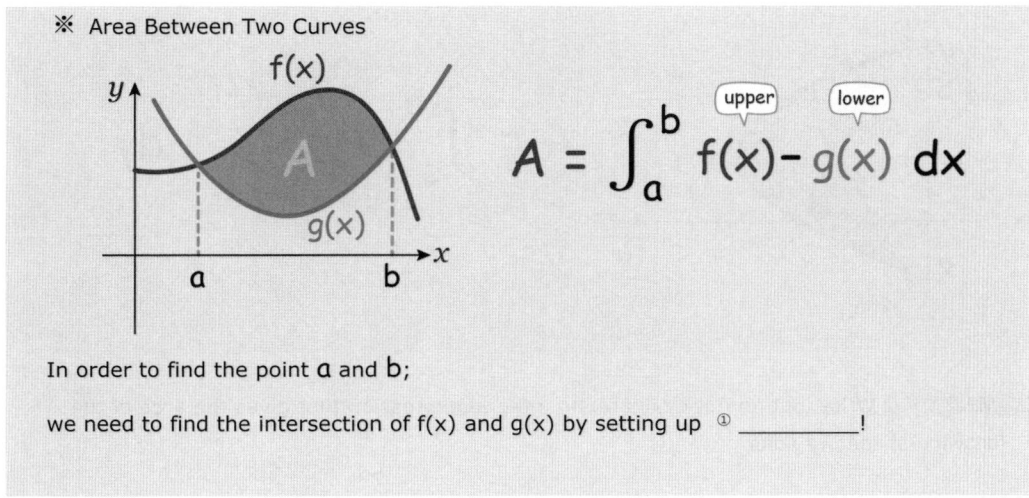

$$A = \int_a^b f(x) - g(x)\, dx$$ (upper) (lower)

In order to find the point **a** and **b**;

we need to find the intersection of f(x) and g(x) by setting up ① _____!

This time let's find the area of the region bounded by $x = f(y)$ and $x = g(y)$, $y = a$ and $y = b$.

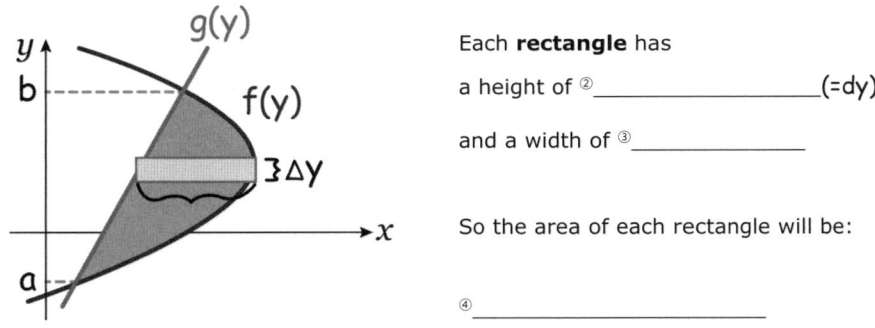

Each **rectangle** has

a height of ② _____ (=dy)

and a width of ③ _____

So the area of each rectangle will be:

④ _____

All we need is to **add up** all these **area of the rectangle** from a to b!

$$A = \boxed{\text{⑤}}$$

(add up) (the area of the rectangles)

Blank : ① f(x) = g(x)   ② △y   ③ f(y) − g(y)   ④ [f(y) − g(y)] dy   ⑤ $\int_a^b [f(y) - g(y)]\, dy$

※ Area Between Two Curves

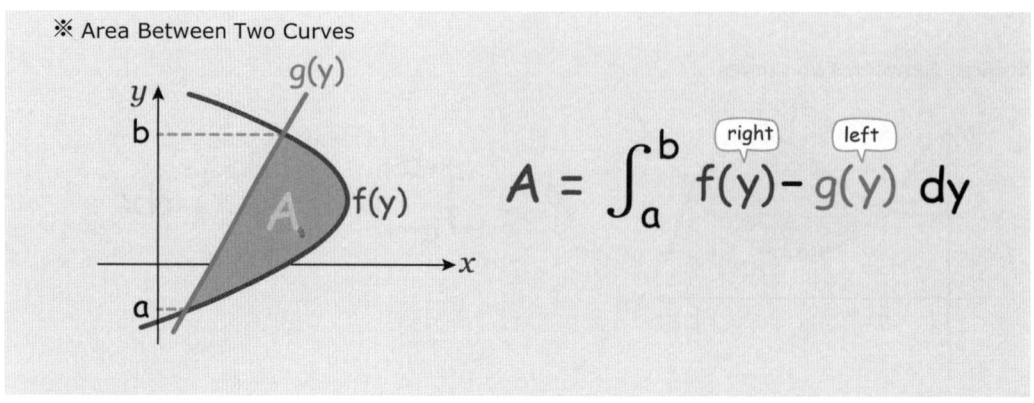

EXAMPLE 1. Write, but do not evaluate, an integral expression that gives the area of the following shaded regions.

①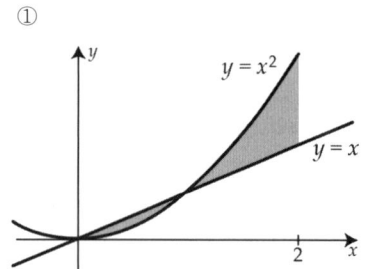

②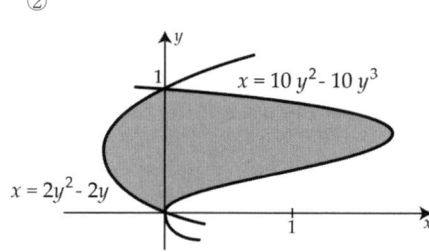

EXAMPLE 2. Find the area of the following shaded regions in terms of

(a) one or more integrals with respect to x, and

(b) one or more integrals with respect to y, if possible.

Write, but do not evaluate, an integral expression.

①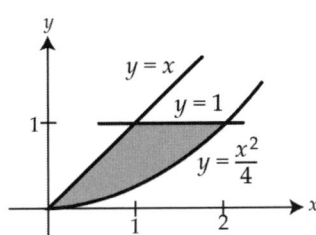

②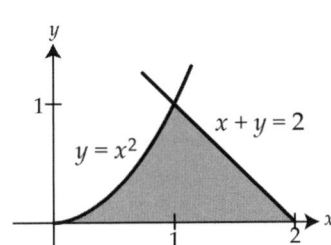

③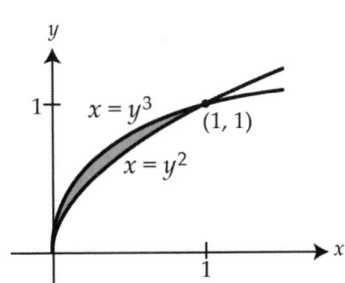

15. Area and Volume

④

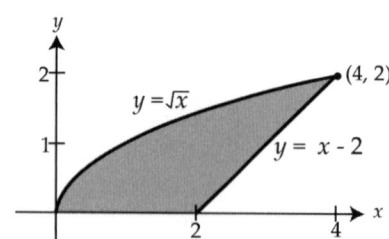

AP Style Problem

1. The area of the region in the first quadrant that is enclosed by the graphs of $y = x^3 + 4$ and $y = x + 4$ is

    A) 1/4
    B) 1/2
    C) 3/4
    D) 65/4
    E) 1

2. The area of the region in the first quadrant that is enclosed by the graphs of $y = \ln x$, y axis, and $y = 2$ is

A) 1

B) $e^2 - 1$

C) $e^2 + 1$

D) e^2

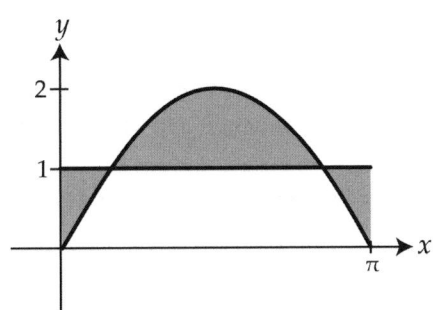

3. The figure above shows the graph of $y = 2 \sin x$ and the line $y = 1$ for $0 \leq x \leq \pi$. Which of the following expressions give the area enclosed by the graphs?

I. $\int_0^\pi (2\sin x - 1)\, dx$

II. $\int_0^{\frac{\pi}{6}} (1 - 2\sin x)\, dx + \int_{\frac{\pi}{6}}^{\frac{5\pi}{6}} (2\sin x - 1)\, dx + \int_{\frac{5\pi}{6}}^{\pi} (1 - 2\sin x)\, dx$

III. $\int_0^\pi |2\sin x - 1|\, dx$

IV. $\left| \int_0^\pi (2\sin x - 1)\, dx \right|$

A) I and II only
B) II and III only
C) II and IV only
D) I, II and III only
E) II, III and IV only

2. Volume Using Cross Section

The **definite integral** comes from the idea :

① _____ up the ② _____ of the rectangles (infinite number of)!

$$A = \lim_{n \to \infty} \sum_{k=1}^{n} f(x) \Delta x$$

$$= \int_a^b f(x)\, dx$$

(add up) (the area of the rectangles)

Finding the **volume** is much like finding the area.

Suppose you have a loaf of bread and you want to find the volume of the loaf. One way to do this is to find the volume of each slice and then add up all the volume of the slices.

The volume of a slice is its **thickness dx** times the **area A(x) of the face of the slice** (= area of the **cross section**).

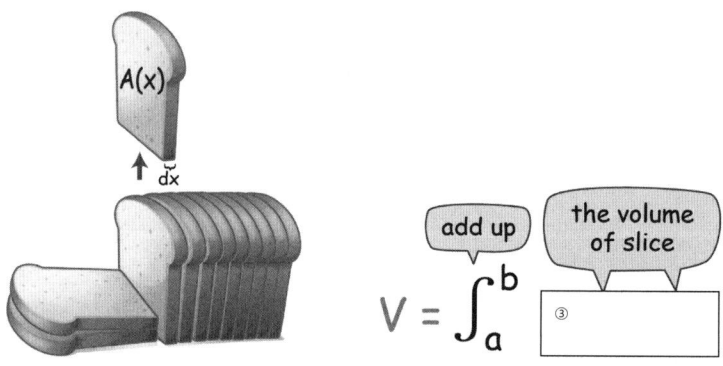

$$V = \int_a^b \boxed{③}$$

We can find a volume by integrating the 'Cross Section Area A(x)'!

Blank : ① adding ② area ③ A(x) dx

※ Volume Using Cross sections

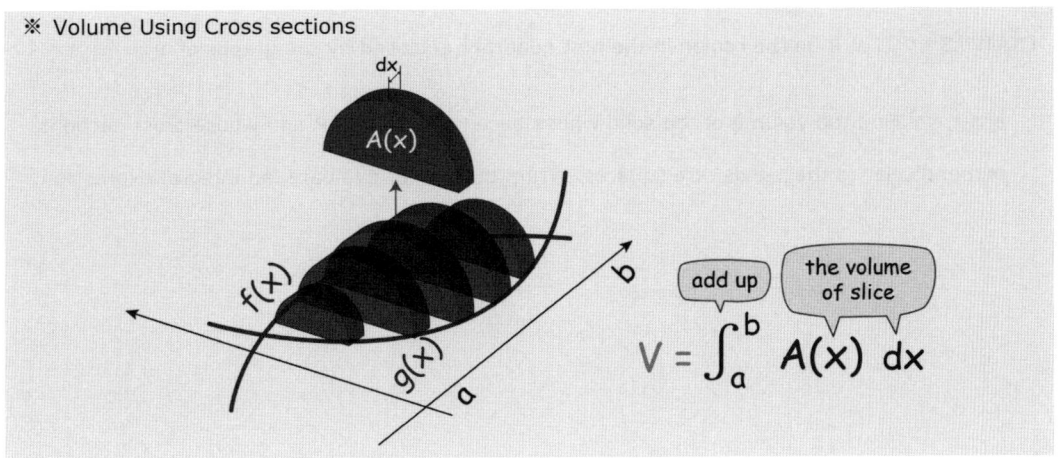

$$V = \int_a^b A(x)\, dx$$

add up · the volume of slice

☺ warm up : Express the distance.

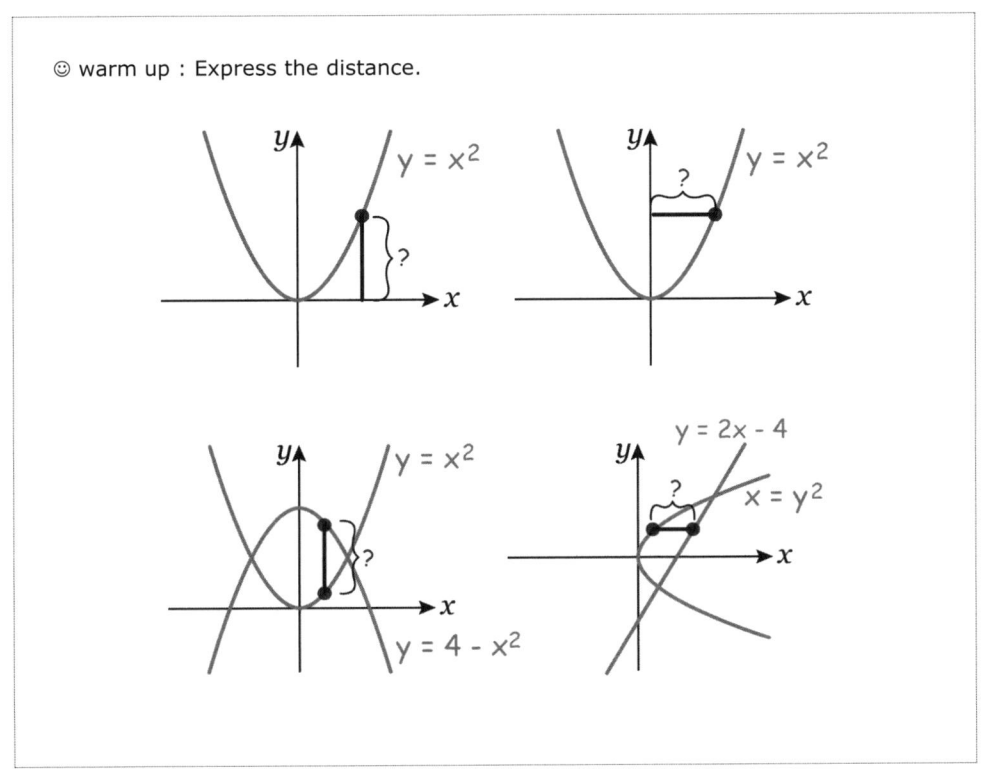

Blank : warm up answer x^2 $\sqrt{y}$ $x^2 - (4 - x^2) = 2x^2 - 4$ $\dfrac{y+4}{2} - y^2$

EXAMPLE 3. Let R be the region in the first quadrant enclosed by the graphs of $y = \dfrac{1}{\sqrt{x}}$, $x = 4$, and $x = 9$. Find the volume of the solid whose base is the region R and whose cross sections, perpendicular to the x-axis, are squares. Write, but do not evaluate, an integral expression.

EXAMPLE 4. The base of the solid is the region enclose by the graphs of $y = 1 - \dfrac{x}{2}$, x-axis and the y-axis. If the cross sections which perpendicular to the x-axis are semicircle, what is the volume of the solid?

EXAMPLE 5. Let R be the region in the first quadrant enclosed by $y = \sin x$, $y = \cos x$, and $x = 0$. Find the volume of the solid generated whose base is the region R and whose cross sections, perpendicular to the x-axis, are squares.

EXAMPLE 6. Find the volume of the solid whose base is the region bounded by $y = x^2$, $y = 2 - x^2$, if the cross sections taken perpendicular to the x axis are equilateral triangles.

EXAMPLE 7. Find the volume of the solid whose base is the region bounded by the lines $x+2y=6$, $x=0$, and $y=0$, if the cross sections taken perpendicular to the y axis are rectangles of height 3.

EXAMPLE 8. Find the volume of the solid whose base is the region bounded by the lines $y=\dfrac{1}{2}x$, $y=2x$, and $y=4$, if the cross sections taken perpendicular to the y axis are squares.

3. Finding Volumes by Revolving

A **solid of revolution** is a solid swept out by rotating a plane area around some straight line (the axis of revolution).

There are three ways to find the volume of solid.

1) Using Disks 2) Using Washers 3) Using Shells

1) Using Disks

If we rotate the region **under the graph y = f(x)** (from a to b) **about the x-axis**, we will have a 3D solid. You can use the disk method to find the volume by cutting that shape into thin ①_____.

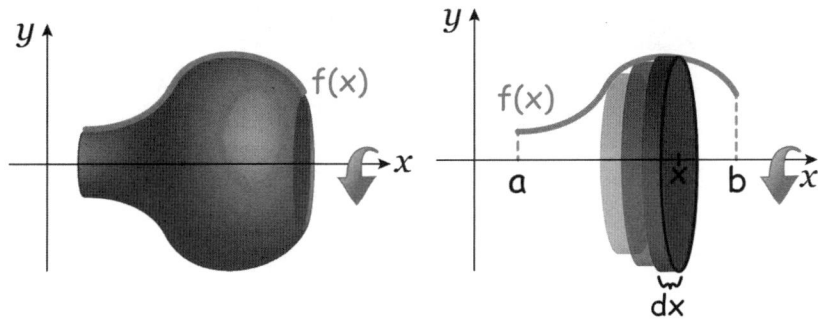

Each **disk** is a has a radius = ②_____

base area $A(x)$ = ③_____

and the thickness of ④_____.

And the volume is found by summing all those disks (from a to b) using Integration;

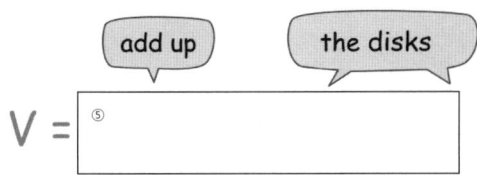

$$V = \text{⑤}$$

☺ Meaning: **Add up** from a to b ($\int_a^b$) the **volume of the disk** which is **thickness dx** times the **area of the circle.**

Blank : ① disk ② f(x) ③ π[f(x)]² ④ dx ⑤ $\int_a^b \pi [f(x)]^2 \, dx$

If we rotate **x = f(y)** about the **y-axis**;

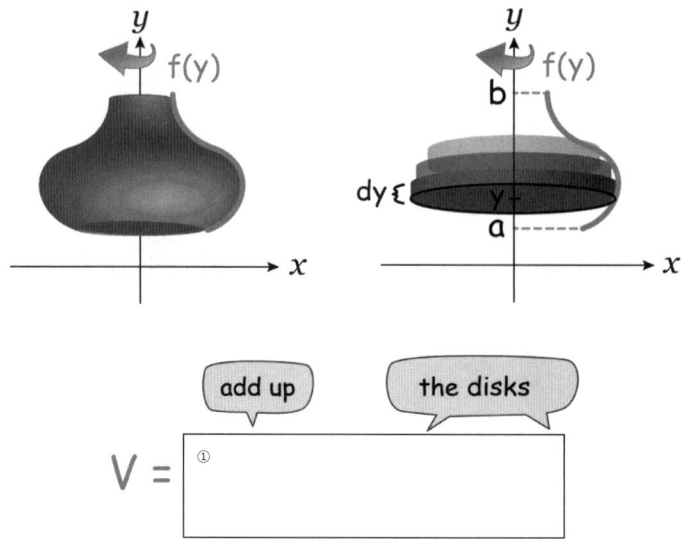

add up   the disks

$$V = \int_a^b \pi [f(y)]^2 \, dy$$

※ Volume Using Disks

We can find a volume by integrating the 'Cross Section Area A(x) = Circle Area'.

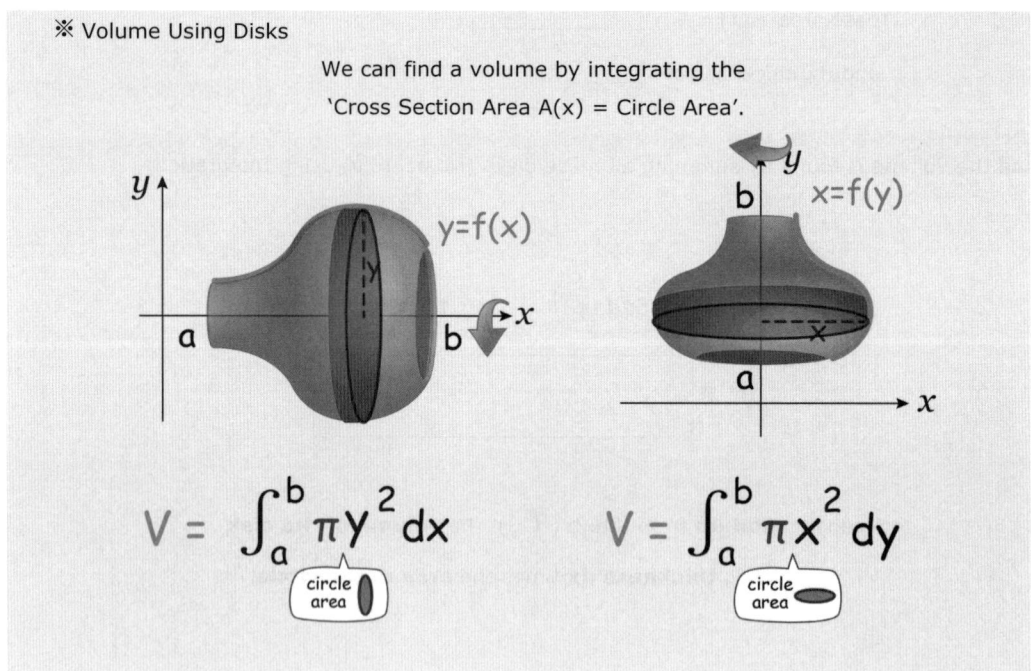

$$V = \int_a^b \pi y^2 \, dx \qquad V = \int_a^b \pi x^2 \, dy$$

circle area   circle area

Blank : ① $\int_a^b \pi [f(y)]^2 \, dy$

EXAMPLE 9. Find the integral expression for the volume. The region is bounded by;

① $y = \sqrt{x}, y = 0, x = 4$,

revolve about x axis

② $y = \sqrt{x}, x = 0, y = 4$,

revolve about y axis

③ $y = e^x, y = 0, x = 0, x = 2$,

revolve about x axis

④ $y = e^x, y = 3, x = 0$,

revolve about y axis

⑤ $y = x^2$ $(x \geq 0)$ $y = 4, x = 0$

revolve about line $y = 4$

⑥ $y = x^2$ $(x \geq 0)$, $y = 0, x = 2$

revolve about line $x = 2$

2) Using Washer

If we rotate the **region between the graph y = f(x) and y = g(x)** (from a to b) **about the x-axis**, we will have a round shape with a hole in the center. You can use the washer method to find the volume by cutting that shape into thin ①_____.

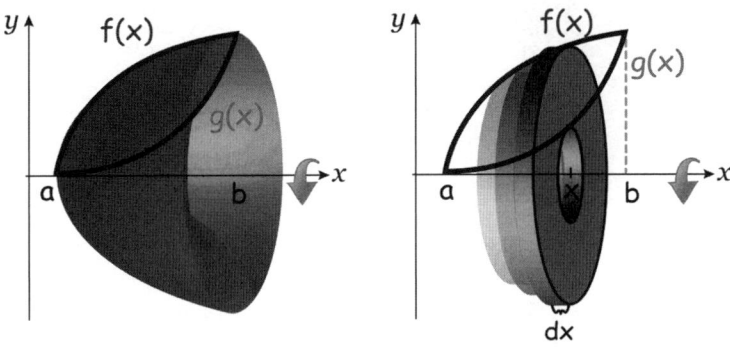

Each **washer** has an **outer radius R** = ②_____

an **inner radius r** = ③_____

base area $A(x)$ = ④_____

and the thickness of ⑤_____.

And the volume is found by summing all those washers (from a to b) using Integration;

add up   the washers

V = ⑥ _____

☺ Meaning: **Add up** from a to b ($\int_a^b$) the **volume of the washer** which is **thickness dx** times the **area of the circle with a hole**.

Blank : ① washer ② f(x) ③ g(x) ④ $\pi[f(x)]^2 - \pi[g(x)]^2$ ⑤ dx ⑥ $\int_a^b \pi[f(x)]^2 - \pi[g(x)]^2 \, dx$

※ Volume Using Washers

We can find a volume by integrating the
'Cross Section Area A(x) = Circle with hole Area'.

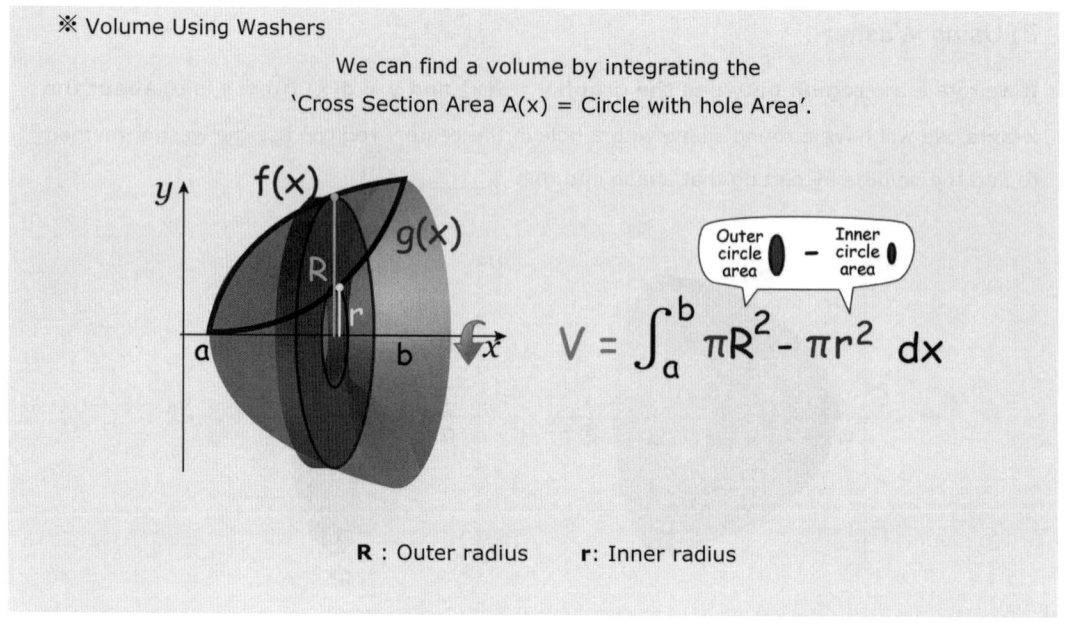

R : Outer radius   r: Inner radius

EXAMPLE 10. Find the volume. Region bounded by $y = x^2, y = \sqrt{x}$, revolve about x axis.

EXAMPLE 11. Find the volume. Region bounded by $y = x^2, y = \sqrt{x}$, revolve about y axis.

EXAMPLE 12. Find the integral expression for the volume. The region is bounded by $y = x^2$
$(x \geq 0)$, $y = 0, x = 2$ and

① revolve about x axis

② revolve about y axis

③ revolve about line $y = 5$

④ revolve about line $x = 3$

⑤ revolve about line $y=-1$

⑥ revolve about line $x=-1$

3) Using Shells

If we rotate the **region under the graph y = f(x)** (from a to b) **about the y-axis**,

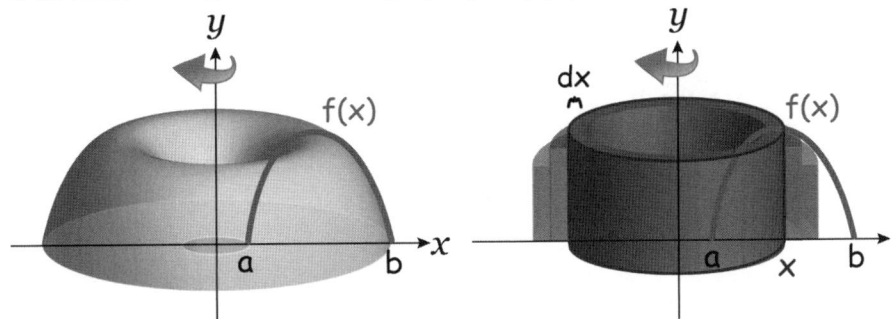

Each **shell** has a circumference of ① _____

, height of ② _____

, and the thickness of ③ _____.

And the volume is found by summing all those shells (from a to b) using Integration;

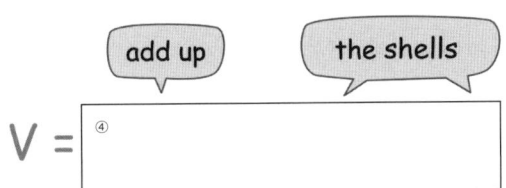

$$V = \text{\textcircled{4}}$$

※ Volume Using Shells

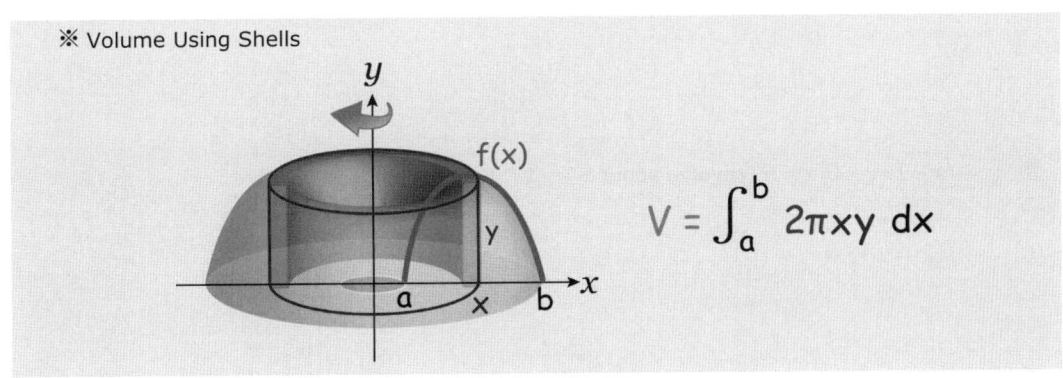

$$V = \int_a^b 2\pi xy \, dx$$

Blank : ① $2\pi x$ ② $f(x)$ ③ dx ④ $\int_a^b 2\pi xy \, dx$

EXAMPLE 13. Find the integral expression for the volume. The region is bounded by;

① $y = \sqrt{x}, y = 0, x = 4$, revolve about y axis

② $y = e^x, y = e^{-x}, x = 4$, revolve about y axis

③ $y = \sqrt{x}, x = 0, y = 4$, revolve about x axis

④ $y = \sqrt{x-1}, y = 0, x = 5$, revolve about $x = -1$

AP Style Problem

1. The region in the first quadrant bounded by $y = \sqrt{9-x^2}$, x = 0, and y = 0 is revolved about the x-axis. The volume of the solid generated is

   A) 9π

   B) 18π

   C) 36π

   D) 72π

2. The region in the bounded above by $y = \frac{1}{2}x$ and $x = y^2$ is rotated about the line y axis. The volume of the solid generated is

   A) $\dfrac{64\pi}{5}$

   B) $\dfrac{32\pi}{5}$

   C) $\dfrac{64\pi}{15}$

   D) $\dfrac{32\pi}{15}$

3. The base of a solid is the region enclosed by the curve $x^2 + 4y^2 = 4$. For the solid, each cross section perpendicular to the x-axis is a semicircle. What is the volume of the solid?

   A) $\pi \int_{-2}^{2} \left(1 - \dfrac{x^2}{4}\right)^2 dx$

   B) $\dfrac{\pi}{2} \int_{-2}^{2} \left(1 - \dfrac{x^2}{4}\right)^2 dx$

   C) $\pi \int_{-2}^{2} \left(1 - \dfrac{x^2}{4}\right) dx$

   D) $\dfrac{\pi}{2} \int_{-2}^{2} \left(1 - \dfrac{x^2}{4}\right) dx$

4. Let R be the region in the first quadrant bounded by the graph of $y = \tan x$, and the vertical line $x = \dfrac{\pi}{4}$. Which of the following gives the volume of the solid generated when region R is revolved about the vertical line $x = \dfrac{\pi}{4}$?

A) $\pi \int_0^{\pi/4} \left(\dfrac{\pi}{4} - \arctan y \right)^2 dy$

B) $\pi \int_0^1 \left(\dfrac{\pi}{4} - \tan y \right)^2 dy$

C) $\pi \int_0^1 \left(\dfrac{\pi}{4} - \arctan y \right)^2 dy$

D) $\pi \int_0^1 \left[\dfrac{\pi^2}{16} - (\arctan y)^2 \right] dy$

5. Let R be the region bounded by the graph of $y = \ln x$, $y = 0$, and $x = e$. Which of the following gives the volume of the solid generated when region R is revolved about the line $x = 1$?

A) $\pi \int_0^1 \left[(e-1)^2 - (\ln y - 1)^2 \right] dy$

B) $\pi \int_0^1 (e^y - 1)^2 \, dy$

C) $\pi \int_0^1 \left[(e-1)^2 - (e^y - 1)^2 \right] dy$

D) $\pi \int_0^1 \left[(1+e)^2 - (1+e^y)^2 \right] dy$

6. Let R be the region bounded by the graph of $y = x^2$ and $y = 4x - x^2$. Which of the following gives the volume of the solid generated when region R is revolved about the line $y = 6$?

A) $\pi \int_0^2 \left(2x^2 - 4x\right)^2 dx$

B) $\pi \int_0^2 \left(4x - 2x^2\right)^2 dx$

C) $\pi \int_0^2 \left[(x^2 - 6)^2 - (4x - x^2 - 6)^2\right] dx$

D) $\pi \int_0^2 \left[(6 - x^2)^2 - (6 - 4x + x^2)^2\right] dx$

7. Let R be the region bounded by the graph of $y = x^2$ and $y = 4x - x^2$. Which of the following gives the volume of the solid generated when region R is revolved about the line $x = 0$?

A) $\pi \int_0^2 \left[x^4 - (4x - x^2)^2\right] dx$

B) $\pi \int_0^2 \left[x^4 - (x^2 - 4x)^2\right] dx$

C) $2\pi \int_0^2 x(4x - x^2) dx$

D) $2\pi \int_0^2 x(4x - 2x^2) dx$

Mia's AP Calculus

16. More Applications and Motion

1. Rate and Net Change

※ When rate of A is given

Given $A'(t)$, what is $A(b) - A(a)$?	①
Given $A'(t)$, what is A at b?	②
Interpret $\int_a^b A'(t)dt$	③

EXAMPLE 1. After t minutes, a chemical is decomposing at the rate of $10e^{-t}$ grams per minute. Find the amount that has decomposed during the first 3 minutes.

EXAMPLE 2. Starting with an initial value of $P(0) = 50$, the population of a prairie dog community grows at a rate of $P'(t) = 10e^{0.5t}$ (in units of prairie dogs/month). Find the population of a prairie dog at $t = 12$ month.

Blank : ① $\int_a^b A'(t)\,dt$ ② $A(b) = A(a) + \int_a^b A'(t)\,dt$ ③ Change of A in [a, b].

AP Style Problem

1. The number of bacteria in a container increases at the rate of $R(t)$ bacteria per hour. If there are 2000 bacteria at the time $t = 2$, which of the following expressions gives the number of bacteria in the container at the time $t = 10$?

   A) $\int_2^{10} R(t)\, dt$

   B) $\frac{1}{8} \int_2^{10} R(t)\, dt$

   C) $2000 + \int_2^{10} R(t)\, dt$

   D) $2000 + \frac{R(10) - R(2)}{10 - 2}$

2. A cake is removed from an oven at midnight once the cake reaches a temperature of 200 degrees Celsius. The temperature of the cake then decreases at a rate given by $r(t)$ degrees Celsius per hour, where t is the number of hours since being removed from the oven. Which of the following is the best interpretation of $\int_0^6 r(t)\, dt$?

   A) The temperature of the cake at 6:00 AM in degrees Celsius
   B) The average temperature of the cake between midnight and 6:00 AM in degrees Celsius.
   C) The change in temperature of the cake between midnight and 6:00 AM in degrees Celsius.
   D) The rate of change in temperature of the cake between midnight and 6:00 AM in degrees Celsius.

2. Motion Along a Straight Line

position $S(t)$ →[d/dt]→ velocity $V(t)$ →[d/dt]→ acceleration $a(t)$

acceleration $a(t)$ →[$\int$]→ velocity $V(t)$ →[$\int$]→ position $S(t)$

1) Total Distance Traveled from a to b

(total amount the object has traveled)

①_____ (②_____ of v(t))

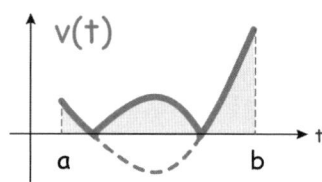

2) Displacement from a to b

(Change of position)

③_____ (④_____ of v(t))

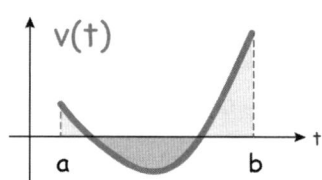

3) Position at $t = b$

(Location of the object)

Displacement = Future Position − Initial Position
Future Position = Initial Position + Displacement

$s(b)$ = ⑤_____

Blank : ① $\int_a^b |v(t)|\, dt$ ② area ③ $\int_a^b v(t)\, dt$ ④ Net area ⑤ $s(a) + \int_a^b v(t)\, dt$

※ Phrases and Motions

Average Velocity from x = a to x = b	given s: given v:
Average acceleration from x = a to x = b	given v: given a:
Displacement (change in position) from x = a to x = b	
Total Distance traveled from x = a to x = b	
Future position at x = b	

Blank : ※ Table Answers are in the answer section

EXAMPLE 3. Below is the graph of a particle's velocity. The particle starts at $x(0) = 4$ at time $t = 0$.

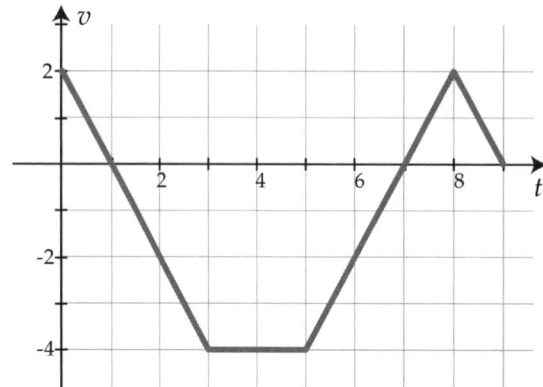

① When is the particle moving backward?

② When does the particle reverse direction?

③ Is the particle speeding up, slowing down, or doing neither at time $t = 6$?

④ Find the total distance covered during the time interval $0 \leq t \leq 9$.

⑤ Find the displacement of the particle during the time interval $0 \leq t \leq 9$.

⑥ Find the position of the particle at $t = 9$.

⑦ At what time in the interval $0 \leq t \leq 9$ is the particle farthest from the initial position? How far from the initial position is the particle at this time?

⑧ Write expressions for the acceleration $a(t)$, velocity $v(t)$, and distance $x(t)$ that are valid for the time interval $0 < t < 3$.

EXAMPLE 4. A particle moves along a line with velocity $v = t^2 - 2t$. When $t = 0$ the particle was at the position 3.

① Find the acceleration $a(t)$ of the particle at any time t.

② Find the position $x(t)$ of the particle at any time t.

③ Find the total distance covered during the time interval $0 \leq t \leq 3$.

④ Find the displacement of the particle during the time interval $0 \leq t \leq 3$.

⑤ Find the position of the particle at $t = 3$.

EXAMPLE 5. A particle moves along the x-axis so that its velocity at any time $t \geq 0$ is given by $v(t) = 1 - \cos(2t)$.

① Find the average velocity over the time interval $0 \leq t \leq \frac{\pi}{2}$.

② Find the average acceleration over the time interval $0 \leq t \leq \frac{\pi}{2}$.

AP Style Problem

1. The graph shows the velocity of a particle during 8 second interval. The graph contains three line segments and a quarter circle.

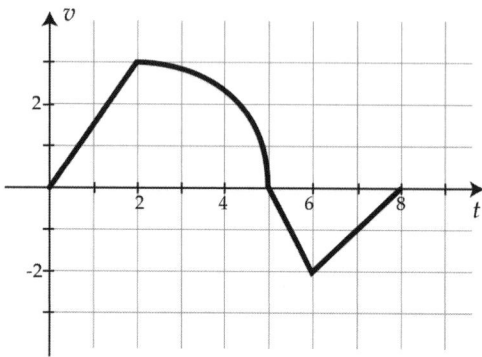

1) The particle reverses direction at $t =$

   A) 3 B) 5 C) 6 D) 8

2) For how many times in the interval (0, 8) is the acceleration undefined?

   A) zero B) one C) two D) three

3) During what time interval does the particle speed up?

   A) $0 < x < 2$ or $6 < x < 8$ sec

   B) $0 < x < 5$ sec

   C) $0 < x < 2$ or $5 < x < 6$ sec

   D) $2 < x < 5$ or $6 < x < 8$ sec

4) What is the average acceleration, in units/sec², during the first 6 seconds?

   A) 1/3   B) – 1/3   C) $\dfrac{8+9\pi}{24}$ D) $\dfrac{16+9\pi}{24}$

5) What is the average velocity, in units/sec, during the first 6 seconds?

   A) 1/3   B) – 1/3   C) $\dfrac{8+9\pi}{24}$ D) $\dfrac{16+9\pi}{24}$

2. The graph shows the velocity of a particle during 8 second interval.

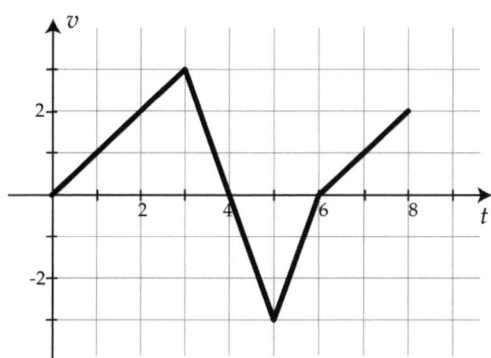

1) What is the displacement of the object during the first 6 seconds?

   A) 3   B) 6   C) 9   D) 0

2) What is the distance traveled during the first 6 seconds?

   A) 3   B) 6   C) 9   D) 0

3) At $t = 0$, the object was at position $x = 5$. At $t = 8$, the object's position was $x =$

   A) -1   B) 8   C) 10   D) 16

4) At $t = 6$, the object was at position $x = 10$. At $t = 4$, the object's position was $x =$

   A) 1   B) 4   C) 7   D) 13

5) The object is farthest from the starting point at $t =$

A) 0   B) 4   C) 6   D) 8

3. An observer recorded the velocity of an object in motion along the x axis for 10 seconds. Initial position of the object is $x = 2$. Based on the table below, use a trapezoidal approximation to estimate the position of the object at $t = 10$.

t	0	2	3	5	7	10
$v(t)$	3	5	1	-1	-3	5

A) 6
B) 12
C) 24
D) 29

4. An observer recorded the velocity of an object in motion along the x axis for 10 seconds. Based on the table below, use a trapezoidal approximation to estimate the total distance traveled during the first 10 sec.

t	0	2	3	5	7	10
$v(t)$	3	5	1	-1	-3	5

A) 6
B) 12
C) 24
D) 29

5. An object traveling on the horizontal line $y = 2$ has position $x(t)$ at time t. The object's velocity $v(t)$ is shown above. Which of the following expression gives the total distance travelled by the object during $0 \le t \le 5$?

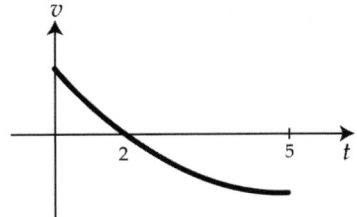

I. $\int_0^5 |v(t)|\, dt$

II. $\int_0^5 v(t)\, dt$

III. $x(2) - x(0) - x(5) + x(2)$

A) I only
B) I, II
C) I, III
D) I, II, and III
E) None of these

Mia's AP Calculus

17. Differential Equation

1. Differential Equations

A **Differential Equation**
is an equation with a function and one or more of its derivatives:

$$y + \frac{dy}{dx} = 5x$$

(differential: $\frac{dy}{dx}$; equation: $= 5x$)

1) Order and Degree

The **Order** is the highest derivative
(is it a first derivative? a second derivative? etc)

The **degree** is the exponent of the highest power.

$$\frac{d^2y}{dx^2} + \frac{dy}{dx} + y = 5x^3 - 10$$

(order 2: $\frac{d^2y}{dx^2}$; degree 3: $5x^3$)

2) General Solution VS Particular Solution

The solution to a differential equation is called ①_____ solution.

To find a ②_____ solution, there must be some initial conditions given.

2. Solving Differential Equations

The classic way to solve a differential equation is taking ③_____ on both sides!

Blank : ① general   ② particular   ③ ∫

306 Mia's AP calculus AB BC

EXAMPLE 1. Find a general solution of the differential equation.

① $\dfrac{dy}{dx} = 2x^2$

② $\dfrac{dy}{dx} = \dfrac{x-5}{x}$

③ $\dfrac{dy}{dx} = \tan^2 x$

EXAMPLE 2. Find the particular solution of

① $\dfrac{dy}{dx} = 2x^2$ when $y = 10$ and $x = 3$.

② $\dfrac{d^2y}{dx^2} = x+2$, initial condition $y(0)=3$, $y'(0)=1$

17. Differential Equation

3. Separation of Variables

Separation of Variables is a special method to solve some Differential Equations.

① Write $y' \to \dfrac{dy}{dx}$	$\dfrac{dy}{dx} = 5xy$
② Move all the y terms (including dy) to one side of the equation, and	$\dfrac{dy}{y\,dx} = 5xy$
③ all the x terms (including dx) to the other side.	$\dfrac{dy}{y\,dx} = 5x\,dx$
④ Take the $\int$ and simplify. (Don't forget **+C**)	$\int \dfrac{dy}{y} = \int 5x\,dx$

EXAMPLE 3. Find the general solution of the following differential equations;

① $y\dfrac{dy}{dx} = \sin x$

② $\dfrac{dy}{dx} = \dfrac{5-x}{y^3}$

③ $xy' = y \ln x$

④ $x\dfrac{dy}{dx} - 2y = 0$

⑤ $\dfrac{dy}{dx} = 3 - y$

EXAMPLE 4. Find the particular solution of the following differential equations;

① $\dfrac{dy}{dx} = xy^3$, initial condition $f(1) = 1$.

② $x^2 dy = (y-1)dx$, initial condition $y(1) = 0$.

③ $yy' = e^x$, initial condition $y(0) = 4$

④ $y(x+1) + y' = 0$, initial condition $y(-2) = 1$

AP Style Problem

1. If $y = f(x)$ is a solution to the differential equation $\dfrac{dy}{dx} = e^{y+1}$ with the initial condition $f(0)=0$, which of the following is true?

    A) $f(x) = e^{y+1}$

    B) $f(x) = e^{-y-1}$

    C) $f(x) = -\ln\left|-x + \dfrac{1}{e}\right| - 1$

    D) $f(x) = -\ln\left|-x + \dfrac{1}{e}\right| + 1$

2. The differential equation is $\dfrac{dy}{dx} = \dfrac{1}{10}(5-y)$. Find $\dfrac{d^2y}{dx^2}$.

    A) $-\dfrac{1}{10}$

    B) $-\dfrac{1}{10}(5-x)$

    C) $-\dfrac{1}{100}(5-x)$

    D) $\dfrac{1}{10}(y-5)$

    E) $\dfrac{1}{100}(y-5)$

3. If $y' = y - 2$, and when $x = 0$, $y = 3$, then $y =$

    A) $-2e^x$

    B) $2e^x$

    C) $e^x + 2$

    D) $e^x - 2$

4. The function $y = \sin(2x) - 2$ is a solution to which of the following differential equation?

   A) $y'' + 4y' + 8 = 0$

   B) $y'' + 4y + 8 = 0$

   C) $y'' + 4y' - 8 = 0$

   D) $y'' + 4y - 8 = 0$

4. Slope Field

Sometimes solving differential equation analytically can be difficult.
But the slope field could help us to find the solution!

Slope field is sometimes called a direction field.

A slope field of a differential equation gives a good picture of what ①_____ looks like.

The slope field of a differential equation $\dfrac{dy}{dx} = -\dfrac{x}{y}$ would be;

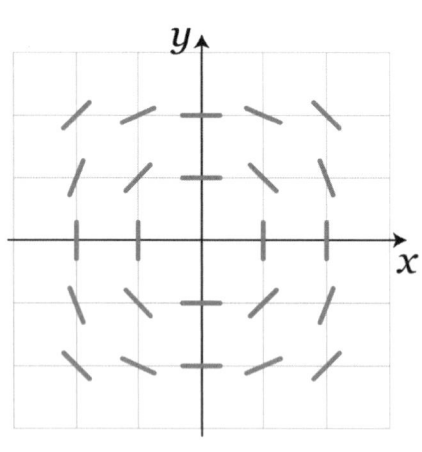

x	y	dy/dx	
1	0	und	|
-1	0	und	|
0	1	②	—
1	1	-1	\
-1	1	1	/
0	-1	0	—
1	-1	1	/
-1	-1	-1	\

at (0,1) slope is 0

Blank : ① general solution   ② 0

EXAMPLE 5. Sketch the slope field for the given differential equation $\dfrac{dy}{dx} = 2x - y$ on the axis provided.

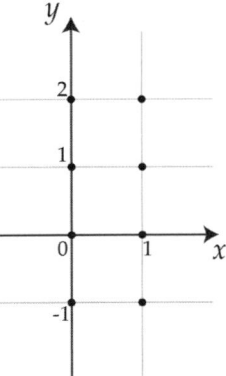

EXAMPLE 6. Consider the differential equation $\dfrac{dy}{dx} = y - 1$.

① Sketch a slope field for the given differential equation on the axis provided.

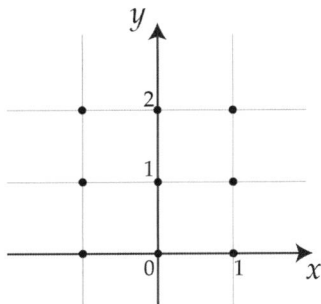

② If $y = f(x)$ is the particular solution to this differential equation with the initial condition $f(-1) = 2$. Find $f(x)$.

EXAMPLE 7. The slope field for the differential equation $\dfrac{dy}{dx} = \dfrac{x}{y^2}$ is shown in the figure.

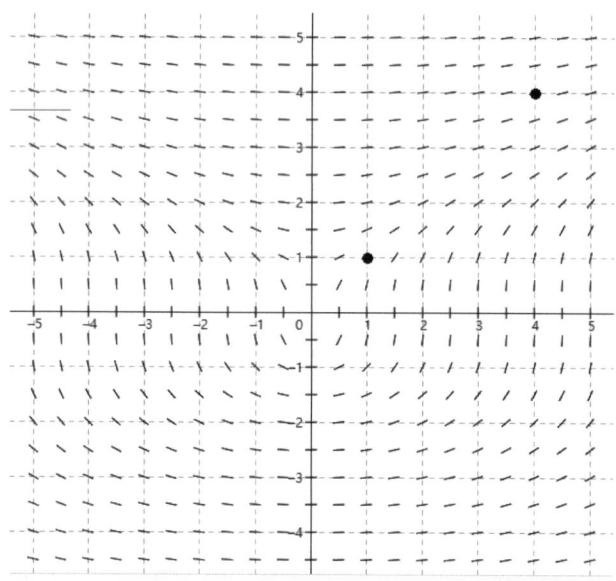

① Draw the particular solution curve that passes through the point (1, 1).

② Draw the particular solution curve that passes through the point (4, 4).

③ Find the general solution for the equation.

AP Style Problem

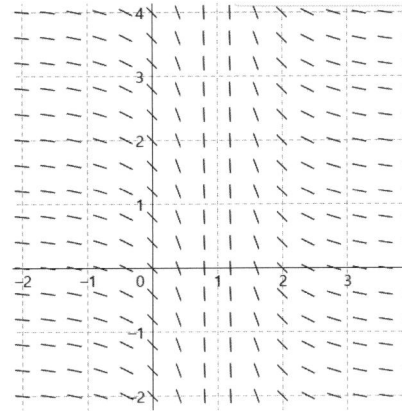

1. The slope field for a certain differential equation is shown in [-2,4]x[-2,4]. Which of the following could be a solution to the differential equation with the initial condition (2, 2)?

A) $y = \sin x$

B) $y = e^x$

C) $y = 1 - x^2$

D) $y = \dfrac{1}{x-1}$

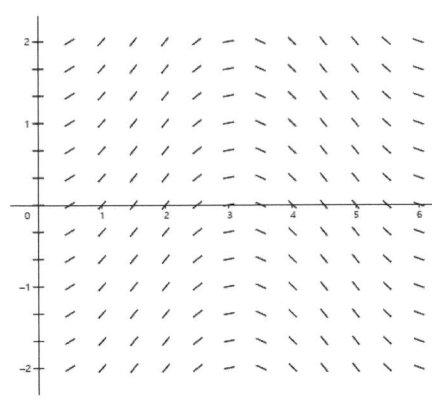

2. The slope field for a certain differential equation is shown [0,6]x[-2,2]. Shown above is a slope field for which of the following differential equations?

A) $y' = \sin x$

B) $y' = \cos x$

C) $y' = -\sin x$

D) $y' = -\cos x$

17. Differential Equation

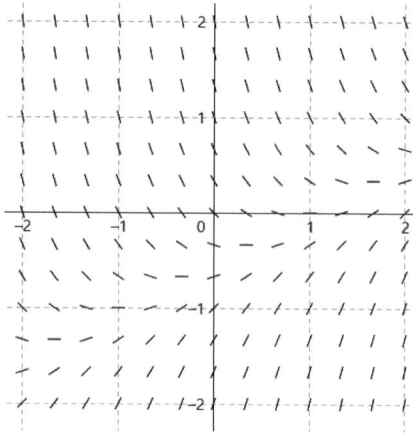

3. Shown above is a slope field for which of the following differential equations?

A) $\dfrac{dy}{dx} = x + 2y + 1$

B) $\dfrac{dy}{dx} = x - 2y - 1$

C) $\dfrac{dy}{dx} = 2x + y - 2$

D) $\dfrac{dy}{dx} = 2x + y + 2$

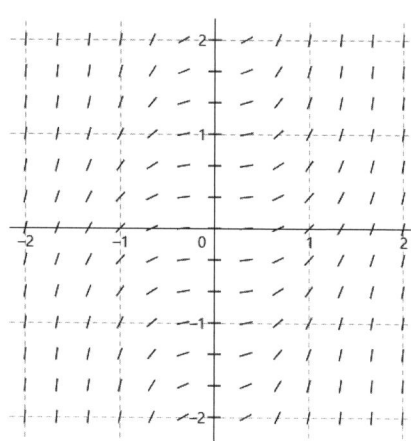

4. Shown above is a slope field for which of the following differential equations?

A) $\dfrac{dy}{dx} = x^2(y^2 + 1)$

B) $\dfrac{dy}{dx} = y^2(x^2 + 1)$

C) $\dfrac{dy}{dx} = x(y + 1)$

D) $\dfrac{dy}{dx} = y(x + 1)$

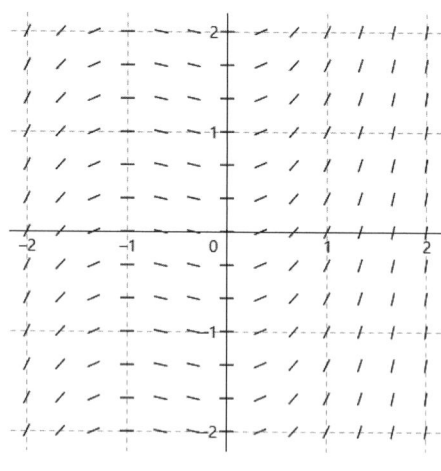

5. Shown above is a slope field for which of the following differential equations?

A) $\dfrac{dy}{dx} = y(x + 1)$

B) $\dfrac{dy}{dx} = x(y + 1)$

C) $\dfrac{dy}{dx} = x(x + 1)$

D) $\dfrac{dy}{dx} = y(y + 1)$

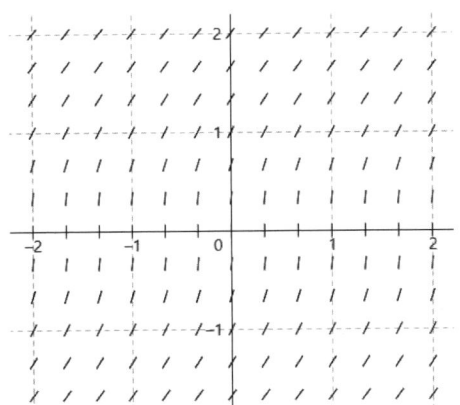

6. Shown above is a slope field for which of the following differential equations?

A) $\dfrac{dy}{dx} = \dfrac{x+1}{y}$

B) $\dfrac{dy}{dx} = \dfrac{x^2+1}{y^2}$

C) $\dfrac{dy}{dx} = \dfrac{y+1}{y}$

D) $\dfrac{dy}{dx} = \dfrac{y^2+1}{y^2}$

7. The slope field for a certain differential equation is shown. Which of the following is true about the solution $y = f(x)$?

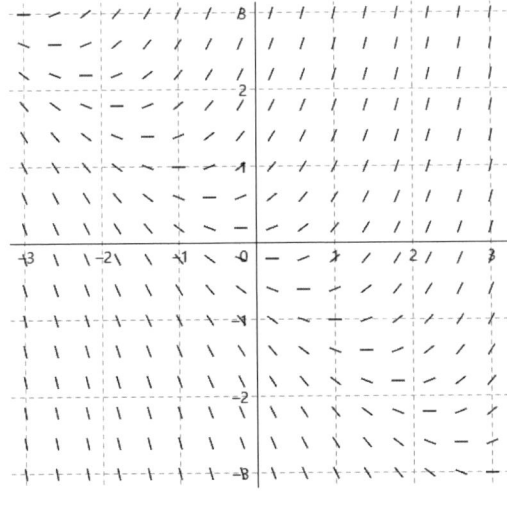

I. The graph of the particular solution that pass through (0, 1) is concave up in $-3 < x < 3$.

II. The graph of the particular solution that pass through (-2, 0) is concave up in $-3 < x < 3$.

III. The graph of the particular solution that pass through (-1, 1) has a relative minimum at $x = -1$.

A) I only
B) I, II
C) I, III
D) I, II, and III
E) None of these

5. Exponential Growth and Decay

☺ Reminder: y is directly proportional to x : ① _____

In our world things change, and describing how they change often ends up as a Differential Equation.

The more rabbits we have the more baby rabbits we will get. Then those rabbits grow up and have babies too! The population will grow faster and faster.

From this situation we can say that;
the **rate of change** is ② _____ to the **amount present** at any given time!

If the amount present is P

the rate of change will be $\dfrac{dP}{dt}$

so the it can be written as; ③ _____

and the general solution to this will be ; ④ _____

Blank : ① $y = kx$ ② proportional   ③ $\dfrac{dP}{dt} = kP$ ④ $P = Ce^{kt}$

※ Exponential growth and decay

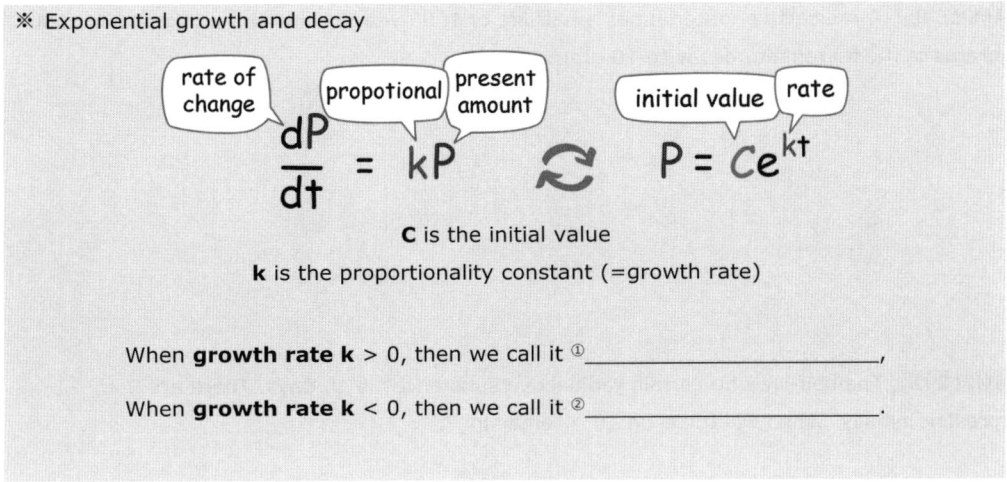

C is the initial value
k is the proportionality constant (=growth rate)

When **growth rate k > 0**, then we call it ① _____,

When **growth rate k < 0**, then we call it ② _____.

EXAMPLE 8. The growth rate of population of rabbits is proportional to the population. In an experiment, it was observed that there were 200 rabbits after the second day and 1000 rabbits after the fourth day. How many rabbits were there in the original population?

EXAMPLE 9. The population of a city is growing at a rate proportional to its population. If the growth rate per year is 4% of the current population, how long will it take for the population to double?

Blank : ① exponential growth   ② exponential decay

EXAMPLE 10. A radioactive material has a half-life of 1000 years. How long will it take for 100 grams of the material to decay to 10 grams?

EXAMPLE 11. The half-life of a certain radioactive substances is 10 days. There are 23g present initially. When will there be 20% remaining?

AP Style Problem

1. The population of a city is growing at a rate proportional to its population. The population doubles in 100 years. After 150 years the ratio of the population to the initial population is

   A) $1 : 3$

   B) $1 : 2\sqrt{2}$

   C) $2\sqrt{2} : 1$

   D) $3 : 1$

2. The rate at which a radioactive material (M) decays is proportional to the amount present at a given time. Which of the following could describe this situation?

   I. $\dfrac{dM}{dt} = -0.25M$

   II. $\dfrac{dM}{dt} = 1.5M$

   III. $\dfrac{dM}{dt} = -0.3t$

   IV. $M = 5e^{-0.5t}$

   A) I, II
   B) I, IV
   C) III, IV
   D) I, II, IV
   E) I, II, III, IV

3. The growth rate of population of a certain insect (I) is proportional to the population. On the first day of the experiment (t = 0), it was observed that there were 1000 insects and the population was increasing at a rate of 50 insects per day.

   1) Which of the following is a differential equation that describes this situation?

   A) $\dfrac{dI}{dt} = \dfrac{t}{10}$ B) $\dfrac{dI}{dt} = \dfrac{I}{10}$

   C) $\dfrac{dI}{dt} = \dfrac{t}{20}$ D) $\dfrac{dI}{dt} = \dfrac{I}{20}$

   2) Which of the following is an expression for I?

   A) $I = 1000e^{t/10}$

   B) $I = e^{t/10} + 1000$

   C) $I = 1000e^{20t}$

   D) $I = 1000e^{t/20}$

Mia's AP Calculus
Free Response Questions (from ch11~17)

(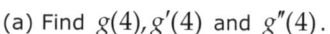 : Do not use calculator,   : Use calculator)

1. ∫ and Graph

The graph of the continuous function f is defined in $0 \le x \le 9$ as shown. Let $g(x) = 3 + \int_{2}^{x} f(t)\, dt$.

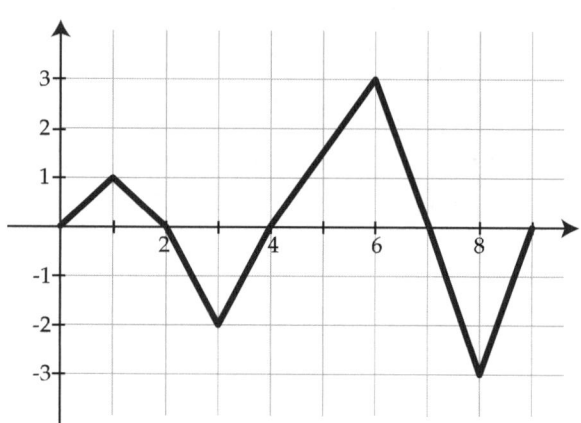

(a) Find $g(4), g'(4)$ and $g''(4)$.

(b) Find the x value(s) of the inflection point of $g(x)$ in $0 \le x \le 9$. Justify your answer.

(c) Find the interval where $g(x)$ is increasing at a decreasing rate. Justify your answer.

(d) Find the absolute minimum value of $g(x)$ over the closed interval $0 \le x \le 9$. Explain your reasoning.

2. 'In rate' & 'Out rate' Problem

※ When (in)′ and (out)′ is given

The rate of the water flowing into the tank (=(in)′) and the rate of the water leaking from the tank (=(out)′) is given.

To find ;

The amount of water that *flows into the tank* : _____

The amount of water that *is leaking from the tank* : _____

The amount of water *in the tank* (A) at $t = b$;

$A(b) = $

When the amount of water in the tank is increasing: _____

When the amount of water in the tank is decreasing: _____

When the amount of water in the tank is max/min: _____

When rate of amount of water in the tank is increasing: _____

The rate at which the water *enters the tank* is $F(t) = 2\sin(t^2)$ where $0 \le t \le 1$. The rate at which the water *leaves the tank* is $G(t) = 4t^3 - 5.3t^2 + 2.1t + 0.03$ where $0 \le t \le 1$. The amount of the water is measured in gallons and t is measured in hour. At $t = 0$, the amount of water *in the tank* is 0.2 gallon.

(a) How many gallons of water enter the tank in the interval $0 \le t \le 1$?

(b) For $0 \le t \le 1$, find the time where the amount of water in the tank is increasing.

(c) For $0 \le t \le 1$, find the minimum amount of water in the tank. Show your work.

3. Motion with Table

t (sec)	0	2	6	14	20
$v(t)$ (feet/sec)	-10	-20	-10	0	10
$a(t)$ (feet/sec²)	1	5	2	1	2

The bicycle's velocity $v(t)$, measured in feet per second, and acceleration $a(t)$, measured in feet per second per second, are continuous functions in the time interval $0 \le t \le 20$ seconds. The table above shows selected values of these functions. The initial position of the bicycle is 6 in the number line.

(a) Is the bicycle speeding up or slowing down at $t = 6$? Explain the reason.

(b) Explain the meaning of $\int_0^{20} |v(t)|\, dt$ in the context of this problem. Use a left Riemann sum with the three subintervals indicated by the data in the table to approximate $\int_0^{20} |v(t)|\, dt$.

(c) Explain the meaning of $\dfrac{1}{20}\int_0^{20} a(t)\, dt$ in the context of this problem. Approximate $\dfrac{1}{20}\int_0^{20} a(t)\, dt$ using a trapezoidal sum with the subintervals indicated by the data in the table.

(d) Approximate the position of the bicycle at $t = 6$ using right Riemann sum with two subintervals. Is the particle moving away from the origin or moving toward the origin at $t = 6$? Justify your answer.

4. Area and Volume

The function $f(x)$ is defined by

$$f(x) = \begin{cases} 3\sin x + 3 & \text{for } -\frac{\pi}{2} \le x < 0 \\ -0.5x + 3 & \text{for } 0 \le x \le 6 \end{cases}.$$

The graph of the continuous function $f(x)$ is shown in the figure. Let R be the region bounded by the graphs of $f(x)$ and the x axis.

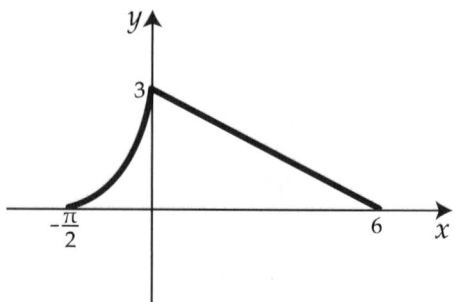

(a) The region R is the base of a solid. For this solid, the cross sections perpendicular to the y-axis are squares. Write, but do not evaluate, an integral expression for the volume of this solid.

(b) Write, but do not evaluate, an integral expression for the volume of the solid generated when R is rotated about the line $y = -1$.

(c) Write, but do not evaluate, an integral expression for the volume of the solid generated when R is rotated about the line $x = 6$.

Part 3
Calculus for BC

Chapter 18~24
(For BC only)

Mia's AP Calculus

18. Euler Method, Logistic Curve (for BC)

1. Euler's Method

Euler' method is a method of ROUGHLY graphing the points of a solution curve of a differential equation.

Sketch the solution of $\dfrac{dy}{dx} = y$ through point y(0) = 1 with stepsize $\Delta x = 1$.

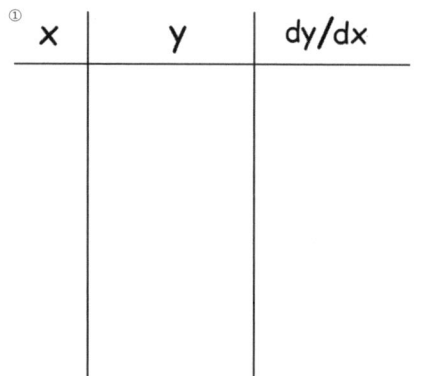
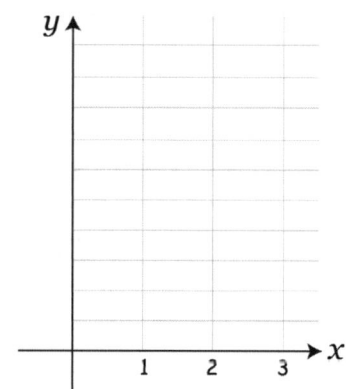

We basically draw a tangent line (with slope 1) from the (0, 1) and then change that line with new tangent line (which has new slope) after each stepsize $\Delta x = 1$.

Blank : ①

x	y	dy/dx
0	1	1
1	2	2
2	4	4

328 Mia's AP calculus AB BC

We already know how to find the exact solution to this problem.

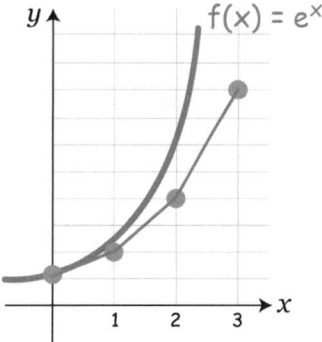

If we compare with our *exact* solution, you will see that it looks quite similar ☺

You will notice that the smaller step size we have the closer will be to our exact solution!

When we are looking for the **New y**,

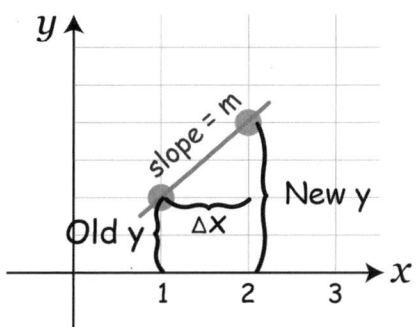

so we could say

New y = ① _____

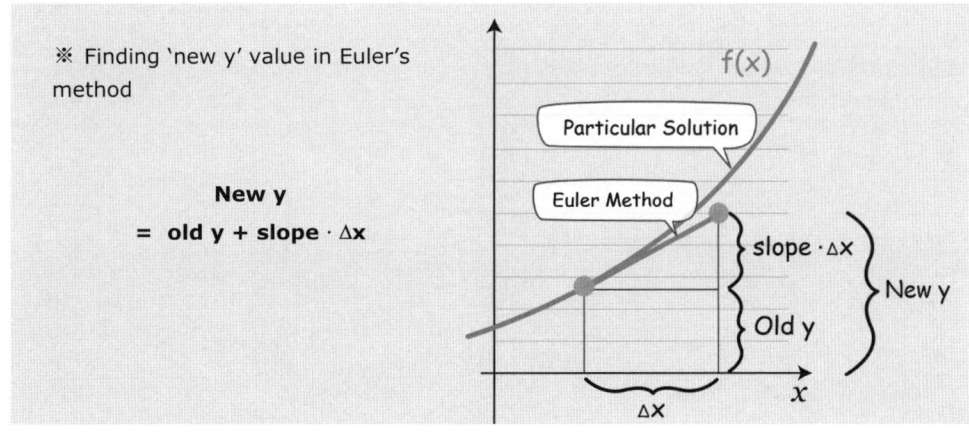

※ Finding 'new y' value in Euler's method

New y
= old y + slope · Δx

Blank : ① old y + slope · △x

18. Euler Method, Logistic Curve(for BC)   329

We can also derive the formula from the definition of derivative!

$$f'(a) \approx \frac{f(a+h) - f(a)}{h}$$

$$f(a+h) \approx \underbrace{f(a)}_{\text{new y}} + \underbrace{h}_{\text{increment}} \underbrace{f'(a)}_{\text{slope}}$$

(new y) (old y)

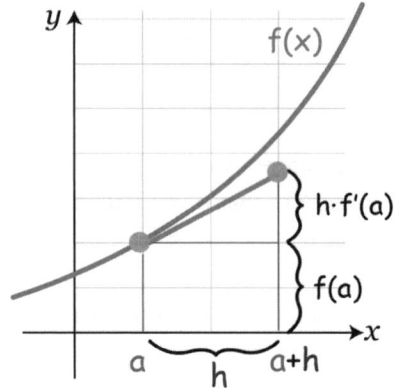

EXAMPLE 1. Use Euler's method with $\Delta x = 0.5$ to approximate y(2) if $\frac{dy}{dx} = y + 1$ and the (1, 1) belongs to the graph of the solution of the differential equation.

EXAMPLE 2. Use Euler's method with $\Delta x = \dfrac{1}{2}$ to approximate y(2) if $\dfrac{dy}{dx} = \dfrac{x+y}{x}$ and y(1) = 2.

AP Style Problem

The table show selected values of the derivative for a differentiable function f.

x	2	3	4	5	6
$f'(x)$	1.5	2	1	-1.5	-0.5

If $f(2) = 10$, what is the approximation to $f(6)$ obtained by using Euler's method with a step size of 2?

A) 12
B) 13.5
C) 14
D) 15
E) 15.5

2. Logistic Growth (BC)

☺ Reminder

When **rate of change** is ①_____ to the **amount present** at any given time :

That growth can't go on forever as they will soon run out of available food.

In many real life applications,
the growth is NOT always unlimited,
but **may have a limit L** which is called

②_____.

Then we will have a slightly different differential equation;

$$\frac{dP}{dt} = kP\left(1 - \frac{P}{L}\right)$$

Limit

which is called **logistic differential equation**.

If the population starts at a value *lower than* the carrying capacity
(P < L) , then the population will ③(increase / decrease).

If the population starts at a value *higher than* the carrying capacity
(P > L) , then the population will ④(increase / decrease).

Blank : ① proportional   ② carrying capacity   ③ increase   ④ decrease

* Now, let's find P.

$$\frac{dP}{dt} = kP\left(1 - \frac{P}{L}\right)$$

$$\frac{dP}{dt} = \frac{k}{L}P(\boxed{})$$

$$\frac{1}{P(\boxed{})}dP = \frac{k}{L}dt$$

$$\boxed{}\int\left(\frac{1}{P} + \frac{1}{L-P}\right)dP = \boxed{}\int k\,dt$$

$$\int\left(\frac{1}{P} + \frac{1}{L-P}\right)dP = \boxed{} + c$$

$$\ln|P| - \boxed{} = \boxed{} + c$$

$$\ln\left|\boxed{}\right| = \boxed{} + c$$

$$\boxed{} = Ce^{kt}$$

$$\boxed{} = Ce^{-kt}$$

$$\boxed{} - 1 = Ce^{-kt}$$

$$\boxed{} = 1 + Ce^{-kt}$$

$$P = \boxed{}$$

※ Logistic growth

$$\frac{dP}{dt} = kP\left(1 - \frac{P}{L}\right) \quad \rightleftarrows \quad P = \frac{L}{1 + Ce^{-kt}}$$

Limit = carrying capacity

Limit = carrying capacity

Where L is carrying capacity.

Blank : ※Blank Answers are in the answer section

※ Facts about logistic curve;

① Population is growing most rapidly at ①_____.

② $\lim_{t \to \infty} y =$ ②⬜

③ $\lim_{t \to 0} y' =$ ③⬜ and
$\lim_{t \to \infty} y' =$ ④⬜

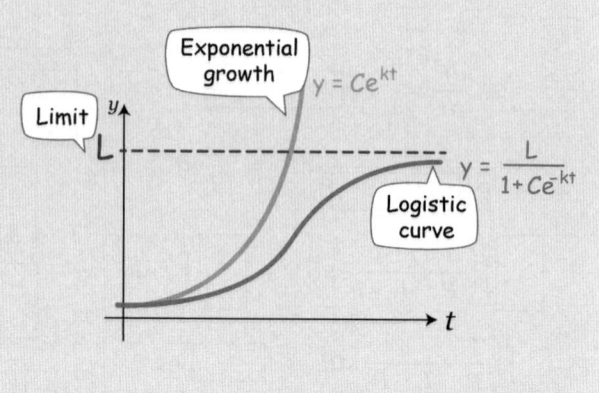

EXAMPLE 3. Which differential equation is logistic? If it is, find the carrying capacity and find the general solution(Do not find C).

① $\dfrac{dy}{dx} = 3y - y^2$

② $\dfrac{dy}{dx} = x^2 - 2x$

③ $\dfrac{dR}{dt} = R^2 + 2R$

④ $\dfrac{dR}{dt} = 6R - \dfrac{R^2}{2}$

Blank: ① $y = \dfrac{L}{2}$ ② L ③ 0 ④ 0

⑤ $\dfrac{dy}{dx} = y(6-y)$ ⑥ $\dfrac{dy}{dx} = x(1-x)$

EXAMPLE 4. Growing of a population is modeled by the following function: (P increases according to the logistic differential equation)

$$\dfrac{dy}{dx} = \dfrac{2}{15} y\left(\dfrac{5}{4} - y\right)$$

① Find the solution if $y(0) = 1$.

② What is $\lim\limits_{x \to \infty} y$?

③ If $y(0) = 1$, for what value of y is the population growing the fastest?

EXAMPLE 5. Let f be a function with $f(0) = 2$ such that all points (x, y) on the graph of f satisfy the logistic differential equation

$$\frac{dy}{dx} = 12y - 2y^2.$$

① Find $y = f(x)$.

② Find $\lim\limits_{x \to \infty} f(x)$, $\lim\limits_{x \to 0} f'(x)$, and $\lim\limits_{x \to \infty} f'(x)$.

③ For what value of y does the graph of f have a point of inflection?

④ For what value of x does the graph of f have a point of inflection?

EXAMPLE 6. A lake is stocked with 500 fish. If the population increases according to the logistic curve $P = \dfrac{10{,}000}{1+10e^{-t/3}}$, where t is measured in months.

① At what rate is the fish population changing at the end of third month?

② After how many months is the population increasing the most rapidly?

AP Style Problem

1. Which of the following differential equation is NOT logistic?

   A) $y' = y - y^2$

   B) $\dfrac{dx}{dt} = 2(x - 4x^2)$

   C) $\dfrac{dy}{dt} = ky - ky^2$

   D) $\dfrac{dG}{dt} = 0.15(100 - G)$

   E) $g'(t) = 10g(t)[1 - g(t)]$

2. The graph shows logistic growth for the grasshopper population G. Which differential equation could be the appropriate model?

   A) $\dfrac{dG}{dt} = 2G - 40G^2$

   B) $\dfrac{dG}{dt} = 2G^2 - 40G$

   C) $\dfrac{dG}{dt} = 0.2G - 0.01G^2$

   D) $\dfrac{dG}{dt} = 0.2G^2 - 0.01G$

   E) $\dfrac{dG}{dt} = 2t^2 - 40t$

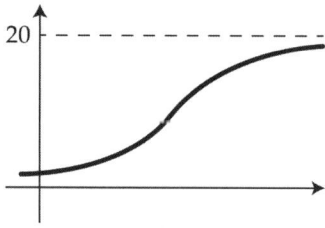

3. Suppose $P(t)$ denotes the size of an animal population at time t and its growth is described by the differential equation $\frac{dP}{dt} = \frac{1}{1000}P(100-P)$, where $P(0) = 10$. Which of the following statements is true?

   I. $\lim_{t \to \infty} P(t) = 100$

   II. $\frac{dP}{dt}$ has maximum value when $t = 50$.

   III. When $P < 50$, P is increasing at a decreasing rate.

   IV. $\frac{dP}{dt} > 0$ for all $t \geq 0$.

A) I, II
B) I, IV
C) I, II, III
D) I, II, IV
E) I, II, III, IV

4. A population of rabbits y changes at a rate modeled by the differential equation $\frac{dy}{dt} = \frac{y}{5}\left(2 - \frac{y}{5}\right)$, where t is measured in years. What is the greatest rate of change of the number of rabbits?

A) 1
B) 5
C) 10
D) 50

Mia's AP Calculus
19. Integration for BC (for BC)

1. Integration by Parts

Integration by Parts is a special method of integration that is often useful when two functions are multiplied together, but is also helpful in other ways.

1) By part type 1

① Choose f and g

$$\int f(x)\,g(x)\,dx$$

② Differentiate f (until you get 0), Integrate g.
Put alternating +'s and -'s in the very left. (always start with +).
Put ∫ sign in the last row.

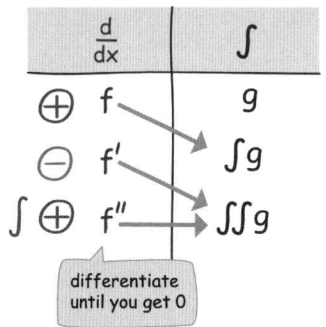

differentiate until you get 0

③ Multiply along the diagonal. Multiply the last row and integrate them.

$$\int f(x)g(x)\,dx = f\int g - f'\iint g + \int (f''\iint g)$$

EXAMPLE 1. Evaluate the integral.

① $\int 4x\sin x \; dx$

② $\int x^2 e^{2x} \; dx$

d/dx	∫

③ $\int y^2 \cos 2y \; dy$

④ $\int x\sin\left(\dfrac{x}{2}\right) dx$

2) By part type 2

① Choose f and g

$$\int f(x)\,g(x)\,dx$$

② Differentiate f (until you get a similar form of f(x)g(x)), Integrate g.
Put alternating +'s and -'s in the very left. (always start with +).
Put ∫ sign in the last row.

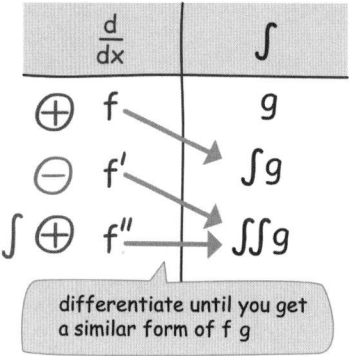

differentiate until you get a similar form of f g

④ Multiply along the diagonal. Multiply the last row and integrate them.

$$\int f(x)g(x)\,dx = f\int g - f'\iint g + \int (f''\iint g)$$

⑤ Simplify for $\int f(x)g(x)\,dx$.

EXAMPLE 2. Evaluate the integral.

① $\displaystyle\int e^{2x} \sin 2x \, dx$

② $\displaystyle\int e^{-x} \cos\left(\frac{x}{2}\right) dx$

3) By part type 3

※ Integration by Parts

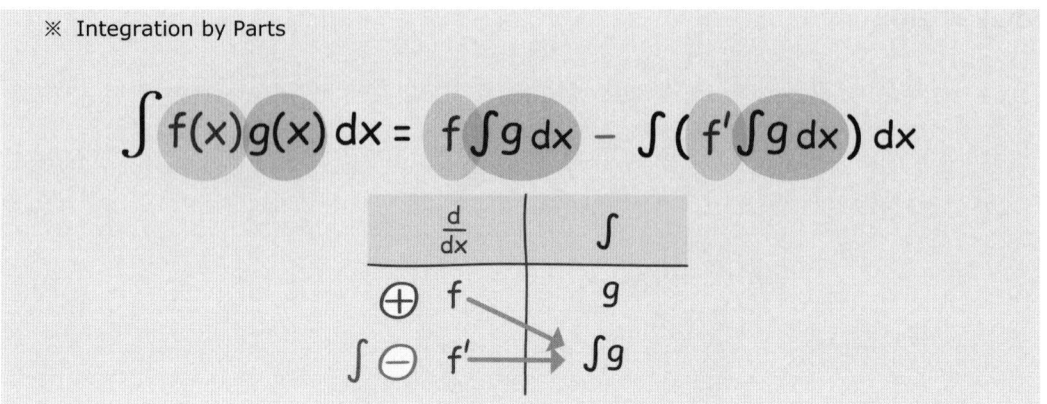

Where did 'integration by parts' come from?
It is based on the product rule for derivatives.

$$(fh)' = f h' + f' h$$

$$\int (fh)' \, dx = \int f h' \, dx + \int f' h \, dx$$

①_____ $= \int f h' \, dx + \int f' h \, dx$

$\int f h' \, dx$ = ②_____ $- \int f' h \, dx$

let $h' = g$ then $h =$ ③_____

$\int f g \, dx$ = ④_____ $- \int f'$ ⑤_____ dx

Blank : ① fh ② fh ③ ∫g dx ④ f(∫g dx) ⑤ ∫g dx

EXAMPLE 3. Evaluate the integral.

> When you have to integrate
> log , inverse trig (u-sub does not work)
> use 'by part' method!

① $\int \ln x \, dx$

② $\int x \ln x \, dx$

③ $\int (\ln x)^2 \, dx$

④ $\int x \ln(x+1) \, dx$

⑤ $\int \arcsin x \, dx$

⑥ $\int \arctan x \, dx$

☺ Tips for Integration by Part

To decide the function to differentiate (f(x) part), we use this order.

I	Inverse Trig (sin⁻¹, tan⁻¹)	
L	Logarithmic (log x, ln x)	↑ d/dx
A	Algebra (x^2, x^3)	
T	Trigonometry (sin x, cos x)	↓ ∫
E	Exponential (e^x)	

(Sometimes T and E can be switched)

How many times do we have to differentiate?

Type	example	How many times do we differentiate?
type 1	$\int$(Algebra)(Trig) $\int$(Algebra)(Exp)	Differentiate *Algebra* part until 0.
type 2	$\int$(Exp)(Trig)	Differentiate *Exp* part twice and then simplify.
type 3	$\int$(Log)(others) $\int$(Inv Trig)(others) or etc	Differentiate *Log, Inv Trig* once.

AP Style Problem

1. $\int x\sin x^2\, dx + \int x\sin x\, dx =$

   A) $-\dfrac{1}{2}\sin x^2 + x\sin x - \cos x + C$

   B) $-\dfrac{1}{2}\sin x^2 - x\cos x + \sin x + C$

   C) $-\dfrac{1}{2}\cos x^2 - x\cos x + \sin x + C$

   D) $-\dfrac{1}{2}\cos x^2 + x\sin x - \cos x + C$

2. $\int \dfrac{\ln}{x^2}\, dx + \int \dfrac{\ln x}{x}\, dx =$

   A) $-\dfrac{\ln x + 1}{x} + \dfrac{\ln^2 x}{2} + C$

   B) $\dfrac{\ln x + 1}{x} + \dfrac{\ln^2 x}{2} + C$

   C) $-\dfrac{\ln x + 1}{x} - \dfrac{\ln^2 x}{2} + C$

   D) $\dfrac{\ln x + 1}{x} - \dfrac{\ln^2 x}{2} + C$

3. $\int \sec^2 x \ln(\tan x + 1)\, dx =$

   A) $\ln(\tan x + 1) - \tan x - 1 + C$
   B) $(\tan x + 1)\ln(\tan x + 1) - \tan x - 1 + C$
   C) $\ln(\tan x + 1) + \tan x + 1 + C$
   D) $(\tan x + 1)\ln(\tan x + 1) + \tan x + 1 + C$

4. $\int_{-1}^{1} xe^x \, dx =$

    A) 2/e

    B) 1/e

    C) e

    D) 2e

5. $\int_{0}^{e-1} \ln(x+1) \, dx$

    A) -3

    B) -1

    C) 1

    D) 3

x	f(x)	f'(x)	g(x)	g'(x)
0	2	0	-1	2
4	4	1	0	-1

6. The table above gives values of $f, f', g,$ and g' for selected values of x. If $\int_{0}^{4} f'(x)g(x) \, dx = 4$, then what is $\int_{0}^{4} f(x)g'(x) \, dx$?

    A) 2

    B) -2

    C) 4

    D) -4

x	$f(x)$	$f'(x)$	$g(x)$	$g'(x)$
0	2	1	-1	2
4	4	1	0	-1

7. The table above gives values of $f, f', g,$ and g' for selected values of x. If $f'(x) = 1$ for all x, then what is $\int_0^4 f(x)g''(x)\,dx$?

A) 8
B) -8
C) 4
D) -9

8. If $g'(x) = g(x)$, then $\int xg(x)\,dx =$

A) $\dfrac{x^2}{2} - g(x)\dfrac{x^2}{2} + C$

B) $\dfrac{x^2}{2} + g(x)\dfrac{x^2}{2} + C$

C) $xg(x) + g(x) + C$

D) $xg(x) - g(x) + C$

2. Partial Fraction

Let's find the "parts" that make the single fraction (the "partial fractions").
It is simpler to integrate the partial fractions rather than the original rational function.

---

① Factor the bottom.

② i) Write one partial fraction for each of those factors

$$\frac{N}{(x-2)(x+3)} = \frac{A}{(x-2)} + \frac{B}{(x+3)}$$

ii) Sometimes you may get a **factor with an exponent,** like $(x+2)^2$

You need a partial fraction for each exponent from 1 up.

$$\frac{N}{(x-2)^2} = \frac{A}{(x-2)} + \frac{B}{(x-2)^2}$$

iii) When you have a **irreducible quadratic binomial factor** (like $x^2 + 3$) you need a linear on the numerator.

$$\frac{Cx+D}{x^2+2}$$ ⟶ linear factor / irreducible quadratic factor

③ Multiply through by the bottom so we no longer have fractions

④ Now find the constants A, B, C or D (by substituting the **roots**)

EXAMPLE 4. Write in partial fractions.

① $\dfrac{N}{x^2 - 2x - 3}$

② $\dfrac{N}{(x-1)^3}$

③ $\dfrac{N}{x(x^2+1)}$

④ $\dfrac{N}{(x-2)(x+2)^2(x^2+2)}$

⑤ $\dfrac{N}{(x^2+1)^2}$

EXAMPLE 5. Find the values of A, B and C that complete the partial fractions.

① $\dfrac{6}{x^2-9} = \dfrac{A}{x-3} + \dfrac{B}{x+3}$

② $\dfrac{x-8}{x^2-4x} = \dfrac{A}{x} + \dfrac{B}{x-4}$

③ $\dfrac{2x-4}{x(x^2+2)} = \dfrac{A}{x} + \dfrac{Bx+C}{(x^2+2)}$

EXAMPLE 6. Evaluate the integral.

① $\displaystyle\int \dfrac{3x+31}{x^2+9x+14}\,dx$

② $\int \dfrac{x+7}{x^2+2x}\,dx$

③ $\int \dfrac{x+1}{(x-1)^2}\,dx$

④ $\int \dfrac{dx}{x^2(x^2-4)}$

⑤ $\int \dfrac{x+1}{x(x^2+1)} dx$

⑥ $\int \dfrac{2x^3+4x}{(x^2+1)^2} dx$

3. Improper Integration

An improper integral is a definite integral where one of the end of the interval is ±∞.

※ Improper Integration

If $f(x)$ is continuous on the interval $[a, \infty)$, then

$$\int_a^\infty f(x)\,dx = \lim_{①} \int_a^p f(x)\,dx$$

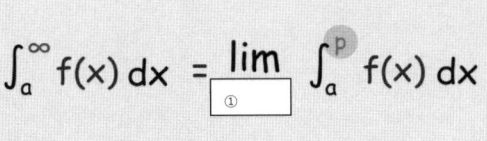

If $f(x)$ is continuous on the interval $(-\infty, b]$, then

$$\int_{-\infty}^b f(x)\,dx = \lim_{②} \int_p^b f(x)\,dx$$

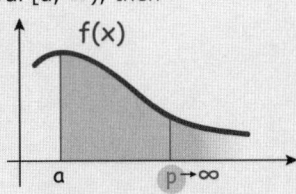

If $f(x)$ is continuous on the interval $(-\infty, \infty)$, then

$$\int_{-\infty}^\infty f(x)\,dx = \int_{-\infty}^c f(x)\,dx + \int_c^\infty f(x)\,dx$$

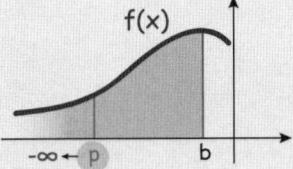

EXAMPLE 7. (a) Express the improper integral as a limit of definite integrals, and (b) evaluate the integrals.

① $\int_1^\infty \dfrac{1}{x}\,dx$

Blank : ① $p \to \infty$ ② $p \to -\infty$

② $\int_0^\infty e^{-x}dx$

③ $\int_1^\infty \dfrac{e^{1/x}}{x^2}dx$

④ $\int_0^\infty xe^{-2x}dx$

⑤ $\int_0^\infty \dfrac{1}{x^2+1}dx$

⑥ $\int_{-\infty}^{-1} \dfrac{dx}{x^2}$

⑦ $\int_{-\infty}^{0} \dfrac{2dx}{x^2 - 4x + 3}$

⑧ $\int_{-\infty}^{\infty} e^{2x} dx$

Sometimes one of the end of the interval has a discontinuity.

※ Improper Integration

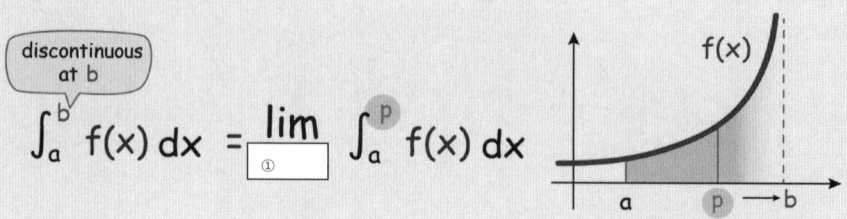

discontinuous at b

$$\int_a^b f(x)\,dx = \lim_{①} \int_a^p f(x)\,dx$$

$$\int_a^b f(x)\,dx = \lim_{②} \int_p^b f(x)\,dx$$

discontinuous at a

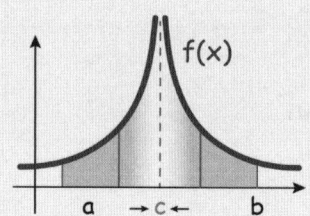

discontinuous at c

$$\int_a^b f(x)\,dx = \int_a^c f(x)\,dx + \int_c^b f(x)\,dx$$

EXAMPLE 8. Evaluate.

① $\int_0^1 \dfrac{1}{x^2}\,dx$

Blank : ① $p \to b^-$ ② $p \to a^+$

358 Mia's AP calculus AB BC

② $\int_1^e \frac{1}{x\ln x}dx$

③ $\int_0^2 \frac{1}{\sqrt{4-x^2}}dx$

④ $\int_0^{\pi/2} \tan x\, dx$

⑤ $\int_{-1}^8 \frac{1}{\sqrt[3]{x}}dx$

AP Style Problem

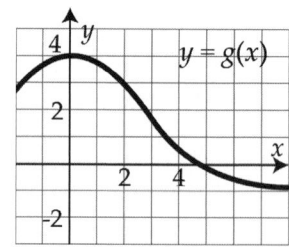

1. If g is a twice-differentiable function and graph of g is given above. There is a horizontal asymptote at $y = -1$. What is $\int_0^\infty g'(x)\, dx =$

   A) 1
   B) -1
   C) -5
   D) ∞

4. Curve Length

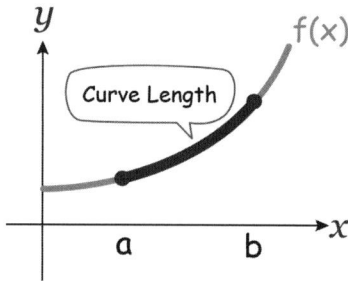

Let's find the length of a curve or line using integration idea.

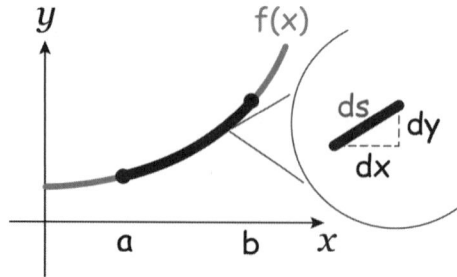

If we want the curve length from a to b, then we can break up to small segments,
and add up all the ds'.

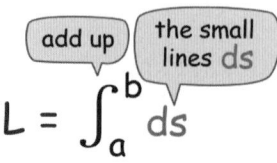

$$L = \int_a^b ds$$

360 Mia's AP calculus AB BC

Using Pythagorean Theorem, $ds = \sqrt{①}$

So,

$$L = \int_a^b ds = \int_a^b \sqrt{(dx)^2 + (dy)^2}$$
$$= \int_a^b \sqrt{(dx)^2\left(1 + ②^2\right)}$$
$$= \int_a^b \sqrt{\left(1 + ③^2\right)}\, dx$$

※ Curve Length

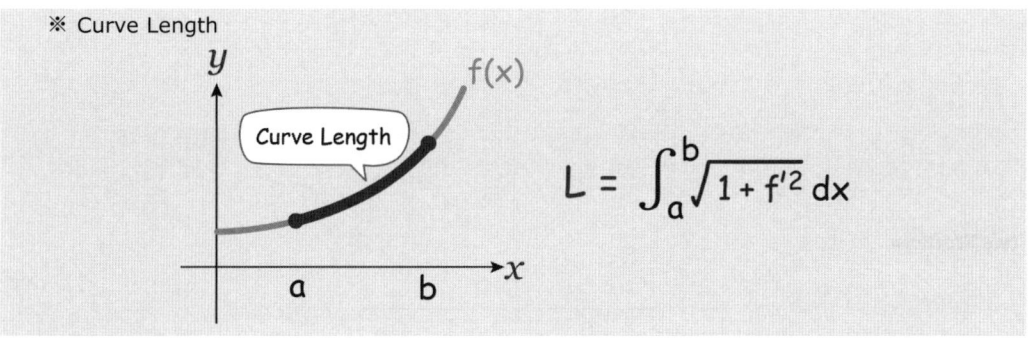

$$L = \int_a^b \sqrt{1 + f'^2}\, dx$$

EXAMPLE 9. Find the length of the curve of the function $y = \dfrac{1}{3}(x^2 + 2)^{3/2}$ over [0, 3].

Blank : ① $(dx)^2 + (dy)^2$ ② $\dfrac{dy}{dx}$ ③ $\dfrac{dy}{dx}$

EXAMPLE 10. Find the length of the curve of the function $y = \dfrac{1}{x+1}$ over [0, 1]. Set up the integral and do not evaluate.

AP Style Problem

x	0	2	4
$f(x)$	2	0	-1
$f'(x)$	-1	1	0

1. The table above gives values of f and f' for selected values of x. Which of the following is an approximation of the length of the graph of f on the interval [0, 4]? Use a left Riemann sum with the subintervals indicated by the data in the table.

A) 0
B) 4
C) $2\sqrt{2}$
D) $4\sqrt{2}$

Mia's AP Calculus
20. Infinite Series (for BC)

1. Sequence

①_____ : set of numbers that are in order.

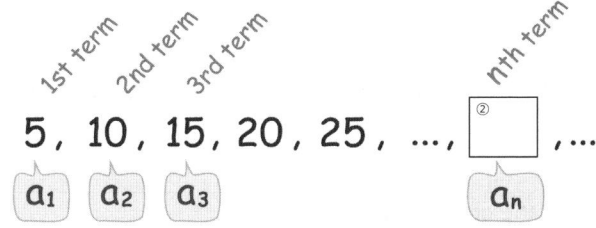

EXAMPLE 1. Write a general term a_n for the sequence.

① $\dfrac{1}{1}, \dfrac{1}{2}, \dfrac{1}{3}, \dfrac{1}{4}, \dots$

② $\dfrac{2}{1}, \dfrac{3}{2}, \dfrac{4}{3}, \dfrac{5}{4}, \dots$

③ $2, 4, 6, 8, 10, \dots$

④ $-1, 1, -1, 1, \dots$

⑤ $7, -14, 21, -28, 35, \dots$

⑥ $1 \cdot 1, 2 \cdot 3, 3 \cdot 5, 4 \cdot 7, \dots$

Blank : ① Sequence ② 5n

A sequence ① _____ when it keeps getting closer and closer to a **certain value**, and we call that *value* the ② _____ of the sequence.

ex) $\dfrac{1}{1}, \dfrac{1}{2}, \dfrac{1}{4}, \dfrac{1}{8}, \ldots, \dfrac{1}{2^{(n-1)}}, \ldots$

A sequence ③ _____ when the Limit of the sequence is **infinite** or **does not exist**.

ex) 1,2,4,8,…

EXAMPLE 2. Determine whether the sequence converges or diverges. If it converges, give the limit.

☺ Tip☞ We can use the rank of the growth rate.

$$\ln x < x^2 < x^4 < e^x < 3^x < x! < x^x$$

① $\dfrac{1}{1}, \dfrac{1}{2}, \dfrac{1}{3}, \dfrac{1}{4}, \ldots$

② $\dfrac{2}{1}, \dfrac{3}{2}, \dfrac{4}{3}, \dfrac{5}{4}, \ldots$

③ 2,4,6,8,10,…

④ −1,1,−1,1,…

⑤ $a_n = (-1)^{n+1} \dfrac{1}{n}$

⑥ $a_n = \dfrac{n^3 + 1}{\sqrt{n} + 4}$

Blank : ① converges ② limit ③ diverges

Mia's AP calculus AB BC

⑦ $a_n = \left(1 + \dfrac{3}{n}\right)^n$ ⑧ $a_n = \tan^{-1} n$

⑨ $a_n = \dfrac{n^3}{\ln n}$ ⑩ $a_n = \dfrac{n^3}{e^n}$

⑪ $a_n = \dfrac{n!}{n^n}$ ⑫ $a_n = \ln(4x-3) - \ln(2x+1)$

2. Summation Notation "Σ"

To **sum up** the terms of a sequence, we use ① _____ Notation;
Σ (called sigma) means **sum up**.

$$\sum_{k=1}^{n} a_k = a_1 + a_2 + a_3 + \cdots + a_n$$

- Sum up
- from 1st term
- to nth term
- of a sequence

Blank : ① Sigma

EXAMPLE 3. Write the sum using sigma notation, assuming the suggested pattern continues.

① $4+5+6+7$

② $1-3+5-7+9-11$

③ $\sin\pi + \sin 2\pi + \sin 3\pi + \sin 4\pi + ...$

④ $3^3 + 4^3 + 5^3 + ... + 10^3$

⑤ $x + x^2 + x^3 + x^4 + ...$

EXAMPLE 4. Write out the sum. Do not evaluate.

① $\sum_{n=1}^{3} \dfrac{5^n}{6^{n+1}}$

② $\sum_{n=0}^{\infty} \left(\dfrac{5}{4}\right) 2^n$

③ $\sum_{n=1}^{\infty} \dfrac{a^{n+1}}{n}$

④ $\sum_{n=0}^{\infty} (-1)^n \dfrac{x^{2n}}{(2n)!}$

3. Infinite Series

Infinite Series is the sum of infinite terms that follow a rule.

$$\sum_{k=1}^{\infty} a_k = a_1 + a_2 + a_3 + \cdots$$

These infinite series could either **converge** or **diverge**.

When the sum approaches a value the series is said to be ① _____,

If the sums do not converge, the series is said to be ② _____.

In this section let's find out whether a given infinite series converge or diverge!

$\sum a_n$ converge ?? diverge ??

Tip☞ We are NOT finding sum,
we are just TESTING whether the sum will converge or diverge!
So it doesn't really matter what the starting point is!

EXAMPLE 5. Determine the convergence or divergence of the series.

① $\sum_{n=1}^{\infty} 1$

② $\sum_{n=3}^{\infty} \frac{1}{2}$

③ $\sum_{n=0}^{\infty} n$

④ $\sum_{n=1}^{\infty} \frac{1}{n^2}$

But what about $\sum_{n=1}^{\infty} \frac{1}{n}$?

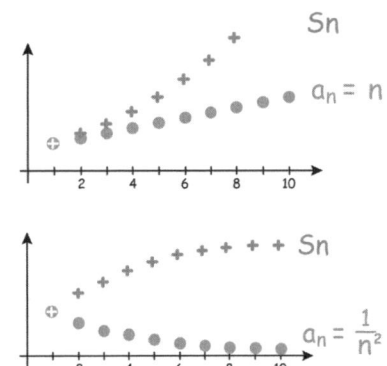

Blank : ① 'converge'   ② 'diverge'

4. How to Test a Series for Convergence and Divergence

1) nth term test (Divergence Test)

If $\lim\limits_{n\to\infty} a_n \neq 0$, then $\sum\limits^{\infty} a_n$ will **diverge**.

If $\lim\limits_{n\to\infty} a_n = 0$, then it is ①_____.

First thing to do! take the limit of a_n and find whether it diverges or not.

Notice that if $\lim\limits_{n\to\infty} a_n = 0$, then it is inconclusive. We need another test.

EXAMPLE 6. Determine the convergence or divergence of the series using nth term test.

① $\sum\limits_{n=1}^{\infty} \dfrac{n}{n+5}$

② $\sum\limits_{n=1}^{\infty} \dfrac{n+1}{n^2}$

③ $\sum\limits_{n=1}^{\infty} \left(\dfrac{3}{2}\right)^n$

④ $\sum\limits_{n=1}^{\infty} \dfrac{2}{3^n}$

⑤ $\sum\limits_{n=1}^{\infty} \dfrac{n^e}{e^n}$

⑥ $\sum\limits_{n=1}^{\infty} \dfrac{3^n}{2^n+1}$

⑦ $\sum\limits_{n=1}^{\infty} \sin\left(\dfrac{1}{n}\right)$

⑧ $\sum\limits_{n=1}^{\infty} \cos\left(\dfrac{1}{n}\right)$

⑨ $\sum\limits_{n=1}^{\infty} (-1)^n e^{1/n}$

Blank : ① Inconclusive

2) Infinite geometric Series

In a ① _____ sequence each term is found by **multiplying** the previous term by a constant.

a, ar, ar^2, ar^3, ... ② _____

(1st term, 2nd term, 3rd term, nth term; ×r, ×r, ×r)

where a is the ③ _____ term, and r is a ④ _____ _____.

Let's add infinite numbers of terms of a geometric sequence, then

$$\sum_{k=1}^{\infty} ar^{n-1} = (a)+(ar)+(ar^2)+\cdots = \;\text{⑤}\;$$

when ⑥ _____

※ **Infinite Geometric Series**

If a_n is geometric Sequence and the common ratio r is ⑦ _____

the series **converges**.

when $-1 < r < 1$

And the sum will be $\displaystyle\sum_{k=1}^{\infty} ar^{n-1} = \dfrac{a}{1-r}$

Blank: ① geometric   ② ar^{n-1} ③ first   ④ common ratio   ⑤ $\dfrac{a}{1-r}$ ⑥ $-1 < r < 1$ ⑦ $|r| < 1$

EXAMPLE 7. Determine whether the infinite geometric series converges or diverges. If it converges, find its sum.

① $1 + \dfrac{1}{2} + \dfrac{1}{4} + \dfrac{1}{8} + ...$

② $\sum_{k=1}^{\infty} 4(0.5)^k$

③ $\sum_{n=0}^{\infty} (-1)^n \dfrac{1}{5^n}$

④ $\sum_{n=1}^{\infty} \left(\dfrac{\pi}{2}\right)^n$

⑤ $\sum_{n=1}^{\infty} \dfrac{2}{3^n}$

⑥ $\sum_{n=0}^{\infty} \left(\dfrac{1}{2^n} + \dfrac{1}{4^n}\right)$

3) Harmonic Series

ex) $\sum_{n=1}^{\infty} \frac{1}{n}$

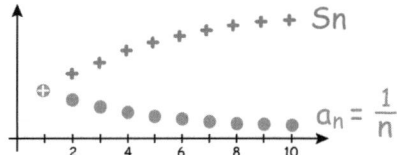

The harmonic series (harmonic) $\sum_{n=1}^{\infty} \frac{1}{n}$ = ① _____

always ②(converges/diverges).

proof☞ ※ Proof will be explained in Mia's AP calculus video from www.masterprep.net.

Blank : ① $1 + \frac{1}{2} + \frac{1}{3} + \frac{1}{4} + \dots$ ② diverge

4) P-Series Test

p series
$$\sum_{n=1}^{\infty} \frac{1}{n^p} = \text{①} \underline{\hspace{4cm}}$$

If $p > 1$, then the series **converges**.

If $0 < p \leq 1$, then the series **diverges**.

☺ Tip☞ See how fast the term decrease!

EXAMPLE 8. Determine the convergence or divergence of the series using p series test.

① $\sum_{n=1}^{\infty} \frac{2}{n}$
② $\sum_{n=1}^{\infty} \frac{2}{n^3}$

③ $\sum_{n=1}^{\infty} \frac{1}{n+2}$
④ $\sum_{n=2}^{\infty} \frac{1}{\sqrt{n}}$

⑤ $\sum_{n=1}^{\infty} \frac{1}{\sqrt[99]{n^{100}}}$
⑥ $\sum_{n=1}^{\infty} \frac{5}{\sqrt[6]{n^5}}$

⑦ $1 + \frac{1}{2\sqrt{2}} + \frac{1}{3\sqrt{3}} + \frac{1}{8} + ...$
⑧ $1 + \frac{1}{4} + \frac{1}{9} + \frac{1}{16} + ...$

Blank : ① $1 + \frac{1}{2^p} + \frac{1}{3^p} + \frac{1}{4^p} + ...$

5) Integral Test

For $\sum_{n=k}^{\infty} a_n$, let $a_n = f(x)$

where $a_n = f(x)$ is positive, continuous and decreasing.

If $\int_{k}^{\infty} f(x)\,dx$ **converges**, then $\sum_{n=k}^{\infty} a_n$ **converges**.

If $\int_{k}^{\infty} f(x)\,dx$ **diverges**, then $\sum_{n=k}^{\infty} a_n$ **Diverges**.

Series and improper integral converge or diverge *together*.

proof☞ ※ Proof will be explained in Mia's AP calculus video from www.masterprep.net.

EXAMPLE 9. Determine the convergence or divergence of the series using integral test.

tip☞ Use u-sub method, and p-series test, if possible!

$$\sum_{n=2}^{\infty} \frac{1}{n(\ln n)^2}$$

① $\sum_{n=1}^{\infty} \dfrac{1}{n+2}$

② $\sum_{n=3}^{\infty} \dfrac{1}{n \ln n}$

③ $\sum_{n=3}^{\infty} \dfrac{1}{n(\ln n)^3}$

④ $\sum_{n=2}^{\infty} \dfrac{5}{n \ln n \left(\ln(\ln n)\right)^2}$

⑤ $\sum_{n=1}^{\infty} \dfrac{4n}{n^2+1}$

⑥ $\sum_{n=1}^{\infty} \dfrac{1}{n^2+1}$

7. $\displaystyle\sum_{n=1}^{\infty} \frac{\ln n}{n}$

8. $\displaystyle\sum_{n=1}^{\infty} \frac{1}{n^2} \cos\left(\frac{1}{n}\right)$

9. $\displaystyle\sum_{n=1}^{\infty} n e^{-n^2}$

10. $\displaystyle\sum_{n=1}^{\infty} \frac{\arctan n}{n^2 + 1}$

6) Comparison Test

When a_n, b_n are nonnegative, and $a_n \leq b_n$ for all n,

if $\sum\limits^{\infty} b_n$ (bigger one) **converges**, then $\sum\limits^{\infty} a_n$ (smaller one) **converges**,

if $\sum\limits^{\infty} a_n$ (smaller one) **diverges**, then $\sum\limits^{\infty} b_n$ (bigger one) **Diverges**.

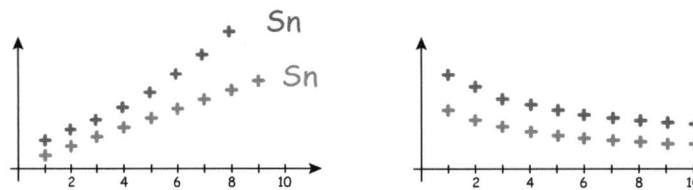

If the bigger one diverges, then we don't know about the smaller one.
If the smaller one converges, then we don't know about the bigger one.

EXAMPLE 10. Determine the convergence or divergence of the series using comparison test.

① $\sum\limits_{n=2}^{\infty} \dfrac{1}{n-1}$

② $\sum\limits_{n=1}^{\infty} \dfrac{1}{\sqrt{n-2}}$

③ $\sum\limits_{n=1}^{\infty} \dfrac{1}{n^2+1}$

④ $\sum\limits_{n=1}^{\infty} \dfrac{1}{n^n}$

⑤ $\sum_{n=1}^{\infty} \dfrac{1}{2^n+1}$

⑥ $\sum_{n=1}^{\infty} \dfrac{n^2}{n^3-3}$

⑦ $\sum_{n=1}^{\infty} \dfrac{3^{n+2}}{2^n}$

Tip ☞

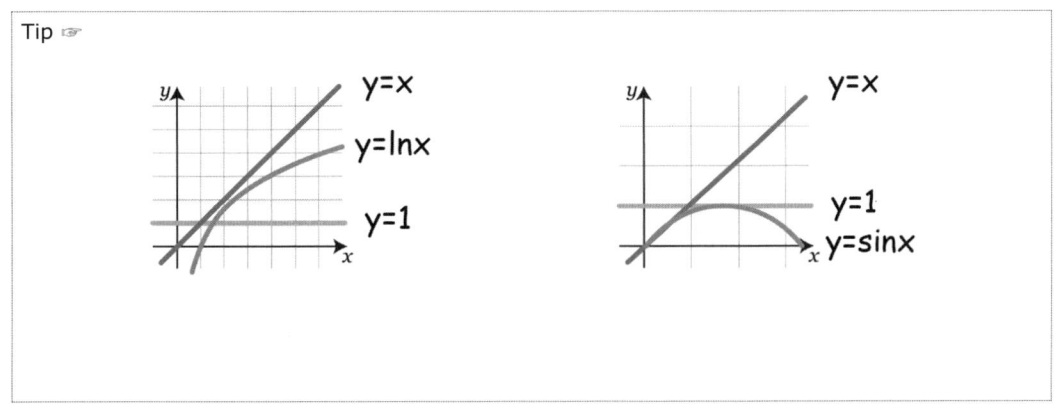

⑧ $\sum_{n=1}^{\infty} \dfrac{1}{\ln n}$

⑨ $\sum_{n=1}^{\infty} \dfrac{1}{n^2 \ln n}$

⑩ $\sum_{n=1}^{\infty} \dfrac{\ln n}{n^3 + n}$

⑪ $\sum_{n=1}^{\infty} \dfrac{\sin \dfrac{\pi}{n}}{n^2}$

⑫ $\sum_{n=1}^{\infty} \sin \dfrac{1}{n^2}$

7) Limit Comparison Test

When Comparison test does not work, we use limit comparison test.

If $\lim_{n \to \infty} \dfrac{a_n}{b_n}$ is positive nonzero number,

then $\sum_{}^{\infty} a_n$ and $\sum_{}^{\infty} b_n$ both converge or both diverge.

EXAMPLE 11. Determine the convergence or divergence of the series using comparison test or limit comparison test.

① $\sum_{n=1}^{\infty} \dfrac{2n}{n^2+1}$

② $\sum_{n=1}^{\infty} \dfrac{\sqrt{n}}{n^2+2}$

③ $\sum_{n=2}^{\infty} \dfrac{n^2+4}{n^4-2}$

④ $\sum_{n=2}^{\infty} \dfrac{n2^n}{n^4+2}$

⑤ $\sum_{n=1}^{\infty} \dfrac{2n-1}{n^2+2n+1}$

⑥ $\sum_{n=1}^{\infty} \dfrac{2^n}{3^n-1}$

⑦ $\sum_{n=1}^{\infty} \sin \dfrac{1}{n}$

8) Ratio Test

When we have $\sum\limits_{}^{\infty} a_n$

if $\lim\limits_{n \to \infty} \left| \dfrac{a_{n+1}}{a_n} \right| <$ ① ___ , then series **converges**.

if $\lim\limits_{n \to \infty} \left| \dfrac{a_{n+1}}{a_n} \right| >$ ② ___ , then series **diverges**.

if $\lim\limits_{n \to \infty} \left| \dfrac{a_{n+1}}{a_n} \right| = 1$, it is ③ _____ .

(absolute value of the ratio btwn consecutive terms)

$\lim\limits_{n \to \infty} \left| \dfrac{a_{n+1}}{a_n} \right| < 1$ means the sequence is getting ④ _____ .

$\lim\limits_{n \to \infty} \left| \dfrac{a_{n+1}}{a_n} \right| > 1$ means the sequence is getting ⑤ _____ .

☺ Tip : We use this test especially when we have $n!$ or n^n.

EXAMPLE 12. Determine the convergence or divergence of the series using ratio test.

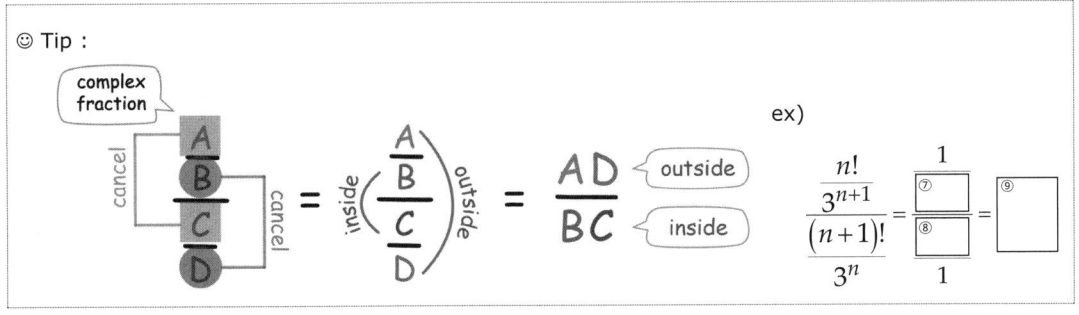

Blank : ① 1   ② 1   ③ Inconclusive   ④ smaller   ⑤ bigger   ⑦ 3   ⑧ (n+1)   ⑨ $\dfrac{1}{3(n+1)}$

① $\sum_{n=1}^{\infty} \dfrac{2^n}{n!}$

② $\sum_{n=1}^{\infty} \dfrac{n^4}{2^n}$

③ $\sum_{n=1}^{\infty} \dfrac{n3^n}{n+4}$

④ $\sum_{n=1}^{\infty} \dfrac{(2n)!}{n+1}$

⑤ $\sum_{n=1}^{\infty} \frac{(n!)^2}{(3n)!}$

⑥ $\sum_{n=1}^{\infty} \frac{n^n}{n!}$

9) Alternating Series Test

A series the terms of which are alternately positive and negative is called the **alternating series**.

$-1 + \frac{1}{2} - \frac{1}{3} + \frac{1}{4} - \frac{1}{5} + \frac{1}{6} - \frac{1}{7} + \cdots$

The alternating series $\sum^{\infty} (-1)^n a_n$ (alternating series) converges

when ① a_n (without $(-1)^n$) ① _____ . ② $\lim_{n \to \infty} a_n =$ ② ☐ (without $(-1)^n$)

(If the number part(no sign) of the terms of an alternating series decreases and approach 0 then that alternating series converges.)

Blank : ① decreasing ② 0

EXAMPLE 13. Determine the convergence or divergence of the series using alternating series test.

① $\sum_{n=1}^{\infty}(-1)^n \dfrac{1}{n}$ ② $\sum_{n=1}^{\infty}(-1)^{n+1}\dfrac{n-1}{n}$

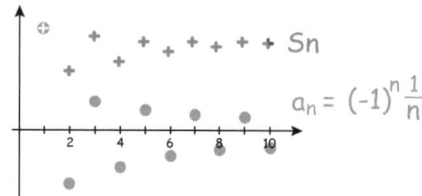

③ $\sum_{n=1}^{\infty}(-1)^{n+1}\dfrac{n}{2^{n-1}}$ ④ $\sum_{n=1}^{\infty}\dfrac{(-1)^n \sqrt{n}}{n+1}$

⑤ $\sum_{n=1}^{\infty}\dfrac{(-1)^n n}{\ln n}$ ⑥ $-1+\dfrac{1}{\sqrt{2}}-\dfrac{1}{\sqrt{3}}+\dfrac{1}{\sqrt{4}}-\cdots$

⑦ $\sum_{n=1}^{\infty}\dfrac{(-n)^{n+1}}{n^{2n}}$ ⑧ $\sum_{n=1}^{\infty}\dfrac{(-n)^{n+1}}{n^2}$

⑨ $\sum_{n=1}^{\infty}\dfrac{\cos(n\pi)}{\sqrt{n}}$ ⑩ $-1+\dfrac{1}{3^2}-\dfrac{1}{2!}+\dfrac{1}{3^3}-\dfrac{1}{3!}+\dfrac{1}{3^4}-\dfrac{1}{4!}+\cdots$

10) Absolute Convergence and Conditional Convergence

When the alternating series $\sum_{}^{\infty} (-1)^n a_n$ (alternating series) Converges,

$\sum_{}^{\infty} (-1)^n a_n$ **absolutely converges**, when $\sum_{}^{\infty} a_n$ converges.

$\sum_{}^{\infty} (-1)^n a_n$ **conditionally converges**, when $\sum_{}^{\infty} a_n$ diverges.

EXAMPLE 14. Determine whether the series is absolute convergence, conditional convergence or divergence for the series.

① $\sum_{n=1}^{\infty} (-1)^n \dfrac{1}{\sqrt{n}}$

② $\sum_{n=1}^{\infty} (-1)^n \dfrac{n^4}{e^n}$

20. Infinite Series (for BC) 385

③ $\sum_{n=1}^{\infty}(-1)^n \dfrac{1}{\sqrt{2n-1}}$ ④ $\sum_{n=1}^{\infty}(-1)^{n+1}\dfrac{1}{n(\ln n)^2}$

⑤ $\sum_{n=1}^{\infty}(-1)^{n+1}\dfrac{1}{\ln n}$ ⑥ $\sum_{n=1}^{\infty}(-1)^{n+1}\dfrac{1}{n\ln n}$

5. Approximating Alternating Series

The **error**(or **remainder**) occurs if we cut off an alternating series after n terms.

true sum
$$S = -1 + \frac{1}{2} - \frac{1}{3} + \frac{1}{4} - \frac{1}{5} + \frac{1}{6} - \frac{1}{7} + \ldots$$

approximate sum
$$S_5 = -1 + \frac{1}{2} - \frac{1}{3} + \frac{1}{4} - \frac{1}{5}$$

The **error**(or **remainder**) between the true sum and approximation

$S - S_5 = $ ①_____ is always less than or equal to ②____

※ Alternating Series error (remainder)

If an alternating series satisfies the conditions of the 'alternating series test', and Sn is used to approximate the sum, then

error
$$|S - S_n| \leq |a_{n+1}|$$

The error is less than or equal to the first term omitted.

Blank : ① $\frac{1}{6} - \frac{1}{7} + \frac{1}{8} - \ldots$ ② $\frac{1}{6}$

EXAMPLE 15. When $\sum_{n=1}^{\infty} \frac{(-1)^{n+1}}{n!}$ is approximated by the sum of its first 10 terms, find the upper bound for the error.

EXAMPLE 16. When $\sum_{n=1}^{\infty} \left(\frac{-1}{5}\right)^n$ is approximated by the sum of its first 15 terms, find the upper bound for the error.

EXAMPLE 17. Consider the alternating series $\sum_{n=1}^{\infty} \frac{(-1)^{n+1}}{n^2}$. Find the smallest value of n for which the nth partial sum approximates the sum of the series within 0.05.

☺Summary

Infinite Series is the sum of infinite terms that follow a rule.

$\sum\limits^{\infty} a_n$ converge ?? diverge ??

These infinite series could either **converge** or **diverge**.
In this section let's find out whether a given infinite series converge or diverge!
(starting point does not matter!)

Is it alternating in sign?
($\sum\limits^{\infty}(-1)^n a_n$ or $\sum\limits^{\infty}\cos(n\pi)a_n$) — Yes! → If $\lim\limits_{n\to\infty} a_n \to$ ① ___ then "converges!" → If $\sum\limits^{\infty} a_n$ converges, then it converges absolutely. If $\sum\limits^{\infty} a_n$ diverges, then it converges conditionally.

↓ No

Is $\lim\limits_{n\to\infty} a_n \to$ NOT ② ___ ? — Yes! → "Diverges!"

↓ No

Is a_n geometric sequence with $-1 < r < 1$?
($\sum\limits^{\infty} a_n = \sum\limits^{\infty} ar^{n-1}$?) — Yes! → "Converges!" to ③ ___

↓ No

Is it a p-series?
($\sum\limits^{\infty} \dfrac{1}{n^p}$?) — Yes! → When $p > 1$, ④ ___
When $0 < p \leq 1$, ⑤ ___
When $p = 1$, it is called ⑥ ___ series.

↓ No

20. Infinite Series (for BC)

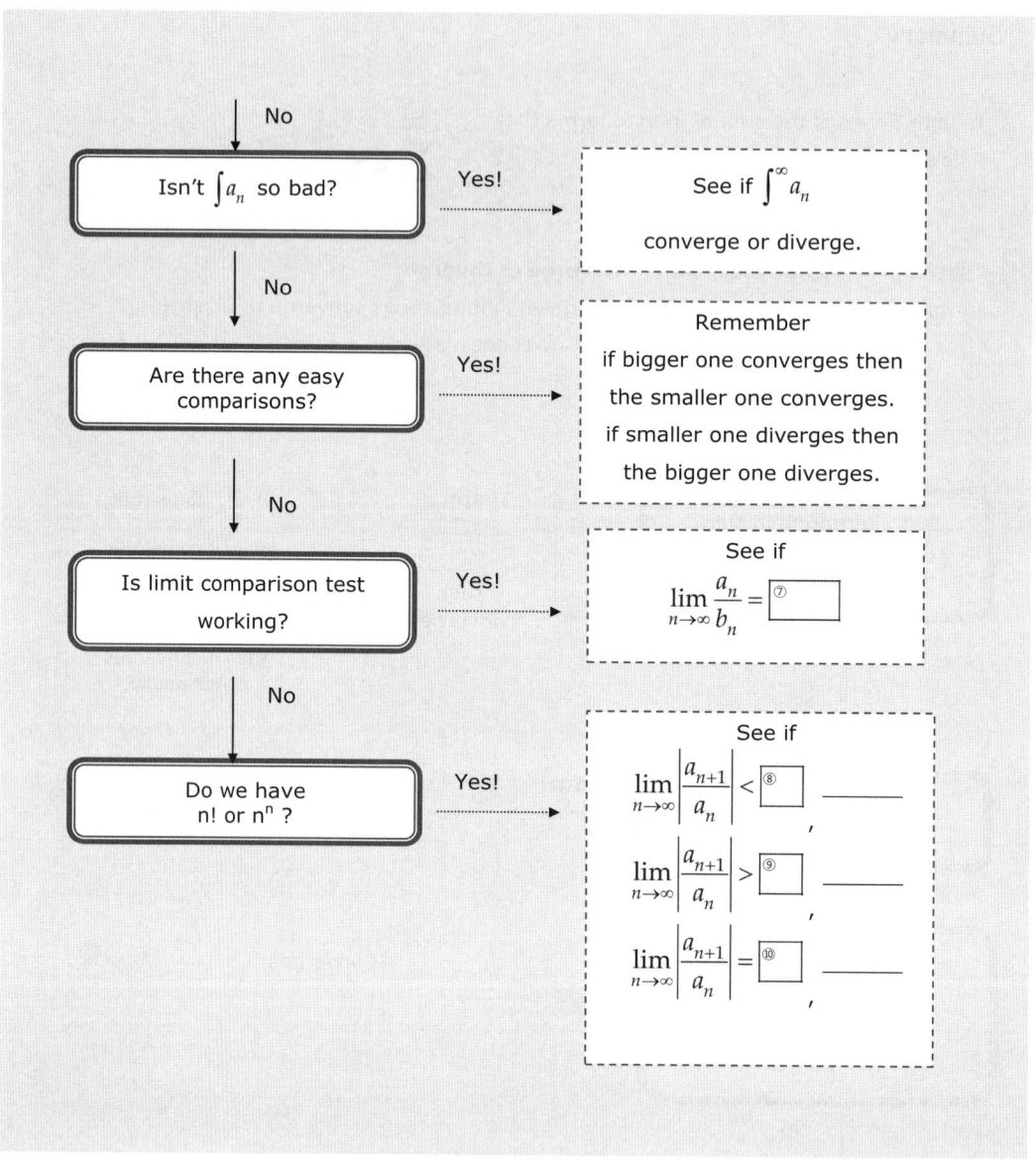

Blank : ① 0   ② 0   ③ $\frac{a}{1-r}$ ④ converge   ⑤ diverge   ⑥ harmonic   ⑦ nonzero positive number (finite)
⑧ 1, converge   ⑨ 1, diverge   ⑩ 1, inconclusive

AP Style Problem

1. Which of the following sequences diverges?

   A) $a_n = \left(\dfrac{2}{3}\right)^n$

   B) $a_n = \dfrac{n^5}{\ln n}$

   C) $a_n = \dfrac{1}{n}$

   D) $a_n = e^{1/n}$

2. Which of the following series converges?

   A) $\displaystyle\sum_{n=1}^{\infty} \dfrac{2n}{3n-5}$

   B) $\displaystyle\sum_{n=1}^{\infty} \dfrac{2n^2}{3n^3+1}$

   C) $\displaystyle\sum_{n=1}^{\infty} \dfrac{2\sqrt{n}}{3n-2}$

   D) $\displaystyle\sum_{n=1}^{\infty} \dfrac{2n}{3n^3-4}$

   E) $\displaystyle\sum_{n=1}^{\infty} \dfrac{2n}{\sqrt{n^2+4}}$

3. Which of the following series converges?

   A) $\displaystyle\sum_{n=1}^{\infty} \dfrac{n!}{10^n}$

   B) $\displaystyle\sum_{n=1}^{\infty} \dfrac{1}{\ln n}$

   C) $\displaystyle\sum_{n=1}^{\infty} \dfrac{2^n}{\ln n}$

   D) $\displaystyle\sum_{n=1}^{\infty} \dfrac{1}{n \ln n}$

   E) $\displaystyle\sum_{n=1}^{\infty} \dfrac{n^{999}}{n!}$

4. Which of the following series does not converges?

A) $\sum_{n=1}^{\infty} \frac{(-1)^{n+1}}{n}$

B) $\sum_{n=1}^{\infty} \frac{\cos n\pi}{\sqrt{n}}$

C) $\sum_{n=1}^{\infty} (-3)^n \frac{1}{2^n}$

D) $\sum_{n=1}^{\infty} (-1)^{n+1} \frac{n}{n^2+1}$

E) $\sum_{n=1}^{\infty} (-1)^{n+1} \frac{(\ln n)^2}{n^2}$

5. Which of the following series diverges?

I. $\frac{1}{\sqrt{2}} - \frac{1}{\sqrt{3}} + \frac{1}{2} - \frac{1}{\sqrt{5}} + \ldots$

II. $\frac{1}{\sqrt{2}} + \frac{1}{\sqrt{3}} + \frac{1}{2} + \frac{1}{\sqrt{5}} + \ldots$

III. $1 - 1.1 + 1.21 - 1.331 + \ldots$

IV. $\frac{1}{2(1)} + \frac{1}{2(2)} + \frac{1}{2(3)} + \frac{1}{2(4)} + \ldots$

A) I, II
B) I, IV
C) I, II, III
D) II, III, IV
E) I, II, III, IV

6. Which of the following series converges according to alternating series test?

   I. $-\dfrac{1}{2}+\dfrac{2}{3}-\dfrac{3}{4}+\dfrac{4}{5}-\dfrac{5}{6}+\ldots$

   II. $1-\dfrac{1}{2}+\dfrac{1}{3}-\dfrac{1}{4}+\dfrac{1}{5}-\dfrac{1}{6}+\ldots$

   III. $1-\dfrac{1}{3}+\dfrac{1}{2}-\dfrac{1}{9}+\dfrac{1}{4}-\dfrac{1}{27}+\dfrac{1}{8}-\dfrac{1}{81}+\ldots$

   A) I B) II
   C) I, II D) II, III E) I, II, III

7. Which of the following series converges conditionally?

   I. $\displaystyle\sum_{n=1}^{\infty}(-1)^{n+1}\dfrac{5+\sqrt{n}}{n}$

   II. $\displaystyle\sum_{n=1}^{\infty}(-1)^{n+1}\dfrac{5+n}{n}$

   III. $\displaystyle\sum_{n=1}^{\infty}(-1)^{n+1}\dfrac{5+n}{n^3}$

   A) I
   B) II
   C) I, II
   D) II, III,
   E) I, II, III

8. Which of the following statements about the series $\sum_{n=1}^{\infty} \frac{\sin n}{n^2}$ is true?

A) $\sum_{n=1}^{\infty} \frac{\sin n}{n^2}$ converges by the comparison test with $\sum_{n=1}^{\infty} \frac{1}{n}$

B) $\sum_{n=1}^{\infty} \frac{\sin n}{n^2}$ diverges by the comparison test with $\sum_{n=1}^{\infty} \frac{1}{n^2}$

C) $\sum_{n=1}^{\infty} \frac{\sin n}{n^2}$ diverges by the comparison test with $\sum_{n=1}^{\infty} \frac{1}{n}$

D) $\sum_{n=1}^{\infty} \frac{\sin n}{n^2}$ converges by the comparison test with $\sum_{n=1}^{\infty} \frac{1}{n^2}$

9. Let a, b are nonzero real number. Find the condition which guarantees that the infinite series $\sum_{n=1}^{\infty} \left(\frac{a}{b}\right)\left(\frac{b}{a}\right)^n$ has a finite sum. And find the sum.

A) $\left|\frac{a}{b}\right| < 1$, $\frac{a^2}{ab - b^2}$

B) $\left|\frac{b}{a}\right| < 1$, $\frac{a^2}{ab - b^2}$

C) $\left|\frac{a}{b}\right| > 1$, $\frac{a}{a - b}$

D) $\left|\frac{b}{a}\right| < 1$, $\frac{a}{a - b}$

E) $\left|\frac{b}{a}\right| > 1$, $\frac{1}{a - b}$

10. What are all values of p for which $\int_1^\infty \frac{1}{n^{p+1}} dx$ and $\sum_{n=1}^\infty \left(\frac{p+1}{2}\right)^n$ converges?

   A) $p > 0$

   B) $p < 0$ or $p > 1$

   C) $p > 1$

   D) $0 < p < 1$

11. Since $f(x) = \frac{1}{\sqrt{x}}$ is a continuous, positive and decreasing for $x > 0$, we can use integral test to determine the divergence of the series. Which of the following inequality is true?

   A) $\sum_{n=1}^\infty \frac{1}{\sqrt{n}} < \int_1^\infty \frac{1}{\sqrt{x}} dx$

   B) $\sum_{n=2}^\infty \frac{1}{\sqrt{n}} < \int_1^\infty \frac{1}{\sqrt{x}} dx$

   C) $\sum_{n=2}^\infty \frac{1}{\sqrt{n}} > \int_1^\infty \frac{1}{\sqrt{x}} dx$

   D) $\sum_{n=1}^\infty \frac{1}{\sqrt{n}} < \sum_{n=2}^\infty \frac{1}{\sqrt{n}}$

12. The infinite series $S = \sum_{n=1}^{\infty}(-1)^{n+1}\dfrac{1}{\sqrt{n}}$ is approximated by the partial sum $P = \sum_{n=1}^{k}(-1)^{n+1}\dfrac{1}{\sqrt{n}}$. Based on the alternating series error bound, what is the smallest value of k for which garantees that $|S-P| < 0.03$?

A) 1110

B) 1111

C) 1112

D) 1113

Mia's AP Calculus

21. Power Series (for BC)

1. Power Series

☺ Reminder

Write the sum using sigma notation, assuming the suggested pattern continues.

$4 + 4^2 + 4^3 + 4^4 + \ldots$ ① _____

$x + x^2 + x^3 + x^4 + \ldots$ ② _____

Now we know that $1 + \dfrac{1}{\sqrt{2}} + \dfrac{1}{\sqrt{3}} + \dfrac{1}{\sqrt{4}} + \ldots = \sum_{n=1}^{\infty} \dfrac{1}{\sqrt{n}}$ ③(converges/diverges).

But what if we have $1 + x + x^2 + x^3 + \ldots = \sum_{n=0}^{\infty}$ ④ $\boxed{}$?

It depends on what x is!

※ Power Series

$$\sum_{n=0}^{\infty} b_n x^n = b_0 + b_1 x + b_2 x^2 + b_3 x^3 + \ldots$$

is called a **power series** and it is centered at 0.

$$\sum_{n=0}^{\infty} b_n (x-c)^n = b_0 + b_1(x-c) + b_2(x-c)^2 + \ldots$$

is called a **power series** and it is centered at C.

Blank : ① $\sum_{n=1}^{\infty} 4^n$ ② $\sum_{n=1}^{\infty} x^n$ ③ diverges   ④ x^n

2. Interval of Convergence

EXAMPLE 1. The geometric series $(2-x)+(2-x)^2+(2-x)^3+\ldots$ converges. What values can x take?

☺ Reminder

> When we have $\sum\limits_{n=1}^{\infty} a_n$
>
> if $\lim\limits_{n\to\infty}\left|\dfrac{a_{n+1}}{a_n}\right| < 1$, then series **converges**.
>
> if $\lim\limits_{n\to\infty}\left|\dfrac{a_{n+1}}{a_n}\right| > 1$, then series **diverges**.
>
> if $\lim\limits_{n\to\infty}\left|\dfrac{a_{n+1}}{a_n}\right| = 1$, it is ①_____.
>
> (absolute value of the ratio btwn consecutive terms)

Blank : ① inconclusive

※ The Convergence Theorem for Power Series

1) Using $\lim\limits_{n \to \infty} \left| \dfrac{a_{n+1}}{a_n} \right| < 1$, we can find that;

power series $\sum\limits_{n=0}^{\infty} a_n = \sum\limits_{n=0}^{\infty} b_n (x-c)^n$ ① _____ when $|x - c| < R$

2) Using $\lim\limits_{n \to \infty} \left| \dfrac{a_{n+1}}{a_n} \right| > 1$, we can find that;

power series $\sum\limits_{n=0}^{\infty} a_n = \sum\limits_{n=0}^{\infty} b_n (x-c)^n$ ② _____ when $|x - c| > R$

3) Using $\lim\limits_{n \to \infty} \left| \dfrac{a_{n+1}}{a_n} \right| = 1$, we can find that;

power series $\sum\limits_{n=0}^{\infty} a_n = \sum\limits_{n=0}^{\infty} b_n (x-c)^n$ may or may not converge when $|x - c| = R$

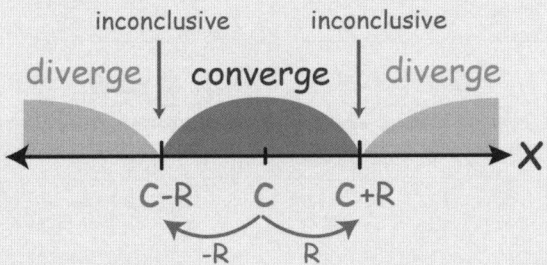

The number R is the **radius of convergence**, and the set of all values of x for which the series converges is the **interval of convergence.**

The convergence at the **endpoints** (where $x = c \pm R$) of the interval of convergence should be tested separately.

Blank : ① converges ② diverges

EXAMPLE 2. Find the radius and the interval of convergence of the power series.

> ☺ Tip : To find the interval of convergence, use $\lim\limits_{n\to\infty} \left|\dfrac{a_{n+1}}{a_n}\right| < 1$ (ratio test) to find $|x-c| < R$.
>
> Test the endpoints separately.

① $\displaystyle\sum_{n=1}^{\infty} \dfrac{(x-2)^n}{4n+2}$

② $\displaystyle\sum_{n=1}^{\infty} \dfrac{x^n}{n^4 2^n}$

③ $\displaystyle\sum_{n=1}^{\infty} \dfrac{(-1)^n (x+1)^n}{3^n}$

④ $\displaystyle\sum_{n=0}^{\infty} \dfrac{(x-2)^n}{n!}$

⑤ $\sum_{n=0}^{\infty} n!(x-1)^n$

⑥ $\sum_{n=1}^{\infty} \frac{(x-3)^n}{(3n)!}$

AP Style Problem

1. The power series $(2x-3) - \frac{(2x-3)^2}{2!} + \frac{(2x-3)^3}{3!} - \frac{(2x-3)^4}{4!} + ...$ diverges

   A) when $x = \frac{3}{2}$ only

   B) when $1 < x \leq 2$

   C) when $x < 1$ or $x \geq 2$

   D) for no real numbers of x

   E) for all real numbers of x

2. The series obtained by differentiating the terms of the series

$$(x-1) + \frac{(x-1)^2}{4} + \frac{(x-1)^3}{9} + \frac{(x-1)^4}{16} + \ldots$$

converges for

A) $0 \leq x < 2$

B) $0 \leq x \leq 2$

C) $0 < x < 2$

C) $1 < x < 3$

D) all real numbers of x

3. Find the radius of convergence of $\sum_{n=1}^{\infty} \frac{(-1)^n (x+1)^n}{2^n}$.

A) 0

B) 1

C) 0.5

D) 2

E) ∞

4. The power series $\sum_{n=0}^{\infty} a_n(x-1)^n$ converges at $x = 4$. Which of the following must be true?

A) $\sum_{n=0}^{\infty} a_n(x-1)^n$ converges at $x = -2$

B) $\sum_{n=0}^{\infty} a_n(x-1)^n$ converges at $x = 3$

C) $\sum_{n=0}^{\infty} a_n(x-1)^n$ diverges at $x = 5$

D) $\sum_{n=0}^{\infty} a_n(x-1)^n$ converges at $x = 6$

Mia's AP Calculus

22. Taylor Series (for BC)

1. Maclaurin Series

We are going to ① _____ a function f(x)

using a polynomial ② _____

starting from x = ③ _____.

We are going to build up a polynomial P(x) so that it looks similar to f(x) around x = 0.

Assume that we know f(0), f'(0), f''(0), f'''(0) ...

We want	Then we can set up P(x) as ...	Does P(x) look like f(x)?
1) ④ _____	$P(x) = f(0)$ Let's check ☞ ⑤	
2) P(0) = f(0) , ⑥ _____	$P(x) = f(0) + f'(0)x$ Let's check ☞ ⑦	

Blank : ① approximate ② P(x) ③ 0 ④ P(0) = f(0) ⑤ let x = 0, then P(0) = f(0) ⑥ P'(0) = f'(0)
⑦ let x = 0, then P(0) = f(0). If we differentiate, then P'(x) = f'(0). let x = 0, then P'(0) = f'(0).

3) $P(0) = f(0)$
, $P'(0) = f'(0)$
, ①

$P(x) = f(0) + f'(0)x + f''(0)\dfrac{1}{2}x^2$

Let's check ☞ ②

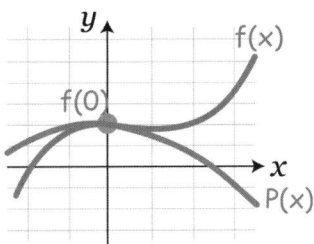

4) $P(0) = f(0)$
, $P'(0) = f'(0)$
, $P''(0) = f''(0)$
③

$P(x) = f(0) + f'(0)x + f''(0)\dfrac{1}{2}x^2$
$\quad + f'''(0)\dfrac{1}{2\cdot 3}x^3$

Let's check ☞ ④

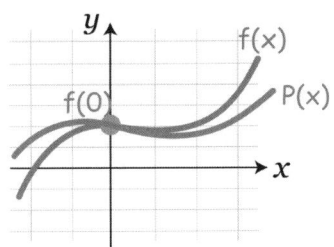

Blank : ① $P''(0) = f''(0)$ ② let x = 0, then P(0) = f(0). If we differentiate, then P'(x) = f'(0) + f''(0)x. let x = 0, then P'(0) = f'(0). If we differentiate, then P''(x) = f''(0). let x = 0, then P''(0) = f''(0).

③ $P'''(0) = f'''(0)$ ④ let x = 0, then P(0) = f(0). If we differentiate, then P'(x) = f'(0) + f''(0)x + f'''(0)1/2x². let x = 0, then P'(0) = f'(0). If we differentiate, then P''(x) = f''(0) + f'''(0)x. let x = 0, then P''(0) = f''(0). If we differentiate, then P'''(x) = f'''(0). let x = 0, then P'''(0) = f'''(0).

If we keep doing this,
(making all the derivatives the same around 0)
we could have better approximation P(x) for f(x)!

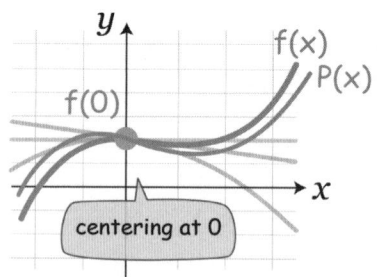

※ Maclaurin Series (centering at 0)

$$f(x) = \underbrace{f(0)}_{\text{centering at 0}} + f'(0)x + f''(0)\frac{x^2}{2!} + f'''(0)\frac{x^3}{3!} + \cdots$$

$$= \sum_{n=0}^{\infty} \boxed{①}$$

EXAMPLE 1. Find the maclaurin series of the function.

① $y = \sin x$

② $y = e^x$

Blank : ① $f^{(n)}(0)\dfrac{x^n}{n!}$

A Taylor Series and Maclaurin Series are an expansion of **a function** into an **infinite sum of terms**, like these ones:

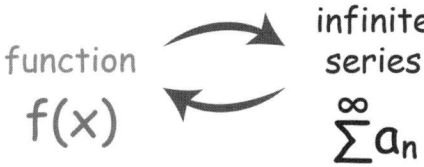

★ Memorize!!

Function	infinite series	General term
$\sin x$	$x - \dfrac{x^3}{3!} + \dfrac{x^5}{5!} - \dfrac{x^7}{7!} + \ldots$	$\displaystyle\sum_{n=0}^{\infty} (-1)^n \dfrac{x^{2n+1}}{(2n+1)!}$
$\cos x$	$1 - \dfrac{x^2}{2!} + \dfrac{x^4}{4!} - \dfrac{x^6}{6!} + \ldots$	$\displaystyle\sum_{n=0}^{\infty} (-1)^n \dfrac{x^{2n}}{(2n)!}$
e^x	$1 + x + \dfrac{x^2}{2!} + \dfrac{x^3}{3!} + \ldots$	$\displaystyle\sum_{n=0}^{\infty} \dfrac{x^n}{n!}$
$\dfrac{1}{1-x}$	$1 + x + x^2 + x^3 + \ldots$	$\displaystyle\sum_{n=0}^{\infty} x^n$
$\tan^{-1} x$	$x - \dfrac{x^3}{3} + \dfrac{x^5}{5} - \dfrac{x^7}{7} + \ldots$	$\displaystyle\sum_{n=0}^{\infty} (-1)^n \dfrac{x^{2n+1}}{2n+1}$

EXAMPLE 2. Find the Maclaurin series for the following functions. Give the first four nonzero terms and the general term.

① $f(x) = \cos\sqrt{x}$

② $f(x) = \sin x^2$

③ $f(x) = \dfrac{\sin x}{x}$

④ $f(x) = \cos^2 x$ (Do not find the general term)

⑤ $f(x) = e^{x^2/2}$

⑥ $f(x) = \dfrac{e^x + e^{-x}}{2}$

⑦ $f(x) = \dfrac{x}{1+x}$

⑧ $f(x) = \dfrac{1}{4+x}$

EXAMPLE 3. Find the Maclaurin series for the *derivative* of the following functions. Give the first three nonzero terms and the general term.

① $f(x) = \dfrac{\cos\sqrt{x}}{x}$

② $f(x) = xe^{x^2}$

③ $f(x) = \dfrac{x^2}{1+x^2}$

EXAMPLE 4. Find a power series that represents $\dfrac{x}{(1-x)^2}$ centered at $x = 0$. Give the first three nonzero terms and the general term.

Hint: what is $\dfrac{d}{dx}\left(\dfrac{1}{1-x}\right)$?

EXAMPLE 5. Find a power series that represents $\ln(1+x)$ centered at $x = 0$. Give the first four nonzero terms and the general term.

Hint: what is $\displaystyle\int_0^x \left(\dfrac{1}{1+t}\right) dt$?

AP Style Problem

1. If $f(x) = 1 + x^2 - \sin x^2$, which of the following is the Maclaurin series?

   A) $1 + \dfrac{x^6}{3!} - \dfrac{x^{10}}{5!} + \ldots$

   B) $1 + 2x^2 - \dfrac{x^6}{3!} \ldots$

   C) $1 + \dfrac{x^3}{3!} - \dfrac{x^5}{5!} + \ldots$

   D) $1 + 2x^2 - \dfrac{x^3}{3!} \ldots$

2. For which function is $\displaystyle\sum_{n=0}^{\infty} \dfrac{(-x)^n}{n!}$ the Taylor series about 0?

   A) e^x

   B) e^{-x}

   C) $\dfrac{1}{1+x}$

   D) $\sin(-x)$

3. If $f(x) = \sin^2 x$, which of the following is the Maclaurin series for f'?

   A) $2 - \dfrac{4}{3}x^2 + \dfrac{4}{15}x^4 + \ldots$

   B) $x^2 - \dfrac{1}{3}x^4 + \dfrac{2}{45}x^6 + \ldots$

   C) $2x - \dfrac{4}{3}x^3 + \dfrac{4}{15}x^5 + \ldots$

   D) $x^2 + \dfrac{1}{3}x^4 + \dfrac{2}{45}x^6 + \ldots$

4. $\int_0^1 e^{t^2} dt =$

A) $2 + \dfrac{1}{2} + \dfrac{1}{6} + \ldots$

B) $1 + \dfrac{1}{2} + \dfrac{1}{4} + \dfrac{1}{6} + \ldots$

C) $1 + \dfrac{1}{3} + \dfrac{1}{10} + \dfrac{1}{42} + \ldots$

D) $1 + \dfrac{1}{3} + \dfrac{1}{5} + \dfrac{1}{7} + \ldots$

5. If $f(x) = e^x(1-x)$, which of the following is the first four nonzero terms of Maclaurin series?

A) $1 - \dfrac{x^2}{2} - \dfrac{x^3}{3} - \dfrac{x^4}{8} + \ldots$

B) $1 + \dfrac{x^2}{2} - \dfrac{x^3}{3} + \dfrac{x^4}{8} + \ldots$

C) $1 + 2x + \dfrac{3x^2}{2} + \dfrac{2x^3}{3} + \ldots$

D) $1 - x + \dfrac{x^2}{2} - \dfrac{x^3}{3} + \ldots$

6. The sum of the series $1+e+\dfrac{e^2}{2!}+\dfrac{e^3}{3!}+\ldots$ is

   A) e^x

   B) e^e

   C) $\dfrac{2}{2-e}$

   D) $\dfrac{e}{2-e}$

7. The Maclaurin series for $\dfrac{1}{1-x}$ is $\sum\limits_{n=0}^{\infty} x^n$. Which of the following is a power series for the derivative of $\dfrac{x^2}{1-x^2}$?

   A) $\sum\limits_{n=0}^{\infty} x^{2n+2}$

   B) $\sum\limits_{n=0}^{\infty} 2nx^{2n-1}$

   C) $\sum\limits_{n=0}^{\infty} 2nx^{2n+1}$

   D) $\sum\limits_{n=0}^{\infty} (2n+2)x^{2n+1}$

   E) $\sum\limits_{n=0}^{\infty} (2n+2)x^{2n-1}$

2. Taylor Series

We are going to ① _____ a function f(x)

using a polynomial ② _____

starting from x = ③ _____ .

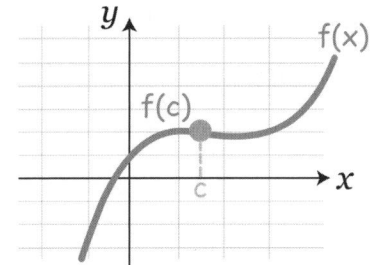

We are going to build up a polynomial P(x) so that it looks similar to f(x) around x = c.

Assume that we know f(c), f'(c), f''(c), f'''(c) ...

We want	Then we can set up P(x) as ...	Does P(x) look like f(x)?
1) ④	$P(x) = f(c)$ Let's check ☞ ⑤	
2) $P(c) = f(c)$, ⑥	$P(x) = f(c) + f'(c)(x - c)$ Let's check ☞ ⑦	

Blank : ① approximate   ② P(x)   ③ c   ④ P(c) = f(c)   ⑤ let x = c, then P(c) = f(c)   ⑥ P'(c) = f'(c)
⑦ let x = c, then P(c) = f(c). If we differentiate, then P'(x) = f'(c). let x = c, then P'(c) = f'(c).

3) $P(c) = f(c)$
, $P'(c) = f'(c)$
, ①

$P(x) = f(c) + f'(c)(x-c)$
$\qquad + f''(c)\frac{1}{2}(x-c)^2$

Let's check ☞ ②

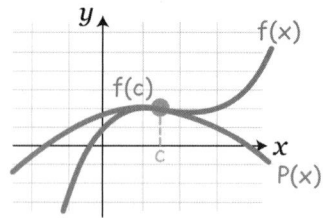

4) $P(c) = f(c)$
, $P'(c) = f'(c)$
, $P''(c) = f''(c)$
, ②

$P(x) = f(c) + f'(c)(x-c)$
$\qquad + f''(c)\frac{1}{2}(x-c)^2$
$\qquad + f'''(c)\frac{1}{2\cdot 3}(x-c)^3$

Let's check ☞ ④

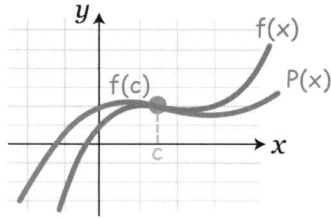

Blank : ① $P''(c) = f''(c)$ ② let x = c, then P(c) = f(c). If we differentiate, then P'(x) = f'(c) + f''(c)(x-c). let x = c, then P'(c) = f'(c). If we differentiate, then P''(x) = f''(c). let x = c, then P''(c) = f''(c).

③ $P'''(c) = f'''(c)$ ④ let x = c, then P(c) = f(c). If we differentiate, then P'(x) = f'(c) + f''(c)(x-c) + f'''(c)1/2(x-c)². let x = c, then P'(c) = f'(c). If we differentiate, then P''(x) = f''(c) + f'''(c)(x-c). let x = c, then P''(c) = f''(c). If we differentiate, then P'''(x) = f'''(c). let x = c, then P'''(c) = f'''(c).

If we keep doing this,
(making all the derivatives the same)
we could have better approximation P(x) for f(x)!

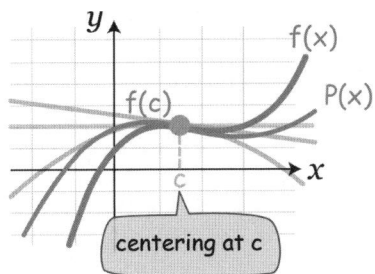

centering at c

※ Taylor Series about c (centering at c)

$$f(x) = f(c) + f'(c)(x-c) + f''(c)\frac{(x-c)^2}{2!} + f'''(c)\frac{(x-c)^3}{3!} + \cdots$$

(centering at c)

$$= \sum_{n=0}^{\infty} \boxed{①}$$

A Maclaurin Series is a Taylor Series where c=0!

An **nth degree Taylor polynomial** (②_____) uses all the Taylor series terms up to and including the term using the ③_____ power.

ex) For $e^x = 1 + x + \frac{x^2}{2!} + \frac{x^3}{3!} + \frac{x^4}{4!} + \cdots$

the 1st degree polynomial ; ④_____

the 3rd degree polynomial ; ⑤_____

first 3 nonzero terms ; ⑥_____

Blank : ① $f^{(n)}(c)\frac{(x-c)^n}{n!}$ ② $P_n(x)$ ③ nth ④ $1+x$ ⑤ $1+x+\frac{x^2}{2!}+\frac{x^3}{3!}$ ⑥ $1+x+\frac{x^2}{2!}$

※ nth degree of Taylor Series about c (centering at c)

$$P_n(x) = f(c) + f'(c)(x-c) + \cdots + f^{(n)}(c)\frac{(x-c)^n}{n!}$$

(until nth)

EXAMPLE 6. Find the 3rd degree taylor polynomial for

① $f(x) = e^{-x}$ centered at $x = 3$.

② $f(x) = x^3$ centered at $x = 4$.

③ $f(x) = \ln x$ generated by $x = 1$.

④ $f(x) = \sin x$ about $x = \pi$.

EXAMPLE 7. Let f be the function given by $f(x) = e^{2x}$, and let $P_3(x)$ be the third-degree Taylor polynomial for f about $x = 1$.

① Find $P_3(x)$.

② Use a third-degree polynomial to approximate the value of $f(1.2)$.

EXAMPLE 8. Let f be a function that has derivatives of all orders for all numbers and $f(2)=1, f'(2)=-2, f''(2)=6$, and $f'''(2)=-6$. Write the third-degree Taylor polynomial for f about $x = 2$ and use it to approximate $f(2.1)$.

EXAMPLE 9. The nth derivative of f at $x = 3$ is given by $f^{(n)}(3) = \dfrac{(-1)^n(n-1)!}{(n+2)}$ and $f(3)=2$.

Write the third-degree Taylor polynomial for f about $x = 3$.

EXAMPLE 10. Let $P(x) = 2 + 3(x-1) - (x-1)^2 - 2(x-1)^3 + 5(x-1)^4$ be the fourth-degree Taylor polynomial for the function f about x = 1.

① Find $f'''(1)$.

② Write the third-degree polynomial for f' about 1. Use it to approximate $f'(1.2)$.

③ Write the third-degree Taylor polynomial for $g(x) = \int_1^x f(t)\,dt$ about 1.

EXAMPLE 11. $f(0)=3,\ f'(0)=1,\ f''(0)=-1,\ f'''(0)=2$

① Write the third degree Taylor polynomial for f about $x = 0$ and use it to approximate $f(0.1)$.

② Write the third degree Taylor polynomial for g, where $g(x) = \int_0^x f(t)\,dt$ about $x = 0$.

③ Write the fourth-degree Taylor polynomial for $h = f(x^2)$ about $x = 0$.

④ From ③, find $h'(0)$ and $h''(0)$. Use it to explain why h must have a relative minimum at $x = 0$.

3. The Lagrange Error of a Taylor Polynomial

☺ Reminder:

true sum
$$S = -1 + \frac{1}{2} - \frac{1}{3} + \frac{1}{4} - \frac{1}{5} + \frac{1}{6} - \frac{1}{7} + \ldots$$

approximate sum
$$S_5 = -1 + \frac{1}{2} - \frac{1}{3} + \frac{1}{4} - \frac{1}{5}$$

$|S - S_5|$ is always less than ①____.

We know that the taylor series for $y = e^x$ centered at $x = 0$ is

$$\underbrace{f(x)}_{e^x} = 1 + x + \frac{x^2}{2!} + \frac{x^3}{3!} + \cdots$$

So we can say that e^3 is

$$\underbrace{f(3)}_{e^3} = 1 + 3 + \frac{3^2}{2!} + \frac{3^3}{3!} + \cdots + \frac{3^9}{9!} + \frac{3^{10}}{10!} + \frac{3^{11}}{11!} + \cdots$$

What will happen if we sum up **only up to 9th degree**?

$$P_9(3) = 1 + 3 + \frac{3^2}{2!} + \frac{3^3}{3!} + \cdots + \frac{3^9}{9!}$$

Then there will be an error② _____.

Blank : ① $\frac{1}{6}$ ② $|f(3) - P_9(3)|$

※ **Lagrange Error Bound (Lagrange Error Theorem)**

If a function f is differentiable through order $n + 1$ and Taylor series for f is expanded about c as;

$$f(x) = \underbrace{f(c) + f'(c)(x-c) + f''(c)\frac{(x-c)^2}{2!} + \cdots + f^{(n)}(c)\frac{(x-c)^n}{n!}}_{P_n(x)} + R_n(x)$$

then there exists **z** (between x and c) such that

$$|R_n(x)| = \underbrace{|f(x) - P_n(x)|}_{\text{true} \quad \text{approximated}} \leq \left| \underbrace{\text{Max } f^{(n+1)}(z)}_{x \leq z \leq c} \cdot \frac{(x-c)^{n+1}}{(n+1)!} \right|$$

Maximum value of $f^{(n+1)}$ between x and c

given x-value / centered value

c is where the equation is centered,
x is the value you evaluate.

This gives us a maximum bound of the error, not exact error.

So according to 'Lagrange Error Bound' the maximum error between

$$\boxed{e^3} \\ f(3) = 1 + 3 + \frac{3^2}{2!} + \frac{3^3}{3!} + \cdots + \frac{3^9}{9!} + \frac{3^{10}}{10!} + \frac{3^{11}}{11!} + \cdots$$

and

$$P_9(3) = 1 + 3 + \frac{3^2}{2!} + \frac{3^3}{3!} + \cdots + \frac{3^9}{9!}$$

will be ①_____

Blank : ① $\underset{0 \leq z \leq 3}{\text{Max }} f^{(10)}(z) \frac{(3-0)^{10}}{10!} = e^3 \frac{3^{10}}{10!}$ (evaluating value $x = 3$, center value $c = 0$.)

EXAMPLE 12. Find the Lagrange error bound when using the 3rd Maclaurin polynomial for function $f(x) = e^{2x}$ to approximate the value $f(0.2)$. Round your answer to five decimal places.

EXAMPLE 13. Find the Lagrange error bound when using the 2nd Taylor polynomial of the function $f(x) = \sqrt{x}$ centered at x = 4 to approximate the value $\sqrt{5}$. Round your answer to five decimal places.

EXAMPLE 14. Let $f(x) = \sin(x)$ and let P(x) be the 4th degree Taylor polynomial for f about x = 1. Use the Lagrange error bound to show that $\left| f\left(\frac{4}{5}\right) - P\left(\frac{4}{5}\right) \right| < \frac{1}{10^5}$.

EXAMPLE 15. Select values of f and its first 4 derivatives are given in the table. The $f'''(x)$ and $f^{(4)}(x)$ are decreasing on the interval $3 < x < 4$.

x	$f(x)$	$f'(x)$	$f''(x)$	$f'''(x)$	$f^{(4)}(x)$
3	2	2	4	3	2
4	5	3	5	2	1

① Write a third degree Taylor Polynomial P(x) for f about 3 and use it to approximate f(3.1).

② Use the Lagrange error bound to show that $\left| f(3.1) - P(3.1) \right| < \frac{1}{10^4}$.

AP Style Problem

1. The third degree Taylor polynomial at $x = \dfrac{\pi}{4}$ for $f(x) = \cos x$ is

   A) $\dfrac{\sqrt{2}}{2}\left[1 - \left(x - \dfrac{\pi}{4}\right) - \dfrac{1}{2}\left(x - \dfrac{\pi}{4}\right)^2 + \dfrac{1}{6}\left(x - \dfrac{\pi}{4}\right)^3\right]$

   B) $\dfrac{\sqrt{2}}{2}\left[1 - \left(x - \dfrac{\pi}{4}\right) - \dfrac{1}{2}\left(x - \dfrac{\pi}{4}\right)^2 + \dfrac{1}{3}\left(x - \dfrac{\pi}{4}\right)^3\right]$

   C) $\dfrac{\sqrt{2}}{2}\left[1 + \left(x - \dfrac{\pi}{4}\right) + \dfrac{1}{2}\left(x - \dfrac{\pi}{4}\right)^2 + \dfrac{1}{6}\left(x - \dfrac{\pi}{4}\right)^3\right]$

   D) $1 - \dfrac{1}{2}\left(x - \dfrac{\pi}{4}\right)^2$

2. The coefficient of x^2 in the Taylor series for the function $\ln(x+1)$ about $x = 0$ is

   A) -2

   B) 2

   C) $\dfrac{1}{2}$

   D) $-\dfrac{1}{2}$

3. The Taylor polynomial for the function f about $x = -2$ is given by

$$f(x) = -\frac{(x+2)^2}{2} + \frac{(x+2)^3}{2^2} - \frac{(x+2)^4}{2^3} + \ldots + (-1)^n \frac{(x+2)^{n+1}}{2^n} + \ldots \quad .$$

What is the value of $f^{(50)}(-2) =$

A) $\dfrac{50!}{2^{50}}$

B) $-\dfrac{50!}{2^{50}}$

C) $\dfrac{50!}{2^{49}}$

D) $-\dfrac{50!}{2^{49}}$

4. Let g be a function for which all derivatives exist at $x = 1$. If $g(1) = g'(1) = g''(1) = g'''(1) = 6$, use the second degree polynomial of $g'(x)$ about $x = 1$ to approximate $g'(2)$.

A) 13
B) 14
C) 15
D) 16

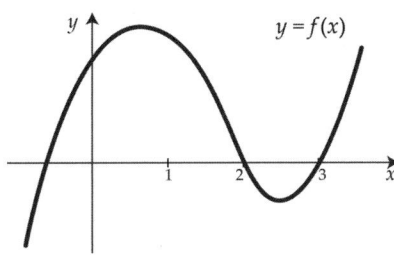

5. The graph of f is shown above. Which of the following could be the Taylor series for f about $x = 2$?

   A) $2+(x-2)+(x-2)^2+\ldots$

   B) $2+(x-2)-(x-2)^2+\ldots$

   C) $2-(x-2)-(x-2)^2+\ldots$

   D) $(x-2)+(x-2)^2+\ldots$

   E) $-(x-2)+(x-2)^2+\ldots$

6. Which of the following could be the 13th degree Taylor polynomial for $y=\sin x$ about $x = 0$?

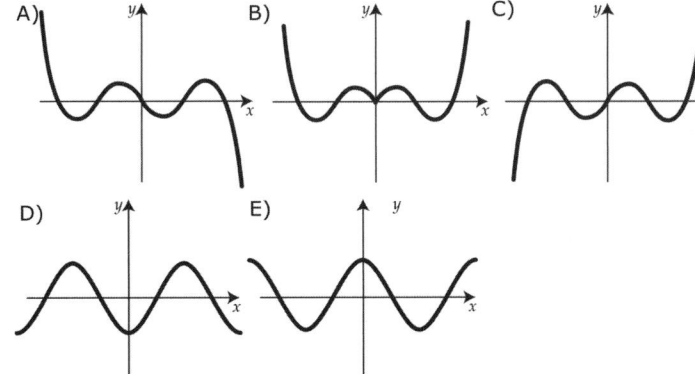

7. Let $P_{10}(x)$ be the tenth-degree Taylor polynomial for f about $x = 0$. The graph of $y = f^{(11)}(x)$ shown above. Which of the following is the smallest value of k for which the Lagrange error bound guarantees that $\left| f\left(\frac{1}{2}\right) - P_{10}\left(\frac{1}{2}\right) \right| \leq k$?

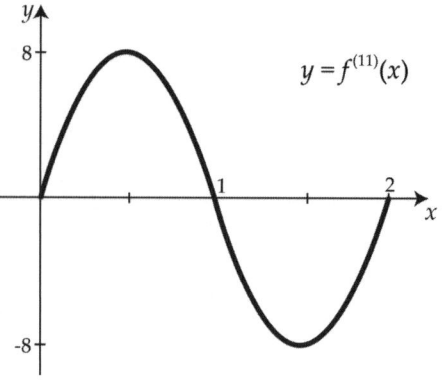

A) $\dfrac{1}{2^8 \cdot 10!}$

B) $\dfrac{1}{2^{10} \cdot 10!}$

C) $\dfrac{1}{2^8 \cdot 11!}$

D) $\dfrac{1}{2^{11} \cdot 11!}$

Mia's AP Calculus

23. Parametric Equation (for BC)

1. Parametric Equation (Precal review)

A **parametric equation** is where the x and y coordinates are both written in terms of another letter.

$$x = f(t), \quad y = g(t)$$

That another letter (usually given the letter t or θ) is called a ①_____.

Finding the Cartesian equation
: Try to eliminate the parameter t or θ by using

②_____ or ③_____.

EXAMPLE 1. Identify the graph of the parametric curve

① $x = 1 - 2t, \quad y = 2 - t$

② $x = 3t, \quad y = t^2 - 2$

③ $x = 2\cos\theta, \quad y = 3\sin\theta, \quad 0 \le \theta \le 2\pi$

④ $x = \sec\theta, \quad y = \tan\theta, \quad 0 \le \theta \le 2\pi$

Blank : ① parameter ② substitution ③ trig identities

If we want to graph $x = t^2 - 2t$, $y = t + 2$;

t	x	y
-2	8	0
-1	①	
0	②	
1	-1	3
2	0	4
3	3	5

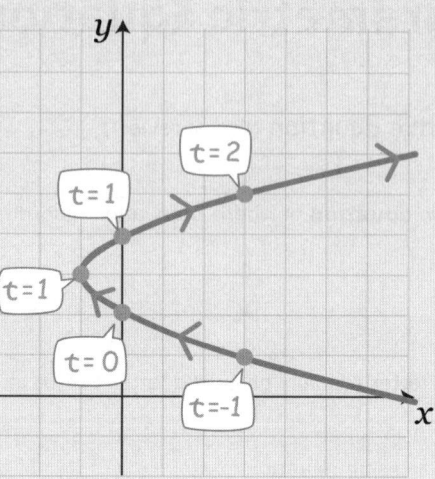

EXAMPLE 2. Sketch the parametric function indicating the orientation.

① $x = 3t + 2, y = t + 1;\ 0 \le t \le 4$

② $x = t - 3,\ y = 2t^2 + 4,\ t \ge -2$

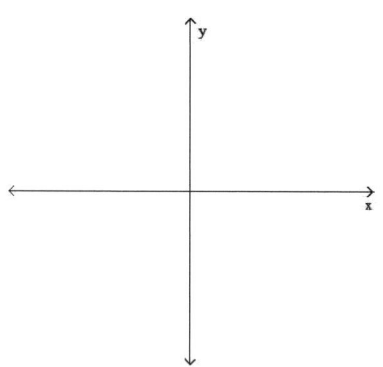
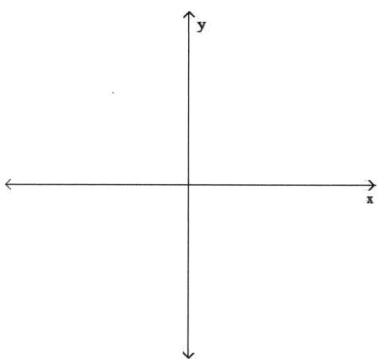

Blank : ① (3, 1) ② (0, 2)

③ $x = 2\cos t,\ y = 3\sin t;\ 0 \le t \le 2\pi$ ④ $x = 2\sin t,\ y = \cos t;\ 0 \le t \le \dfrac{\pi}{2}$

2. Derivative of Parametric Curve

If we have a parametric equation $x = f(t),\ y = g(t)$

the first derivative will be:

$$\dfrac{dy}{dx} = \dfrac{\dfrac{dy}{\boxed{①}}}{\dfrac{dx}{\boxed{②}}} = \dfrac{\dfrac{dy}{dt}}{\dfrac{dx}{dt}}$$

the second derivative will be:

$$\dfrac{d^2y}{dx^2} = \dfrac{d}{dx}\left(\dfrac{\boxed{③}}{\boxed{④}}\right) = \dfrac{d\left(\dfrac{dy}{dx}\right)}{dx} = \dfrac{\dfrac{d}{\boxed{⑤}}\left(\dfrac{dy}{dx}\right)}{\dfrac{dx}{\boxed{⑥}}} = \dfrac{\dfrac{d}{dt}\left(\dfrac{dy}{dx}\right)}{\dfrac{dx}{dt}}$$

Blank : ① dt ② dt ③ dy ④ dx ⑤ dt ⑥ dt

※ The derivative of Parametric Function

$$\frac{dy}{dx} = \frac{dy/dt}{dx/dt} \qquad \frac{d^2y}{dx^2} = \frac{\frac{d}{dt}\left(\frac{dy}{dx}\right)}{\frac{dx}{dt}}$$

EXAMPLE 3. Find $\dfrac{dy}{dx}$ and $\dfrac{d^2y}{dx^2}$ in terms of t.

① $x = \sqrt{t},\ y = t^2$

② $x = 4\sin t,\ y = -2\cos t$

③ $x = \ln(7t),\ y = e^{7t}$

EXAMPLE 4. Find the equation of the tangent to $x = \cos t$, $y = 2\sin^2 t$ at the point where $t = \dfrac{\pi}{3}$.

EXAMPLE 5. A curve is given by $x = \sqrt{t}$ and $y = \dfrac{t^2 - 4}{4}$ $(t \geq 0)$. Find the slope and concavity at the point (2, 3).

EXAMPLE 6. The curve C is given by the parametric equations $x = t^3 - 3t^2, y = t^2 - 8t$.

① Find $\dfrac{dy}{dx}$ in terms t.

② Find the point at which the curve C has a horizontal tangent.

③ Find the point at which the curve C has a vertical tangent.

3. Vectors (Precal review)

A **vector** has ①_____ (how long it is)

and ②_____ :

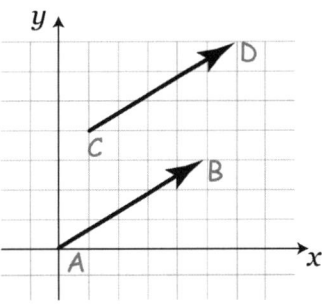

The length of the line shows its ③_____

and the arrowhead points in the **direction**.

We can write the vector is as ④_____.

1) Equivalent vectors

Equivalent vectors :
two vectors that have **equal length** and the **same direction**.

2) Vectors Notation (Component form)

If a vector has an arrow from the ⑤_____ through out to a point (x, y), then we can write the vector as $\vec{v}$ = **v** = ⑥_____.

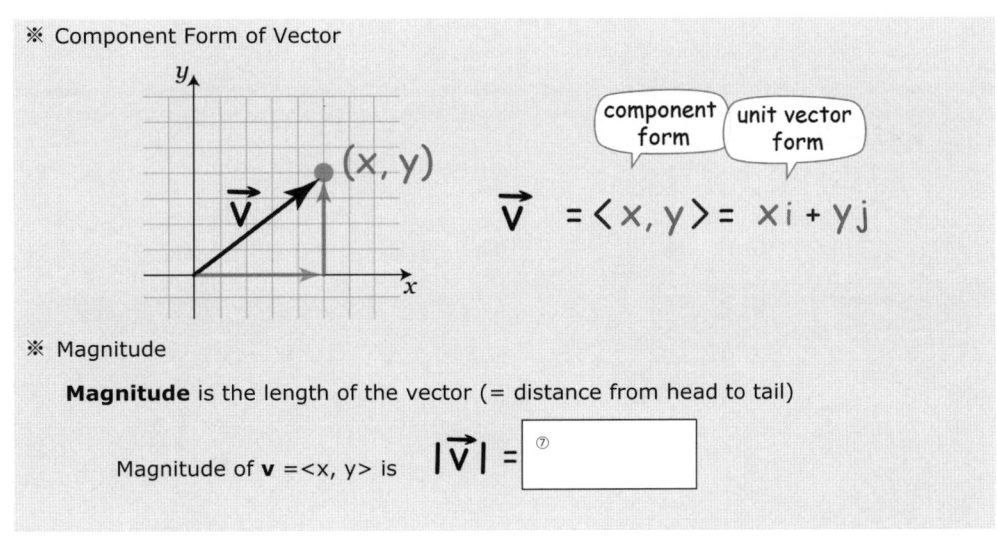

※ Component Form of Vector

$\vec{v} = \langle x, y \rangle = xi + yj$

※ Magnitude

Magnitude is the length of the vector (= distance from head to tail)

Magnitude of **v** =<x, y> is $|\vec{v}|$ = ⑦□

Blank : ① magnitude ② direction ③ magnitude ④ $\vec{v}$ or **v** ⑤ origin ⑥ <x, y> ⑦ $\sqrt{x^2 + y^2}$

EXAMPLE 7. Write the illustrated vectors in component form and in unit vector form. Find the magnitude of the vector.

① vector **a**

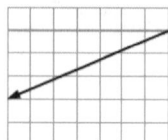

② vector **b**

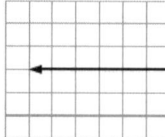

③ vector **c**

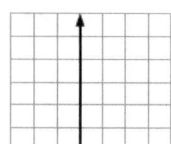

④ vector **d**

EXAMPLE 8. Find the magnitude of the given vector.

① **a** = <-1, 5>

② $-3i + j$

③ **v** = $2i + 2j$

3. Parametric Curve and Velocity Vector

※ Velocity and Acceleration Vector

Suppose a particle moves along a smooth curve in the plane so that its position at any time t is (x(t), y(t)), where x and y are differentiable functions of t.

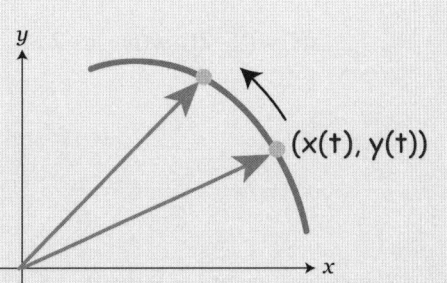

position vector $R(t) = \langle x(t), y(t) \rangle$

velocity vector $v(t) = \langle x'(t), y'(t) \rangle$

acceleration vector $a(t) = \langle x''(t), y''(t) \rangle$

The particle's **speed** is the ①_____ of velocity vector,

which is **speed** $|v| = \sqrt{(x'(t))^2 + (y'(t))^2}$

(Speed is a scalar, not a vector.)

Blank : ① magnitude

An ice skater Yuna is gliding around on a frozen coordinate plane. At time t (in seconds) Yuna's position on the coordinate plane is given by $(x(t), y(t))$ where

$$x(t) = t^2 - 2t, \quad y(t) = t + 2.$$

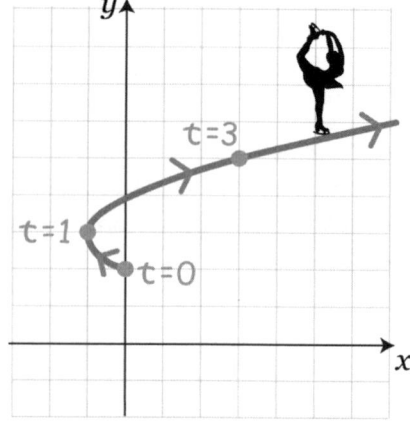

What is Yuna's position at $t = 0$, $t = 1$, $t = 3$?

What is Yuna's velocity vector at $t = 0$, $t = 1$, $t = 3$?

What is Yuna's acceleration vector at $t = 0$, $t = 1$, $t = 3$?

EXAMPLE 9. A particle travels in the plane with position vector $r(t)$. Find the velocity vector $v(t)$ and acceleration vector $a(t)$. Find the particle's velocity vector, acceleration vector, speed at the given value of t.

① $r(t) = \left\langle 4t^2 - 2, \dfrac{t^3}{3} \right\rangle$, $t = 1$

② $r(t) = \langle \cos 5t, 3\sin t \rangle$, $t = \dfrac{\pi}{2}$

EXAMPLE 10. A particle moves according to the equations $x = 2\cos t$, $y = 4\sin t$.

① Find a single equation in x and y for the path of the particle and sketch the curve.

② Find the velocity and acceleration vectors at any time t.

③ Find the velocity vector and acceleration vector when (i) $t = \dfrac{\pi}{6}$, (ii) $t = \pi$, and draw them on the sketch.

④ Is the particle moving to the left or to the right when $t = \dfrac{\pi}{6}$? Is the particle moving up or down when $t = \dfrac{\pi}{6}$? Justify each answer.

⑤ Find the speed of the particle at $t = \dfrac{\pi}{6}$.

EXAMPLE 11. A particle moves in the xy-plane with position vector $x(t)$, $y(t)$ such that
$x(t) = t^3 - 6t^2 + 9t + 2$ and $y(t) = -t^2 + 2t$ in the time interval $0 \le t \le 5$.

① Find the velocity vector of the particle at $t = 5$.

② Is the particle moving to the left or to the right when $t = 5$? Is the particle moving up or down when $t = 5$? Justify each answer.

③ Find the equation of the tangent line to the path of the particle when $t = 5$.

④ At what time is the particle at rest?

⑤ Find the acceleration vector at the time when the particle is at rest.

⑥ How fast is the particle moving when $t = 5$?

4. Parametric Curve and Integration

☺ Reminder: Given v(t), what is

the displacement from a to b? ① _____

the total distance traveled from a to b? ② _____

the position at b? ③ _____

Suppose a particle moves along a path in the plane so that its velocity at any time t is [velocity vector] $v(t) = \langle x'(t), y'(t) \rangle$

, then the **displacement** from $t = a$ to $t = b$ is given by the vector

[displacement] $\left\langle \int_a^b x'(t)\,dt , \quad \boxed{④} \right\rangle$

The **distance traveled** from $t = a$ to $t = b$ is

[total distance] $\int_a^b \boxed{⑤}\,dt = \int_a^b \sqrt{(x'(t))^2 + (y'(t))^2}\,dt$

The **position** at $t = b$ is (Future position = Initial position + displacement)

[position of x] $x(b) = x(a) + \int_a^b x'(t)\,dt$

[position of y] $y(b) = \boxed{⑥}$

Blank: ① $\int_a^b v\,dt$ ② $\int_a^b |v|\,dt$ ③ $s(b) = s(a) + \int_a^b v\,dt$ ④ $\int_a^b y'(t)\,dt$ ⑤ $|v|$ ⑥ $y(a) + \int_a^b y'(t)\,dt$

EXAMPLE 12. The velocity $v(t)$ of a particle moving in the plane is given, along with the position of the particle at time $t = 0$. Find;

(a) the position of the particle at time $t = 3$, and

(b) the distance the particle travels from $t = 0$ to $t = 3$.

① $v(t) = \langle 3t^2 - t, \cos \pi t \rangle$, initial position (1, 2)

② $v(t) = \langle e^t - t, e^t + t \rangle$, initial position (1, 3)

EXAMPLE 13. An object moving along a curve in the xy-plane has position $< x(t), y(t) >$ at time t with $\dfrac{dx}{dt} = t^2 - 2t$, $\dfrac{dy}{dt} = t^3$ for $0 \leq t \leq 3$. At time $t = 1$, the object is at position (4, 5).

① Write an equation for the line tangent to the curve at (4, 5).

② Is the particle moving to the left or to the right when $t = 1$? Is the particle moving up or down when $t = 1$? Justify each answer.

③ Find the speed of the object at time $t = 1$.

④ Find the displacement of the object over the time interval $0 \leq t \leq 1$.

⑤ Find the total distance traveled by the object over the time interval $0 \leq t \leq 1$. Set up the integral, do not evaluate.

⑥ Find the position of the object at time $t = 0$.

5. Curve Length of Parametric

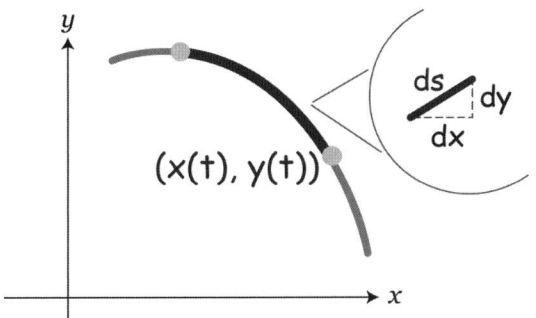

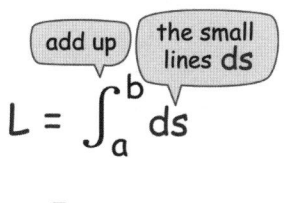

We can break up to small segments, and add up all the ds'.

add up the small lines ds

$$L = \int_a^b ds$$

$$= ①\underline{\qquad\qquad}$$

※ **Curve Length of Parametric Function**

If a smooth curve C is given by $x = f(t)$ and $y = g(t)$, then the curve length over the interval $a \le t \le b$ is

$$L = \int_a^b \sqrt{\left(\frac{dx}{dt}\right)^2 + \left(\frac{dy}{dt}\right)^2}\, dt$$

Same with 'total distance' formula!

EXAMPLE 14. Find the length of the curve. Set up the integral, do not evaluate.

① $x = \sin t,\ y = \cos t,\ [0, \pi]$

Blank : ① $\int_a^b \sqrt{dx^2 + dy^2} = \int_a^b \sqrt{\frac{dx^2}{dt^2} + \frac{dy^2}{dt^2}}\, dt$

② $x = t^2$, $y = 2t$, $[0,2]$

③ $x = e^{-t}\cos t$, $y = e^{-t}\sin t$, $[0, \pi/2]$

AP Style Problem

1. If $x = -t^2 + 2$, $y = t^3 - 1$, then, when $t = 1$, what is $\dfrac{d^2y}{dx^2}$?

   A) $\dfrac{3}{4t}$

   B) $\dfrac{3}{4}$

   C) 0

   D) $\dfrac{3}{t}$

2. $\left\langle 3\sin\frac{\pi}{4}t,\ 2\cos\frac{\pi}{4}t+1 \right\rangle$ is the position vector $\langle x, y \rangle$ from the origin to a moving point (x, y) at time t.

1) The slope of the curve along the particle moves when $t = 2$ is

   A) does not exist
   B) 0
   C) 1
   D) -1

2) What is the speed of the particle when $t = 4$

   A) $\dfrac{\pi}{2}$

   B) $\dfrac{3\pi}{4}$

   C) $\dfrac{3}{4}$

   D) $\dfrac{1}{2}$

3) How far does it travel during $0 \le t \le 4$?

   A) $\displaystyle\int_0^4 \sqrt{\frac{9\pi^2}{16}\cos^2\left(\frac{\pi}{4}t\right)+\frac{\pi^2}{4}\sin^2\left(\frac{\pi}{4}t\right)}\ dt$

   B) $\displaystyle\int_0^4 \sqrt{\frac{3\pi}{4}\cos^2\left(\frac{\pi}{4}t\right)+\frac{\pi}{2}\sin^2\left(\frac{\pi}{4}t\right)}\ dt$

   C) $\displaystyle\int_0^4 \sqrt{9\sin^2\left(\frac{\pi}{4}t\right)+4\cos^2\left(\frac{\pi}{4}t\right)}\ dt$

   D) $\displaystyle\int_0^4 \sqrt{3\sin^2\left(\frac{\pi}{4}t\right)+2\cos^2\left(\frac{\pi}{4}t\right)}\ dt$

3. The object moves in the xy plane with position vector $\langle x,y \rangle = \langle 4t^3 - 6t^2, 2t^2 - 4t \rangle$. Find where the particle is at rest.

A) (1, 0)

B) (-2, -2)

C) (0, 0)

D) (2, 0)

4. An object moves along the line $y = 2x + 4$ for $0 \leq t \leq 3$, with the horizontal velocity given by $\frac{dy}{dt} = 4t^2 - 2$. What is the speed of the object at $t = 1$?

A) $\sqrt{5}$

B) $\sqrt{2}$

C) 4

D) 1

5. A particle, initially at rest, moves with an acceleration vector $a(t) = \langle 3t^2, e^{-t} \rangle$. If the initial position is (2, 1), then what is the position of the particle when $t = 4$?

A) $\left(68, e^{-4} + 1\right)$

B) $\left(66, e^{-4} + 4\right)$

C) $\left(11, e^{-3} + 3\right)$

D) $\left(68, e^{-3} + 3\right)$

Mia's AP Calculus
24. Polar Equation (for BC)

1. Polar Coordinates (Precal Review)

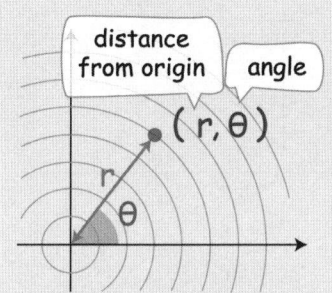

Polar Coordinate is a way to pinpoint where you are on a map or graph by **how far away**, and at **what angle** the point is.

※ Converting Cartesian ↔ Polar

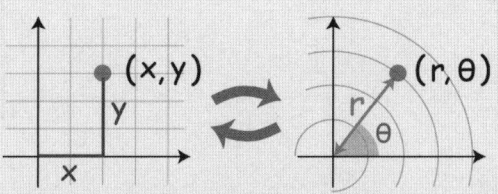

($-r$, θ) is the reflection over the origin of (r, θ)

※ Formulas for Polar Coordinates

$$r = \sqrt{x^2 + y^2} \qquad \theta = \tan^{-1}\left(\frac{y}{x}\right)$$

$$y = r \times \sin\theta \qquad x = r \times \cos\theta$$

EXAMPLE 1. Plot the point having the given polar coordinates.

① $\left(4, 225°\right)$

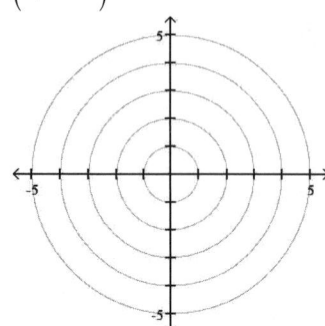

② $\left(-2, -330°\right)$

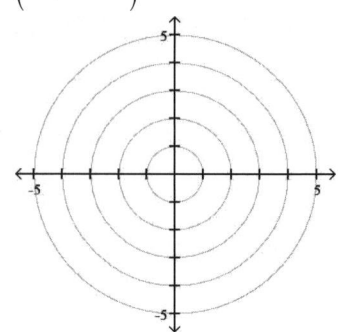

③ $\left(3, \dfrac{7\pi}{4}\right)$

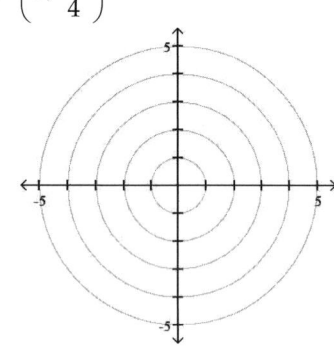

④ $\left(2, -\dfrac{5\pi}{4}\right)$

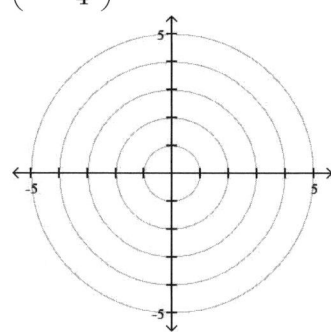

⑤ $\left(-1, -\dfrac{7\pi}{4}\right)$

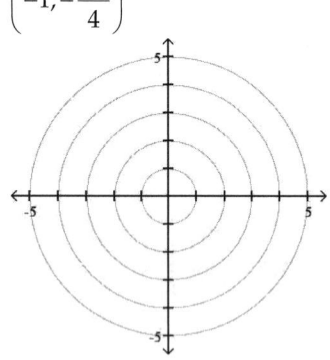

⑥ $\left(-2, -\dfrac{5\pi}{3}\right)$

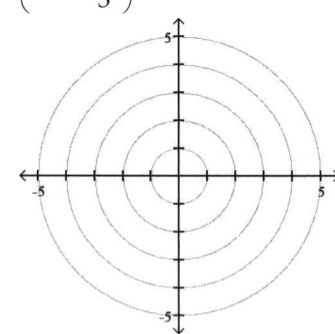

EXAMPLE 2. Convert the given polar coordinates of the point to rectangular coordinates.

① $\left(-6, 225°\right)$

② $\left(-7, \dfrac{5\pi}{3}\right)$

EXAMPLE 3. Convert the rectangular coordinates of the point to polar coordinates (r, θ) with r > 0 and $0 \leq \theta < 2\pi$.

① $\left(6, -6\sqrt{3}\right)$

② $(-1, 1)$

EXAMPLE 4. Find an equivalent equation in rectangular coordinates.

① $r(\cos\theta - \sin\theta) = 3$

② $r = 10\sin\theta$

③ $r = \dfrac{2}{4\sin\theta + 5\cos\theta}$

EXAMPLE 5. Find an equivalent equation in polar coordinates.

① $y = 7$ ② $x + y = 3$

③ $x^2 + y^2 = 4$

2. Polar Curve (Precal Review)

A **polar equation** is a curve with an equation of the form $r = f(\theta)$.

Examples:

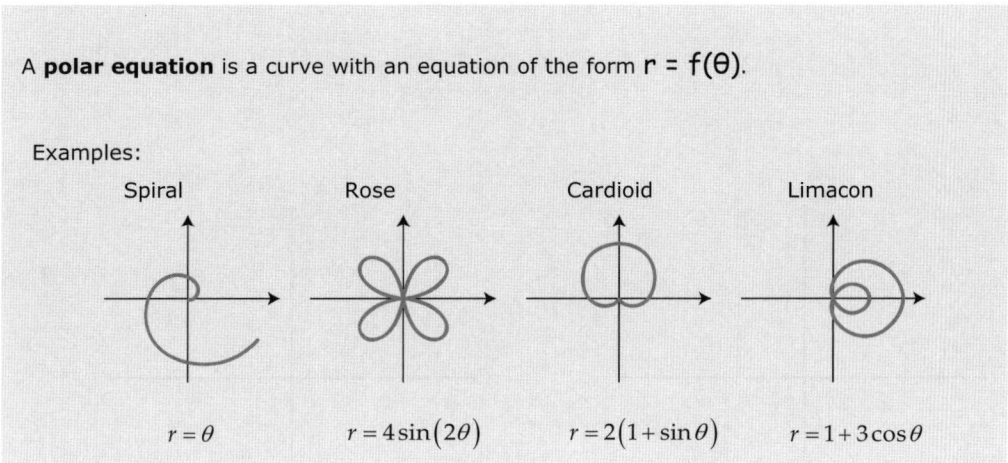

    Spiral   Rose   Cardioid   Limacon

$r = \theta$ $r = 4\sin(2\theta)$ $r = 2(1+\sin\theta)$ $r = 1+3\cos\theta$

EXAMPLE 6.   Graph in the polar system.

① $r = 1 + \cos\theta$ ② $r = 2 - \sin\theta$

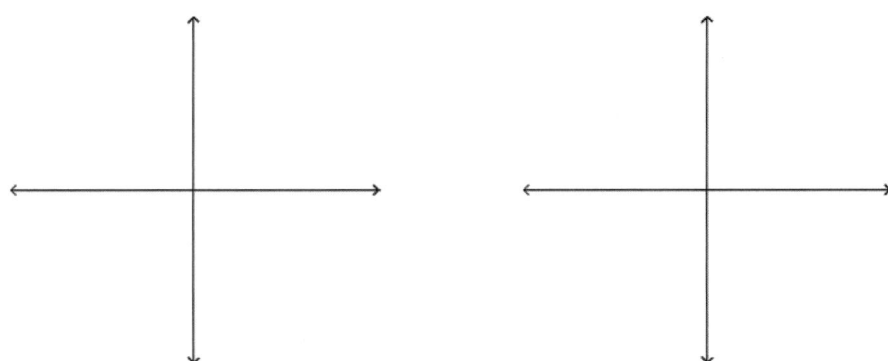

③ $r = 2 - 3\sin\theta$ ④ $r = 2$

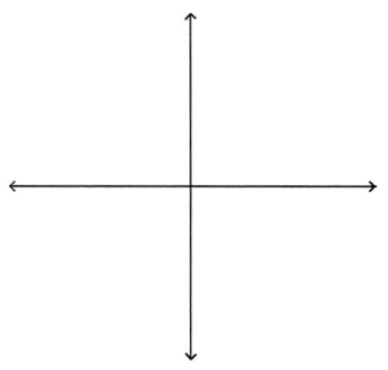 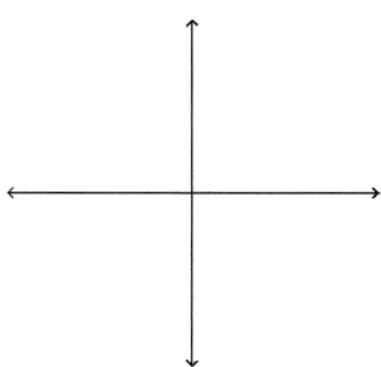

⑤ $r = 3\cos 2\theta$ ⑥ $r = 5\sin 3\theta$

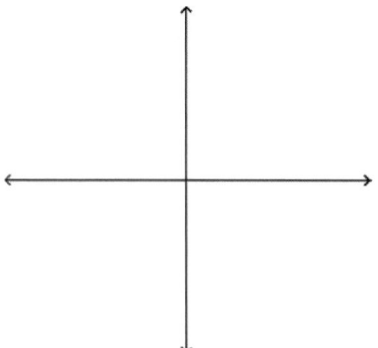 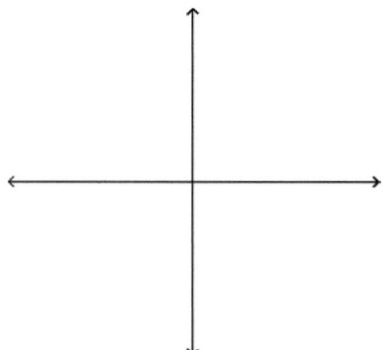

⑦ $r^2 = 9\sin(2\theta)$ ⑧ $r = 4\sin\theta$

* Polar Curve All in All (a, b is a constant)

If it is r = f(sin θ), then it is symmetric over line $\theta = \dfrac{\pi}{2}$ (y-axis).

If it is r = f(cos θ), then it is symmetric over polar axis(x-axis).

Shape	Equation	Notes	
Line	θ = a		
Circle	r = a	radius is **a**	
	r = a cos θ	diameter is **a**	

Rose	$r = a \cos n\theta$	If n is even, we have **2n** patals.	
		If n is odd, we have **n** patals.	
Cardiod or Limacon	$r = a \pm b \cos \theta$	If a > b, then Dimpled Limacon	
		If a = b, then Cardioid	
		If a < b, then Limacon with loop	
Lemniscate	$r^2 = a^2 \cos 2\theta$		
Spiral	$r = \theta$		

3. Slope of a Polar Curve

When we have a polar curve $r=f(\theta)$, we can express the curve in parametric form.

$$x = r\cos\theta = \text{①}\underline{\quad\quad}\cos\theta$$

$$y = r\sin\theta = \text{②}\underline{\quad\quad}\sin\theta$$

Then the derivative of $r=f(\theta)$ at the point (r, θ) is

$$\frac{dy}{dx} = \frac{\frac{dy}{d\theta}}{\frac{dx}{d\theta}} = \frac{\text{③}\underline{\quad\quad}}{\text{④}\underline{\quad\quad}} = \frac{\text{⑤}\underline{\quad\quad}}{\text{⑥}\underline{\quad\quad}}$$

※ Derivative of Polar curve

$$\frac{dy}{dx} = \frac{dy/d\theta}{dx/d\theta} = \frac{(r\sin\theta)'}{(r\cos\theta)'}$$

EXAMPLE 7. Find the slope of the polar curve at the indicated point.

① $r = 1 - \sin\theta, \quad \theta = 0$

② $r = 5\cos 3\theta, \quad \theta = \dfrac{\pi}{3}$

Blank : ① f(θ) ② f(θ) ③ (f(θ)sin θ)' ④ (f(θ)cos θ)' ⑤ f '(θ) sin θ + f(θ) cos θ ⑥ f '(θ) cos θ - f(θ) sin θ

③ $r = \theta^2$, $\theta = \pi$ ④ $r = 5$, $\theta = \dfrac{\pi}{4}$

EXAMPLE 8. A particle is moving along the polar curve $r = \sin\theta$ such that $\dfrac{d\theta}{dt} = 2$. If its position at time t is $(x(t), y(t))$,

① what is the value of $\dfrac{dy}{dt}$ at $\theta = \dfrac{\pi}{3}$?

② what is the value of $\dfrac{dx}{dt}$ at $\theta = \dfrac{\pi}{3}$?

4. Area in Polar Coordinates

☺ Reminder: Area of a sector (θ is in radian) = ① _____

Let's find the area enclosed by the graph of r = f (θ) on the interval [α, β] is;

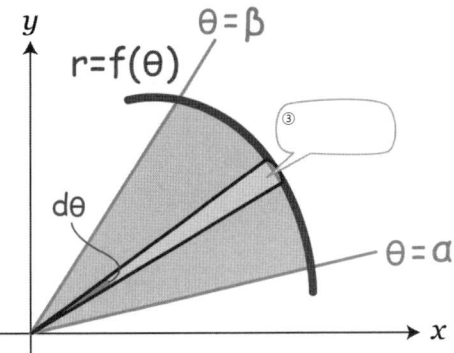

We can break up to small ② _____,
and add up all the area of the sectors.

※ Area of a polar curve

If f is continuous and nonnegative on the interval [α, β] (α,β are both angles), then the area enclosed by the graph of $r = f(\theta)$ on the interval [α, β] is

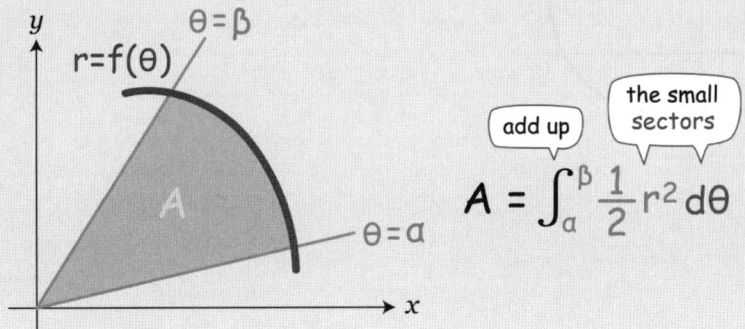

$$A = \int_\alpha^\beta \frac{1}{2} r^2 \, d\theta$$

Blank : ① $\frac{1}{2}r^2\theta$ ② sectors ③ $\frac{1}{2}r^2 d\theta$ (dθ means small θ)

EXAMPLE 9. Find the area bounded by the graph of $r = 2 + 2\cos\theta$

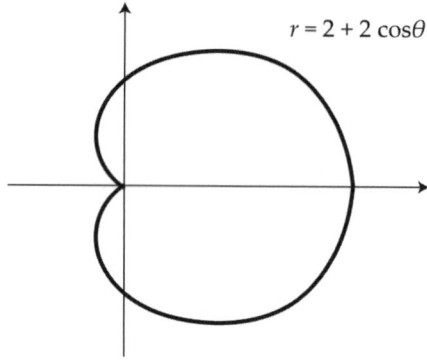

$r = 2 + 2\cos\theta$

EXAMPLE 10. Find the area bounded by the graph of $r = 2 + \sin\theta$

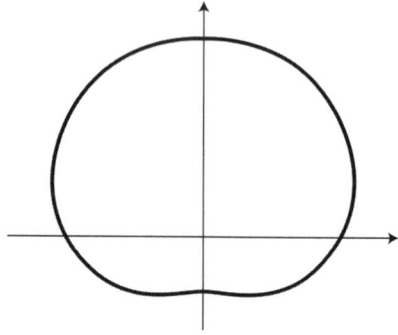

EXAMPLE 11. Find the area of one petal of $r = 2\sin 3\theta$

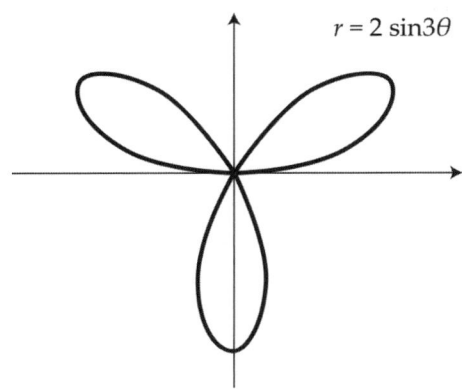

EXAMPLE 12. Sketch the curve $r = 4\cos 2\theta$. Find the area of one petal of $r = 4\cos 2\theta$. Set up the integral do not evaluate.

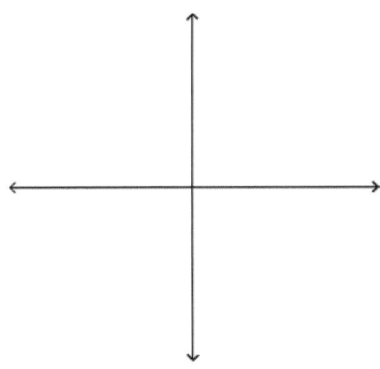

EXAMPLE 13. Sketch the curve $r^2 = 4\cos 2\theta$. Find the area inside the loops of $r^2 = 4\cos 2\theta$. Set up the integral do not evaluate.

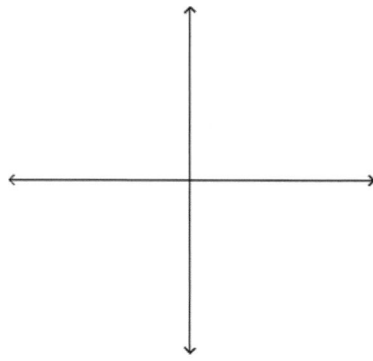

EXAMPLE 14. Sketch the polar curve $r=1+2\cos\theta$. For each question, set up the integral do not evaluate.

① Find the area of the inner loop of $r=1+2\cos\theta$.

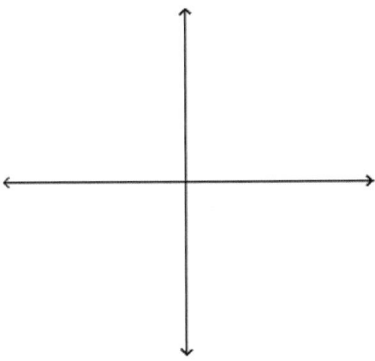

② Find the area of between the loops of $r=1+2\cos\theta$.

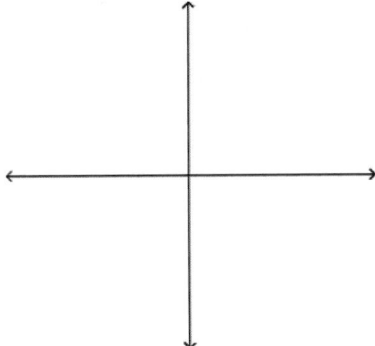

5. Area Between Two Polar Curves

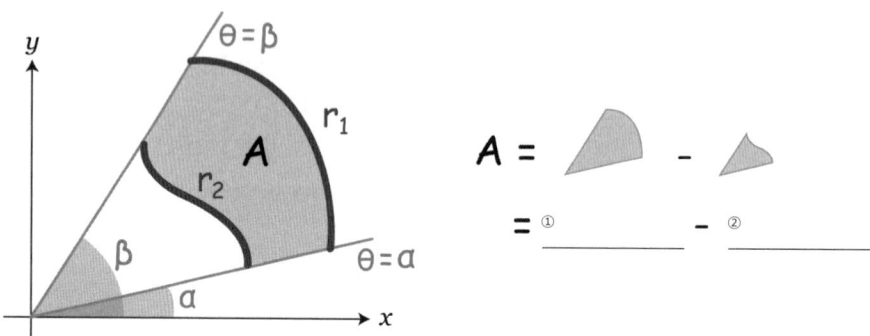

$$A = \text{⬠} - \text{△}$$

$$= \underline{\text{①}} - \underline{\text{②}}$$

※ Area between two polar curves

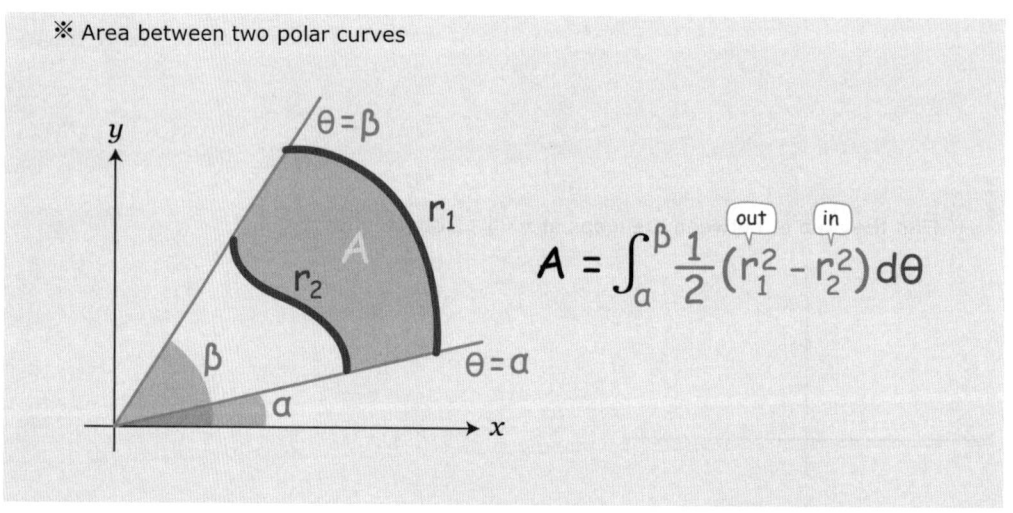

$$A = \int_\alpha^\beta \frac{1}{2}(r_1^2 - r_2^2)\,d\theta \quad \text{(out)} \; r_1^2 \;\; \text{(in)} \; r_2^2$$

Blank : ① $\dfrac{1}{2}\int_\alpha^\beta r_1^2\,d\theta$ ② $\dfrac{1}{2}\int_\alpha^\beta r_2^2\,d\theta$

EXAMPLE 15. The polar curve $r = 2 - 2\sin\theta$ and $r = 2$ is shown. For each question, set up the integral do not evaluate.

① Determine the area that lies inside $r = 2 - 2\sin\theta$ and outside $r = 2$.

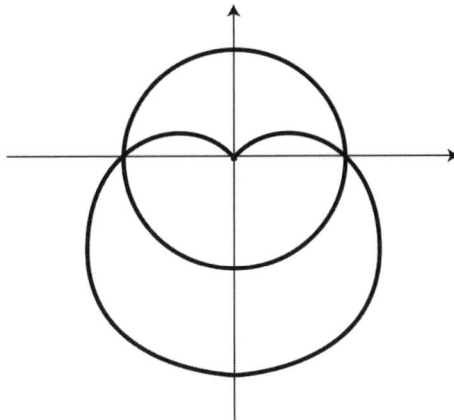

② Determine the area that lies outside $r = 2 - 2\sin\theta$ and inside $r = 2$.

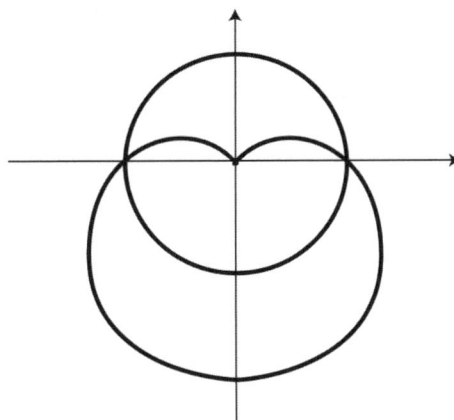

③ Determine the area that is inside both $r = 2 - 2\sin\theta$ and $r = 2$.

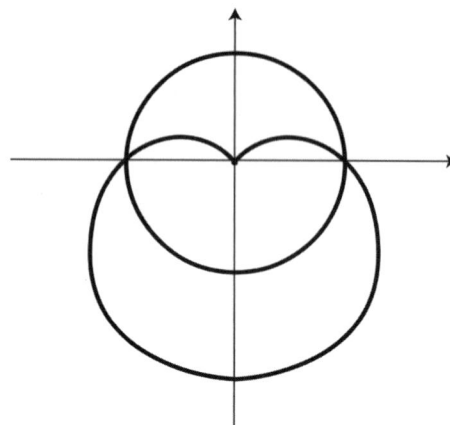

EXAMPLE 16.   Sketch the polar curve $r = 1 + \cos\theta$. And $r = 3\cos\theta$. For each question, set up the integral do not evaluate.

① Find the area inside $r = 3\cos\theta$ and outside $r = 1 + \cos\theta$.

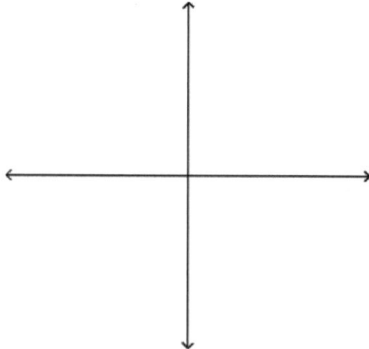

② Find the area inside both the circle $r = 3\cos\theta$ and the $r = 1+\cos\theta$.

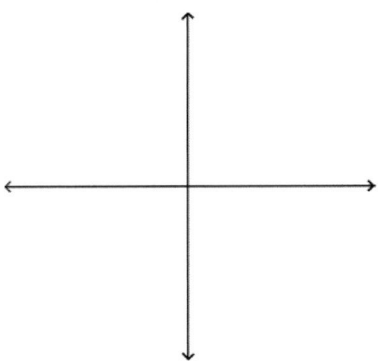

③ Find the area outside $r = 3\cos\theta$ and inside $r = 1+\cos\theta$.

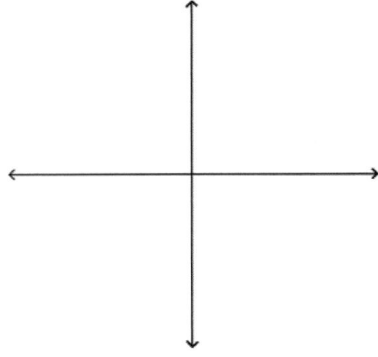

EXAMPLE 17. Find the area of the common interior of $r = 3\cos\theta$ and $r = 3\sin\theta$. Set up the integral do not evaluate.

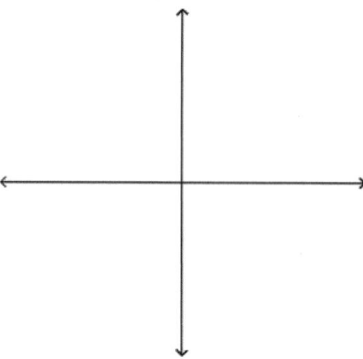

EXAMPLE 18. Find the common area of $r = 4\sin 2\theta$ and $r = 2$. Set up the integral do not evaluate.

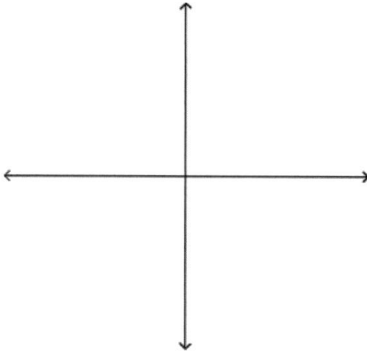

AP Style Problem

1. What is the equation of the line tangent of $r = \theta$ at $\theta = \pi$?

   A) $y = \pi x + \pi^2$

   B) $y = \pi x - \pi^2$

   C) $y = \dfrac{1}{\pi}x + \pi^2$

   D) $y = \dfrac{1}{\pi}x - \pi^2$

2. A particle moves along the polar curve $r = \sin\theta$ so that at time t seconds, $\theta = t^2$. Find the time t in the interval $1 \leq t \leq 2$ for which the y-coordinate of the particle's position is 1.

   A) $\sqrt{\dfrac{\pi}{2}}$

   B) $\sqrt{\dfrac{\pi}{4}}$

   C) $\dfrac{\pi}{2}$

   D) $\dfrac{\pi}{4}$

3. Let R be the region bounded by the graph of the polar curve $r = \theta$ and $\theta = 1$ as shown in the figure above. What is the area of R?

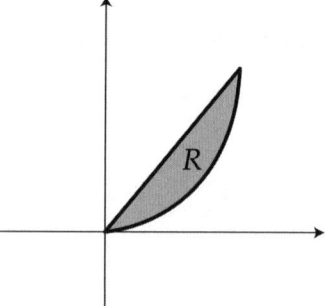

A) $\dfrac{1}{6}$

B) $\dfrac{1}{3}$

C) $\dfrac{1}{2}$

D) π

4. Given the curve $r = \theta - \cos 2\theta$, find the angle θ in the interval $0 \leq \theta \leq \pi$ where the curve is farthest from the origin.

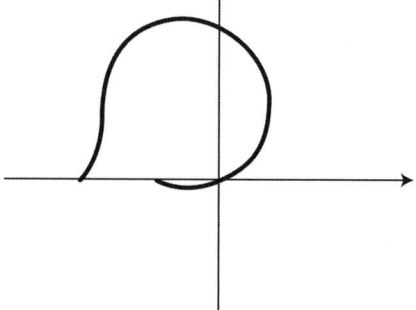

A) $\dfrac{7\pi}{6}$

B) $\dfrac{11\pi}{12}$

C) $\dfrac{11\pi}{6}$

D) $\dfrac{7\pi}{12}$

5. The inner loop of the polar curve $r = 2\sin\theta - 1$ is graphed for $0 \le \theta \le \pi$. Let R be the region enclosed by the curve as shown in the figure. What is the area of R?

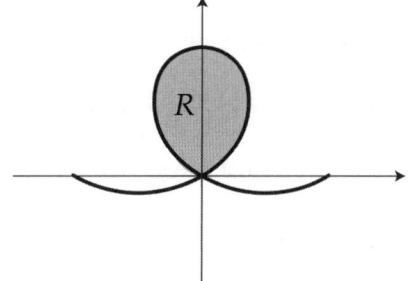

A) $\dfrac{1}{2}\int_0^{\pi}(2\sin\theta - 1)^2\, d\theta$

B) $\dfrac{1}{2}\int_0^{\pi/2}(2\sin\theta - 1)^2\, d\theta$

C) $\int_{\pi/6}^{\pi/2}(2\sin\theta - 1)^2\, d\theta$

D) $\int_0^{\pi/2}(2\sin\theta - 1)^2\, d\theta$

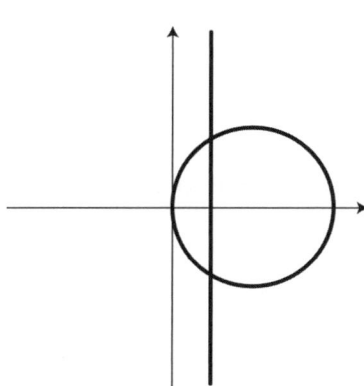

6. The area inside the circle $r = 4\cos\theta$ and to the left of the line $r = \sec\theta$ is given by the definite integral

A) $\int_0^{\pi/3}(\sec\theta)^2\, d\theta + \int_{\pi/3}^{\pi/2}(4\cos\theta)^2\, d\theta$

B) $\int_0^{\pi/2}(\sec\theta)^2 - (4\cos\theta)^2\, d\theta$

C) $\int_0^{\pi/2}(4\cos\theta)^2 - (\sec\theta)^2\, d\theta$

D) $\int_0^{\pi/2}(\sec\theta)^2 + (4\cos\theta)^2\, d\theta$

Mia's AP Calculus
Free Response Questions (from ch18~24)

(: Do not use calculator, : Use calculator)

1. Series

 A function f is defined as

$$f(x) = \sum_{n=1}^{\infty} \frac{nx^n}{n^2+1} = \frac{1}{2}x + \frac{2}{5}x^2 + \frac{3}{10}x^3 + \dots$$

for all x in the interval of convergence of the given power series.

(a) Find the interval of convergence for this power series. Show the work that leads to your answer.

(b) Use the first two terms to approximate $f(-1)$. Show that this approximation differs from $f(-1)$ by less than 0.5.

(c) The function g has first derivative given $g'(x) = f(x)$ where $g(0) = 1$. Using the third degree polynomial of g, approximate $g(-1)$.

(d) The function h is defined by $h(x) = e^x f(x)$ where e^x is the Taylor polynomial about $x = 0$. Write the first three terms of the polynomial $h(x)$.

2. Series with Table

x	f	f'	f''
2	3	5	-10

The function f is twice differentiable for $x > 0$. Values of f, f' and f'' of $x = 2$ are given in the table above and $\left|f^{(3)}(x)\right| \leq 20$.

(a) Write a first degree polynomial of f about $x = 2$. Use it to approximate $f(2.2)$. Determine whether your answer is an underestimation or an overestimation.

(b) Let $f'(2.1) = 6$. Use Euler's method, starting at $x = 2$ with two steps of equal size, to approximate $f(2.2)$.

(c) Write a second degree polynomial of f about $x = 2$. Use it to approximate $f(2.2)$.

(d) Use the Lagrange error bound to show that the approximation in (c) differs from $f(2.2)$ by less than $\dfrac{1}{25}$.

3. Parametric Curve

A moving particle has a position $(x(t), y(t))$ and the velocity vector of the particle is $\left\langle \sqrt{t}+2,\ 1-t \right\rangle$ for $t \geq 0$. The position of the particle is (2, -8) at $t = 1$.

(a) Find the acceleration vector at $t = 2$.

(b) Find the position of y at $t = 2$.

(c) What is the slope of the line tangent to the path of the particle at $t = 2$?

(d) Write, but do not evaluate, an integral expression for the total distance of the particle from $t = 0$ to $t = 6$.

(e) Write, but do not evaluate, an integral expression for the average speed of the particle from $t = 0$ to $t = 6$.

4. Polar Curve

The graphs of the polar curves $r = 2$ and $r = 3 + 2\sin\theta$ are shown in the figure above.

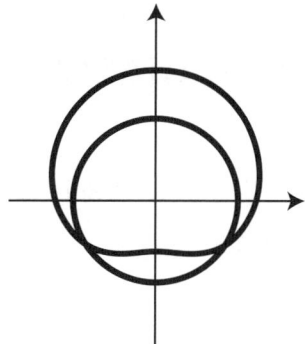

(a) Write, but do not evaluate, an integral expression for the area of the region that lies inside the $r = 3 + 2\sin\theta$ but outside the $r = 2$.

(b) Write, but do not evaluate, an integral expression for the area of the region that lies inside the $r = 3 + 2\sin\theta$ and also inside the $r = 2$.

(c) Find the slope of the tangent line to the polar curve $r = 3 + 2\sin\theta$ at $\theta = 0$.

(d) A partible moves along the curve $r = 3 + 2\sin\theta$ so that its position at time t is $(x(t), y(t))$ and such that $\dfrac{d\theta}{dt} = 3$ for all times. Find $\dfrac{dr}{dt}$ at $\theta = 0$. Interpret the meaning where r is measured in units and t is measured in seconds.

Mia's AP Calculus

Calculator Skills (for Ti 84, Ti nspire CAS)

1. Calculator Skills for Ti-84

1) Basics

Clear All data	2nd – + – 4 – **ENTER** 2nd – + – 7 – 1 – 2
Insert a symbol	2nd – **DEL**(insert) – **ENTER**
Recall the expression	2nd – **ENTER**(entry) or use ▼ or ▲ button to highlight the expression, then **ENTER**
BASIC SETUP	**MODE** Normal Sci Eng Float 0123456789 Radian Degree Func Par Pol Seq Connected Dot Sequential Simul Real a+bi re^θi Full Horiz G-T
Degree Radian mode	**MODE** - ▼ - ▼
To **return to the 'home' screen** at any time	2nd – **MODE**(QUIT)
To enter a **rational expression**	**(**numerator **)/(**denominator**)**
Negative vs **subtract** sign	negative button:**(-)** subtract button:**-**
To change a **decimal →fraction**	**MATH** – **ENTER** – **ENTER**

478   Mia's AP calculus AB BC

To find or enter the **absolute value**	**MATH** – ▶ (NUM) – 1:abs
sin cos tan	**sin**, **cos**, **tan**
csc sec cot	1 / **sin**, 1 / **cos**, 1 / **tan**
arcsin, arccos, arctan	**2nd** – **sin**, **2nd** – **cos**, **2nd** – **tan**

2) Graphing functions

To **graph** an equation	**Y=** – enter the equation – **GRAPH**

3) Window adjusting

To **change the viewing window** for a graph	**WINDOW** enter values and desired scales WINDOW Xmin=-10 Xmax=10 Xscl=1 Ymin=-10 Ymax=10 Yscl=1 Xres=1 (xscl,yscl means distance between tick marks)
Going back to the **standard size** of the window setting	**ZOOM**–6:ZStandard

EXAMPLE 1. Graph the function $y = x^3 - 12x^2 + 30x + 30$, $-10 \leq x \leq 10$, $-20 \leq y \leq 60$.

4) Finding Zeros

To find the **x-intercept**(s) (an equation must be entered)	**2ⁿᵈ** – **TRACE**(CALC) – **2:ZERO** - **ENTER** Use ▶ or ◀ and move cursor to the LEFT of the point. **ENTER** Use ▶ or ◀ and move cursor to the RIGHT of the point. **ENTER** Guess? **ENTER** 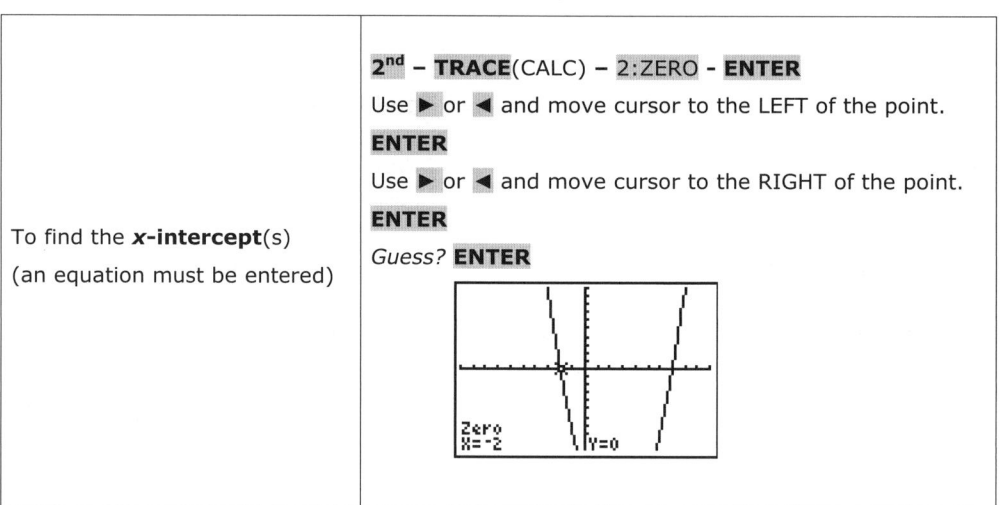

EXAMPLE 2. Graph the function $y = x^3 - 12x^2 + 30x + 30$. Find the Zeros.

5) Finding Max or Min

To find the **maximum (minimum) point** (an equation must be entered.)	**2nd – TRACE**(CALC) – **3:MAXIMUM** – **ENTER** Use ▶ or ◀ and move cursor to the LEFT of the point. **ENTER** Use ▶ or ◀ and move cursor to the RIGHT of the point. **ENTER** **ENTER**

EXAMPLE 3. Graph the function $y = x^3 - 12x^2 + 30x + 30$. Find the max and min.

6) Finding Intersections

To find the **intersection of 2 graphs** (2 equations must be entered)	**2nd – TRACE**(CALC) – **5:INTERSECT** – **ENTER** Use ▶ or ◀ to move cursor close to the point. **ENTER – ENTER – ENTER** (press enter 3 times) NOTE: Your x value must be within your viewing window. 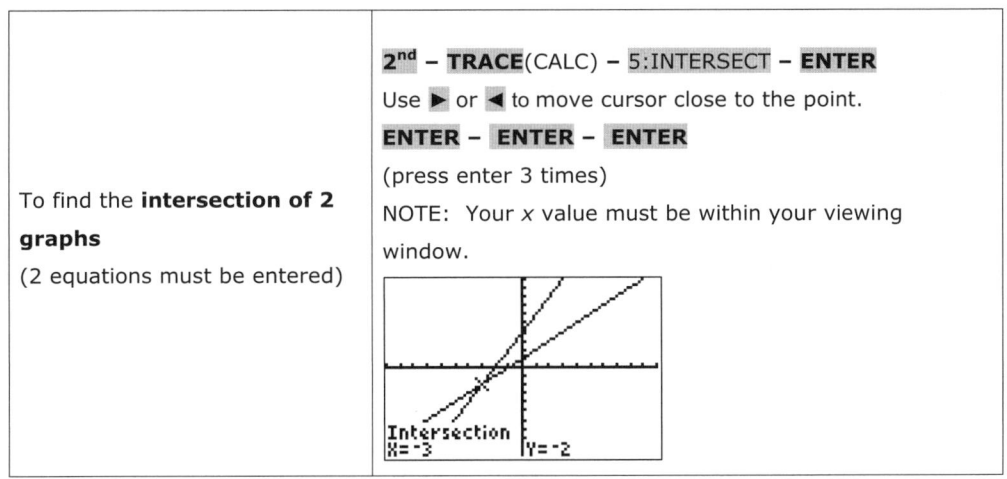

To **solve an equation by graphing** (2 equations must be entered)	**Y=** Enter left-hand side of equation in **y1 =** ; right-hand side in **y2 =** Graph and find the point(s) of **intersection**.
Window setting [-2π, 2π] when you have a trig functions	**Zoom – trig**

EXAMPLE 4. Find the least positive x that satisfy $\frac{1}{4} + \sin(\pi x) = 4^{-x}$.

EXAMPLE 5. Find the intersection of $y = 2$ and $y = \dfrac{20}{1+x^2}$.

7) Calculating Derivatives

Finding Derivative	**MATH – 8:nDeriv** – variable x, function ,value $\frac{d}{dx}(\Box)\vert_{x=\Box}$
Bringing the function	**Alpha–Trace** or **VARS** – **y Vars** – **1:Function**

EXAMPLE 6. Find $f'(2)$ when $f(x) = e^{\cos^2 x}$.

EXAMPLE 7. Find the slope of the tangent of $y = \dfrac{20}{1+x^2}$ at x = 2

8) Calculating Definite Integrations

Finding Definite Integral	MATH – 9:fnInt – starting value, ending value, function, variable x 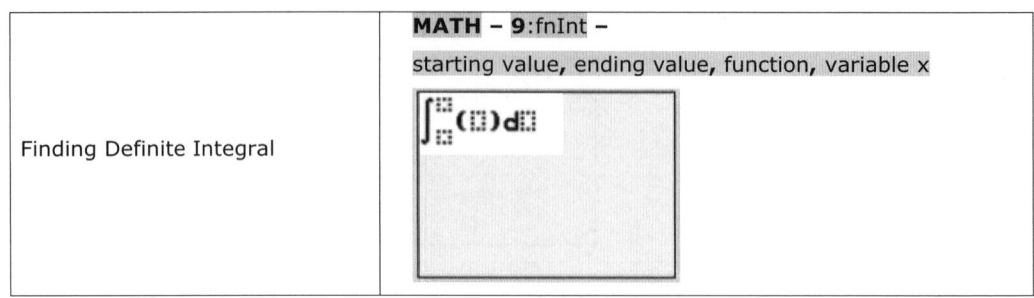

EXAMPLE 8. Let R be the region in the first and second quadrants bounded above the graph $y = 2$ and below the graph $y = \dfrac{20}{1+x^2}$. Find the area between two graphs.

9) Graphing Polar or Parametric Curves

Parametric mode	**MODE** – select par
Enter the parametric equation and graph it	**Y=** enter the function
Polar mode	**MODE** – select pol
Enter the polar equation and graph it	**Y=** enter the function

EXAMPLE 9. Graph polar curve $r = 2 - 2\sin\theta$.

2. Calculator Skills for Ti-nspire CAS

1) Basics

Home screen	press [⌂ on]. *Home screen showing Scratchpad (A: Calculate, B: Graph) and Documents (1: New Document, 2: My Documents, 3: Recent, 4: Current, 5: Settings).*
Change Setting	On Home screen, select **5. Settings**. *Menu showing 1: Change Language, 2: Settings, 3: Handheld Setup, 4: Status, 5: Login.*
General settings for AP calculus	Change the 'General settings' to **Float** and **Radian**. Make Default. *General Settings dialog: Display Digits: Float, Angle: Radian, Exponential Format: Normal, Real or Complex: Real, Calculation Mode: Auto, Vector Format: Rectangular.* Change the 'Graphs & Geometry' settings to **Float** and **Radian**. Make Default. (If you cannot see the 'Graphs & Geometry' settings, then open the graph document, and then menu – 9:settings)

Opening Calculator Document	On Home screen, select 1. New Document – 1:Add Calculator Or press **ctrl** – **doc** – 1:Add Calculator
Opening Graph Document	On Home screen, select 1. New Document – 2:Add Graphs Or press **ctrl** – **doc** – 2:Add Graphs
Closing Documents	Press [x] button at the very right top. Or **ctrl** – **W** (All the documents will be closed.)
Moving to next Document	**ctrl** – ▶ or ◀

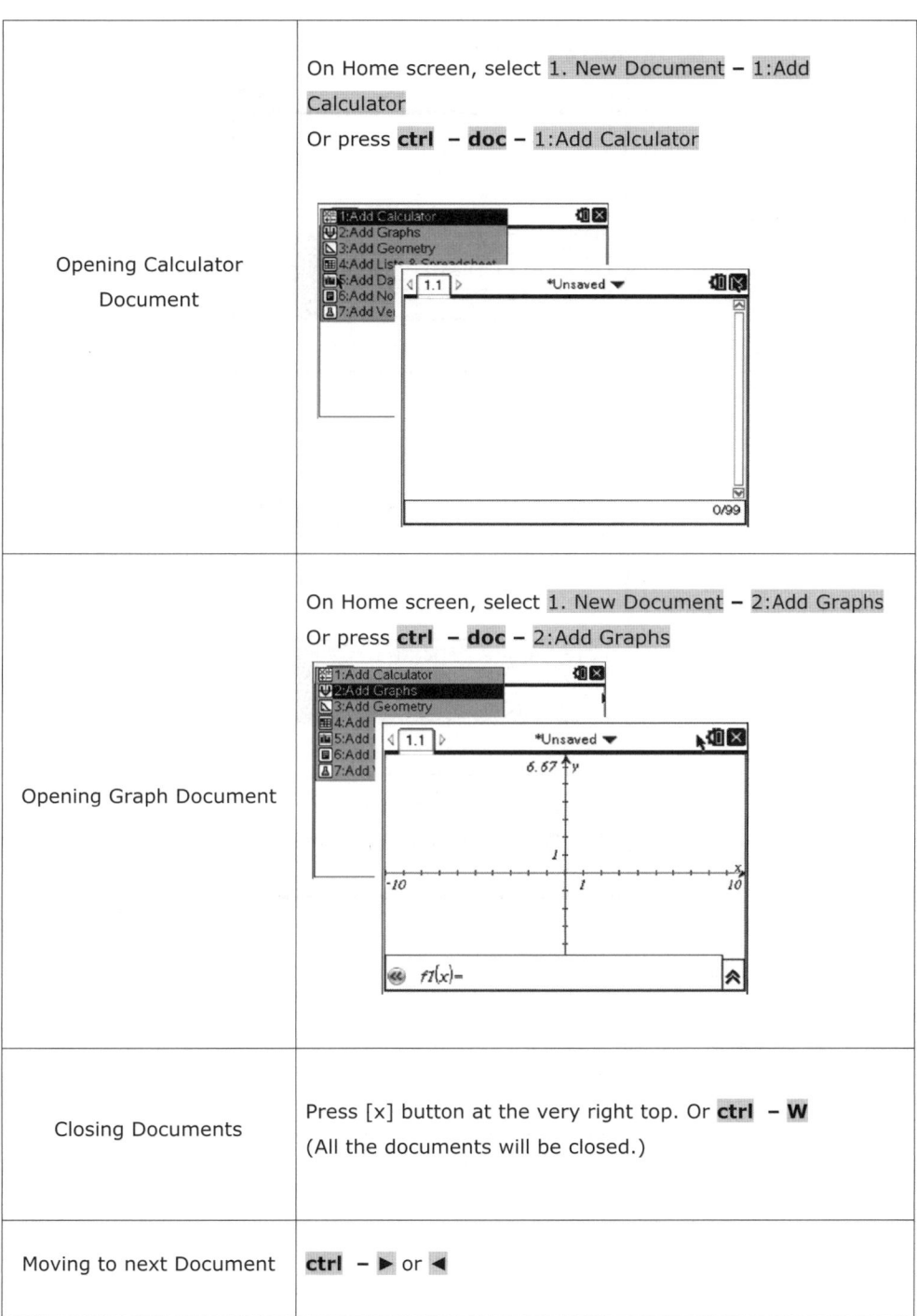

Entering special characters	Press **ctrl** – 📖
Entering math expressions	press [icon].
Finding approximate value	**Enter** gives you exact value **ctrl** – **Enter** gives you approximate value (decimals)

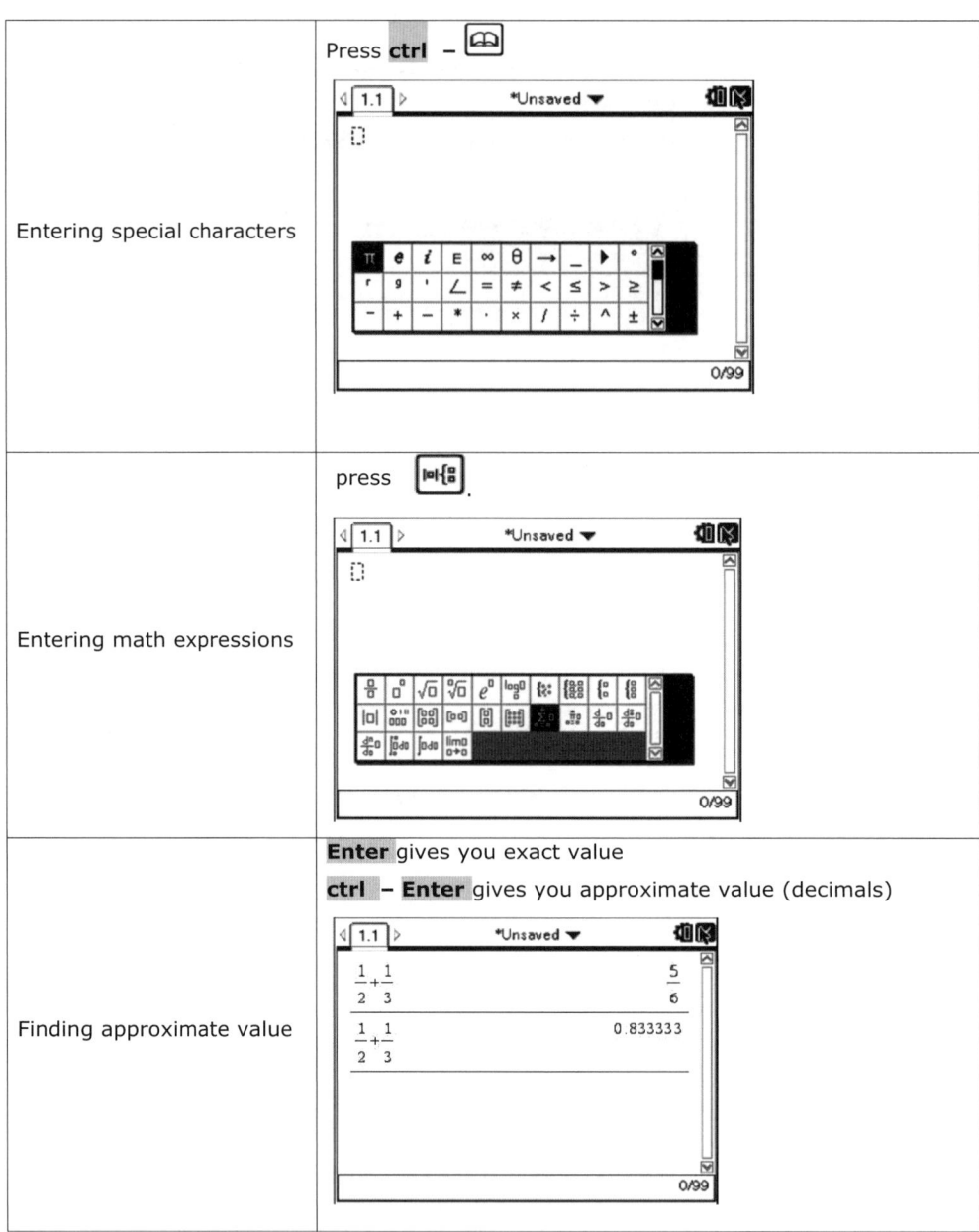

2) Graphing functions

To **graph** an equation	**ctrl** – **doc** – 2:Add Graphs – enter the function in f1 – **Enter** 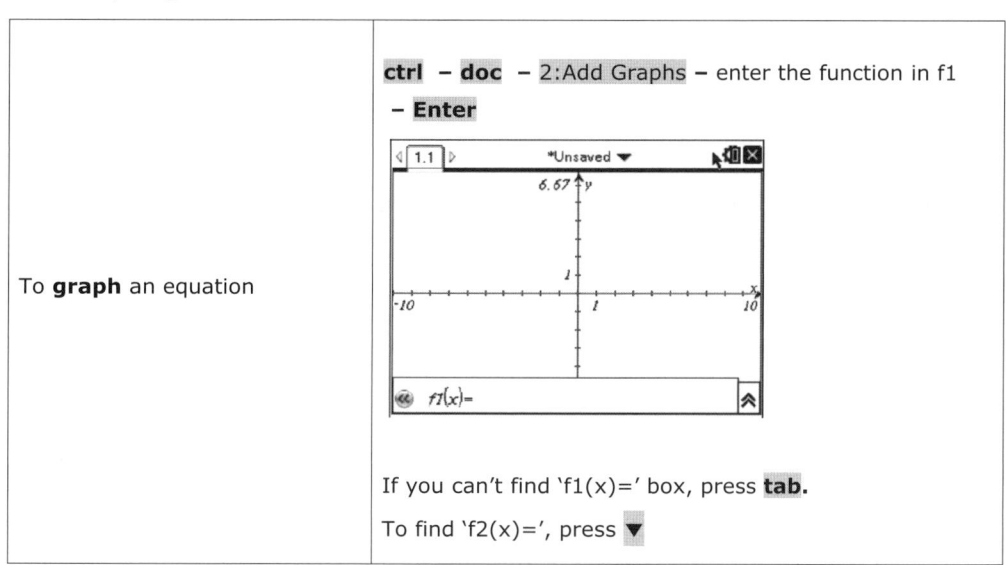 If you can't find 'f1(x)=' box, press **tab**. To find 'f2(x)=', press ▼

3) Window adjusting

To **change the viewing window** for a graph	**menu** – 4:Window/Zoom – 1: Window Settings 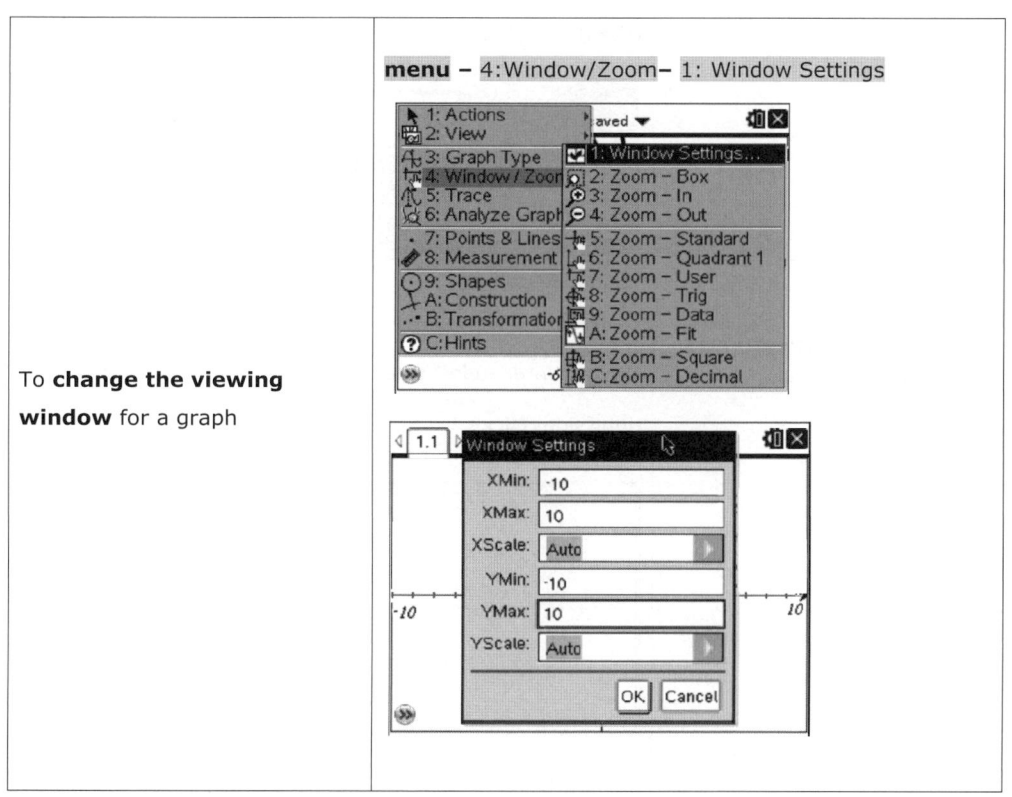

Calculator Skills (for Ti 84, Ti nspire CAS) 489

Going back to the **standard size** of the window setting	**menu** – 4:Window/Zoom– 5: Zoom Standard

EXAMPLE 10. Graph the function $y = x^3 - 12x^2 + 30x + 30$, $-10 \leq x \leq 10$, $-20 \leq y \leq 60$.

4) Finding Zeros

To find the **x-intercept**(s) (an equation must be entered)	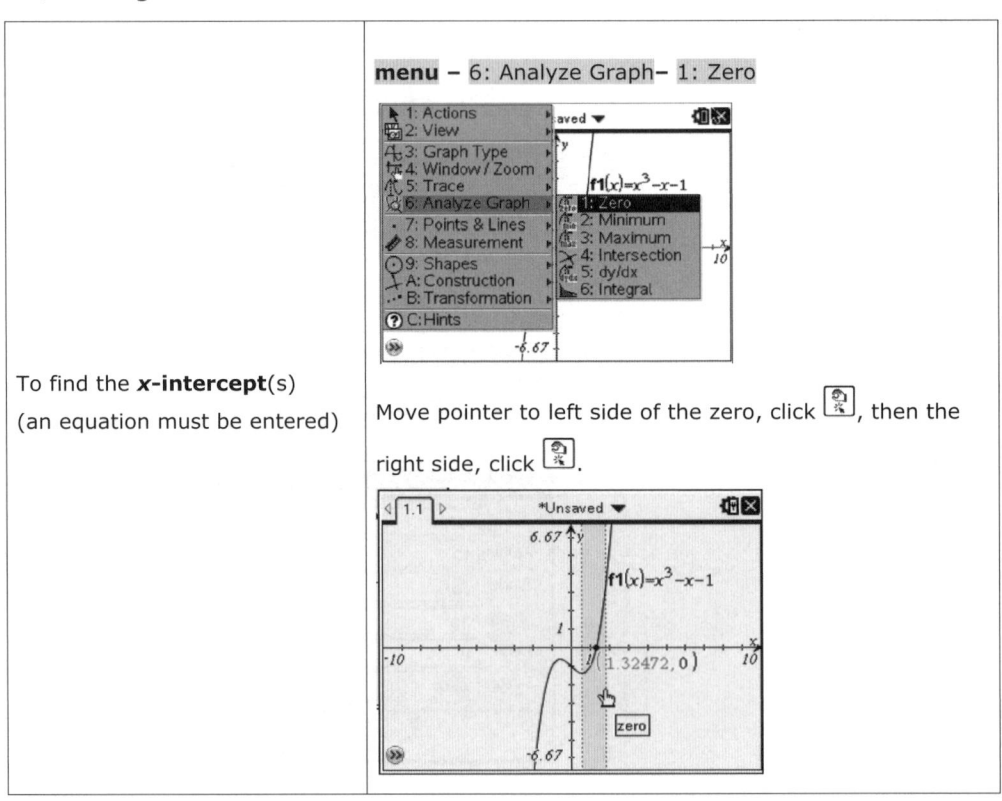

	Highlight the x coordinate – press **var** – Type the variable name (any alphabet is possible)
Saving x coordinate of the zero	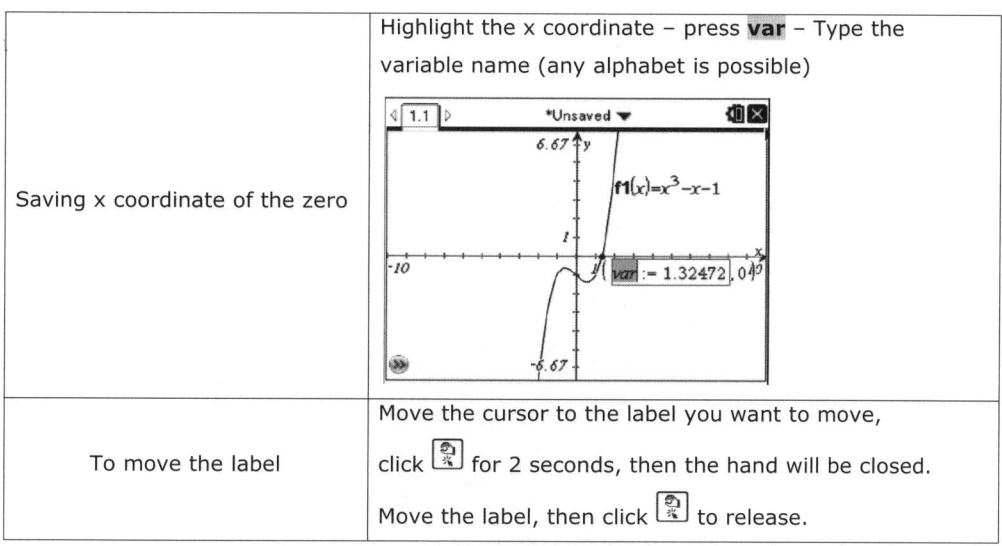
To move the label	Move the cursor to the label you want to move, click 🖑 for 2 seconds, then the hand will be closed. Move the label, then click 🖑 to release.

EXAMPLE 11. Graph the function $y = x^3 - 12x^2 + 30x + 30$. Find the Zeros.

5) Finding Max or Min

To find the **maximum (minimum) point** (an equation must be entered.)	**menu** – 6: Analyze Graph – 3: Minimum or 4: Maximum

EXAMPLE 12. Graph the function $y = x^3 - 12x^2 + 30x + 30$. Find the max and min.

6) Finding Intersections

To find the **intersection of 2 graphs** (2 equations must be entered)	**ctrl** – **doc** – 2:Add Graphs – enter the 1st function in f1 – enter the 2nd function in f2 – **menu** – 6: Analyze Graph – 4: Intersection – Move pointer to left side of the zero, click 🔲, then the right side, click 🔲.
To **solve an equation by graphing** (2 equations must be entered)	**Y=** Enter left-hand side of equation in **y1 =** ; right-hand side in **y2 =** Graph and find the point(s) of intersection.
Window setting [-2π, 2π] when you have a trig functions	**menu** – 4:Window/Zoom– 8: Zoom Trig
Solving Equation	**menu** – 3:Algebra – 1:Solve – enter the equation (with =) , variable 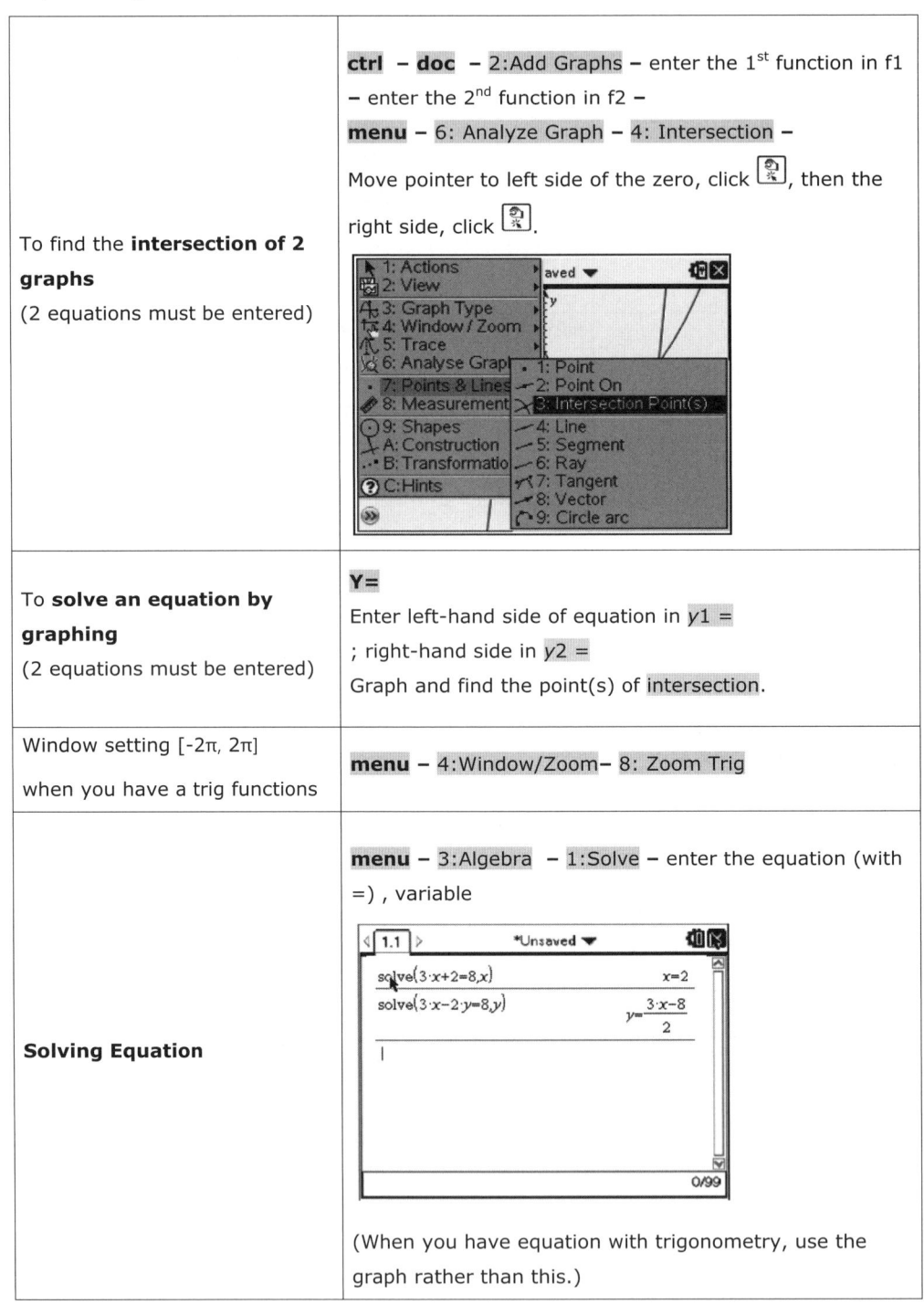 (When you have equation with trigonometry, use the graph rather than this.)

EXAMPLE 13. Find the least positive x that satisfy $\frac{1}{4} + \sin(\pi x) = 4^{-x}$.

EXAMPLE 14. Find the intersection of $y = 2$ and $y = \frac{20}{1+x^2}$.

7) Calculating Derivatives

Finding Derivative	**ctrl** – **doc** – 1:Add Calculator Press [📋] – [d/d□] 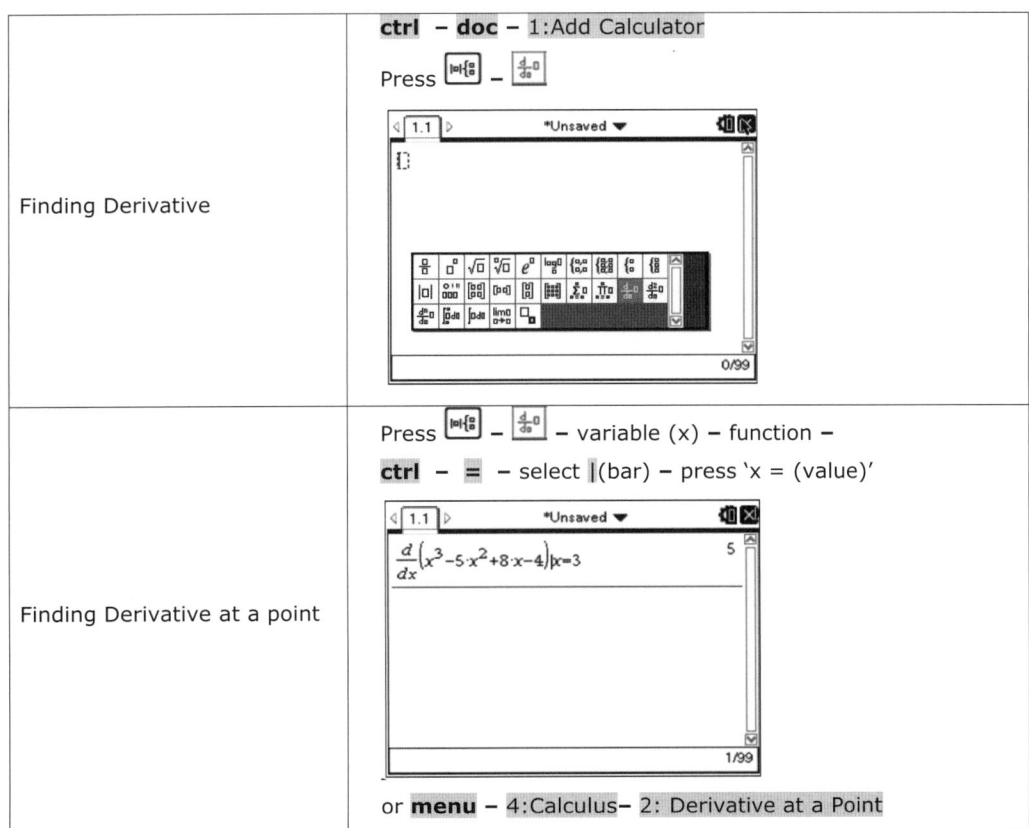
Finding Derivative at a point	Press [📋] – [d/d□] – variable (x) – function – **ctrl** – **=** – select |(bar) – press 'x = (value)' or **menu** – 4:Calculus– 2: Derivative at a Point

| Bringing the function | Press **var** – select the function we saved 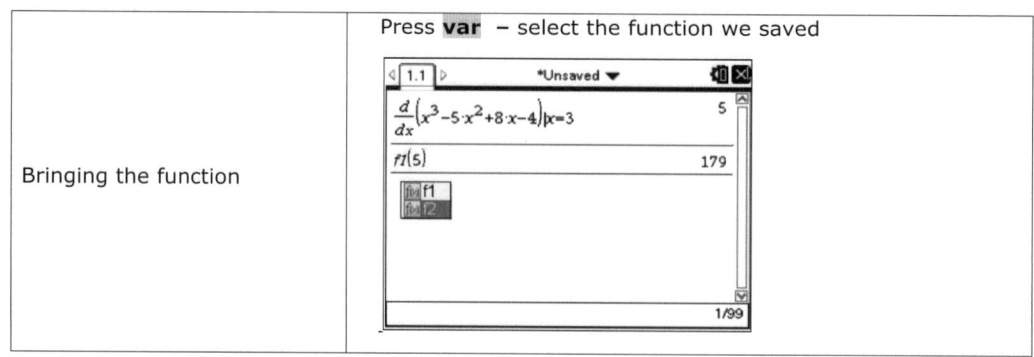 |

EXAMPLE 15. Find $f'(2)$ when $f(x) = e^{\cos^2 x}$.

EXAMPLE 16. Find the slope of the tangent of $y = \dfrac{20}{1+x^2}$ at x = 2

8) Calculating Definite Integrations

Finding Indefinite Integral	Press [templates] – [∫□d□] 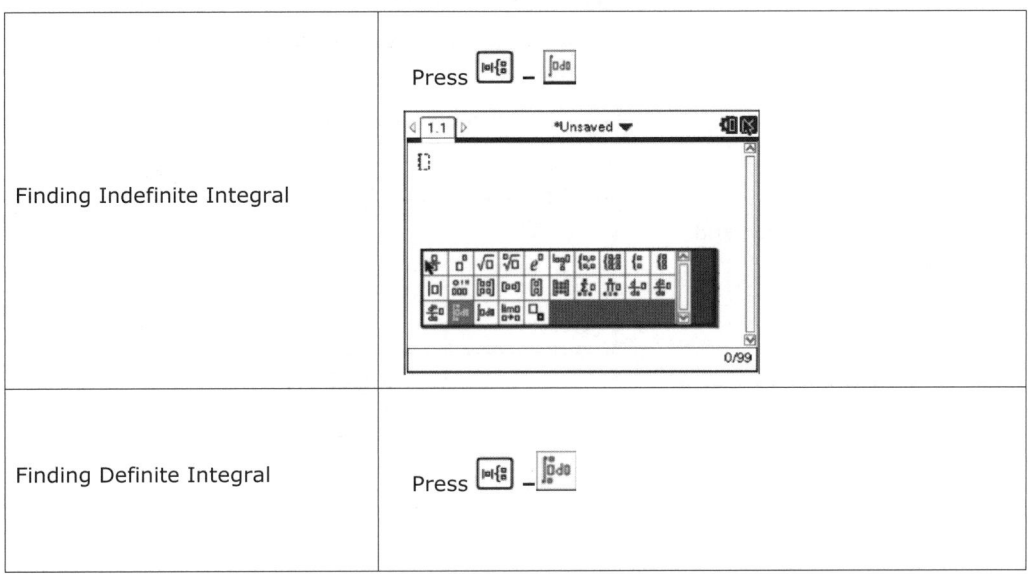
Finding Definite Integral	Press [templates] – [∫ᵇₐ □d□]

EXAMPLE 17. Let R be the region in the first and second quadrants bounded above the graph $y = 2$ and below the graph $y = \dfrac{20}{1+x^2}$. Find the area between two graphs.

9) Graphing Polar or Parametric Curves

Enter the parametric equation and graph it	**ctrl** – **doc** – 2:Add Graphs – **menu** – 3: Graph Type – 2: Parametric – Enter the parametric equation Note: Do not put x as your variable! Put t !

Calculator Skills (for Ti 84, Ti nspire CAS) 495

Enter the polar equation and graph it	ctrl – doc – 2:Add Graphs – menu – 3: Graph Type – 3: Polar – Enter the polar equation Note: Do not put x as your variable! Put θ ! 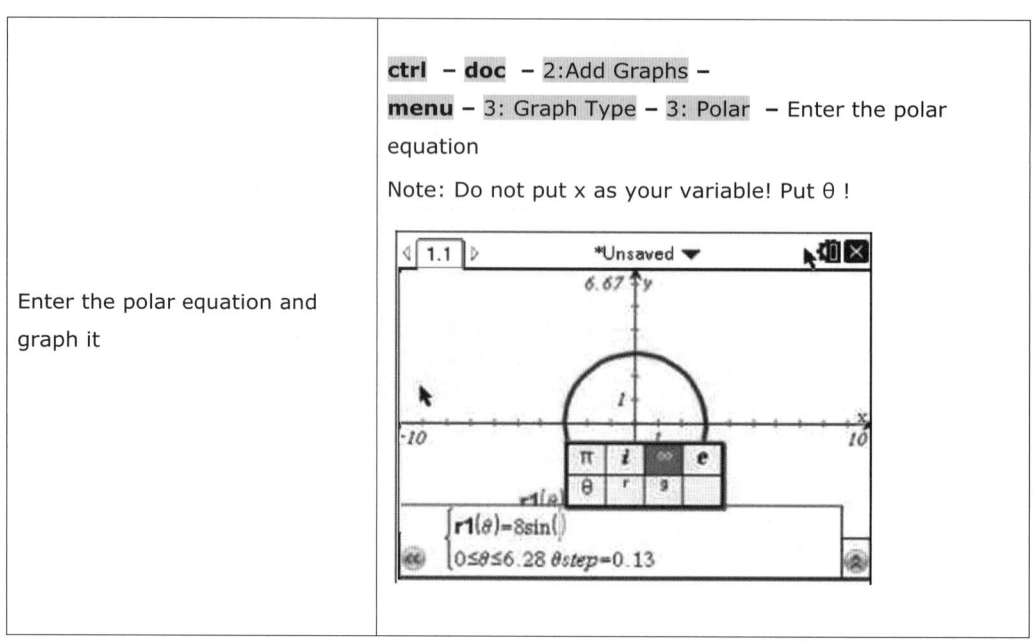

EXAMPLE 18. Graph polar curve $r = 2 - 2\sin\theta$.

3. Calculator Question for Derivative

1. If $f(x) = \ln x \cos x$, what is the slope of the normal line at x = 3?
   A) -2.062
   B) 0.485
   C) -0.485
   D) 2.062

2. The derivative of the function f is given by $f'(x) = \cos^2 x - \dfrac{1}{x}$. How many critical values does f have in the interval 0 < x ≤ 10?
   A) 3
   B) 4
   C) 5
   D) 6

3. Let the derivative of f be the function given by $f'(x) = x^2 \sin 2x$. What is the number of x at which the graph of f changes concavity in [-3.5, 3.5]?
   A) 2
   B) 3
   C) 4
   D) 5

4. Let f be the function given by $f(x) = e^x - 3x^2$. Which of the following values of x does the line tangent to the graph of f have the least slope?

A) 0.103
B) 0.204
C) 1.792
D) 2.833

5. How close does the curve $y = e^{2x}$ come to the point (2, 1)?

A) 0.012
B) 0.224
C) 0.582
D) 1.864

6. The velocity of an object is given by $v(t) = \sqrt{1 + \sin t}$ for $t \geq 0$. Which of the following describes the motion of the object at $t = 2$?

A) The particle is moving to the right and speeding up.
B) The particle is moving to the right and speeding down.
C) The particle is moving to the left and speeding up.
D) The particle is moving to the left and speeding down.

4. Calculator Question for Integration

1. Let $G(x)$ be an antiderivative of $e^{\sqrt{x}+x}$. If $G(4) = 10$, then $G(0)=$
   A) -215.855
   B) -302.855
   C) 322.855
   D) 215.855

2. Which is the greatest positive value of x that $10\int_0^x \cos 2t\, dt = \int_0^x e^t dt$?
   A) 1.024
   B) 1.292
   C) 1.982
   D) 2.086

3. What is the area of the region in the first quadrant enclosed by the graph of $y = \sqrt{1+\sin x}$ and $y = x$?
   A) 0.024
   B) 0.314
   C) 0.485
   D) 0.779

4. The average rate of change of the function $f(x) = \int_1^x e^{\sin t} dt$ over the interval [1, 3] is

A) 0.415
B) 0.792
C) 4.425
D) 2.212

5. Let g be the function given by $g(x) = \int_0^x (t - t^2)\sin t \, dt$. Which of the following statements about g is NOT true?

   I. g is increasing in (0, 1)

   II. g has a minimum at x = 0

   III. g has an inflection point around x = 2.414

   IV. $g(4) > 0$

A) I only
B) II only
C) II and III only
D) II and IV only

6. If $g(x) = \int_1^{x^2} e^{\sqrt{t}+1} dt$, what is the value of x in the interval [0, 1] such that the instantaneous rate of change of g is equal the average rate of change of g on that interval?

A) 0.428
B) 0.567
C) 0.124
D) 0.851

7. The object is moving on a line with a velocity $v(t) = 2\sqrt{t} - t^3$ m per seconds. How many meters did the object travel from t = 0 to t = 2?

A) -0.229
B) 0.129
C) 1.245
D) 2.755

8. The region bounded by $y = \sec x$, x-axis, $x = 0$, and $x = k$ is revolved about the x-axis. If the volume of the solid generated is 3, then $k =$

A) 0.412
B) 0.762
C) 0.808
D) 0.901

Mia's AP Calculus
MCQ Mock Test for AB

CALCULUS AB
SECTION I, Part A
Time—1 hour
Number of questions—30

CALCULATOR MAY NOT BE USED ON THIS PART OF THE EXAM.

Directions: Solve each of the following problems, using the available space for scratch work. After examining the form of the choices, decide which is the best of the choices given and fill in the corresponding circle on the answer sheet. No credit will be given for anything written in the exam book. Do not spend too much time on any one problem.

In this exam:
(1) Unless otherwise specified, the domain of a function f is assumed to be the set of all real numbers x for which $f(x)$ is a real number.

(2) The inverse of a trigonometric function f may be indicated using the inverse function notation f^{-1} or with the prefix "arc" (e.g. $\sin^{-1} x = \arcsin x$,).

GO ON TO THE NEXT PAGE.

A A A A A A A A A A A A A A A A A A A A A A A A A

1. $\int \tan x \, dx =$

   A) $\ln|\cos x| + C$

   B) $\ln|\sin x| + C$

   C) $\ln|\sec x| + C$

   D) $\dfrac{1}{\ln|\sin x|} + C$

   E) $\dfrac{1}{\ln|\cos x|} + C$

2. Find the slope of the curve with equation $x^4 - x^2y + y^4 = 1$ where $x = -1$.

   A) $\dfrac{2}{3}$

   B) $\dfrac{1}{2}$

   C) $\dfrac{4}{3}$

   D) $\dfrac{3}{2}$

   E) $\dfrac{1}{3}$

GO ON TO THE NEXT PAGE.

3. Which of the following functions are differentiable for all real numbers x ?

   I. $f(x) = x^{2/3}$

   II. $f(x) = e^x$

   III. $f(x) = \tan x$

   A) I only
   B) I and II only
   C) II only
   D) none of these
   E) I and III only

4. What is the horizontal asymptotes of $y = \dfrac{6 + 2^x}{3 - 4^x}$?

   A) $y = 0$ and $y = 2$
   B) $y = 0$
   C) $y = 2$
   D) $y = -1$ and $y = 0$
   E) none

GO ON TO THE NEXT PAGE.

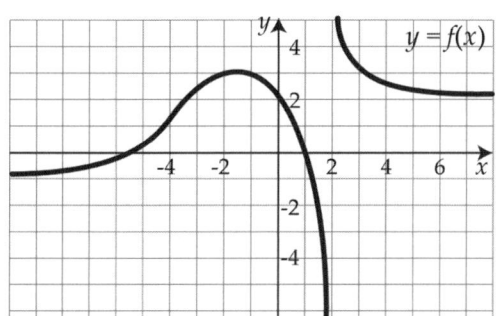

5. Graph of f is shown which has a horizontal asymptotes at $y = -1$ and $y = 2$, and a vertical asymptote at $x = 2$. Which of the following is NOT true?

A) $\lim_{x \to 2} f(x)$ does not exist.

B) $f'(-1.5)$ is approximately 0.

C) $f(0) > \lim_{h \to 0} \dfrac{f(4+h) - f(4)}{h}$

D) $\lim_{x \to \infty} f'(x) = 2$

E) $\lim_{x \to -\infty} f(f^2(x)) = 0$

6. Let f be the function defined by the following.

$$f(x) = \begin{cases} \dfrac{\sin x}{x} & ,-2 \le x < 0 \\ x^2 - x & ,0 \le x < 2 \\ 4\sin\left(\dfrac{x\pi}{12}\right) & ,2 \le x < 6 \\ x^2 + x & ,x \ge 6 \end{cases}$$

For what values of x is f NOT continuous?

A) 0 only

B) 2 only

C) 6 only

D) 0 and 6 only

E) 2 and 6 only

7. If $h(x) = e^{4\ln x^2}$ then $\lim\limits_{x \to 1} \dfrac{h(x) - h(1)}{x - 1} =$

A) $8x$

B) x^2

C) 4

D) 8

E) 16

8. Given that $x \arctan y = 1$, $\dfrac{dy}{dx} = $.

   A) $-\dfrac{1+y^2}{x^2}$

   B) $1+y^2$

   C) $-\dfrac{x \arctan y}{1+y^2}$

   D) $\dfrac{1+y^2}{x}$

   E) $1+x^2$

9. $f(x) = \begin{cases} -2x & , x < 1 \\ x^2 - 4x + 2 & , x \geq 1 \end{cases}$

   Let $f(x)$ be the function above. Which of the following statements are true?

   I. $\lim\limits_{x \to 1} f(x)$ exists.

   II. f is continuous at $x = 1$.

   III. f is differentiable at $x = 1$.

   A) I only

   B) I and II only

   C) III only

   D) none of these

   E) I and III only

10. A particle moves along the curve $x^2y = 4$. When $x = 2$, then $\frac{dx}{dt} = 1$. What is the value of $\frac{dy}{dt}$ when $x = 2$?

A) 0

B) -1

C) 2

D) 1

E) 3

11. If $f(0) = 1$, $f'(1) = 4$, $f'(2) = 3$, and $\int_0^2 f'(x)\, dx = -1$, then $(f^{-1})'(0) =$

A) $\dfrac{1}{4}$

B) $\dfrac{1}{3}$

C) $-\dfrac{1}{4}$

D) $-\dfrac{1}{3}$

E) Not exist

GO ON TO THE NEXT PAGE.

12. Let $g(x)$ be a twice differentiable function. If $g'(0) = -10$ and $g'(5) = 10$, which of the following must be true on the interval $0 \le x \le 5$?

A) $g'(x) = 20$ for some x in the interval

B) $g'(x) = 0$ for some x in the interval

C) $g(x) = 0$ for some x in the interval

D) $g(x) = 4$ for some x in the interval

E) $g(x) > 0$ for some x in the interval

13. The derivative of f is $e^x(x-2)^2(x+1)^3$. At how many points will the graph of f have a relative minimum?

A) None

B) Four

C) Two

D) One

E) Three

14. Let f be the function defined by $f(x) = \tan x$. Using the tangent line of f at the point $x = \dfrac{\pi}{4}$, find the approximation for $f\left(\dfrac{\pi}{3}\right)$.

A) $\dfrac{\pi}{3} + 3$

B) $\dfrac{\pi}{3} + 1$

C) $\dfrac{\pi}{6} + 1$

D) $\dfrac{\pi}{6} + 3$

E) $\dfrac{\pi}{2} + 2$

15. The position of a particle moving along the x-axis is given by $x(t) = -2t^3 + 24t^2 - 90t + 14$ meters where t is in seconds, $t > 0$. At what times is the particle's speed decreasing?

A) $0 \leq t < 4$

B) $3 < t < 4$ or $t > 5$

C) $0 \leq t < 3$ or $t > 4$

D) $0 \leq t < 3$ or $4 < t < 5$

E) $t > 5$

GO ON TO THE NEXT PAGE.

16. A student attempted to use L'Hopital's Rule as follows. In which step does an error first appear?

$$\lim_{x\to\infty} \frac{\sin(1/x)}{e^{1/x}}$$ Step 1
$$= \lim_{x\to\infty} \frac{-x^{-2}\cos(1/x)}{-x^{-2}e^{1/x}}$$ Step 2
$$= \lim_{x\to\infty} \frac{\cos(1/x)}{e^{1/x}}$$ Step 3
$$= \frac{1}{1}$$
$$= 1$$ Step 4

A) Step 1
B) Step 2
C) Step 3
D) Step 4
E) No error.

17. A cone shaped cup is made by a circular piece of paper of radius 2 by cutting out a sector and joining the cut edges. Find the maximum capacity of such a cup.

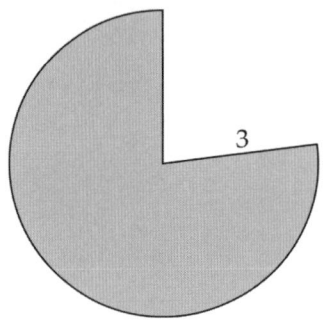
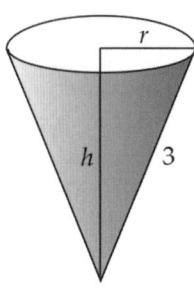

A) $\sqrt{3}\pi$

B) 3π

C) $3\sqrt{3}\pi$

D) $4\sqrt{3}\pi$

E) $2\sqrt{3}\pi$

18. $\int_{1}^{4} \dfrac{5e^{\frac{1}{y}}}{y^2} dy = ?$

A) $-5\int_{1}^{0.25} e^y \, dy$

B) $-\int_{1}^{0.25} e^y \, dy$

C) $-5\int_{1}^{4} e^y \, dy$

D) $-\int_{1}^{4} e^y \, dy$

E) $\int_{1}^{4} e^y \, dy$

GO ON TO THE NEXT PAGE.

19. An observer recorded the velocity of an object in motion along the x axis for 10 seconds. Based on the table below, use a trapezoidal approximation to estimate how far from its starting point the object came at the end of this time.

t	0	2	3	5	7	10
$v(t)$	3	5	1	-1	-3	5

A) 6
B) 12
C) 24
D) 29
E) 34

20. The graph above shows the derivative of function f. The numbers represents the areas of each region. What is the value of x at which the minimum of f occurs in the interval $0 \leq x \leq 12$?

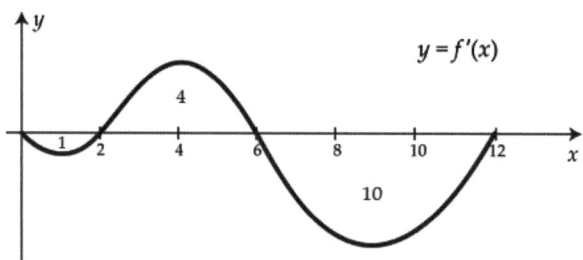

A) 0
B) 2
C) 6
D) 9
E) 12

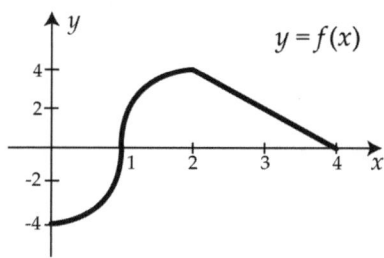

21. Graph of $f(x)$ is shown and let h be the function $h(x) = \int_0^{\sqrt{x}} f(t)\, dt$. Which of the following is an equation for the line tangent to the graph of h at the point where $x = 4$?

A) $y = x + 2$

B) $y = x - 4$

C) $y = x - 2$

D) $y = x + 4$

E) $y = x$

22. If $y = f(x)$ is a solution to the differential equation $\dfrac{dy}{dx} = e^{x^2+1}$ with the initial condition $f(0)=1$, which of the following is true?

A) $f(x) = e^{x^2+1}$

B) $f(x) = 2xe^{x^2+1}$

C) $f(x) = 1 + \int_0^x e^{t^2+1}\, dt$

D) $f(x) = 1 + \int_1^x e^{t^2+1}\, dt$

E) $f(x) = \int_0^x e^{t^2+1}\, dt$

23. On the closed interval [0, 2], which of the following could be the graph of a function f with the average value of 2?

I. 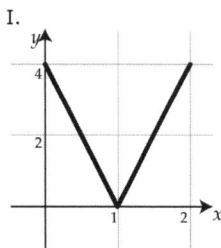 II. 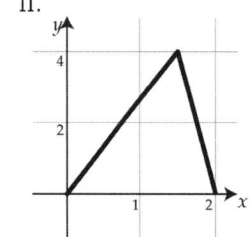 III.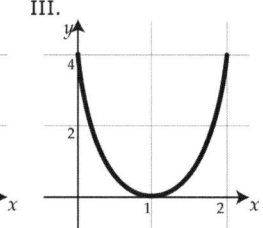

A) I only

B) I and II only

C) III only

D) none of these

E) I and III only

24. By using the substitution $u = 1 + \sqrt{x}$, $\dfrac{1}{2}\displaystyle\int \dfrac{\sqrt{x}}{1+\sqrt{x}}\,dx$ is same with

A) $\displaystyle\int 1\,du$

B) $\displaystyle\int \dfrac{(u-1)^2}{u}\,du$

C) $\displaystyle\int \dfrac{(\sqrt{u}-1)^2}{u}\,du$

D) $\displaystyle\int \dfrac{(\sqrt{u}+1)^2}{u}\,du$

E) $\displaystyle\int \dfrac{(u+1)^2}{u}\,du$

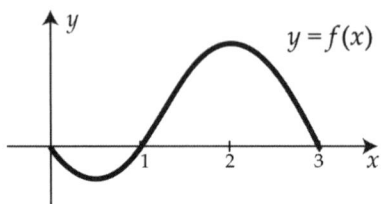

25. The graph of a function f is shown. Which of the following shows the inequality between $\int_0^1 f(x)\,dx$, $\int_0^3 f(x)\,dx$, and $\int_3^1 f(x)\,dx$?

A) $\int_0^3 f(x)\,dx < \int_0^1 f(x)\,dx < \int_3^1 f(x)\,dx$

B) $\int_0^1 f(x)\,dx < \int_0^3 f(x)\,dx < \int_3^1 f(x)\,dx$

C) $\int_0^1 f(x)\,dx < \int_3^1 f(x)\,dx < \int_0^3 f(x)\,dx$

D) $\int_3^1 f(x)\,dx < \int_0^1 f(x)\,dx < \int_0^3 f(x)\,dx$

E) $\int_3^1 f(x)\,dx < \int_0^3 f(x)\,dx < \int_0^1 f(x)\,dx$

26. If $\dfrac{dy}{dx} = 1 - y$, and if $x = 1$ and $y = 0$, then $y =$

   A) $y = e^x + 1$

   B) $y = e^{1+x} + 1$

   C) $y = e^{1-x} + 1$

   D) $y = 1 - e^{1+x}$

   E) $y = 1 - e^{1-x}$

27. Which of the following limits is equal to $\displaystyle\int_2^5 x^3 \, dx$?

   A) $\displaystyle\lim_{n \to \infty} \sum_{k=1}^{n} \left(2 + \dfrac{5k}{n}\right)^3 \dfrac{1}{n}$

   B) $\displaystyle\lim_{n \to \infty} \sum_{k=1}^{n} \left(2 + \dfrac{3k}{n}\right)^3 \dfrac{1}{n}$

   C) $\displaystyle\lim_{n \to \infty} \sum_{k=1}^{n} \left(2 + \dfrac{3k}{n}\right)^3 \dfrac{3}{n}$

   D) $\displaystyle\lim_{n \to \infty} \sum_{k=1}^{n} \left(2 + \dfrac{5k}{n}\right)^3 \dfrac{5}{n}$

   E) $\displaystyle\lim_{n \to \infty} \sum_{k=1}^{n} \left(2 + \dfrac{k}{n}\right)^3 \dfrac{5}{n}$

GO ON TO THE NEXT PAGE.

28. A ferris wheel has a radius of 15 meters and is rotating at the rate of 2 radians per minutes. How fast is the carriage rising when the carriage is 12 meters higher than the center of the ferris wheel?

A) 9 m/min
B) 18 m/min
C) 36 m/min
D) 48 m/min
E) 52 m/min

29. Let $g(x)$ be a continuous and differentiable for all x. If $g(1) = g'(1) = 0$, and $g''(1) = 2$, then what is $\lim_{x \to 1} \dfrac{\int_1^{x^2} g(t)\, dt}{g(x)}$?

A) 0
B) 1
C) -1
D) 2
E) 4

30. Let f be differentiable function, and $f(2+x) = f(2-x)$ for all x. Which of the following must be true?

   I. $f'(1) = f'(3)$.
   II. $f'(2) = 0$.
   III. $\int_0^2 f(x)\, dx = \int_2^4 f(x)\, dx$.

A) I only
B) I and II only
C) III only
D) none of these
E) II and III only

CALCULUS AB
SECTION I, Part B
Time—45 minutes
Number of questions—15

A GRAPHING CALCULATOR IS REQUIRED FOR SOME QUESTIONS ON THIS PART OF THE EXAM.

Directions: Solve each of the following problems, using the available space for scratch work. After examining the form of the choices, decide which is the best of the choices given and fill in the corresponding circle on the answer sheet. No credit will be given for anything written in the exam book. Do not spend too much time on any one problem.

BE SURE YOU FILL IN THE CIRCLES ON THE ANSWER SHEET THAT CORRESPOND TO QUESTIONS NUMBERED 76–90.

YOU MAY NOT RETURN TO QUESTIONS NUMBERED 1–30.

In this exam:

(1) The exact numerical value of the correct answer does not always appear among the choices given. When this happens, select from among the choices the number that best approximates the exact numerical value.

(2) Unless otherwise specified, the domain of a function f is assumed to be the set of all real numbers x for which $f(x)$ is a real number.

(3) The inverse of a trigonometric function f may be indicated using the inverse function notation f^{-1} or with the prefix "arc" (e.g. $\sin^{-1} x = \arcsin x$,).

GO ON TO THE NEXT PAGE.

76. The rate at which motor oil is leaking from an automobile is modeled by the function L defined by $L(t) = 500e^{-0.5t}$ gal/hr for time $t \geq 0$. How much oil leaks out of the automobile during the first 2 hour?

A) 240.450

B) 314.740

C) 542.451

D) 632.121

E) 512.121

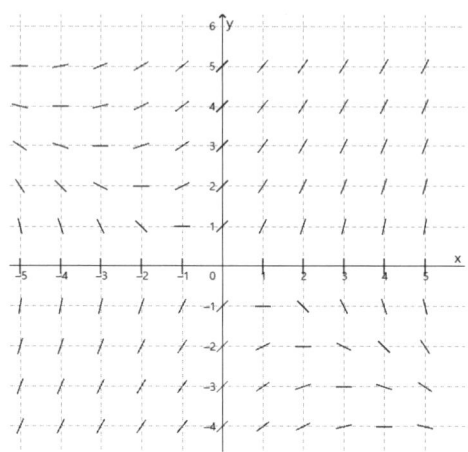

77. Shown above is a slope field for which of the following differential equations?

A) $\dfrac{dy}{dx} = \dfrac{x-y}{y}$

B) $\dfrac{dy}{dx} = \dfrac{x+y}{y}$

C) $\dfrac{dy}{dx} = \dfrac{x-y}{x}$

D) $\dfrac{dy}{dx} = \dfrac{x+y}{x}$

E) $\dfrac{dy}{dx} = \dfrac{2+y}{y}$

GO ON TO THE NEXT PAGE.

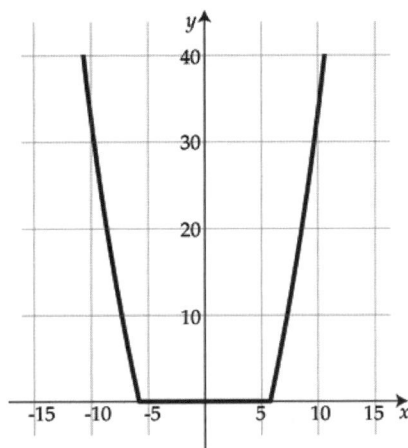

78. The vertical cross-section of a flower vase is shown in the figure. The curved sides of the cross section are given by the equation $y = 0.5x^2 - 16$. The horizontal cross sections are circular. The depth of the container is 40cm. If the flower vase is fully filled with water, what is the volume of the water?

A) 3220π

B) 2880π

C) 1440π

D) 8640π

E) 6440π

B B B B B B B B B

79. An object is moving along a straight line so that the position is $s(t)$, the velocity is $v(t)$ and the acceleration is $a(t)$. Which of the following gives the average acceleration of the particle in the interval $1 \le t \le 5$?

A) $\dfrac{1}{4}\displaystyle\int_1^5 v(t)\,dt$

B) $\dfrac{a(5)-a(1)}{4}$

C) $\dfrac{v(5)-v(1)}{4}$

D) $\displaystyle\int_1^5 a(t)\,dt$

E) $\dfrac{1}{4}\displaystyle\int_1^5 s(t)\,dt$

80. Let $f(x)=\dfrac{\ln(3x)}{x}$ for $0<x\le 3$. Point $A\left(\dfrac{1}{3},0\right)$ and point B are on the curve f. The tangent to the curve of f at A is perpendicular to the tangent at B. The x coordinate of B is

A) 0.014
B) 0.148
C) 1.016
D) 1.127
E) 2.045

GO ON TO THE NEXT PAGE.

81. Let f be the function with derivative $f'(x) = \sqrt{x^2 + 1}$. If $f(2) = 5$, what is the value of $f(7)$?

A) 21.454

B) 24.244

C) 14.201

D) 28.113

E) 30.113

82. Let R be the region in the first quadrant bounded by the graph of $y = \sin x$, and the vertical line $x = 1$. Which of the following gives the volume of the solid generated when region R is revolved about the vertical line $x = \dfrac{\pi}{2}$?

A) $\pi \int_0^1 (\arcsin x - 1)^2 dx$

B) $\pi \int_0^1 \left(\arcsin x - \dfrac{\pi}{2}\right)^2 - \left(1 - \dfrac{\pi}{2}\right)^2 dx$

C) $\pi \int_0^{\sin 1} \left(\arcsin x - \dfrac{\pi}{2}\right)^2 - \left(1 - \dfrac{\pi}{2}\right)^2 dx$

D) $\pi \int_0^{\sin 1} \left(\dfrac{\pi}{2} - \arcsin x\right)^2 - \left(\dfrac{\pi}{2} - 1\right)^2 dx$

E) $\pi \int_0^1 \left(\dfrac{\pi}{2} - \arcsin x\right)^2 - \left(\dfrac{\pi}{2} - 1\right)^2 dx$

83. Let $f(x) = \int_0^x \cos(e^t)\, dt$. In which of the following intervals is the graph of f concave down in $0 \leq x \leq 2$?

    A) $0.452 < x < 1.838$

    B) $0.452 < x < 1.550$

    C) $0 < x < 0.452$ or $1.550 < x < 2$

    D) $1.145 < x < 1.838$

    E) $0 < x < 1.145$ or $1.838 < x < 2$

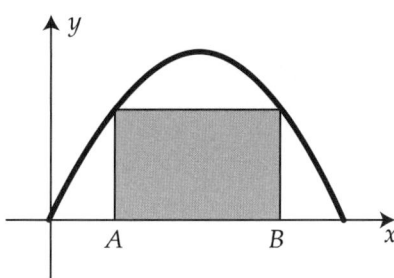

84. A rectangle is inscribed in the curve $y = \sin x$ and the x axis as shown in the figure. The vertex A has a coordinate $(x, 0)$. Find expression that gives the x value which will maximize the area of the rectangle.

A) $\tan x = \pi - 2x$

B) $2\tan x = \pi - 2x$

C) $\tan x = \dfrac{\pi}{2} - 2x$

D) $2\tan x = \dfrac{\pi}{2} - 2x$

E) $\tan x = \dfrac{\pi}{4}$

85. The velocity of a particle moving along the x axis is given by $v(t) = \sin(\sqrt{x}) - e^x$ for $t \geq 0$.

Which of the following statements could NOT describes the movement of the particle at $t = 2$?

A) Moves to the left

B) Moving down

C) Velocity is decreasing

D) Speed is increasing.

E) Acceleration is increasing

86. What is the area of the region in the first quadrant enclosed by the graph of $y = \sqrt{1 + \cos x}$ and $y = x$?

A) 0.415

B) 0.779

C) 0.877

D) 0.478

E) 0.315

87. If the derivative of f is defined by $f'(x) = x\sin(x^2)$, how many times does the concavity of f change in $-2 < x < 2$?

A) 0
B) 1
C) 2
D) 3
E) 4

88. The population of a city y is growing at a rate proportional to its population. If the population doubles every 5 years, then in how many years will the population triple?

A) $\dfrac{5\ln 2}{\ln 3}$

B) $\dfrac{5\ln 3}{\ln 2}$

C) $\dfrac{\ln 3}{\ln 2}$

D) $\dfrac{\ln 2}{\ln 5}$

E) $\dfrac{\ln 32}{\ln 3}$

x	$f(x)$	$f'(x)$	$g(x)$	$g'(x)$
1	4	6	-1	2

89. The table gives the values of the differentiable functions f and g and their derivatvies at $x = 1$. If $h(x) = \dfrac{xf(x)}{g(x)}$, what is $h'(1)$?

A) -8

B) -10

C) -14

D) -18

E) -20

x	0.0	0.1	0.2
$f(x)$	2	4	8

90. Function f is a continuous function and f' is increasing for all x. Selected values of f is shown in the table. Which of the following must be true about $f'(0.1)$?

A) $30 < f'(0.1) < 50$

B) $f'(0.1) < 0$

C) $f'(0.1) < 20$

D) $20 < f'(0.1) < 40$

E) $f'(0.1) > 20$

GO ON TO THE NEXT PAGE.

Mia's AP Calculus
MCQ Mock Test for BC

CALCULUS BC
SECTION I, Part A
Time—1 hour
Number of questions—30

A CALCULATOR MAY NOT BE USED ON THIS PART OF THE EXAM.

Directions: Solve each of the following problems, using the available space for scratch work. After examining the form of the choices, decide which is the best of the choices given and fill in the corresponding circle on the answer sheet. No credit will be given for anything written in the exam book. Do not spend too much time on any one problem.

In this exam:
(1) Unless otherwise specified, the domain of a function f is assumed to be the set of all real numbers x for which $f(x)$ is a real number.

(2) The inverse of a trigonometric function f may be indicated using the inverse function notation f^{-1} or with the prefix "arc" (e.g. $\sin^{-1} x = \arcsin x$,).

GO ON TO THE NEXT PAGE.

A A A A A A A A A A A A A A A A A A A A A A A A A A

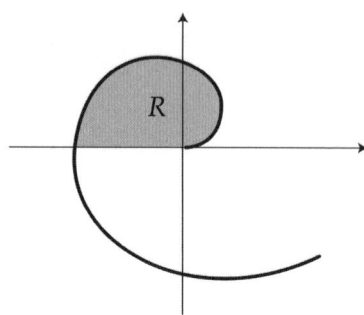

1. The polar curve $r = \theta$ is graphed. Let R be the region enclosed by the curve as shown in the figure. What is the area of R?

   A) $\dfrac{\pi^3}{12}$

   B) $\dfrac{\pi^3}{6}$

   C) $\dfrac{\pi^3}{3}$

   D) $\dfrac{\pi^3}{4}$

   E) $\dfrac{\pi^3}{8}$

2. Find the slope of the curve with equation $x^4 - x^2y + y^4 = 1$ where $x = -1$.

   A) $\dfrac{2}{3}$

   B) $\dfrac{1}{2}$

   C) $\dfrac{4}{3}$

   D) $\dfrac{3}{2}$

   E) $\dfrac{1}{3}$

GO ON TO THE NEXT PAGE.

3. Which of the following functions are differentiable for all real numbers x ?

   I. $f(x) = x^{2/3}$

   II. $f(x) = e^x$

   III. $f(x) = \tan x$

A) I only
B) I and II only
C) II only
D) none of these
E) I and III only

4. What is the horizontal asymptotes of $y = \dfrac{6 + 2^x}{3 - 4^x}$?

A) $y = 0$ and $y = 2$
B) $y = 0$
C) $y = 2$
D) $y = -1$ and $y = 0$
E) none

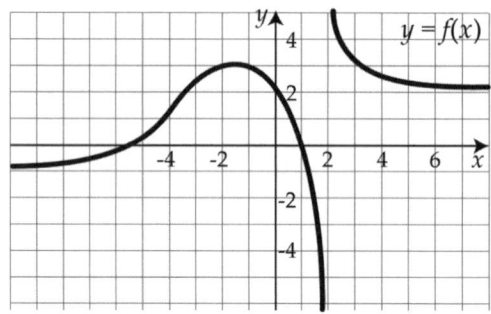

5. Graph of f is shown which has a horizontal asymptotes at $y = -1$ and $y = 2$, and a vertical asymptote at $x = 2$. Which of the following is NOT true?

A) $\lim\limits_{x \to 2} f(x)$ does not exist.

B) $f'(-1.5)$ is approximately 0.

C) $f(0) > \lim\limits_{h \to 0} \dfrac{f(4+h) - f(4)}{h}$

D) $\lim\limits_{x \to \infty} f'(x) = 2$

E) $\lim\limits_{x \to -\infty} f(f^2(x)) = 0$

6. $\int \dfrac{2}{x^2 - 4x + 3}\, dx =$

   A) $\ln\left|\dfrac{x-3}{x-1}\right| + C$

   B) $\ln\left|\dfrac{x-1}{x-3}\right| + C$

   C) $\ln\left|x^2 - 4x + 3\right|$

   D) $2\ln\left|\dfrac{x-3}{x-1}\right| + C$

   E) $2\ln\left|x^2 - 4x + 3\right|$

7. The power series $-\dfrac{(x-2)}{5} + \dfrac{(x-2)^2}{2(5^2)} - \dfrac{(x-2)^3}{3(5^3)} + \dfrac{(x-2)^4}{4(5^4)} - \ldots$ converges for

   A) $-3 < x < 7$

   B) $-3 \leq x < 7$

   C) $-3 < x \leq 7$

   D) $-3 \leq x \leq 7$

   E) All real numbers

8. Given that $x\arctan y = 1$, $\dfrac{dy}{dx} = $.

   A) $-\dfrac{1+y^2}{x^2}$

   B) $1+y^2$

   C) $-\dfrac{x\arctan y}{1+y^2}$

   D) $\dfrac{1+y^2}{x}$

   E) $1+x^2$

9. $f(x) = \begin{cases} -2x & , x < 1 \\ x^2 - 4x + 2 & , x \geq 1 \end{cases}$

   Let $f(x)$ be the function above. Which of the following statements are true?

   I. $\lim\limits_{x \to 1} f(x)$ exists.

   II. f is continuous at $x = 1$.

   III. f is differentiable at $x = 1$.

   A) I only

   B) I and II only

   C) III only

   D) none of these

   E) I and III only

10. A particle moves along the curve $x^2y = 4$. When $x = 2$, then $\frac{dx}{dt} = 1$. What is the value of $\frac{dy}{dt}$ when $x = 2$?

A) 0

B) -1

C) 2

D) 1

E) 3

11. If $f(0) = 1$, $f'(1) = 4$, $f'(2) = 3$, and $\int_0^2 f'(x)\, dx = -1$, then $(f^{-1})'(0) =$

A) $\frac{1}{4}$

B) $\frac{1}{3}$

C) $-\frac{1}{4}$

D) $-\frac{1}{3}$

E) Not exist

12. Let $g(x)$ be a twice differentiable function. If $g'(0) = -10$ and $g'(5) = 10$, which of the following must be true on the interval $0 \leq x \leq 5$?

   A) $g'(x) = 20$ for some x in the interval

   B) $g'(x) = 0$ for some x in the interval

   C) $g(x) = 0$ for some x in the interval

   D) $g(x) = 4$ for some x in the interval

   E) $g(x) > 0$ for some x in the interval

13. The derivative of f is $e^x(x-2)^2(x+1)^3$. At how many points will the graph of f have a relative minimum?

   A) None
   B) Four
   C) Two
   D) One
   E) Three

A A A A A A A A A A A A A A A A A A A A A A A A A

14. Let f be the function defined by $f(x) = \tan x$. Using the tangent line of f at the point $x = \dfrac{\pi}{4}$, find the approximation for $f\left(\dfrac{\pi}{3}\right)$.

A) $\dfrac{\pi}{3} + 3$

B) $\dfrac{\pi}{3} + 1$

C) $\dfrac{\pi}{6} + 1$

D) $\dfrac{\pi}{6} + 3$

E) $\dfrac{\pi}{2} + 2$

15. Which of the following series converges?

A) $\sum\limits_{n=1}^{\infty} (-1)^n \dfrac{n+1}{n}$

B) $\sum\limits_{n=1}^{\infty} \dfrac{3}{n+2}$

C) $\sum\limits_{n=1}^{\infty} \dfrac{1}{\ln n}$

D) $\sum\limits_{n=1}^{\infty} \dfrac{2^n x^n}{n!}$

E) $\sum\limits_{n=1}^{\infty} \dfrac{2^n n!}{x^n}$

GO ON TO THE NEXT PAGE.

16. A student attempted to use L'Hopital's Rule as follows. In which step does an error first appear?

$$\lim_{x \to \infty} \frac{\sin(1/x)}{e^{1/x}}$$ Step1

$$= \lim_{x \to \infty} \frac{-x^{-2}\cos(1/x)}{-x^{-2}e^{1/x}}$$ Step2

$$= \lim_{x \to \infty} \frac{\cos(1/x)}{e^{1/x}}$$ Step3

$$= \frac{1}{1}$$
$$= 1$$ Step4

A) Step 1

B) Step 2

C) Step 3

D) Step 4

E) No error.

17. A cone shaped cup is made by a circular piece of paper of radius 2 by cutting out a sector and joining the cut edges. Find the maximum capacity of such a cup.

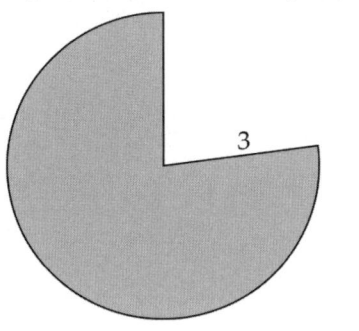
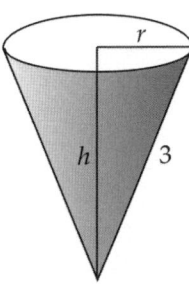

A) $\sqrt{3}\pi$

B) 3π

C) $3\sqrt{3}\pi$

D) $4\sqrt{3}\pi$

E) $2\sqrt{3}\pi$

18. Let g be a function for which all derivatives exist at $x = 1$. If $g(1) = g'(1) = g''(1) = g'''(1) = 6$, use the third degree polynomial of $g(x)$ about $x = 1$ to approximate $g(2)$.

   A) 13
   B) 14
   C) 15
   D) 16
   E) 17

19. An observer recorded the velocity of an object in motion along the x axis for 10 seconds. Based on the table below, use a trapezoidal approximation to estimate how far from its starting point the object came at the end of this time.

t	0	2	3	5	7	10
$v(t)$	3	5	1	-1	-3	5

   A) 6
   B) 12
   C) 24
   D) 29
   E) 34

20. The graph above shows the derivative of function f. The numbers represents the areas of each region. What is the value of x at which the minimum of f occurs in the interval $0 \le x \le 12$?

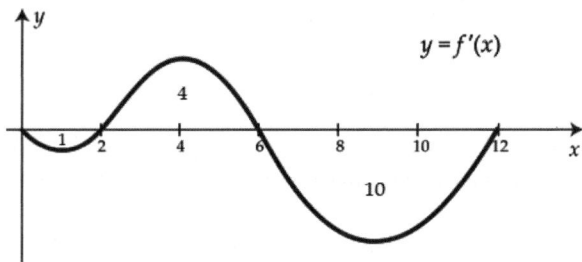

A) 0
B) 2
C) 6
D) 9
E) 12

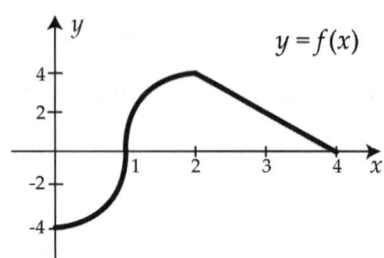

21. Graph of f(x) is shown and let h be the function $h(x) = \int_0^{\sqrt{x}} f(t)\,dt$. Which of the following is an equation for the line tangent to the graph of h at the point where $x = 4$?

A) $y = x + 2$

B) $y = x - 4$

C) $y = x - 2$

D) $y = x + 4$

E) $y = x$

22. Which of the following must be true about $\sum_{n=1}^{\infty} \frac{1}{n \ln n}$?

A) $\sum_{n=1}^{\infty} \frac{1}{n \ln n}$ diverges, and $\int_{1}^{\infty} \frac{1}{x \ln x} dx < \sum_{n=1}^{\infty} \frac{1}{n \ln n}$

B) $\sum_{n=1}^{\infty} \frac{1}{n \ln n}$ diverges, and $\int_{1}^{\infty} \frac{1}{x \ln x} dx > \sum_{n=1}^{\infty} \frac{1}{n \ln n}$

C) $\sum_{n=1}^{\infty} \frac{1}{n \ln n}$ converges, and $\int_{1}^{\infty} \frac{1}{x \ln x} dx < \sum_{n=1}^{\infty} \frac{1}{n \ln n}$

D) $\sum_{n=1}^{\infty} \frac{1}{n \ln n}$ converges, and $\int_{1}^{\infty} \frac{1}{x \ln x} dx > \sum_{n=1}^{\infty} \frac{1}{n \ln n}$

E) $\sum_{n=1}^{\infty} \frac{1}{n \ln n} = 0$

A A A A A A A A A A A A A A A A A A A A A A A A A

23. On the closed interval [0, 2], which of the following could be the graph of a function f with the average value of 2?

I.
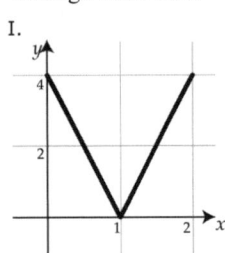

II.
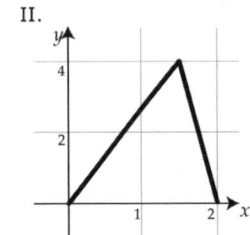

III.
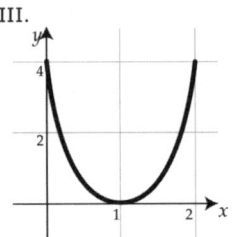

A) I only

B) I and II only

C) III only

D) none of these

E) I and III only

24. By using the substitution $u = 1 + \sqrt{x}$, $\dfrac{1}{2}\int \dfrac{\sqrt{x}}{1+\sqrt{x}}\,dx$ is same with

A) $\int 1\,du$

B) $\int \dfrac{(u-1)^2}{u}\,du$

C) $\int \dfrac{(\sqrt{u}-1)^2}{u}\,du$

D) $\int \dfrac{(\sqrt{u}+1)^2}{u}\,du$

E) $\int \dfrac{(u+1)^2}{u}\,du$

GO ON TO THE NEXT PAGE.

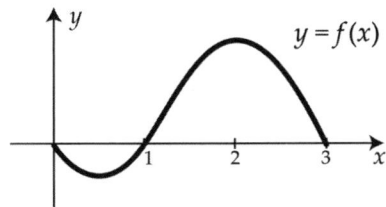

25. The graph of a function f is shown. Which of the following shows the inequality between $\int_0^1 f(x)\,dx$, $\int_0^3 f(x)\,dx$, and $\int_3^1 f(x)\,dx$?

A) $\int_0^3 f(x)\,dx < \int_0^1 f(x)\,dx < \int_3^1 f(x)\,dx$

B) $\int_0^1 f(x)\,dx < \int_0^3 f(x)\,dx < \int_3^1 f(x)\,dx$

C) $\int_0^1 f(x)\,dx < \int_3^1 f(x)\,dx < \int_0^3 f(x)\,dx$

D) $\int_3^1 f(x)\,dx < \int_0^1 f(x)\,dx < \int_0^3 f(x)\,dx$

E) $\int_3^1 f(x)\,dx < \int_0^3 f(x)\,dx < \int_0^1 f(x)\,dx$

GO ON TO THE NEXT PAGE.

A A A A A A A A A A A A A A A A A A A A A A A A A

26. If $\dfrac{dy}{dx} = 1 - y$, and if $x = 1$ and $y = 0$, then $y =$

   A) $y = e^x + 1$

   B) $y = e^{1+x} + 1$

   C) $y = e^{1-x} + 1$

   D) $y = 1 - e^{1+x}$

   E) $y = 1 - e^{1-x}$

27. Which of the following limits is equal to $\int_2^5 x^3\, dx$?

   A) $\lim\limits_{n \to \infty} \sum\limits_{k=1}^{n} \left(2 + \dfrac{5k}{n}\right)^3 \dfrac{1}{n}$

   B) $\lim\limits_{n \to \infty} \sum\limits_{k=1}^{n} \left(2 + \dfrac{3k}{n}\right)^3 \dfrac{1}{n}$

   C) $\lim\limits_{n \to \infty} \sum\limits_{k=1}^{n} \left(2 + \dfrac{3k}{n}\right)^3 \dfrac{3}{n}$

   D) $\lim\limits_{n \to \infty} \sum\limits_{k=1}^{n} \left(2 + \dfrac{5k}{n}\right)^3 \dfrac{5}{n}$

   E) $\lim\limits_{n \to \infty} \sum\limits_{k=1}^{n} \left(2 + \dfrac{k}{n}\right)^3 \dfrac{5}{n}$

GO ON TO THE NEXT PAGE.

28. What is the sum of the series $1 + 2\ln x + \frac{(2\ln x)^2}{2!} + \frac{(2\ln x)^3}{3!} + \ldots$

A) x

B) $\frac{1}{1-2\ln x}$

C) e^x

D) e^{x^2}

E) x^2

29. Let $g(x)$ be a continuous and differentiable for all x. If $g(1) = g'(1) = 0$, and $g''(1) = 2$, then what is $\lim_{x \to 1} \frac{\int_1^{x^2} g(t)\, dt}{g(x)}$?

A) 0

B) 1

C) -1

D) 2

E) 4

30. Let f be differentiable function, and $f(2+x) = f(2-x)$ for all x. Which of the following must be true?

   I. $f'(1) = f'(3)$.

   II. $f'(2) = 0$.

   III. $\int_0^2 f(x)\,dx = \int_2^4 f(x)\,dx$.

A) I only
B) I and II only
C) III only
D) none of these
E) II and III only

CALCULUS BC
SECTION I, Part B
Time—45 minutes
Number of questions—15

A GRAPHING CALCULATOR IS REQUIRED FOR SOME QUESTIONS ON THIS PART OF THE EXAM.

Directions: Solve each of the following problems, using the available space for scratch work. After examining the form of the choices, decide which is the best of the choices given and fill in the corresponding circle on the answer sheet. No credit will be given for anything written in the exam book. Do not spend too much time on any one problem.

BE SURE YOU FILL IN THE CIRCLES ON THE ANSWER SHEET THAT CORRESPOND TO QUESTIONS NUMBERED 76–90.

YOU MAY NOT RETURN TO QUESTIONS NUMBERED 1–30.

In this exam:
(1) The exact numerical value of the correct answer does not always appear among the choices given. When this happens, select from among the choices the number that best approximates the exact numerical value.

(2) Unless otherwise specified, the domain of a function f is assumed to be the set of all real numbers x for which $f(x)$ is a real number.

(3) The inverse of a trigonometric function f may be indicated using the inverse function notation f^{-1} or with the prefix "arc" (e.g. $\sin^{-1} x = \arcsin x$,).

GO ON TO THE NEXT PAGE.

76. The number of students in a school who have listened to Kpop music at time t hours is modeled by the function P as shown in the graph, the solution to a logistic differential equation. Which differential equation could be the appropriate model?

A) $\dfrac{dP}{dt} = 2000P - 2P^2$

B) $\dfrac{dP}{dt} = 2000P - 1000P^2$

C) $\dfrac{dP}{dt} = 2P^2 - 2000P$

D) $\dfrac{dP}{dt} = 1000P^2 - 2000P$

E) $\dfrac{dP}{dt} = 2P^2 - 500P$

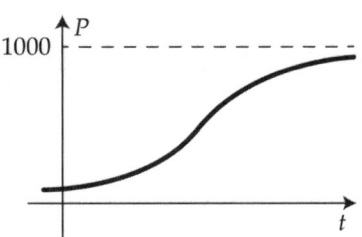

77. The length of the curve path described by the parametric equation $x(t) = \sin 3x$, $y(t) = t^2 - 1$ from $t = 0$ to $t = 3$ is

A) $\displaystyle\int_0^3 \sqrt{9\sin^2 3t + 4t^2}\, dt$

B) $\displaystyle\int_0^3 \sqrt{3\cos^4 3t + 4t^2}\, dt$

C) $\displaystyle\int_0^3 \sqrt{9\cos^2 3t + 4t^2}\, dt$

D) $\displaystyle\int_0^3 \sqrt{3\cos^2 3t + 2t^2}\, dt$

E) $\displaystyle\int_0^3 \sqrt{9\sin^2 3t + 2t^2}\, dt$

GO ON TO THE NEXT PAGE.

B   B   B   B   B   B   B   B   B

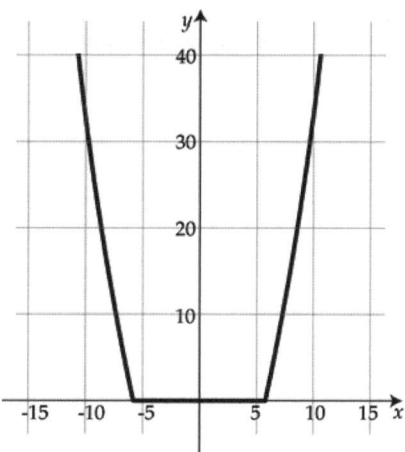

78. The vertical cross-section of a flower vase is shown in the figure. The curved sides of the cross section are given by the equation $y = 0.5x^2 - 16$. The horizontal cross sections are circular. The depth of the container is 40cm. If the flower vase is fully filled with water, what is the volume of the water?

A) 3220π

B) 2880π

C) 1440π

D) 8640π

E) 6440π

GO ON TO THE NEXT PAGE.

79. An object is moving along a straight line so that the position is $s(t)$, the velocity is $v(t)$ and the acceleration is $a(t)$. Which of the following gives the average acceleration of the particle in the interval $1 \leq t \leq 5$?

A) $\dfrac{1}{4}\displaystyle\int_1^5 v(t)\,dt$

B) $\dfrac{a(5)-a(1)}{4}$

C) $\dfrac{v(5)-v(1)}{4}$

D) $\displaystyle\int_1^5 a(t)\,dt$

E) $\dfrac{1}{4}\displaystyle\int_1^5 s(t)\,dt$

80. Let $f(x)=\dfrac{\ln(3x)}{x}$ for $0<x\leq 3$. Point $A\left(\dfrac{1}{3},0\right)$ and point B are on the curve f. The tangent to the curve of f at A is perpendicular to the tangent at B. The x coordinate of B is

A) 0.014

B) 0.148

C) 1.016

D) 1.127

E) 2.045

GO ON TO THE NEXT PAGE.

81. An object moving along a curve in the xy-plane has position $x(t) = e^{t^2 - t + 1}$, $y(t) = t^3 - 2t^2$ at time t. Write an equation for the line tangent to the curve at $t = 1$.

A) $y + 1 = -\dfrac{1}{e}(x - 1)$

B) $y + 1 = -\dfrac{1}{e}(x - e)$

C) $y + 1 = -e(x - e)$

D) $y = -x$

E) $y = x$

82. Let R be the region in the first quadrant bounded by the graph of $y = \sin x$, and the vertical line $x = 1$. Which of the following gives the volume of the solid generated when region R is revolved about the vertical line $x = \dfrac{\pi}{2}$?

A) $\pi \displaystyle\int_0^1 (\arcsin x - 1)^2 \, dx$

B) $\pi \displaystyle\int_0^1 \left(\arcsin x - \dfrac{\pi}{2}\right)^2 - \left(1 - \dfrac{\pi}{2}\right)^2 \, dx$

C) $\pi \displaystyle\int_0^{\sin 1} \left(\arcsin x - \dfrac{\pi}{2}\right)^2 - \left(1 - \dfrac{\pi}{2}\right)^2 \, dx$

D) $\pi \displaystyle\int_0^{\sin 1} \left(\dfrac{\pi}{2} - \arcsin x\right)^2 - \left(\dfrac{\pi}{2} - 1\right)^2 \, dx$

E) $\pi \displaystyle\int_0^1 \left(\dfrac{\pi}{2} - \arcsin x\right)^2 - \left(\dfrac{\pi}{2} - 1\right)^2 \, dx$

83. The table show selected values of the derivative for a differentiable function f.

x	1	1.5	2
$f'(x)$	-0.5	-1.2	-2.3

If $f(1) = 10$, what is the approximation to $f(2)$ obtained by using Euler's method with a step size 0.5?

A) 12
B) 8.35
C) 9.15
D) 9.45
E) 10.21

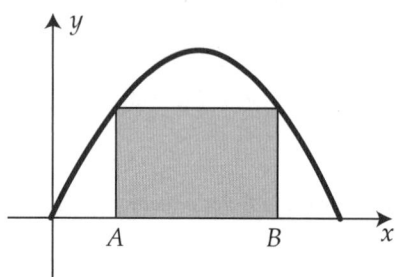

84. A rectangle is inscribed in the curve $y = \sin x$ and the x axis as shown in the figure. The vertex A has a coordinate $(x, 0)$. Find expression that gives the x value which will maximize the area of the rectangle.

A) $\tan x = \pi - 2x$

B) $2\tan x = \pi - 2x$

C) $\tan x = \dfrac{\pi}{2} - 2x$

D) $2\tan x = \dfrac{\pi}{2} - 2x$

E) $\tan x = \dfrac{\pi}{4}$

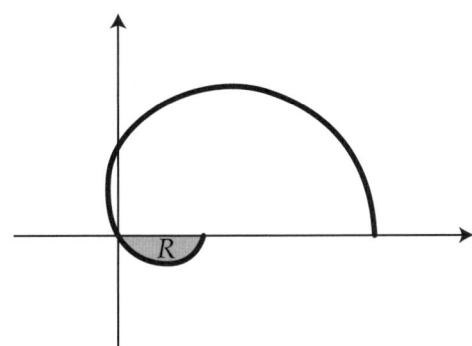

85. The polar curve $r = 1 + 2\cos\theta$ is graphed for $0 \le \theta \le \pi$. Let R be the region enclosed by the curve as shown in the figure. What is the area of R?

A) $\dfrac{1}{2}\int_{\pi}^{\pi/2}(1+2\cos\theta)^2\, d\theta$

B) $\dfrac{1}{2}\int_{2\pi/3}^{\pi}(1+2\cos\theta)^2\, d\theta$

C) $\dfrac{1}{2}\int_{3\pi/2}^{\pi}(1+2\cos\theta)^2\, d\theta$

D) $\dfrac{1}{2}\int_{0}^{\pi}(1+2\cos\theta)^2\, d\theta$

E) $\int_{0}^{\pi/2}(1+2\cos\theta)^2\, d\theta$

86. What is the area of the region in the first quadrant enclosed by the graph of $y = \sqrt{1 + \cos x}$ and $y = x$?

A) 0.415

B) 0.779

C) 0.877

D) 0.478

E) 0.315

87. If the derivative of f is defined by $f'(x) = x \sin(x^2)$, how many times does the concavity of f change in $-2 < x < 2$?

A) 0

B) 1

C) 2

D) 3

E) 4

For question 88-89, use the table. The table gives the values of the differentiable functions f and g and their derivatvies at $x = 1$ and 3.

x	$f(x)$	$f'(x)$	$g(x)$	$g'(x)$
1	4	6	-1	2
3	0	5	4	3

88. If $h(x) = \dfrac{xf(x)}{g(x)}$, what is $h'(1)$?

   A) -8

   B) -10

   C) -14

   D) -18

   E) -20

89. If $\int_0^3 g(x)\,dx = 7$ and $\int_0^1 g(x)\,dx = 2$, then what is $\int_1^3 xg'(x)\,dx = ?$

   A) 6   B) 8   C) 13   D) 18   E) 21

90. Consider the alternating series $\sum_{n=1}^{\infty} \frac{(-1)^n}{\ln(n^2+1)}$. Find the smallest value of n for which the nth partial sum approximates the sum of the series within 0.1.

A) 146

B) 147

C) 148

D) 149

E) 150

Mia's AP Calculus
Answers

1. Limit

Ex1.	① i) 3 ii) 1 iii) 1 iv) 1 ② i) 8 ii) 5 iii) 8 iv) DNE ③ i) und ii) 5 iii) 3 iv) DNE ④ i) und ii) 5 iii) 5 iv) 5
Ex2.	① 1 ② ∞ ③ $-\infty$ ④ 0 ⑤ $-\infty$ ⑥ $-\infty$ ⑦ ∞ ⑧ ∞ ⑨ ∞ ⑩ $-\infty$
Ex3.	① DNE ② 0 ③ 2
Ex4.	① 19 ② -2 ③ $\frac{1}{2}$ ④ $\frac{1}{4}$ ⑤ 12 ⑥ $\frac{\sqrt{3}}{6}$ ⑦ $-\frac{1}{6}$
AP	1. C 2. B 3. A 4. D 5. D
Ex5.	① 19 ② 28 ③ $-\frac{1}{2}$ ④ $4\sqrt{7}$ ⑤ e^7
AP	1. C 2.1)B 2.2)B
Ex6.	① a) 1 b) DNE c) 2 d) 1 ② a) 4 b) $\frac{1}{2}$ c) $\frac{1}{2}$ d) $\frac{1}{2}$ ③ 1 ④ -1 ⑤ 8 ⑥ -8
Ex7.	① ∞ ② $-\infty$ ③ $-\infty$ ④ ∞ ⑤ ∞ ⑥ $-\infty$ ⑦ ∞ ⑧ $-\infty$
AP	1. B 2. B 3. C
Ex8.	① 0 ② 0 ③ 0 ④ 0 ⑤ 0 ⑥ 3 ⑦ $-\infty$ ⑧ -2
Ex9.	① $-\infty$ ② ∞ ③ 0 ④ $\frac{3}{5}$ ⑤ ∞ ⑥ ∞ ⑦ 2 ⑧ $\frac{1}{2}$ ⑨ ∞ ⑩ -4 ⑪ $\frac{2}{3}$ ⑫ 0 ⑬ 0
Ex10.	$y = 3$ and $y = -3$
Ex11.	① ∞ ② 5 ③ -6 ④ -8 ⑤ 3
AP	1.C 2.C
Ex12.	① $\frac{2}{3}$ ② 1 ③ $\frac{3}{2}$ ④ $\frac{1}{2}$ ⑤ $\frac{1}{3}$ ⑥ 2 ⑦ 0 ⑧ 2 ⑨ $\frac{\pi}{2}$
Ex13.	$-\frac{1}{x} \leq \frac{\sin x}{x} \leq \frac{1}{x}$ $\lim\limits_{x \to \infty} -\frac{1}{x} = 0$, $\lim\limits_{x \to \infty} \frac{1}{x} = 0$ According to squeeze theorem, $\lim\limits_{x \to \infty} \frac{\sin x}{x} = 0$

2. Continuity and Discontinuity

Ex1.	$x = -1$: jump $x = 1$, removable $x = 2$, removable
Ex2.	When $x = -1$ (a) $f(-1) = 0$, (b) $\lim\limits_{x \to -1^+} f(x) = 0$, $\lim\limits_{x \to -1^-} f(x) = 1$ $\lim\limits_{x \to -1} f(x) = DNE$ (c) $\lim\limits_{x \to -1} f(x) \neq f(-1)$ (d) second, third condition When $x = 1$ (a) $f(1) = 2$, (b) $\lim\limits_{x \to 1^+} f(x) = 1$, $\lim\limits_{x \to 1^-} f(x) = 1$ $\lim\limits_{x \to 1} f(x) = 1$ (c) $\lim\limits_{x \to 1} f(x) \neq f(1)$ (d) third condition When $x = 2$ (a) $f(2) = $ und, (b) $\lim\limits_{x \to 2^+} f(x) = 0$, $\lim\limits_{x \to 2^-} f(x) = 0$ $\lim\limits_{x \to 2} f(x) = 0$ (c) $\lim\limits_{x \to 2} f(x) \neq f(2)$ (d) first, third condition
Ex3.	$f(2) = 0$
Ex4.	① Not continuous ($f(2)$ is und) ② Continuous ③ Continuous ④ Not continuous $(\lim\limits_{x \to 1} \dfrac{x^3 - 1}{x^2 + 2x - 3} \neq f(1))$
Ex5.	① $a = \dfrac{4}{3}$ ② $a = 5$ ③ $a = -2, b = 1$
AP	1. B 2. B 3. E

3. Differentiation

Ex1.	① 11 ② $-\dfrac{3}{7}$
Ex2.	① $f'(x)$ $= \lim\limits_{h \to 0} \dfrac{(x+h)^2 + 2(x+h) - x^2 - 2x}{h}$ $= 2x + 2$ ② $\dfrac{dy}{dx}$ $= \lim\limits_{h \to 0} \dfrac{\sqrt{x+h} - \sqrt{x}}{h}$ $= \dfrac{1}{2\sqrt{x}}$ ③ $\dfrac{ds}{dt}$ $= \lim\limits_{h \to 0} \dfrac{\frac{t+h}{2(t+h)+1} - \frac{t}{2t+1}}{h}$ $= \dfrac{1}{(2t+1)^2}$
Ex3.	① i) $f'(5)$ $= \lim\limits_{h \to 0} \dfrac{\sqrt{5+h} - \sqrt{5}}{h} = \dfrac{1}{2\sqrt{5}}$ ii) $f'(5)$ $= \lim\limits_{x \to 5} \dfrac{\sqrt{x} - \sqrt{5}}{x - 5} = \dfrac{1}{2\sqrt{5}}$ ② i) $f'(2)$ $= \lim\limits_{h \to 0} \dfrac{[(2+h)^2 + 3] - 7}{h} = 4$ ii) $f'(2)$ $= \lim\limits_{x \to 2} \dfrac{[x^2 + 3] - 7}{x - 2} = 4$
Ex4.	① $y' = 0$ ② $y' = 2x$ ③ $y' = 8x + 2$ ④ $y' = x - \dfrac{1}{3}$ ⑤ $y' = 3t^2 - 4t + 4$ ⑥ $y' = ex^{e-1} - e$ ⑦ $y' = -\dfrac{1}{x^2} - \dfrac{2}{x^3}$

	⑧	$y' = -\dfrac{6}{x^4} + \dfrac{1}{3x^2}$
	⑨	$y' = \dfrac{1}{2\sqrt{a}} - \dfrac{1}{2\sqrt{a^3}}$
	⑩	$y' = \dfrac{8}{3}\sqrt[3]{x} - \dfrac{1}{5\sqrt{x^3}}$
	⑪	$y' = 2x - \dfrac{2}{x^3}$
	⑫	$y' = 4x - 1$
	⑬	$y' = 4\cos x$
	⑭	$y' = -\pi \sin x$
	⑮	$y' = \sec^2 x$
	⑯	$y' = -\csc^2 x$
	⑰	$y' = \tan x \sec x - \cot x \csc x$
	⑱	$y' = \cot x \csc x$
	⑲	$y' = ex^{e-1} + e^x$
	⑳	$y' = \dfrac{e^x}{5}$
	㉑	$y' = \dfrac{1}{x}$
	㉒	$y' = \dfrac{2}{3x}$
	㉓	$y' = 2^x \ln 2 + e^x + 2x$
	㉔	$y' = \left(\dfrac{\ln x}{\ln 2}\right)' = \dfrac{1}{x \ln 2}$
	㉕	$y' = (4 \ln x)' = \dfrac{4}{x}$
	㉖	$y' = (e^{-2} e^x)' = e^{x-2}$
Ex5.	①	$a = 2, f(x) = x^4, f'(2) = 32$
	②	$a = 9, f(x) = \sqrt{x}, f'(9) = \dfrac{1}{6}$
	③	$a = 2, f(x) = \dfrac{1}{x}, f'(2) = -\dfrac{1}{4}$
	④	$a = 0, f(x) = e^x, f'(0) = 1$
	⑤	$a = 0, f(x) = \sin x, f'(0) = 1$
	⑥	$a = 1, f(x) = x^5, f'(1) = 5$

AP	1. B	2. I, III, IV	3. A	4.1) B
	4.2) B	4.3) A		4.4) I, III
	5. C	6. D		

4. Technique of Differentiation

Ex1.	①	$-6(-x+1)^2$
	②	$\dfrac{1}{\sqrt{2x-1}}$
	③	$\dfrac{-6x}{(3x^2+1)^2}$
	④	$\dfrac{15x}{\sqrt{(1-x^2)^5}}$
	⑤	$2\cos 2x$
	⑥	$-6\sin 3x$
	⑦	$2x\cos x^2$
	⑧	$2\sin x \cos x = \sin 2x$
	⑨	$\tan(\tan x)\sec(\tan x)\sec^2 x$
	⑩	$4x\sec^2(2x^2+1)$
	⑪	$-2\csc^2 x \cot x$
	⑫	$\dfrac{2}{3}e^{2x/3}$
	⑬	e^{x-1}
	⑭	$-2e^{-\sin x - 1}\cos x$
	⑮	$\dfrac{1}{x}$
	⑯	$\dfrac{6}{x}$
	⑰	$\dfrac{2}{x}(1 + \ln x)$
	⑱	$\dfrac{1}{2x}\left(\dfrac{1}{\sqrt{\ln x}} + 1\right)$
	⑲	$-\ln 3(3^{\cos x})\sin x$
Ex2.	①	$-6\cos^2 2x \sin 2x$
	②	$6x^2 \sec^2 x^3 \tan x^3$
	③	$3x^2 e^{\sin x^3} \cos x^3$
	④	$3e^{\sin^3 x} \sin^2 x \cos x$
	⑤	$24\sin 3x \cos 3x (1 + \sin^2 3x)^3$
	⑥	$\dfrac{e^{2x} \cos e^{2x}}{\sqrt{\sin e^{2x}}}$

Ex3.	① $2(2x+3)(4x^2+3x+2)$
	② $-2(1-t)(2t^2-t+1)$
	③ $e^{2x}(2\sin x + \cos x)$
	④ $-2e^{-x}\sin x$
	⑤ $1+\ln x$
	⑥ $\dfrac{4x}{(x^2+1)^2}$
	⑦ $\dfrac{x\cos x - 2\sin x}{x^3}$
	⑧ $\dfrac{1-\ln x}{x^2}$
	⑨ $\dfrac{15(x-2)^2}{(2x+1)^4}$
	⑩ $\dfrac{-x^3+4}{2(x^3+2)^{3/2}}$
Ex4.	$3\ln 4$
Ex5.	-4
Ex6.	$\dfrac{\pi}{4}, \dfrac{5\pi}{4}$
Ex7.	$a=12, b=18$
Ex8.	$\dfrac{12x^2}{x^3-1} + \dfrac{3}{2(3x-1)} - \dfrac{2x}{x^2+4}$
Ex9.	① $\dfrac{-x}{y}$
	② $\dfrac{y-3x^2}{4y-x}$
	③ $\dfrac{y^2-2xy}{x^2-2xy}$
	④ $\dfrac{1}{1-\csc^2 y}$
	⑤ $\dfrac{\sec^2(x+y)}{1-\sec^2(x+y)}$
	⑥ $\dfrac{y-2xy^2}{x}$
Ex10.	$-\dfrac{1}{2}$
Ex11.	$\dfrac{6}{7}$
Ex12.	$-\dfrac{1}{2}$
Ex13.	(a) $(0,5),(0,-2)$

	(b) $\left(\dfrac{7}{2},\dfrac{3}{2}\right),\left(-\dfrac{7}{2},\dfrac{3}{2}\right)$
Ex14.	① $\dfrac{1}{1+x^2}$
	② $\dfrac{2}{4+x^2}$
	③ $\dfrac{1-x}{\sqrt{1-x^2}}$
	④ $4x^2\left(3\sin^{-1}x + \dfrac{x}{\sqrt{1-x^2}}\right)$
	⑤ $\dfrac{6\tan^{-1}3x}{1+9x^2}$
	⑥ 0
Ex15.	① $6f'(x) - g'(x)$
	② $2f(x)f'(x)$
	③ $f'(f(x))f'(x)$
	④ $g'(f(x^2))f'(x^2)\cdot 2x$
	⑤ $\dfrac{f'(x^3)3x^2(g(x)+1) - f(x^3)g'(x)}{(g(x)+1)^2}$
	⑥ $f'(x+g(x))(1+g'(x))$
	⑦ $f'(x)g(x^2) + f(x)g'(x^2)2x$
	⑧ $f'(x)g^2(x) + f(x)\cdot 2g(x)g'(x)$
Ex16.	$\dfrac{d^3y}{dx^3}=6, \dfrac{d^4y}{dx^4}=0$
Ex17.	① T
	② F
Ex18.	① $\dfrac{2(y-1)}{(1+x)^2}$
	② $\dfrac{2y^2-x^2}{4y^3}$
Ex19.	$-n^{99}\cos nx$
AP	1.1) A 1.2) D 1.3) E 2. A
	3. B 4. E 5. B 6. E
	7. D 8. D 9. A

5. Differentiability and tangent line

Ex1.	① tang: $y-3=\dfrac{1}{2}(x-2)$
	norm: $y-3=-2(x-2)$
	② tang: $y-2=\dfrac{2}{e}(x-e)$
	norm: $y-2=-\dfrac{e}{2}(x-e)$
	③ tang: $y=0$
	norm: $x=\dfrac{\pi}{2}$
Ex2.	$y-3=-5(x-1)$
	$y=-5x+8$
AP	1. A 2. A 3. B 4. B
Ex3.	$\dfrac{1}{10}$
Ex4.	e^2
AP	1. B 2. C 3. C
Ex5.	(a) e, g (b) e, f, g, h (c) b – h
	(d) b, c, d (e) e – h
Ex6.	① continuous, not differentiable
	② discontinuous, not differentiable
	③ continuous, differentiable
	④ continuous, not differentiable
	⑤ continuous, not differentiable
	⑥ continuous, differentiable
AP	1. D 2. A 3. D 4. D 5. A

Free Response Question (from ch1~5)

1.	(a) $\lim\limits_{x\to 1}g(f(x))=g(\lim\limits_{x\to 1}f(x))=g(1^-)$
	$=\lim\limits_{x\to 1^-}g(x)=2$
	(b) $h(1)=f(3)g(1)=4$
	$\lim\limits_{x\to 1^+}f(x+2)g(x)=(1)(4)=4$
	$\lim\limits_{x\to 1^-}f(x+2)g(x)=(2)(2)=4$
	$\lim\limits_{x\to 1}f(x+2)g(x)=4$
	$h(1)=\lim\limits_{x\to 1}f(x+2)g(x)=4$
	Therefore, h is continuous at x = 1.
	(c) $\lim\limits_{h\to 0^+}\dfrac{f(1+h)-f(1)}{h}=-1$
	$\lim\limits_{h\to 0^-}\dfrac{f(1+h)-f(1)}{h}=1$
	Since
	$\lim\limits_{h\to 0^+}\dfrac{f(1+h)-f(1)}{h}\neq\lim\limits_{h\to 0^-}\dfrac{f(1+h)-f(1)}{h}$
	Therefore
	$\lim\limits_{h\to 0}\dfrac{f(1+h)-f(1)}{h}=f'(1)=undefined$
2.	(a) $f'(2)=4e^{g(2)}+4e^{g(2)}g'(2)=-4e$
	(b) $P'(2)=\dfrac{f'(2)g(2^2)-f(2)g'(2^2)(2)(2)}{\left[g(2^2)\right]^2}=e$
	(c) $Q'(1)=f'(\sqrt{g(1)})\dfrac{1}{2\sqrt{g(1)}}g'(1)=-e$
	(d) Point: $(4,g^{-1}(4))=(4,1)$
	Slope: $[g^{-1}(4)]'=\dfrac{1}{g'(g^{-1}(4))}=\dfrac{1}{g'(1)}=1$
	Therefore, $y-1=x-4\Rightarrow y=x-3$
	(e) $2y\dfrac{dy}{dx}=g'(xy+x)(y+x\dfrac{dy}{dx}+1)$
	If we plug in (1, 0)
	$\dfrac{dy}{dx}=-1$

6. Extrema and the First Derivative

Ex1.	seven
Ex2.	① $x = 0, 2$ ② $x = 0$ ③ $x = 3$
Ex3.	① max $y(1) = 10$ min $y(2) = 9$ ② min $y(-2) = -4$ ③ max $y(1) = e^{-1}$ ④ min $y(1) = \dfrac{1}{2}$ max $y(5) = \dfrac{1}{10}$ ⑤ max $y(\pi/6) = \dfrac{\pi}{12} + \dfrac{\sqrt{3}}{2}$ min $y(5\pi/6) = \dfrac{5\pi}{12} - \dfrac{\sqrt{3}}{2}$ ⑥ max $y(0) = 0$ min $y(2/5) = -\dfrac{3}{5}\left(\dfrac{2}{5}\right)^{2/3}$
AP	1. C 2. A 3. A 4. D
Ex4.	① Abs max = -11 Abs min = -15 ② Abs max = $e^2 - 2$ Abs min = 1
AP	1. E
Ex5.	① ② ③ ④
AP	1. B
Ex6.	① The height of the rocket is increasing at the rate of 30 km/min at t = 2 min ② The time it takes for a chemical reaction is increasing at the rate of 2.2 min/ml when a = 20ml. ③ The rate at which the temperature is changing is decreasing by 10 Fahrenheit per hour per hour when h = 5 hours.
Ex7.	$20e^2$ The rate of consumption of milk in the US is increasing by $20e^2$ millions of gallon per year per year in 2010.
Ex8.	-30 The rate of decay of radioactive substance is decreasing by 30 grams per min per min when t = 5 min.

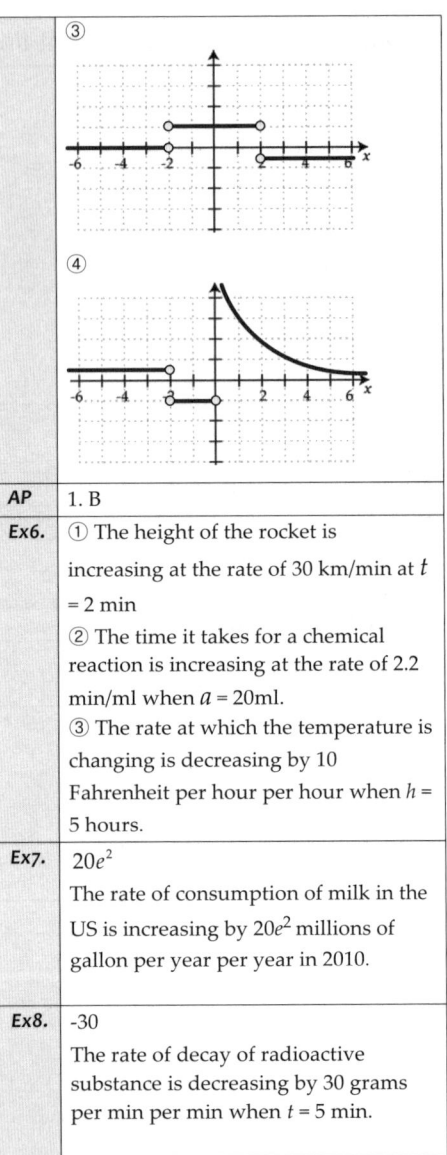

7. Concavity and the Second Derivative

Ex1.									
	f'	+	-	-	+	-	+	+	-
	f''	-	-	+	+	+	+	-	-

Ex2.	inflection point is at x = a, d
Ex3.	① $(2,-4)$ ② No inflection point ③ $(-3,0)$ ④ No inflection point ⑤ $\left(e^{\frac{5}{6}}, \dfrac{5}{6e^{5/3}}\right)$
Ex4.	$a = -12$, $b = -4$
Ex5.	(a) max at $x = 3$ (b) $x = 1$ (c) (y value does not matter)
Ex6.	(a) $x = 1$ (b) No inflection point (c)
AP	1. C 2. E 3. C 4. C 5. D 6. A
Ex7.	
Ex8.	

Ex9.	(a) [-3, -2) ∪ (0, 2) ∪ (2, 3] (∵ f' is positive) (b) max at x = -2 (∵ f' is change + to −) min at x = 0 (∵ f' is change − to +) (c) (-1, 1) ∪ (2, 3] (∵ f' is increasing) (d) x = -1, 1, 2 (∵ f' changes from increasing to decreasing, vice versa)
Ex10.	(a) [0, 1) ∪ (3, 4) ∪ (5, 6] (∵ f' is positive) (b) max at x = 1, 4 min at x = 3, 5 (c) (2, 6] (∵ f' is increasing) (d) $x = 2$ (∵ f' changes from decreasing to increasing)
Ex11.	(a) O, B (b) concave down (c) increasing
Ex12.	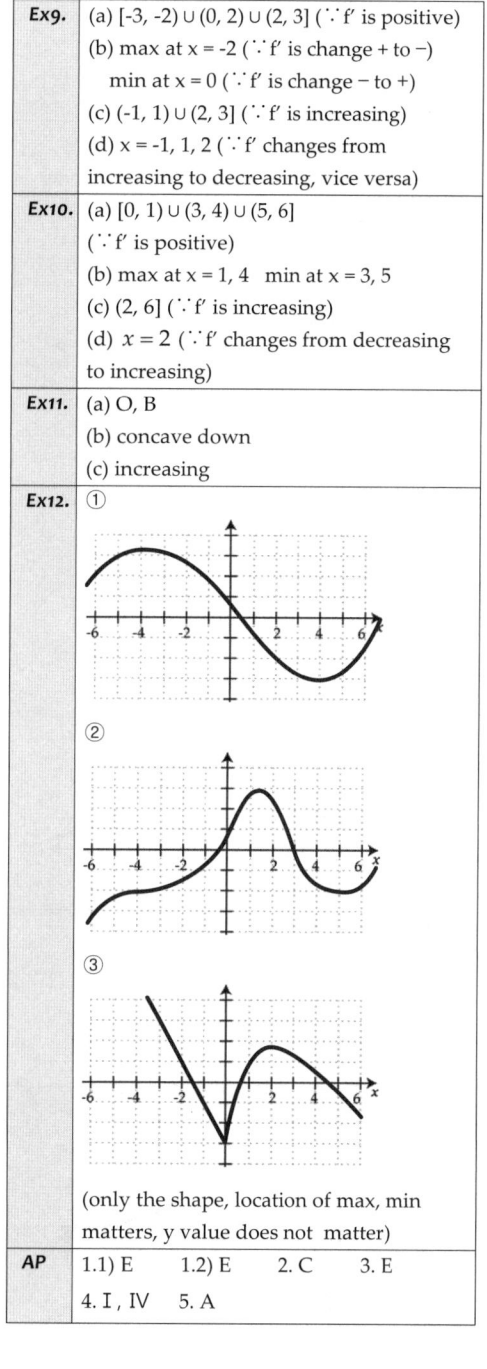 ① ② ③ (only the shape, location of max, min matters, y value does not matter)
AP	1.1) E 1.2) E 2. C 3. E 4. I, IV 5. A

Ex13.	Domain: All real numbers Asymptotes: none intercepts: (0, 0) (27/8, 0) Critical points and max, min: max at x = 1, min at x = 0 Inflection points and concavity: none

Ex14.	Domain: All real numbers
	Asymptotes: y = 0
	intercepts: (0, 1)
	Critical points and max, min:
	  max at x = 0
	Inflection points and concavity:
	  at $x = \pm \frac{\sqrt{2}}{2}$

Ex15.	Domain: x > 0 Asymptotes: x = 0, y = 0 intercepts: (1, 0) Critical points and max, min: max at x = e Inflection points and concavity: at $x = e^{3/2}$

8. Motions and Derivatives

※ Blank answer

Displacement	$s(b) - s(a)$
Average Velocity	$\frac{s(b) - s(a)}{b - a}$
initial	$t = 0$
initial position	$s(0)$
initial velocity	$v(0)$
at the origin point	$s = 0$
is stationary	$v = 0$
is at rest, is standing still	$v = 0$
changes direction, reverse	$v = 0$
reaches its maximum/minimum height	$v = 0$
moving forward	$v > 0$
moving backward	$v < 0$
velocity is increasing	$v' > 0 \ (a > 0)$
velocity is decreasing	$v' < 0 \ (a < 0)$
Speed up, Speed increasing	v, a has same sign
Slow down, Speed decreasing	v, a has different sign
constant speed	$a = 0$

Ex1.	a) 36 ft b) 12 ft/sec
Ex2.	① forward [0,1), backward (1,7) ∪ (7, 9) ② 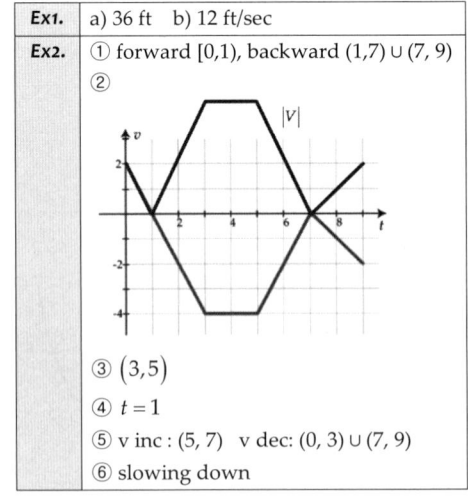 ③ (3, 5) ④ $t = 1$ ⑤ v inc : (5, 7) v dec: (0, 3) ∪ (7, 9) ⑥ slowing down

Ex3.	① forward: (0, 1) ∪ (4, 6) backward: (2, 3) standing still: (1, 2) ∪ (3, 4) ② 2 m ③ 1 m/s ④ 1 m/s
Ex4.	① $v(t) = 3t^2 - 8t - 3$, -3 km/hr ② $t = 3$ ③ $t > \dfrac{4}{3}$ ④ $0 \le t < \dfrac{4}{3}$ or $t > 3$
Ex5.	① $-1 + e^{1-t}$ ② $-e^{1-t}$ ③ speed is increasing ④ $t = 1$ ⑤ $-4 - \dfrac{1}{e^3} + e$ ⑥ $e + \dfrac{1}{e^3}$
AP	1.1) A 1.2) B 1.3) C 2. A 3. C 4. D

AP-5	$\dfrac{32}{e^2}$
AP-6	4
AP-7	$\dfrac{\sqrt{5}}{2}$
AP-8	$\sqrt{3}$ mi from nearest point
AP-9	$\dfrac{\pi}{6}$
Ex2.	−6
AP-10	(a) 4π cm/s (b) 40π cm²/s
AP-11	$\dfrac{1}{10\pi}$ m/min
AP-12	$\dfrac{1}{2\pi}$ m/sec
AP-13	(a) $-\dfrac{3}{2}$ ft/sec (b) 7 ft²/sec (c) $-\dfrac{1}{8}$ rad/sec
AP-14	(a) $\dfrac{2}{5}h = r$ (b) $-\dfrac{5}{4\pi}$ ft/min (c) -2 ft²/min
AP-15	$\dfrac{2}{25}$ rad/sec
AP-16	−8 cm/sec
AP-17	$k = \dfrac{1}{4}$

9. Optimization and Related Rates

Ex1.	① max at x = 0, min at x = 4 ② min at x = $-\sqrt[3]{\dfrac{1}{2}}$ ③ min at x = 0
AP-1	$20\sqrt{5}$ by $10\sqrt{5}$
AP-2	$r = \dfrac{12}{4 + \pi}$ ∵ $Area''\left(\dfrac{12}{4+\pi}\right) < 0$
AP-3	$r = \dfrac{3}{\sqrt[3]{2\pi}}$ ∵ $Surface\ Area''\left(\dfrac{3}{\sqrt[3]{2\pi}}\right) > 0$
AP-4	4, 2 by 2

10. Application of Diff

Ex1.	f is continuous in [0, 1]. f(0) = -3 < 0, f(1) = 3 > 0 According IVT, there must be at least one zero in [0, 1].
Ex2.	h is continuous in $\left[0, \dfrac{\pi}{2}\right]$. h(0) = -2 < 0, h(π/2) > 0 According IVT, there must be at least one zero in $\left[0, \dfrac{\pi}{2}\right]$

Ex3.	f is continuous in [0, 2]. f(0) = 1 < 2, f(2) = 27 > 2 According IVT, there must be at least one x such that f(x) = 2 in [0, 2].
Ex4.	① 1 ② 2 ③ cannot use MVT
Ex5.	$\dfrac{2}{\ln 3}$

Ex6.	① $c = \sqrt{2}$
	② cannot use Rolle's theorem
	    (Not continuous at $x = 0$)
	③ cannot use Rolle's theorem
	    (Not differential at $x = 3$)

Ex7.	① 3 ② 2 ③ f is differentiable, therefore continuous in [0, 10]. f(0) = -2 < 0, f(10) = 1 > 0 According IVT, there must be at least one c such that f(c) = 0 in [0, 10]. ④ f is differentiable and continuous in [0, 10]. $\dfrac{f(10) - f(0)}{10 - 0} = \dfrac{1-(-2)}{10} = 0.3$ According MVT, there must be at least one c such that f'(c) = 0.3 in (0, 10). ⑤ f is differentiable and continuous in [1, 10]. $\dfrac{f(10) - f(1)}{10 - 1} = \dfrac{1-1}{9} = 0$ According MVT(Rolle's thm), there must be at least one c such that f'(c) = 0 in (1, 10).
AP	1. E 2. E 3. C 4. D
Ex8.	① 6 ② 1 ③ 2 ④ 2 ⑤ $\dfrac{2}{3}$ ⑥ −1

	⑦ 0 ⑧ 0 ⑨ 1
AP	1. B 2. B
Ex9.	1.1
Ex10.	0.02
Ex11.	$\dfrac{\pi}{4} - 0.05$
Ex12.	73.6, underestimate
Ex13.	91/30, overestimate
AP	1. C 2. C 3. D 4. B 5. B 6. B

Free Response Question (from ch6~10)

1.	(a) $x = 3, 6$ (b) $x = 2, 4, 5$ (c) [0,7] (d) $[0,2) \cup (4,5)$ (e) $x = 7$

2.	(a) $G'(2) \approx \dfrac{2-5}{3-0} = -1$
	The rate at which the height of the water is rising in the can is decreasing by about 1 mm per day per day at t = 2.
	(b) G is differentiable $\Rightarrow$ continuous
	$G(5) = 1 > 0.5$, $G(9) = -1 < 0.5$
	According to Intermediate Value Theorem, there must be a time where $G(t) = 0.5$ in $5 \le t \le 9$.
	(c) G is differentiable $\Rightarrow$ continuous
	$\dfrac{G(9) - G(5)}{9 - 5} = -0.5$
	According to Mean Value Theorem, there must be a time where $G'(t) = -0.5$ in $5 < t < 9$.
	(d) Point: $(3, h(3)) = (3, 6)$
	    Slope: $h'(3) = G(3) = 2$
	    $h \approx 6 + 2(t - 3)$
	    $h(4) \approx 6 + 2(4 - 3) = 8\,mm$

3. (a) $h'(2) = 0.909$

    The amount of hay in the bin is increasing at the rate of 0.909 pound per hour at 14:00.

    (b) $h''(2) = -1.248$

    The rate of the amount of hay is decreasing by 1.248 pound per hour per hour at 14:00.

    (c) $t = 2.342$

    (d) $(1.849, 2.342)$

11. Antiderivative

Ex1.
① $\dfrac{x^4}{4}+c$

② $7x-\dfrac{x^2}{2}-x^3+c$

③ $13x-2x^3+\dfrac{x^6}{6}+c$

④ $\dfrac{x^6}{6}-\dfrac{1}{x}+c$

⑤ $\dfrac{-3}{x}-\dfrac{2}{x^2}+c$

⑥ $\dfrac{2}{3}\sqrt{x^3}+\dfrac{3}{4}\sqrt[3]{x^4}+\dfrac{3}{5}\sqrt[3]{x^5}+c$

⑦ $\dfrac{2\sqrt{x^5}}{5}+\sqrt{x}+c$

⑧ $\dfrac{2\sqrt{x^3}}{3}+12\sqrt{x}+c$

⑨ $-\dfrac{1}{x}-\dfrac{1}{x^2}+\dfrac{1}{x^3}+c$

Ex2.
① $7\ln|x|+c$

② $\dfrac{x^2}{2}-3x+\dfrac{1}{5}\ln|x|+\dfrac{2}{x}+c$

③ $\dfrac{1}{3}e^x+c$

④ $3e^x+\dfrac{x^{e+1}}{e+1}+c$

Ex3.
① $-\cos x+\sin x+c$
② $-2\csc x+c$
③ $\tan x+x+c$
④ $\tan x+c$
⑤ $\sec x+c$
⑥ $-2\cot x+c$

Ex4.
① $\dfrac{1}{6}(2x-3)^3+c$

② $\dfrac{3}{4}(x-5)^4+c$

③ $-\sqrt{(1-2y)^3}+c$

④ $-\dfrac{1}{(2x+1)^2}+c$

⑤ $-\dfrac{1}{2}\cos 2x+c$

⑥ $\pi\tan\left(\dfrac{x}{\pi}-2\right)+c$

⑦ $-4\csc\dfrac{x}{2}+c$

⑧ $\ln|x+2|+c$

⑨ $-\dfrac{1}{3}\ln|2-3x|+c$

⑩ $-e^{-x}+c$

⑪ $\dfrac{2}{3}e^{3x/2}+c$

⑫ $-\dfrac{1}{5}e^{-5x-4}+c$

Ex5.
① $\ln|x^2+2|+c$

② $\dfrac{1}{2}\ln|x^2+4|+c$

③ $\dfrac{3}{4}(x^2-1)^4+c$

④ $\sqrt{t^2+1}+c$

⑤ $\dfrac{2}{15}\sqrt{(x^3-2)^5}+c$

⑥ $-\dfrac{1}{2}e^{-x^2}+c$

⑦ $-\dfrac{1}{6}(\cos 2x)^3+c$

⑧ $-\dfrac{1}{\sin x}+c$

⑨ $-\dfrac{2}{3}\cot^{\frac{3}{2}} t+c$

⑩ $\dfrac{1}{4}\tan^4 y+c$

⑪ $2e^{\sqrt{x}}+c$

⑫ $-\dfrac{1}{2}\left(1+\dfrac{1}{x}\right)^2+c$

⑬ $\ln|\ln x|+c$

Ex6. $-\dfrac{1}{3}(\cos^2\theta+1)^{\frac{3}{2}}+c$

Ex7. $\dfrac{\ln^3(\sin x)}{3}+c$

Ex8.
① $\dfrac{2}{5}(x+1)^{\frac{5}{2}}-\dfrac{2}{3}(x+1)^{\frac{3}{2}}+c$

② $(x-1)+2\ln|x-1|-\dfrac{1}{x-1}+c$

	③ $2(1+\sqrt{x}-\ln|1+\sqrt{x}|)+c$
Ex9.	① $-\cos x + c$
	② $\frac{1}{2}\left(x-\frac{1}{2}\sin 2x\right)+c$
	③ $-\cos x + \frac{\cos^3 x}{3}+c$
	④ $\frac{1}{2}\left(x+\frac{1}{2}\sin 2x\right)+c$
Ex10.	① $\ln|\sec x|+c$
	② $\tan x - x + c$
	③ $\frac{\tan^2 x}{2}-\ln|\sec x|+c$
	④ $\ln|\sin x|+c$
	⑤ $\ln|\tan x + \sec x|+c$
	⑥ $-\ln|\cot x + \csc x|+c$
Ex11.	① $\frac{1}{2}\arcsin 2x + c$
	② $\frac{1}{2}\arctan 2x + c$
	③ $\arcsin x + c$
	④ $-\sqrt{1-x^2}+c$
	⑤ $\arcsin\frac{x}{2}+c$
	⑥ $\frac{1}{4}\arctan\frac{x}{4}+c$
	⑦ $\frac{1}{6}\tan^{-1}\frac{3x}{2}+c$
	⑧ $\frac{1}{2}\arcsin\frac{2x-1}{3}+c$
	⑨ $\arctan(x-1)+c$
	⑩ $\frac{1}{2}\arctan\frac{x-2}{2}+c$
	⑪ $\frac{1}{4}\tan^{-1}\frac{e^{2x}}{2}+c$
	⑫ $\frac{1}{6}\tan^{-1}\left(\frac{2}{3}\ln x\right)+c$
Ex12.	① $-\sqrt{1-x^2}+\arcsin x + c$
	② $\frac{1}{2}\ln|x^2+1|+\arctan x + c$
	③ $\ln|x^2+4x+5|-4\arctan(x+2)+c$
	④ $\frac{1}{2}\ln|x^2+6x+13|+\arctan\frac{x+3}{2}+c$

Ex13.	① $y=-\frac{1}{x}+\frac{x^2}{2}-\frac{3}{2}$
	② $y=9x^{\frac{1}{3}}+14$
	③ $y=\cos\pi\theta -1$
	④ $y=2x+4$
AP	1. A 2. C

12. Definite Integral

Ex1.	① 75
	② $10-2\sqrt{2}$
	③ $\frac{4}{3}\ln 13$
	④ $\frac{2}{3}$
	⑤ 4
	⑥ $\frac{1}{2}\left(\frac{\pi}{2}-1\right)$
Ex2.	① $\ln\frac{4}{3}$
	② $\frac{1}{3}\left(5^{\frac{3}{2}}-1\right)$
	③ $\frac{7}{3}$
	④ $\ln 2$
	⑤ e^4-1
Ex3.	① 12
	② -5
	③ -12
	④ 0
	⑤ -5
	⑥ 36
	⑦ 33
Ex4.	① 12
	② 3
	③ 2π
	④ 4
Ex5.	① $-\pi$
	② $4-2\pi$
	③ $2\pi-5$
	④ $5+2\pi$
	⑤ $25-2\pi$
	⑥ $2-2\pi$

Ex6.	① $\int_1^3 2x+1\,dx$
	② $2\int_0^\pi 1-\sin\left(x-\dfrac{\pi}{2}\right)dx$
	③ $\int_0^2 4-x^2\,dx - \int_2^3 4-x^2\,dx$ or $\int_0^3 |4-x^2|\,dx$
	④ $-\int_2^3 x^2-4x+3\,dx + \int_3^4 x^2-4x+3\,dx$ or $\int_2^4 |x^2-4x+3|\,dx$
Ex7.	① 0
	② $\dfrac{64}{3}$
	③ $\dfrac{2}{5}$
	④ 1
AP	1. B 2. B 3. B 4. E
	5. C 6. B 7. C 8. D
	9. E 10. E
Ex8.	① 10
	② 12
	③ 8
	④ 6
	⑤ 2
	⑥ −1
	⑦ interval $(-4, 0)$
	⑧ interval $(-2, 2)$
Ex9.	① −90
	② −6
	③ 10
	④ 13
	⑤ −1
AP	1. A 2. E 3. B 4. E 5. D

13. Fundamental Theorem of Calculus

Ex1.	(a)
	<table><tr><td>x</td><td>0</td><td>1</td><td>3</td><td>4</td><td>5</td><td>7</td><td>8</td></tr><tr><td>F(x)</td><td>0</td><td>1</td><td>5</td><td>6</td><td>5</td><td>2</td><td>3</td></tr></table>
	(b) x = 4
	(c) x = 7
Ex2.	(a) x = 0, 4, 8
	(b) max at x = 2, 6 min at x = 4, 8
	(c)
	(d) x = 4, 8, 0
AP	1. E 2. D 3. A
Ex3.	① $\sqrt{2x-1}$
	② $\dfrac{1}{5x+6}$
	③ $-\cos x$
	④ $\sec^2 z$
	⑤ $2x\sin^2 x^2$
	⑥ $\sqrt{\sin x}\cos x$
	⑦ $-4\cos^2 2x \sin 2x$
	⑧ −1
	⑨ $f(c)$
Ex4.	① 5
	② 5
	③ -4
	④ 0
	⑤ 3
	⑥ 0
	⑦ und
	⑧ -3
	⑨ interval (0, 5) (∵ g′= f is positive)
	⑩ interval (4, 6) (∵ g′= f is decreasing)
	⑪ x = 4 (∵ g′= f changes inc→dec)
	⑫ y − 5 = 3(x − 4)
	⑬ $\dfrac{13}{2}$
Ex5.	① 0
	② +

	③ +				
	④ −				
	⑤ +				
	⑥ 0				
	⑦ −				
	⑧ +				
AP	1. D	2. B	3. D	4. D	
	5. A	6. D	7. E	8. A	
	9. D	10. C			
Ex6.	① $\frac{1}{3}$				
	② 2				
	③ 2				
	④ 2				
AP	1. A	2. B	3. B	4. D	

Ex7.	① $\int_1^4 x^2 dx$
	② $\int_0^2 x^3 dx$
	③ $\frac{1}{9}\int_1^4 x^2 dx$
	④ $\int_0^1 x^2 dx$
	⑤ $\int_0^1 \sqrt{x}\, dx$
	⑥ $\int_1^2 \frac{1}{x} dx$
AP	1. A 2. B

14. Approximating Area

Ex1.	① L(6) = 2120
	② R(6) = 2320
	③ T(6) = 2220
	④ M(3) = 1640
Ex2.	① L(5) = 1830
	② R(5) = 2110
	③ T(5) = 2070
Ex3.	① $R(5) = 2(3\sqrt{2} + \sqrt{6} + \sqrt{10} + 2)$
	② $L(5) = 2(2 + 3\sqrt{2} + \sqrt{6})$
	③ $T(5) = 6\sqrt{2} + 2\sqrt{6} + 4 + \sqrt{10}$
Ex4.	$L(n) < \int_a^b f(x)\,dx < T(n) < R(n)$
Ex5.	$R(n) < T(n) < \int_a^b f(x)\,dx < L(n)$
AP	1. B 2. C 3. A 4. B
Ex6.	① $\Delta x = \frac{4-1}{n} = \frac{3}{n}$
	② $\left[1, 1+\frac{3}{n}\right], \left[1+\frac{3}{n}, 1+\frac{3(2)}{n}\right], \left[1+\frac{3(2)}{n}, 1+\frac{3(3)}{n}\right], \ldots$
	③ $f\left(1+\frac{3k}{n}\right) \cdot \frac{3}{n}$
	④ $\lim_{n \to \infty} \sum_{k=1}^n f\left(1+\frac{3k}{n}\right) \cdot \frac{3}{n}$
	$\int_1^4 f(x)\,dx$

15. Area, Volume

Ex1.	① $\int_0^1 x - x^2 dx + \int_1^2 x^2 - x\, dx$
	② $\int_{y=0}^{y=1} 10y^2 - 10y^3 - (2y^2 - 2y)\,dy$
Ex2.	① (a) $\int_0^1 x - \frac{x^2}{4} dx + \int_1^2 1 - \frac{x^2}{4} dx$
	(b) $\int_0^1 2\sqrt{y} - y\, dy$
	② (a) $\int_0^1 x^2 dx + \int_1^2 2 - x\, dx$
	(b) $\int_0^1 2 - y - \sqrt{y}\, dy$
	③ (a) $\int_0^1 \sqrt[3]{x} - \sqrt{x}\, dx$
	(b) $\int_0^1 y^2 - y^3\, dy$
	④ (a) $\int_0^4 \sqrt{x}\, dx - 2$
	(b) $\int_0^2 2 + y - y^2 dy$
AP	1. A 2. B 3. B
Ex3.	$\int_4^9 \left(\frac{1}{\sqrt{x}}\right)^2 dx$
Ex4.	$\frac{\pi}{2}\int_0^2 \left(\frac{1}{2} - \frac{x}{4}\right)^2 dx$
Ex5.	$\int_0^{\frac{\pi}{4}} (\cos x - \sin x)^2 dx$

Ex6.	$\int_{-1}^{1} \frac{\sqrt{3}}{4}(2-2x^2)^2 dx$
Ex7.	$\int_{0}^{3} 3(6-2y) dy$
Ex8.	$\int_{0}^{4} \left(2y - \frac{1}{2}y\right)^2 dy$
Ex9.	① $\pi \int_{0}^{4} (\sqrt{x})^2 dx$ ② $\pi \int_{0}^{4} (y^2)^2 dy$ ③ $\pi \int_{0}^{2} e^{2x} dx$ ④ $\pi \int_{1}^{3} (\ln y)^2 dy$ ⑤ $\pi \int_{0}^{2} (4-x^2)^2 dx$ ⑥ $\pi \int_{0}^{4} (2-\sqrt{y})^2 dy$
Ex10.	$\int_{0}^{1} \pi(\sqrt{x})^2 - \pi(x^2)^2 dx$
Ex11.	$\int_{0}^{1} \pi(\sqrt{y})^2 - \pi(y^2)^2 dy$
Ex12.	① $\pi \int_{0}^{2} (x^2)^2 dx$ ② $\int_{0}^{4} \pi(2)^2 - \pi(\sqrt{y})^2 dy$ $= \pi \int_{0}^{4} (2)^2 - (\sqrt{y})^2 dy$ ③ $\int_{0}^{2} \pi 5^2 - \pi(5-x^2)^2 dx$ $= \pi \int_{0}^{2} 5^2 - (5-x^2)^2 dx$ ④ $\int_{0}^{2} \pi(3-\sqrt{y})^2 - \pi(1)^2 dy$ $= \pi \int_{0}^{2} (3-\sqrt{y})^2 - 1 \, dy$ ⑤ $\int_{0}^{2} \pi(x^2+1)^2 - \pi(1)^2 dx$ $= \pi \int_{0}^{2} (x^2+1)^2 - 1 \, dx$ ⑥ $\int_{0}^{4} \pi(3)^2 - \pi(\sqrt{y}+1)^2 dy$ $= \pi \int_{0}^{4} 9 - (\sqrt{y}+1)^2 dy$
Ex13.	① $\int_{0}^{4} 2\pi x\sqrt{x} dx$ ② $\int_{0}^{4} 2\pi x(e^x - e^{-x}) dx$ ③ $\int_{0}^{4} 2\pi y \cdot y^2 dy$

	④ $\int_{1}^{5} 2\pi(x+1)\sqrt{x-1} dx$
AP	1. B 2. C 3. D 4. C 5. C 6. D 7. D

16. More Apps and Motion

※ Blank answer

Average Velocity from x = a to x = b	given s:	$\frac{s(b)-s(a)}{b-a}$
	given v:	$\frac{\int_{a}^{b} v(t) dt}{b-a}$
Average acceleration from x = a to x = b	given v:	$\frac{v(b)-v(a)}{b-a}$
	given a:	$\frac{\int_{a}^{b} a(t) dt}{b-a}$
Displacement (change in position) from x = a to x = b		$\int_{a}^{b} v(t) dt$
Total Distance traveled from x = a to x = b		$\int_{a}^{b} |v(t)| dt$
Future position at x = b		$s(b) = s(a) + \int_{a}^{b} v(t) dt$

Ex1.	$10 - \frac{10}{e^3}$
Ex2.	$20e^6 + 30$
AP	1. C 2. C
Ex3.	① (1, 7) ② t = 1, 7 ③ slow down ④ 19 ⑤ −13 ⑥ −9 ⑦ −15 ⑧ $x(t) = -t^2 + 2t + 4$, $v(t) = -2t + 2$, $a(t) = -2$

Ex4.	① $2t-2$
	② $\dfrac{t^3}{3}-t^2+3$
	③ $\dfrac{8}{3}$
	④ 0
	⑤ 3
Ex5.	① 1
	② $\dfrac{4}{\pi}$
AP	1.1) B 1.2) D 1.3) C 1.4) B
	1.5) C 2.1) A 2.2) C 2.3) C
	2.4) D 2.5) B 3. B 4. D
	5. C

17. Differential Equation

Ex1.	① $y=\dfrac{2x^3}{3}+c$
	② $y=x-5\ln|x|+c$
	③ $y=\tan x-x+c$
Ex2.	① $y=\dfrac{2x^3}{3}-8$
	② $y=\dfrac{x^3}{6}+x^2+x+3$
Ex3.	① $y=\pm\sqrt{-2\cos x+2c}$
	② $y=\pm\sqrt[4]{20x-2x^2+4c}$
	③ $y=Ce^{(\ln x)^2/2}$
	④ $y=Cx^2$
	⑤ $y=-Ce^{-x}+3$
Ex4.	① $y=\sqrt{\dfrac{1}{-x^2+2}}$
	② $y=-e^{1-\tfrac{1}{x}}+1$
	③ $y=\sqrt{2e^x+14}$
	④ $y=e^{\tfrac{-x^2}{2}-x}$
AP	1. C 2. E 3. C 4. B

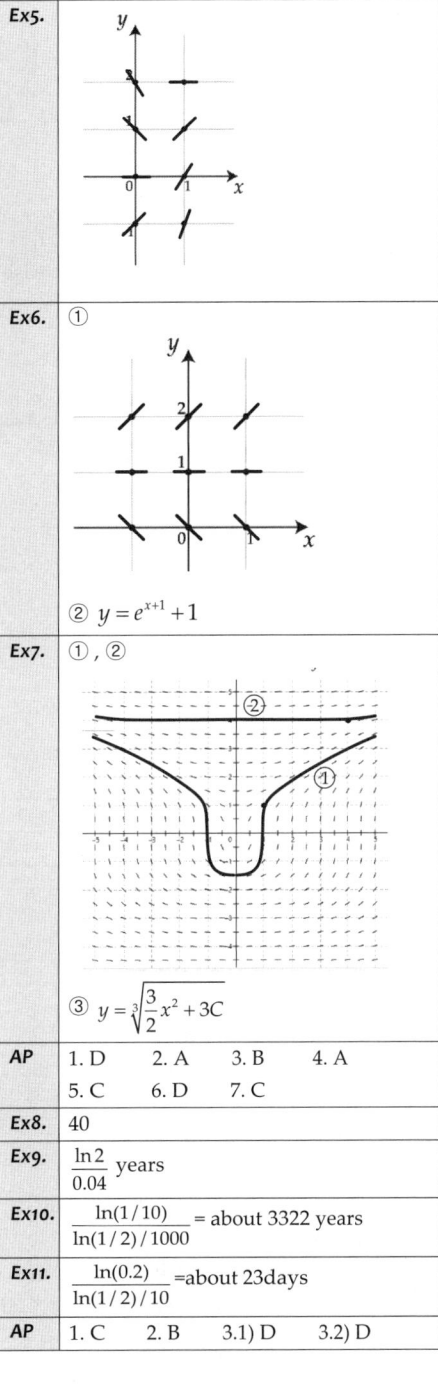

Ex5.	(slope field graph)
Ex6.	① (slope field graph)
	② $y=e^{x+1}+1$
Ex7.	①, ② (slope field with curves)
	③ $y=\sqrt[3]{\dfrac{3}{2}x^2+3C}$
AP	1. D 2. A 3. B 4. A
	5. C 6. D 7. C
Ex8.	40
Ex9.	$\dfrac{\ln 2}{0.04}$ years
Ex10.	$\dfrac{\ln(1/10)}{\ln(1/2)/1000}$ = about 3322 years
Ex11.	$\dfrac{\ln(0.2)}{\ln(1/2)/10}$ = about 23 days
AP	1. C 2. B 3.1) D 3.2) D

Answers 581

Free Response Question
(from ch11~17)

1.
(a) $g(4) = 1$
$g'(4) = f(4) = 0$
$g''(4) = f'(4) = undefined$

(b) $x = 1, 3, 6, 8$
$g'(x) = f(x)$ changes from increasing to decreasing, decreasing to increasing at $x = 1, 3, 6, 8$.

(c) $(1, 2) \cup (6, 7)$
$g'(x) = f(x)$ is positive and decreasing in $(1, 2) \cup (6, 7)$.

(d) $g(0) = 3 + \int_2^0 f(t)\, dt = 2$
$g(4) = 1$
$g(9) = 3 + \int_2^9 f(t)\, dt = 2.5$
minimum value : 1

2.
(a) $\int_0^1 F(t)\, dt = 0.621\, gal$

(b) $(0.377, 1]$

(c) $F(t) = G(t) \Rightarrow t = 0.377$

t	Amount of water in tank
0	0.2
0.377	$0.2 + \int_0^{0.377} F(t) - G(t)\, dt$ = 0.1495...
1	$0.2 + \int_0^1 F(t) - G(t)\, dt$ = 0.5072...

Minimum amount of water in the tank: $0.15\, gal$

3.
(a) $v(6) = -10 < 0,\ a(6) = 2 > 0$
Slowing down

(b) The total distance traveled in $0 \le t \le 20$.
$2(10) + 4(20) + 8(10) + 6(0) = 180\, ft$

(c) Average acceleration in $0 \le t \le 20$.
$\dfrac{1}{20} \cdot \dfrac{1}{2}[2(6) + 4(7) + 8(3) + 6(3)] = \dfrac{41}{20}\, ft/\sec^2$

(d) $s(6) \approx 6 + [2(-20) + 4(-10)] = -74$
$v(6) = -10 < 0$

The position of the bicycle is at left side of the origin at $t = 6$, and the bicycle is moving backwards at $t = 6$. Therefore, the bicycle is moving away from the origin at $t = 6$.

4.
(a) $\int_0^3 \left[(-2y + 6) - \sin^{-1}\dfrac{y-3}{3}\right]^2 dy$

(b) $\pi \int_{-\frac{\pi}{2}}^0 (3\sin x + 4)^2 - 1^2\, dx$
$+ \pi \int_0^6 (-0.5x + 4)^2 - 1^2\, dx$

(c) $\pi \int_0^3 \left(6 - \sin^{-1}\dfrac{y-3}{3}\right)^2 - (2y)^2\, dy$

18. Euler method and Logistic Curve (BC)

※ Blank answer

$\dfrac{dP}{dt} = kP\left(1 - \dfrac{P}{L}\right)$

$\dfrac{dP}{dt} = \dfrac{k}{L}P(L-P)$

$\dfrac{1}{P(L-P)}dP = \dfrac{k}{L}dt$

$\dfrac{1}{L}\int\left(\dfrac{1}{P} + \dfrac{1}{L-P}\right)dP = \dfrac{1}{L}\int k\,dt$

$\int\left(\dfrac{1}{P} + \dfrac{1}{L-P}\right)dP = kt + c$

$\ln|P| - \ln|L-P| = kt + c$

$\ln\left|\dfrac{P}{L-P}\right| = kt + c$

$\dfrac{P}{L-P} = Ce^{kt}$

$\dfrac{L-P}{P} = Ce^{-kt}$

$\dfrac{L}{P} - 1 = Ce^{-kt}$

$\dfrac{L}{P} = 1 + Ce^{-kt}$

$P = \dfrac{L}{1 + Ce^{-kt}}$

Ex1.	$y(2) \approx 3.5$
Ex2.	$y(2) \approx \dfrac{31}{6}$
AP	1. D
Ex3.	① $L = 3,\ y = \dfrac{3}{1 + Ce^{-3x}}$ ② Not logistic ③ Not logistic ④ $L = 12,\ R = \dfrac{12}{1 + Ce^{-6t}}$ ⑤ $L = 6,\ y = \dfrac{6}{1 + Ce^{-6x}}$ ⑥ Not logistic

Ex4.	① $y = \dfrac{5/4}{1 + \dfrac{1}{4}e^{-1/6x}} = \dfrac{5}{4 + e^{-1/6x}}$ ② $\dfrac{5}{4}$ ③ $\dfrac{5}{8}$
Ex5.	① $y = \dfrac{6}{1 + 2e^{-12x}}$ ② 6, 0, 0 ③ 3 ④ $\dfrac{\ln(0.5)}{-12} \approx 0.058$
Ex6.	① $\dfrac{100{,}000}{3e(1 + 10e^{-1})^2}$ ② $-3\ln\dfrac{1}{10} \approx 6.908$
AP	1. D 2. C 3. B 4. A

19. Integration for BC (BC)

Ex1.	① $-4x\cos x + 4\sin x + C$ ② $\dfrac{x^2}{2}e^{2x} - \dfrac{x}{2}e^{2x} + \dfrac{1}{4}e^{2x} + C$ ③ $\dfrac{y^2}{2}\sin 2y + \dfrac{y}{2}\cos 2y - \dfrac{1}{4}\sin 2y + C$ ④ $-2x\cos\dfrac{x}{2} + 4\sin\dfrac{x}{2} + C$
Ex2.	① $-\dfrac{e^{2x}}{4}\cos 2x + \dfrac{e^{2x}}{4}\sin 2x + C$ ② $\dfrac{1}{5}\left(2e^{-x}\sin\dfrac{x}{2} - 4e^{-x}\cos\dfrac{x}{2}\right) + C$
Ex3.	① $x\ln x - x + C$ ② $\dfrac{x^2}{2}\ln x - \dfrac{x^2}{4} + C$ ③ $x(\ln x)^2 - 2(x\ln x - x) + C$ ④ $\dfrac{x^2}{2}\ln(x+1) - \dfrac{1}{2}\left[\dfrac{(x+1)^2}{2} - 2(x+1) + \ln|x+1|\right] + C$ ⑤ $x\arcsin x + \sqrt{1 - x^2} + C$ ⑥ $x\arctan x - \dfrac{1}{2}\ln\left|1 + x^2\right| + C$

AP	1. C 2. A 3. B 4. A 5. C
	6. B 7. D 8. D
Ex4.	① $\dfrac{A}{x-3}+\dfrac{B}{x+1}$
	② $\dfrac{A}{x-1}+\dfrac{B}{(x-1)^2}+\dfrac{C}{(x-1)^3}$
	③ $\dfrac{A}{x}+\dfrac{Bx+C}{x^2+1}$
	④ $\dfrac{A}{x-2}+\dfrac{B}{x+2}+\dfrac{C}{(x+2)^2}+\dfrac{Dx+E}{x^2+2}$
	⑤ $\dfrac{Ax+B}{x^2+1}+\dfrac{Cx+D}{(x+1)^2}$
Ex5.	① $A=1,\ B=-1$
	② $A=2,\ B=-1$
	③ $A=-2,\ B=2,\ C=2$
Ex6.	① $5\ln|x+2|-2\ln|x+7|+C$
	$=\ln\left|\dfrac{(x+2)^5}{(x+7)^2}\right|+C$
	② $\dfrac{7}{2}\ln|x|-\dfrac{5}{2}\ln|x+2|+C$
	$=\ln\left|\dfrac{\sqrt{x^7}}{\sqrt{(x+2)^5}}\right|+C$
	③ $\ln|x-1|-\dfrac{2}{x-1}+C$
	④ $\dfrac{1}{4x}-\dfrac{\ln|x+2|}{16}+\dfrac{\ln|x-2|}{16}+C$
	⑤ $\ln|x|-\dfrac{1}{2}\ln|x^2+1|+\arctan x+C$
	⑥ $\ln|x^2+1|-\dfrac{1}{x^2+1}+C$
Ex7.	① (a) $\lim_{p\to\infty}\int_1^p \dfrac{1}{x}dx$ (b) ∞
	② (a) $\lim_{p\to\infty}\int_0^p e^{-x}dx$ (b) 1
	③ (a) $\lim_{p\to\infty}\int_1^p \dfrac{e^{\frac{1}{x}}}{x^2}dx$ (b) $e-1$
	④ (a) $\lim_{p\to\infty}\int_1^p xe^{-2x}dx$ (b) $\dfrac{1}{4}$
	⑤ (a) $\lim_{p\to\infty}\int_0^p \dfrac{1}{1+x^2}dx$ (b) $\dfrac{\pi}{2}$
	⑥ (a) $\lim_{p\to-\infty}\int_p^{-1} \dfrac{1}{x^2}dx$ (b) 1

	⑦ (a) $\lim_{p\to-\infty}\int_p^0 \dfrac{2}{x^2-4x+3}dx$ (b) $\ln 3$
	⑧ (a) $\lim_{p\to-\infty}\int_p^0 e^{2x}dx+\lim_{p\to\infty}\int_0^p e^{2x}dx$ (b) ∞
Ex8.	① ∞
	② ∞
	③ $\dfrac{\pi}{2}$
	④ ∞
	⑤ $\dfrac{9}{2}$
AP	1. C
Ex9.	12
Ex10.	$\int_0^1 \sqrt{1+\dfrac{1}{(x+1)^4}}\,dx$
AP	1. D

20. Infinite Series (BC)

Ex1.	① $\dfrac{1}{n}$
	② $\dfrac{n+1}{n}$
	③ $2n$
	④ $(-1)^n$
	⑤ $(-1)^{n+1}7n$
	⑥ $n(2n-1)$
Ex2.	① converge to 0
	② converge to 1
	③ diverge
	④ diverge
	⑤ converge to 0
	⑥ diverge
	⑦ converge to e^3
	⑧ converge to $\dfrac{\pi}{2}$
	⑨ diverge
	⑩ converge to 0
	⑪ converge to 0
	⑫ converge to $\ln 2$

Ex3.	① $\sum_{n=4}^{7} n$
	② $\sum_{n=1}^{6}(-1)^{n+1}(2n-1)$
	③ $\sum_{n=1}^{\infty}\sin n\pi$
	④ $\sum_{n=3}^{10} n^3$
	⑤ $\sum_{n=1}^{\infty} x^n$
Ex4.	① $\dfrac{5}{6^2}+\dfrac{5^2}{6^3}+\dfrac{5^3}{6^4}$
	② $\dfrac{5}{4}+\dfrac{5}{4}\cdot 2+\dfrac{5}{4}\cdot 2^2+\dfrac{5}{4}\cdot 2^3+\cdots$
	③ $a^2+\dfrac{a^3}{2}+\dfrac{a^4}{3}+\cdots$
	④ $1-\dfrac{x^2}{2!}+\dfrac{x^4}{4!}-\dfrac{x^6}{6!}+\cdots$
Ex5.	① diverge
	② diverge
	③ diverge
	④ converge
Ex6.	① diverge
	② inconclusive
	③ diverge
	④ inconclusive
	⑤ inconclusive
	⑥ diverge
	⑦ inconclusive
	⑧ diverge
	⑨ diverge
Ex7.	① converge to 2
	② converge to 4
	③ converge to $\dfrac{5}{6}$
	④ diverge
	⑤ converge to 1
	⑥ converge to $\dfrac{10}{3}$
Ex8.	① diverge
	② converge
	③ diverge
	④ diverge
	⑤ converge
	⑥ diverge

	⑦ converge
	⑧ converge
Ex9.	① diverge
	② diverge
	③ converge
	④ converge
	⑤ diverge
	⑥ converge
	⑦ diverge
	⑧ converge
	⑨ converge
	⑩ converge
Ex10.	① diverge, compare to $\sum_{n=1}^{\infty}\dfrac{1}{n}$
	② diverge, compare to $\sum_{n=1}^{\infty}\dfrac{1}{\sqrt{n}}$
	③ converge, compare to $\sum_{n=1}^{\infty}\dfrac{1}{n^2}$
	④ converge, compare to $\sum_{n=1}^{\infty}\dfrac{1}{n^2}$
	⑤ converge, compare to $\sum_{n=1}^{\infty}\left(\dfrac{1}{2}\right)^n$
	⑥ diverge, compare to $\sum_{n=1}^{\infty}\dfrac{1}{n}$
	⑦ diverge, compare to $\sum_{n=1}^{\infty}\left(\dfrac{3}{2}\right)^n$
	⑧ diverge, compare to $\sum_{n=1}^{\infty}\dfrac{1}{n}$
	⑨ converge, compare to $\sum_{n=1}^{\infty}\dfrac{1}{n^2}$
	⑩ converge, compare to $\sum_{n=1}^{\infty}\dfrac{n}{n^3+n}$
	⑪ converge, compare to $\sum_{n=1}^{\infty}\dfrac{1}{n^2}$
	⑫ converge, compare to $\sum_{n=1}^{\infty}\dfrac{1}{n^2}$
Ex11.	① diverge, compare to $\sum_{n=1}^{\infty}\dfrac{2}{n}$
	② converge, compare to $\sum_{n=1}^{\infty}\dfrac{1}{n^{3/2}}$
	③ converge, compare to $\sum_{n=1}^{\infty}\dfrac{1}{n^2}$

	④ diverge, compare to $\sum_{n=1}^{\infty} \frac{2^n}{n^3}$
	⑤ diverge, compare to $\sum_{n=1}^{\infty} \frac{2}{n}$
	⑥ converge, compare to $\sum_{n=1}^{\infty} \left(\frac{2}{3}\right)^n$
	⑦ diverge, compare to $\sum_{n=1}^{\infty} \frac{1}{n}$
Ex12.	① converge $\left(\lim_{n\to\infty}\left|\frac{a_{n+1}}{a_n}\right|=0\right)$
	② converge $\left(\lim_{n\to\infty}\left|\frac{a_{n+1}}{a_n}\right|=\frac{1}{2}\right)$
	③ diverge $\left(\lim_{n\to\infty}\left|\frac{a_{n+1}}{a_n}\right|=3\right)$
	④ diverge $\left(\lim_{n\to\infty}\left|\frac{a_{n+1}}{a_n}\right|=\infty\right)$
	⑤ converge $\left(\lim_{n\to\infty}\left|\frac{a_{n+1}}{a_n}\right|=0\right)$
	⑥ diverge $\left(\lim_{n\to\infty}\left|\frac{a_{n+1}}{a_n}\right|=e\right)$
Ex13.	① converge
	② diverge
	③ converge
	④ converge
	⑤ diverge
	⑥ converge
	⑦ converge
	⑧ diverge
	⑨ converge
	⑩ inconclusive (Cannot use alternating series test)
Ex14.	① converge conditionally
	② converge absolutely
	③ converge conditionally
	④ converge absolutely
	⑤ converge conditionally
	⑥ converge conditionally
Ex15.	$\frac{1}{11!}$
Ex16.	$\frac{1}{5^{16}}$

Ex17.	4			
AP	1. B	2. D	3. E	4. C
	5. D	6. B	7. A	8. D
	9. D	10. D	11. B	12. B

21. Power Series (BC)

Ex1.	$1 < x < 3$			
Ex2.	① $R=1$, $1 \le x < 3$			
	② $R=2$, $-2 \le x \le 2$			
	③ $R=3$, $-4 < x < 2$			
	④ $R=\infty$, $-\infty < x < \infty$			
	⑤ $R=0$, $x=1$			
	⑥ $R=\infty$, $-\infty < x < \infty$			
AP	1. D	2. B	3. D	4. B

22. Taylor Series (BC)

Ex1.	① $x - \frac{x^3}{3!} + \cdots$
	② $1 + x + \frac{x^2}{2!} + \frac{x^3}{3!} + \cdots$
Ex2.	① $1 - \frac{x}{2!} + \frac{x^2}{4!} - \frac{x^3}{6!} + \cdots (-1)^n \frac{x^n}{(2n)!}$
	② $x^2 - \frac{x^6}{3!} + \frac{x^{10}}{5!} - \frac{x^{14}}{7!} + \cdots$
	$\cdots + (-1)^n \frac{x^{4n+2}}{(2n+1)!} + \cdots$
	③ $1 - \frac{x^2}{3!} + \frac{x^4}{5!} - \frac{x^6}{7!} + \cdots$
	$\cdots + (-1)^n \frac{x^{2n}}{(2n+1)!} + \cdots$
	④ $1 - \frac{2x^2}{2!} + \frac{8x^4}{4!} - \frac{32x^6}{6!} + \cdots$
	⑤ $1 + \frac{x^2}{2} + \frac{x^4}{8} + \frac{x^6}{48} + \cdots + \frac{1}{n!}\left(\frac{x^2}{2}\right)^n + \cdots$
	⑥ $1 + \frac{x^2}{2!} + \frac{x^4}{4!} + \cdots + \frac{x^n + (-x)^n}{2[(n)!]} + \cdots$
	⑦ $x - x^2 + x^3 - x^4 + \cdots + (-1)^n x^{n+1} + \cdots$
	⑧ $\frac{1}{4} - \frac{x}{16} + \frac{x^2}{64} - \frac{x^3}{256} + \cdots + (-1)^n \frac{x^n}{4^{n+1}} + \cdots$

Ex3.	① $-\dfrac{1}{x^2}+\dfrac{1}{4!}-\dfrac{2x}{6!}+\cdots+(-1)^n\dfrac{(n-1)x^{n-2}}{(2n)!}+\cdots$
	② $1+3x^2+\dfrac{5x^4}{2}-\cdots+(2n+1)\dfrac{x^{2n}}{n!}+\cdots$
	③ $2x-4x^3+6x^5+\cdots+(-1)^n(2n+2)x^{2n+1}+\cdots$
Ex4.	$x+2x^2+3x^3+\cdots+nx^n+\cdots$
Ex5.	$x-\dfrac{x^2}{2}+\dfrac{x^3}{3}-\dfrac{x^4}{4}+\cdots+(-1)^n\dfrac{x^{n+1}}{n+1}+\ldots$
AP	1. A 2. B 3. C 4. C 5. A 6. B 7. D
Ex6.	① $e^{-3}\left[1-(x-3)+\dfrac{(x-3)^2}{2!}-\dfrac{(x-3)^3}{3!}\right]$
	② $64+48(x-4)+12(x-4)^2+(x-4)^3$
	③ $(x-1)-\dfrac{(x-1)^2}{2}+\dfrac{(x-1)^3}{3}$
	④ $-(x-\pi)+\dfrac{(x-\pi)^3}{3!}$
Ex7.	① $e^2+2e^2(x-1)+2e^2(x-1)^2+\dfrac{4}{3}e^2(x-1)^3$
	② $e^2+2e^2(0.2)+2e^2(0.2)^2+\dfrac{4}{3}e^2(0.2)^3$ ≈ 11.015
Ex8.	$1-2(x-2)+3(x-2)^2-(x-2)^3$ $1-2(0.1)+3(0.1)^2-(0.1)^3=0.829$
Ex9.	$2-\dfrac{1}{3}(x-3)+\dfrac{1}{8}(x-3)^2-\dfrac{1}{15}(x-3)^3$
Ex10.	① -12
	② $3-2(x-1)-6(x-1)^2+20(x-1)^3$ $3-2(0.2)-6(0.2)^2+20(0.2)^3=2.52$
	③ $2(x-1)+\dfrac{3}{2}(x-1)^2-\dfrac{1}{3}(x-1)^3$
Ex11.	① $3+x-\dfrac{x^2}{2}+\dfrac{x^3}{3}$ $3+(0.1)-\dfrac{(0.1)^2}{2}+\dfrac{(0.1)^3}{3}\approx 3.095$
	② $3x+\dfrac{x^2}{2}-\dfrac{x^3}{6}$
	③ $3+x^2-\dfrac{x^4}{2}$

	④ $h'(0)=0$ $h''(0)=2>0$ $\therefore h$ has min at $x=0$
Ex12.	$16e^{0.4}\dfrac{(0.2)^4}{4!}\approx 0.00159$
Ex13.	$\dfrac{3}{8\cdot 2^5}\cdot\dfrac{1}{3!}\approx 0.00195$
Ex14.	$\cos\left(\dfrac{4}{5}\right)\cdot\dfrac{\left(\dfrac{4}{5}-1\right)^5}{5!}\approx 0.00000186<0.00001$
Ex15.	① $2+2(x-3)+2(x-3)^2+\dfrac{1}{2}(x-3)^3$ $2+2(0.1)+2(0.1)^2+\dfrac{1}{2}(0.1)^3=2.2205$
	② $\dfrac{1}{12\cdot 10^4}<\dfrac{1}{10^4}$
AP	1. A 2. D 3. D 4. C 5. E 6. C 7. C

23. Parametric Functions (BC)

Ex1.	① $x-2y=-3$ (linear)
	② $y=\left(\dfrac{x}{3}\right)^2-2$ (quadratic)
	③ $\left(\dfrac{y}{3}\right)^2+\left(\dfrac{x}{2}\right)^2=1$ (ellipse)
	④ $x^2-y^2=1$ (hyperbola)
Ex2.	① 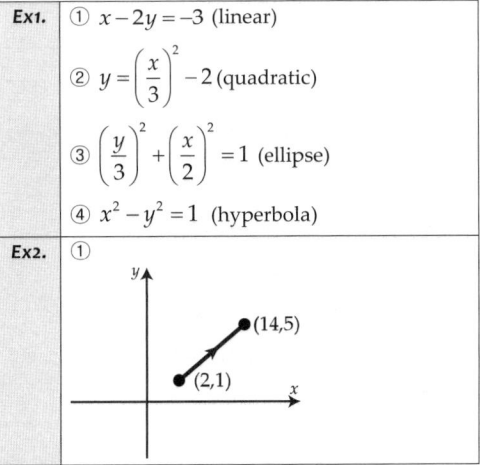

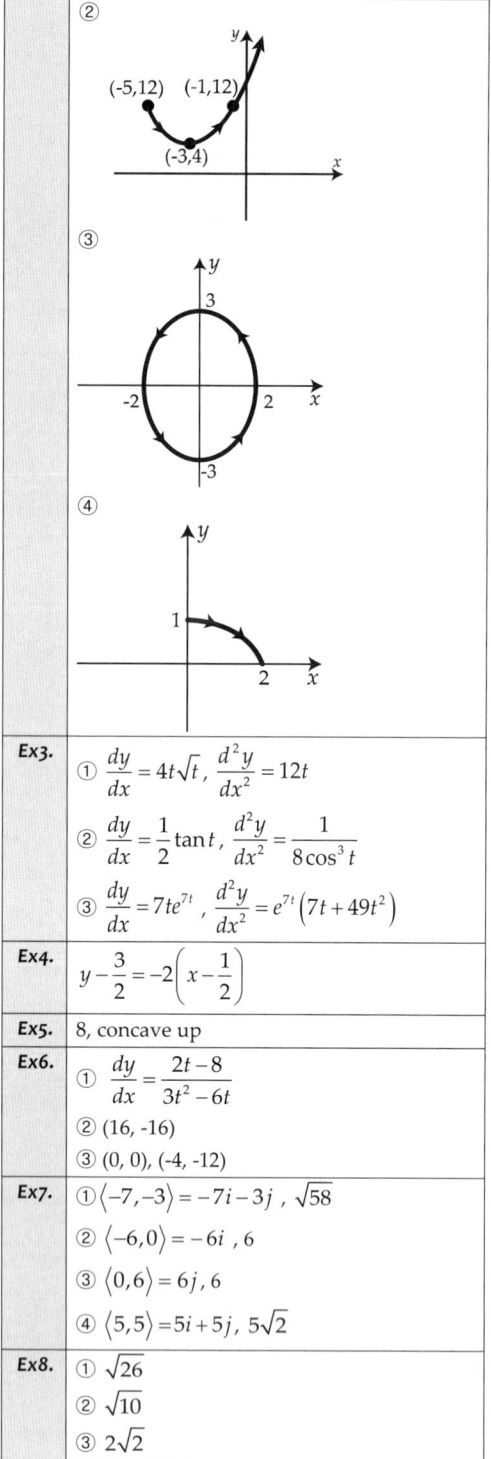

Ex9.	① $v(t) = \langle 8t, t^2 \rangle, a(t) = \langle 8, 2t \rangle$ $v(1) = \langle 8,1 \rangle, a(1) = \langle 8,2 \rangle, |v(t)| = \sqrt{65}$ ② $v(t) = \langle -5\sin 5t, 3\cos t \rangle$, $a(t) = \langle -25\cos 5t, -3\sin t \rangle$, $v\left(\dfrac{\pi}{2}\right) = \langle -5, 0 \rangle, a\left(\dfrac{\pi}{2}\right) = \langle 0, -3 \rangle, |v(t)| = 5$
Ex10.	① ② $v(t) = \langle -2\sin t, 4\cos t \rangle$, $a(t) = \langle -2\cos t, -4\sin t \rangle$ ③ $v\left(\dfrac{\pi}{6}\right) = \langle -1, 2\sqrt{3} \rangle, a\left(\dfrac{\pi}{6}\right) = \langle -\sqrt{3}, -2 \rangle$ $v(\pi) = \langle 0, -4 \rangle, a(\pi) = \langle 2, 0 \rangle$ velocity vector acceleration vector ④ left and up ⑤ $\sqrt{13}$
Ex3.	① $\dfrac{dy}{dx} = 4t\sqrt{t}$, $\dfrac{d^2y}{dx^2} = 12t$ ② $\dfrac{dy}{dx} = \dfrac{1}{2}\tan t$, $\dfrac{d^2y}{dx^2} = \dfrac{1}{8\cos^3 t}$ ③ $\dfrac{dy}{dx} = 7te^{7t}$, $\dfrac{d^2y}{dx^2} = e^{7t}(7t + 49t^2)$
Ex4.	$y - \dfrac{3}{2} = -2\left(x - \dfrac{1}{2}\right)$
Ex5.	8, concave up
Ex6.	① $\dfrac{dy}{dx} = \dfrac{2t-8}{3t^2-6t}$ ② (16, -16) ③ (0, 0), (-4, -12)
Ex7.	① $\langle -7, -3 \rangle = -7i - 3j$, $\sqrt{58}$ ② $\langle -6, 0 \rangle = -6i$, 6 ③ $\langle 0, 6 \rangle = 6j$, 6 ④ $\langle 5, 5 \rangle = 5i + 5j$, $5\sqrt{2}$
Ex8.	① $\sqrt{26}$ ② $\sqrt{10}$ ③ $2\sqrt{2}$
Ex11.	① $v(5) = \langle 24, -8 \rangle$ ② right and down ③ $y + 15 = -\dfrac{1}{3}(x - 22)$ ④ $t = 1$ ⑤ $a(1) = \langle -6, -2 \rangle$ ⑥ $8\sqrt{10}$
Ex12.	① (a) (23.5, 2) (b) about 23 ② (a) (15.586, 26.586) (b) 27.791
Ex13.	① $y - 5 = -(x - 4)$ ② left, up ③ $\sqrt{2}$

	④ $\left\langle -\dfrac{2}{3}, \dfrac{1}{4} \right\rangle$
	⑤ $\int_0^1 \sqrt{\left(t^2-2t\right)^2 + \left(t^3\right)^2}\, dt$
	⑥ $\left(\dfrac{14}{3}, \dfrac{19}{4} \right)$
Ex14.	① $\int_0^\pi \sqrt{(\cos t)^2 + (-\sin t)^2}\, dt$
	② $\int_0^2 \sqrt{(2t)^2 + 2^2}\, dt$
	③ $\int_0^{\frac{\pi}{2}} \sqrt{\left(-e^{-t}\cos t - e^{-t}\sin t\right)^2 + \left(-e^{-t}\sin t + e^{-t}\cos t\right)^2}\, dt$
AP	1. B 2.1) A 2.2) B 2.3) A
	3. B 4. A 5. B

24. Polar Coordinates (BC)

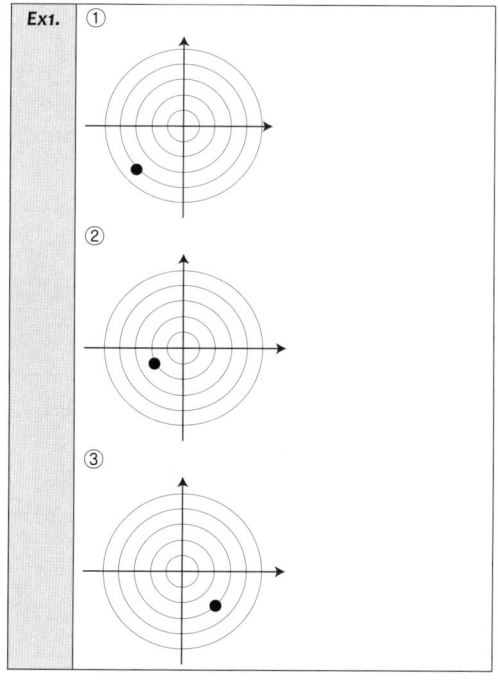

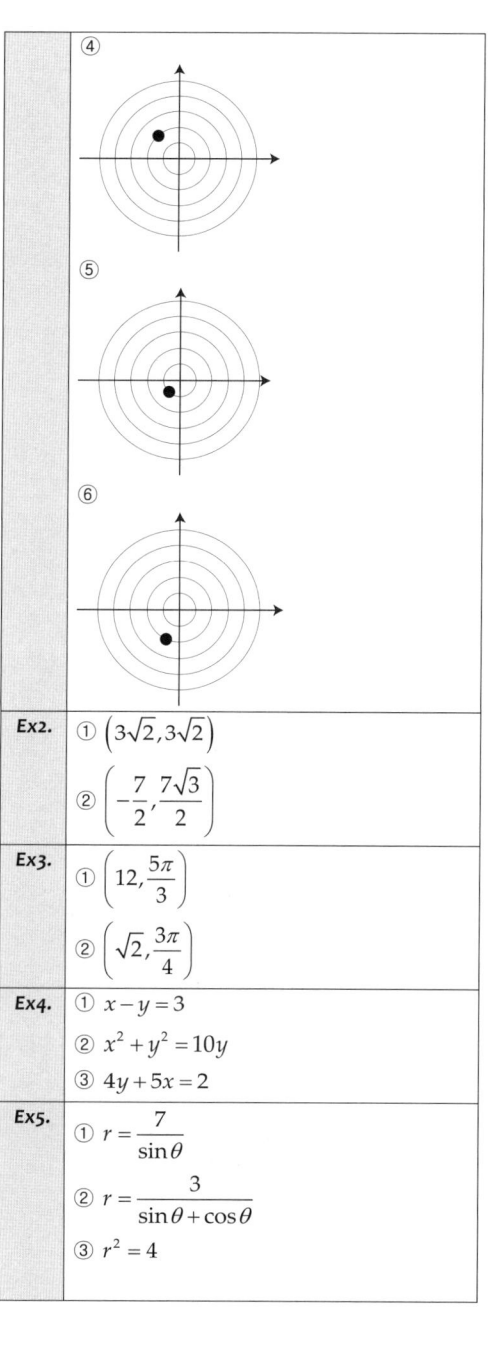

Ex2.	① $\left(3\sqrt{2}, 3\sqrt{2} \right)$
	② $\left(-\dfrac{7}{2}, \dfrac{7\sqrt{3}}{2} \right)$
Ex3.	① $\left(12, \dfrac{5\pi}{3} \right)$
	② $\left(\sqrt{2}, \dfrac{3\pi}{4} \right)$
Ex4.	① $x - y = 3$
	② $x^2 + y^2 = 10y$
	③ $4y + 5x = 2$
Ex5.	① $r = \dfrac{7}{\sin\theta}$
	② $r = \dfrac{3}{\sin\theta + \cos\theta}$
	③ $r^2 = 4$

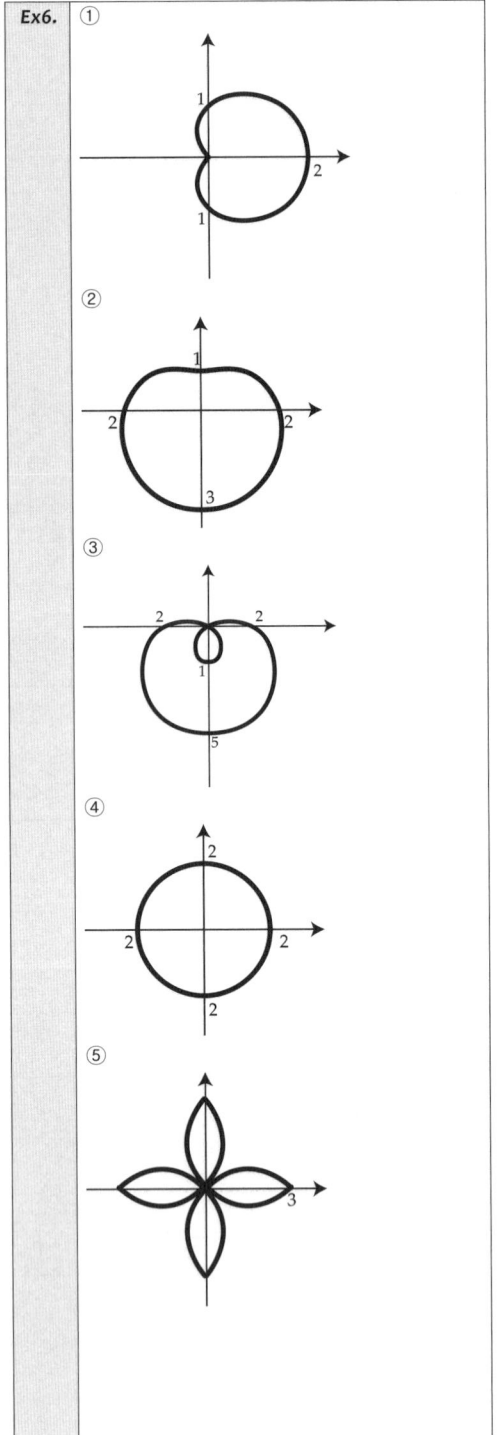
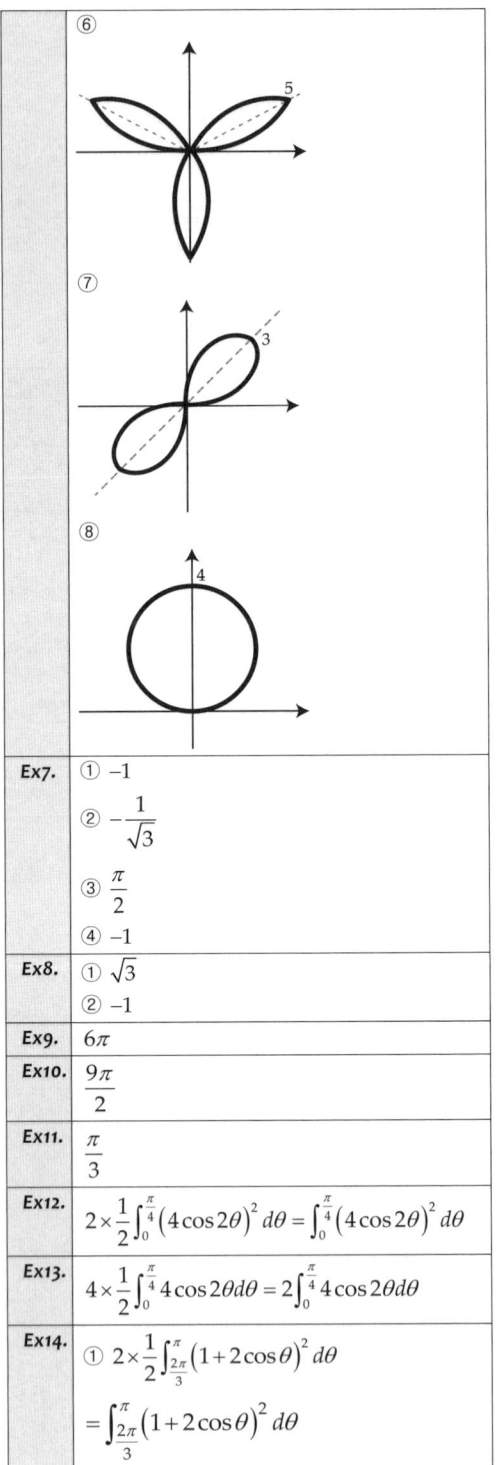

Ex7.	① -1
	② $-\dfrac{1}{\sqrt{3}}$
	③ $\dfrac{\pi}{2}$
	④ -1
Ex8.	① $\sqrt{3}$
	② -1
Ex9.	6π
Ex10.	$\dfrac{9\pi}{2}$
Ex11.	$\dfrac{\pi}{3}$
Ex12.	$2\times\dfrac{1}{2}\int_{0}^{\frac{\pi}{4}}(4\cos 2\theta)^{2}\,d\theta=\int_{0}^{\frac{\pi}{4}}(4\cos 2\theta)^{2}\,d\theta$
Ex13.	$4\times\dfrac{1}{2}\int_{0}^{\frac{\pi}{4}}4\cos 2\theta\,d\theta=2\int_{0}^{\frac{\pi}{4}}4\cos 2\theta\,d\theta$
Ex14.	① $2\times\dfrac{1}{2}\int_{\frac{2\pi}{3}}^{\pi}(1+2\cos\theta)^{2}\,d\theta$
	$=\int_{\frac{2\pi}{3}}^{\pi}(1+2\cos\theta)^{2}\,d\theta$

	② $2\times\left(\dfrac{1}{2}\int_0^{\frac{2\pi}{3}}(1+2\cos\theta)^2\,d\theta - \dfrac{1}{2}\int_{\frac{2\pi}{3}}^{\pi}(1+2\cos\theta)^2\,d\theta\right)$ $=\int_0^{\frac{2\pi}{3}}(1+2\cos\theta)^2\,d\theta - \int_{\frac{2\pi}{3}}^{\pi}(1+2\cos\theta)^2\,d\theta$
Ex15.	① $2\times\dfrac{1}{2}\int_{-\frac{\pi}{2}}^{0}(2-2\sin\theta)^2 - 2^2\,d\theta$ $=\int_{-\frac{\pi}{2}}^{0}(2-2\sin\theta)^2 - 2^2\,d\theta$ ② $2\times\dfrac{1}{2}\int_{0}^{\frac{\pi}{2}}2^2 - (2-2\sin\theta)^2\,d\theta$ $=\int_{0}^{\frac{\pi}{2}}2^2 - (2-2\sin\theta)^2\,d\theta$ ③ $2\times\left[\dfrac{1}{2}\int_{0}^{\frac{\pi}{2}}(2-2\sin\theta)^2\,d\theta + \pi\right]$
Ex16.	① $2\times\dfrac{1}{2}\int_{0}^{\frac{\pi}{3}}(3\cos\theta)^2 - (1+\cos\theta)^2\,d\theta$ $=\int_{0}^{\frac{\pi}{3}}(3\cos\theta)^2 - (1+\cos\theta)^2\,d\theta$ ② $2\times\left[\dfrac{1}{2}\int_{0}^{\frac{\pi}{3}}(1+\cos\theta)^2\,d\theta + \dfrac{1}{2}\int_{\frac{\pi}{3}}^{\frac{\pi}{2}}(3\cos\theta)^2\,d\theta\right]$ $=\int_{0}^{\frac{\pi}{3}}(1+\cos\theta)^2\,d\theta + \int_{\frac{\pi}{3}}^{\frac{\pi}{2}}(3\cos\theta)^2\,d\theta$ ③ $2\times\left[\dfrac{1}{2}\int_{\frac{\pi}{3}}^{\pi}(1+\cos\theta)^2\,d\theta - \dfrac{1}{2}\int_{\frac{\pi}{3}}^{\frac{\pi}{2}}(3\cos\theta)^2\,d\theta\right]$ $=\int_{\frac{\pi}{3}}^{\pi}(1+\cos\theta)^2\,d\theta - \int_{\frac{\pi}{3}}^{\frac{\pi}{2}}(3\cos\theta)^2\,d\theta$
Ex17.	$2\times\dfrac{1}{2}\int_{0}^{\frac{\pi}{4}}(3\sin\theta)^2\,d\theta$ $=\int_{0}^{\frac{\pi}{4}}(3\sin\theta)^2\,d\theta$
Ex18.	$8\times\left(\dfrac{1}{2}\int_{\frac{\pi}{12}}^{\frac{\pi}{4}}2^2\,d\theta + \dfrac{1}{2}\int_{0}^{\frac{\pi}{12}}(4\sin 2\theta)^2\,d\theta\right)$
AP	1. A 2. A 3. A 4. D 5. C 6. A

Free Response Question (from ch18~24)

1.

(a) $\lim\limits_{n\to\infty}\left|\dfrac{a_{n+1}}{a_n}\right| = \lim\limits_{n\to\infty}\left|\dfrac{\dfrac{(n+1)x^{n+1}}{(n+1)^2+1}}{\dfrac{nx^n}{n^2+1}}\right| =$

$\lim\limits_{n\to\infty}\left|\dfrac{x(n+1)(n^2+1)}{n[(n+1)^2+1]}\right| = |x| < 1$

$\Rightarrow -1 < x < 1$

When $x = -1$, $\sum\limits_{n=1}^{\infty}(-1)^n\dfrac{n}{n^2+1}$

converges (alternating series test)

When $x = 1$, $\sum\limits_{n=1}^{\infty}\dfrac{n}{n^2+1}$ diverges

(harmonic series)

Therefore, $-1 \le x < 1$.

(b) $f(-1) \approx -\dfrac{1}{2} + \dfrac{2}{5} = -\dfrac{1}{10}$

$\left|f(-1) - \left(-\dfrac{1}{10}\right)\right| \le \left|-\dfrac{3}{10}\right| = \dfrac{3}{10} < \dfrac{5}{10} = 0.5$.

(c) $g(x) = 1 + \dfrac{x^2}{4} + \dfrac{2x^3}{15} + \ldots$

$g(-1) \approx 1 + \dfrac{1}{4} - \dfrac{2}{15} = \dfrac{67}{60}$

(d)

$h(x) = \left(1 + x + \dfrac{x^2}{2!} + \ldots\right)\left(\dfrac{x}{2} + \dfrac{2x^2}{5} + \dfrac{3x^3}{10} + \ldots\right)$

$= \dfrac{x}{2} + \left(\dfrac{2}{5}x^2 + \dfrac{x^2}{2}\right) + \left(\dfrac{3}{10}x^3 + \dfrac{2}{5}x^3 + \dfrac{x^3}{4}\right) + \ldots$

$= \dfrac{x}{2} + \dfrac{9}{10}x^2 + \dfrac{19}{20}x^3 + \ldots$

2.

(a) $f(x) \approx f(2) + f'(2)(x-2) = 3 + 5(x-2)$

$f(2.2) \approx 3 + 5(2.2 - 2) = 4$

Since $f''(2) = -10 < 0$, it is overestimated.

(b)

x	y	dy/dx
2	3	5
2.1	$3 + 5(0.1) = 3.5$	6
2.2	$3.5 + 6(0.1) = 4.1$	

Therefore, $f(2.2) \approx 4.1$

(c)
$$f(x) \approx f(2) + f'(2)(x-2) + f''(2)\frac{(x-2)^2}{2!}$$
$$= 3 + 5(x-2) - 5(x-2)^2$$
$$f(2.2) \approx 3 + 5(2.2-2) - 5(2.2-2)^2 = 3.8$$

(d) $|f(2.2) - 3.8| \leq \text{Max } f^{(3)}(z)\frac{(2.2-2)^3}{3!}$

$$= 20\frac{(0.2)^3}{3!} = \frac{2}{75} < \frac{3}{75} = \frac{1}{25}$$

3.

(a) $\left\langle \frac{\sqrt{2}}{4}, -1 \right\rangle$

(b) $y(2) = -8 + \int_1^2 (1-t)\, dt = -8.5$

(c) $\dfrac{dy/dt}{dx/dt} = \dfrac{1-t}{\sqrt{t}+2}$

$\left.\dfrac{dy/dt}{dx/dt}\right|_{t=2} = \dfrac{-1}{2+\sqrt{2}} = \dfrac{\sqrt{2}-2}{2}$

(d) $\int_0^6 \sqrt{(\sqrt{t}+2)^2 + (1-t)^2}\, dt$

(e) $\dfrac{1}{6}\int_0^6 \sqrt{(\sqrt{t}+2)^2 + (1-t)^2}\, dt$

4.

(a) $\dfrac{1}{2}\int_{-\pi/6}^{7\pi/6} (3+2\sin\theta)^2 - 2^2\, d\theta$

(b) $\dfrac{1}{2}\int_{7\pi/6}^{11\pi/6} (3+2\sin\theta)^2 d\theta + \dfrac{1}{2} 2^2 \left(\dfrac{4\pi}{3}\right)$

(c) $\dfrac{dy/d\theta}{dx/d\theta} =$

$\dfrac{(2\cos\theta)\sin\theta + (3+2\sin\theta)\cos\theta}{(2\cos\theta)\cos\theta + (3+2\sin\theta)(-\sin\theta)}$

$\left.\dfrac{dy/d\theta}{dx/d\theta}\right|_{\theta=0} = \dfrac{3}{2}$

(d) $\dfrac{dr}{dt} = 2\cos\theta\dfrac{d\theta}{dt}$

$\left.\dfrac{dr}{dt}\right|_{\theta=0} = 2(\cos 0)(3) = 6$

The distance from the origin is increasing at the rate of 6 unit per second at $\theta = 0$.

Calculator Skills

Ex1.	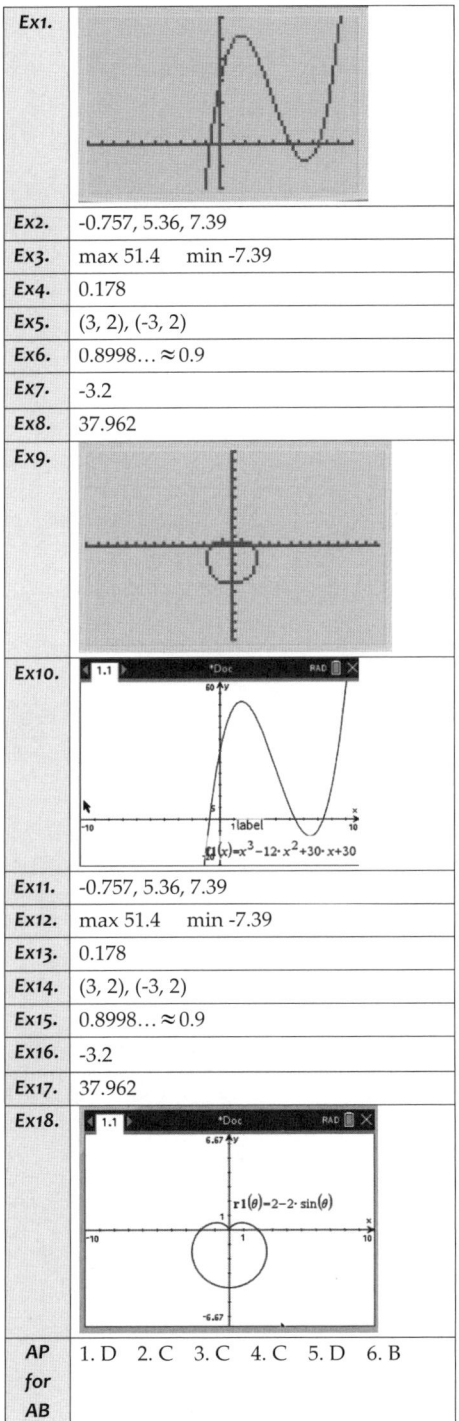
Ex2.	-0.757, 5.36, 7.39
Ex3.	max 51.4 min -7.39
Ex4.	0.178
Ex5.	(3, 2), (-3, 2)
Ex6.	0.8998… ≈ 0.9
Ex7.	-3.2
Ex8.	37.962
Ex9.	
Ex10.	
Ex11.	-0.757, 5.36, 7.39
Ex12.	max 51.4 min -7.39
Ex13.	0.178
Ex14.	(3, 2), (-3, 2)
Ex15.	0.8998… ≈ 0.9
Ex16.	-3.2
Ex17.	37.962
Ex18.	
AP for AB	1. D 2. C 3. C 4. C 5. D 6. B

AP for BC	1. B 2. B 3. D 4. D 5. B 6. B
	7. D 8. B

Multiple Choice

MCQ for AB (Noncal)	1. C	2. A	3. C
	4. A	5. D	6. C
	7. D	8. A	9. D
	10. B	11. B	12. B
	13. D	14. C	15. B
	16. A	17. E	18. A
	19. D	20. E	21. B
	22. C	23. B	24. B
	25. D	26. E	27. C
	28. B	29. A	30. E
MCQ for AB (Cal)	76. D	77. B	78. B
	79. C	80. C	81. D
	82. D	83. E	84. B
	85. E	86. C	87. C
	88. B	89. D	90. D
MCQ for AB (Noncal)	1. B	2. A	3. C
	4. A	5. D	6. A
	7. C	8. A	9. D
	10. B	11. B	12. B
	13. D	14. C	15. D
	16. A	17. E	18. D
	19. D	20. E	21. B
	22. A	23. B	24. B
	25. D	26. E	27. C
	28. E	29. A	30. E
MCQ for AB (Cal)	76. A	77. C	78. B
	79. C	80. C	81. B
	82. D	83. C	84. B
	85. B	86. C	87. C
	88. D	89. B	90. C

Answers 593

memo

memo